Get a FREE eBook

To register this book, scan the code or go to
www.manning.com/freebook/morgan3

By registering you get

- **FREE eBook copy**
  download in PDF and ePub

- **FREE online access**
  to Manning's liveBook platform

- **FREE audio**
  read and listen online in liveBook

- **FREE AI Assistant**
  it knows the contents (and your exact location) when it answers

- **FREE in-book testing**
  fun tests to lock in your knowledge

In Manning's liveBook platform you can share discussions and comments with other readers, add your own bookmarks and highlights, insert personal notes anywhere on the page, see color versions of all the book's graphics, download source code and other resources, and more!
To register, scan the code or go to www.manning.com/freebook/morgan3

MANNING

Coding with AI

Coding with AI

EXAMPLES IN PYTHON

JEREMY C. MORGAN

MANNING

SHELTER ISLAND

For online information and ordering of this and other Manning books, please visit www.manning.com. The publisher offers discounts on this book when ordered in quantity.

For more information, please contact

> Special Sales Department
> Manning Publications Co.
> 20 Baldwin Road
> PO Box 761
> Shelter Island, NY 11964
> Email: orders@manning.com

Manning Publications Co.
20 Baldwin Road
PO Box 761
Shelter Island, NY 11964

Development editor:	Doug Rudder
Technical editor:	Richard J. Vaughan
Review editor:	Dunja Nikitović
Production editor:	Kathy Rossland
Copy editor:	Lana Todorovic-Arndt
Proofreader:	Keri Hales
Typesetter:	Tamara Švelić Sabljić
Cover designer:	Marija Tudor

ISBN 9781633437272

I dedicate this book to my amazing family.
Without them, this book would not have been possible.

brief contents

contents

I've been blessed to make a living doing something I'd do as a hobby. For decades, coding has been my passion. When I started programming, learning was tough—hardcopy books, dogpile.com, and newsgroups were our lifelines. You had to really want it.

My journey began with Perl, watching HTML come to life for the first time. Although tedious and frustrating, the results had me hooked. PHP changed everything, letting me build applications in days rather than months. The real high came from watching users' eyes light up when their clunky spreadsheet workflow transformed into a sleek HTML form overnight.

Back then, documentation was scarce, and Google was in its infancy. Without old head programmers helping us, we may never have finished anything. My code got the job done but was often ugly behind the scenes, something I'd be proud of on Monday and embarrassed about by Friday.

I gravitated toward backend development—its deterministic nature felt more intuitive. Like everyone else, I sought better ways to build code faster. Our team briefly adopted a rapid-application-development generator that promised miracles. It worked initially, cranking out features at warp speed. Then reality hit: when requirements changed, we spent twice as long untangling the generated mess. Less than a year later, we abandoned it.

Lesson learned: Fast development is only fun if you never plan on maintaining it.

Python was my next breakthrough—offering speed without sacrificing readability or maintainability. Later, C# provided similar efficiency gains. But I never matched the raw speed of that ill-fated PHP generator.

Then generative AI crashed the party. With ChatGPT and GitHub Copilot, I tackled a C# side project. I watched AI spit out boilerplate and tests before my pizza cooled.

Work I'd blocked off for two weekends wrapped up before Sunday brunch. It felt like rediscovering that early PHP generator magic—only faster, with guardrails.

Now the hype cycle is in full swing. Vibe coding promises amazing software from a few prompts. This is genuinely possible—but beware creating complex code nobody understands. It's fine for a weekend project but not ideal for mission-critical applications.

This book aims to use this silver bullet properly. AI can enhance productivity, but heavy reliance brings trouble. You'll learn to manage expectations: AI can generate about 80% of an application, but the remaining 20% is up to you.

You don't need to be taught how to vibe code. Instead, you'll learn how each tool works and when to use it effectively. Today's tooling—cloud IDEs, auto-generated tests, and AI pair-programmers—means shipping faster with fewer tradeoffs than ever before.

Whether you're an old head like me who remembers the struggles or a beginner facing different challenges, these tools will accelerate your journey. The best time to build was yesterday; the second-best time is right now.

acknowledgments

Although very fun to write, this book was a lot of work. I hope you'll enjoy what we've put together here. There are quite a few folks I'd like to thank for helping me along the way.

First, I would like to thank my wife Amber. You've always believed in me and gave up so much time with me to get this done. You also provided lots of helpful encouragement, even if it was, "Go work on that book! Hurry up!" I love you and I'm eternally thankful.

Also, thanks to my mother Robbin Fariss and father Rocky Morgan, and my stepfather Russ Peckham and stepmother Tina Chambliss. They all raised me to believe in myself and not quit when times get tough. I never heard them say, "You can't do that," no matter what crazy ambition I had. They shaped me into who I am today. And thanks to my four children Austin, Hayley, Rory, and Kendra, and grandchildren Brynlee, Aubrie, Wittly, Aurora, Brantley, Cody, and Octavia. You are the folks who keep me grounded and motivated to keep going strong every day. You are my *why* and part of the reason I had to write this book.

At Manning, I'd like to thank my development editor Doug Rudder for all the patience and guidance throughout this process. I'll never match your knowledge of writing, but I appreciate you lending it so often. And your way of delivering feedback is fantastic. I'd like to thank my acquisitions editor Michael Stephens for your guidance, knowledge, and tough conversations. Without your help, this book wouldn't be nearly as good. In addition, thanks to the entire production team who helped shepherd this book into its final format.

Thanks to the reviewers who have taken time to read my manuscript at various stages and help me with feedback: Tom Massey, Sean Collins, Xavier Morera, Lars Klint, Steve

Buchanan, Dave McCollough, Santosh Yadav, Danny Nunez, Steven Senkus, Renjith Ramachandran, and Roger Rizk. I'd also like to thank Roger for all the tips and tricks with Blackbox AI to make sure we got the most from it. I'd like to thank the team from Tabnine for all their help with questions and guidance.

Also, thanks to Abir Qasem, Advait Patel, Anandaganesh Balakrishnan, Arik Leonidov, Asterios Raptis, Bin Hu, Christopher Forbes, Clifford Thurber, David Allen Blubaugh, David Goldfarb, Debasish Ghosh, Emre Sevinç, Estera Kot, Franklin Neves, Giampiero Granatella, Greg Grimes, Ian Walker, Ioannis Atsonios, Jacek Sokulski, Jason Nelson, Jesús Juárez, Jiri Pik, John Abela, Julien Pohie, Manohar Sai Jasti, Michael Bright, Mike Metzger, Nadeem Lalani, Nakul Pandey, Ninoslav Cerkez, Oliver Korten, Pasquale Zirpoli, Paul Soh, Piotr Jastrzebski, Ramani Natarajan, Rambabu Posa, Samuel Lawrence, Sanjana Kandi, Saurabh Aggarwal, Shiroshica Kulatilake, Simeon Leyzerzon, Sriram Macharla, Steve Steiner, Thomas Jaensch, Tony Holdroyd, Vlad Bezden, Vladislav Bilay, Walter Alexander Mata López, and William Whitehead. Your suggestions helped make this a better book.

Special thanks to technical editor Richard Vaughan. Richard is a highly experienced engineer, who is CTO at Purple Monkey Collective—a research focused startup delivering machine learning and cloud guidance services.

Finally, I'd like to thank my mother, Robbin Farris, for letting me use her work computer back in the 1980s and get hooked on tech. But most importantly, I am grateful she has always believed in me, telling me my entire life that anything is possible.

about this book

This book empowers you to harness AI's full potential and improve your coding. My goal is to help you save time by developing features faster and getting higher quality code as a result. The book covers practical uses of tools such as GitHub Copilot, Tabnine, Blackbox AI, and ChatGPT. You'll see how these technologies can help you code faster, solve problems better, and cut down on repetitive tasks. You won't just learn how to use these tools but also discover when and why to use them in your development process.

Who should read this book

This book is for Python developers who want to use generative AI tools in their work. But the techniques can be applied to many other languages as well. If you're an experienced developer aiming to increase your productivity or a team lead exploring AI tools for your team, you'll find helpful guidance and real-world examples. While some knowledge of Python is helpful, developers of all skill levels will learn how these tools can enhance their skills instead of replacing them.

How this book is organized: A road map

The book consists of 10 chapters:

- Chapter 1 covers generative AI for coding. It explains how large language models predict and create code. It also distinguishes between integrated tools, such as GitHub Copilot, and standalone tools, such as ChatGPT. These technologies boost developer productivity by automating routine tasks, letting developers focus more on problem-solving and design.

- Chapter 2 introduces AI-assisted coding with GitHub Copilot. It explains how Copilot works and shows different ways to use it, such as code completion, chat, and prompts. The chapter also includes a practical Python project that analyzes word frequency in text. This project shows developers how to integrate Copilot into their workflow effectively.

- Chapter 3 describes how to use ChatGPT for project design and discovery. It explains how to write effective prompts. These prompts help set AI roles, create detailed software design documents, and develop user stories. The focus is on a Python web application that offers randomized practice tests for HAM radio license exams.

- Chapter 4 demonstrates how to begin coding an application with AI assistance by extracting requirements from design documents using both ChatGPT and Gemini, setting up a Python virtual environment, creating a structured Flask application with AI-suggested file organization, and implementing code stubs that provide the skeleton of the application before adding functionality.

- Chapter 5 demonstrates how to build a functional Flask application for HAM radio practice tests using Blackbox AI, showing how to connect to an SQLite database, implement separation of concerns through refactoring, create database sessions to track test progress, generate random question sets, and build the core functionality, while highlighting when human intervention is necessary to improve AI-generated code.

- Chapter 6 focuses on building a question engine for the HAM radio practice test application, using Tabnine to troubleshoot bugs in session management, implement persistent browser cookies to maintain user state across page refreshes, refactor code to properly handle question sets associated with specific sessions, and create a simple user interface that allows users to end test sessions and start new ones.

- Chapter 7 demonstrates how to create a user interface for the HAM radio practice test application using AI tools such as ChatGPT, Google Gemini, and Blackbox AI to generate design strategies, wireframes, flowcharts, and functional HTML/CSS code, transforming a basic application into one with a professional appearance, while following proper Flask templating practices.

- Chapter 8 explores how to use generative AI tools to create effective test suites for Python applications, comparing GitHub Copilot, Tabnine, and Blackbox AI for generating both `unittest` and `pytest` code, setting up in-memory databases for testing isolation, and demonstrating how each tool approaches the creation of test fixtures, assertions, and database interactions with varying degrees of context awareness.

- Chapter 9 explains prompt engineering techniques for working with generative AI tools, covering basic concepts like context, clear instructions, and examples. In addition, it explores advanced approaches such as chain of thought prompting, recursive prompting, context manipulation, instruction refinement, and output control, before concluding with 30 specific prompt techniques tailored for software developers.

- Chapter 10 explores vibe coding, a fast-evolving approach to programming based on natural language prompts. It further demonstrates how to build a retro arcade-based game using this technique.

I recommend reading the chapters in order, as each builds on concepts from previous chapters. However, experienced developers may choose to focus on specific chapters addressing their immediate needs.

About the code

This book contains many examples of source code both in numbered listings and in line with normal text. In both cases, source code is formatted in a `fixed-width font` `like this` to separate it from ordinary text.

In many cases, the original source code has been reformatted; we've added line breaks and reworked indentation to accommodate the available page space in the book. In rare cases, even this was not enough, and listings include line-continuation markers ( ). Additionally, comments in the source code have often been removed from the listings when the code is described in the text.

You can get executable snippets of code from the liveBook (online) version of this book at https://livebook.manning.com/book/coding-with-ai. The complete code for the examples in the book is available for download from the Manning website at https://www.manning.com/books/coding-with-ai, and from GitHub at https://github .com/JeremyMorgan/HAM-Radio-Practice-Web.

liveBook discussion forum

Purchase of *Coding with AI* includes free access to liveBook, Manning's online reading platform. Using liveBook's exclusive discussion features, you can attach comments to the book globally or to specific sections or paragraphs. It's a snap to make notes for yourself, ask and answer technical questions, and receive help from the author and other users. To access the forum, go to https://livebook.manning.com/book/ coding-with-ai/discussion.

Manning's commitment to our readers is to provide a venue where a meaningful dialogue between individual readers and between readers and the author can take place. It is not a commitment to any specific amount of participation on the part of the author, whose contribution to the forum remains voluntary (and unpaid). We suggest you try asking the author some challenging questions lest his interest stray! The forum and the archives of previous discussions will be accessible from the publisher's website as long as the book is in print.

about the author

JEREMY C. MORGAN is on a mission to help developers get better at what they do. He's a senior training architect for KodeKloud and an avid tech blogger and speaker. He has two decades of experience as an engineer building software for everything from Fortune 100 companies to tiny startups. He's been immersed in generative AI and machine learning projects for the last couple of years and enjoys teaching through his popular tech blog, www.jeremymorgan.com. Jeremy is an NVIDIA-Certified Associate for Generative AI and LLMS (NCA-GENL Certification) and holds the GitHub Foundations and GitHub Copilot certifications. He also contributes to open source as a .NET Foundation Member and DevOps Institute Ambassador, and serves on the DevNetwork AI/ML Advisory Board.

about the cover illustration

The figure on the cover of *Coding with AI*, titled "Le Créole (Petit blanc)," or "Creole (Small white)," is taken from a book by Louis Curmer published in 1841. Each illustration is finely drawn and colored by hand.

In those days, it was easy to identify where people lived and what their trade or station in life was just by their dress. Manning celebrates the inventiveness and initiative of the computer business with book covers based on the rich diversity of regional culture centuries ago, brought back to life by pictures from collections such as this one.

Part 1

Getting started with AI-assisted coding

Have you ever stared at a blank code editor, unsure how to start your next project? It's like writer's block for developers. Have you spent hours writing boring boilerplate code that feels like busy work? If so, you've felt the friction that generative AI tools aim to remove. Today, software developers around the world are finding that AI coding assistants such as GitHub Copilot, ChatGPT, and Tabnine can change their workflow. They can cut coding time by 30% or more, while also improving code quality. They're also taking care of much of the boring boilerplate coding.

The revolution is here. Professional developers use AI to generate functions, create documentation, write tests, and design entire application architectures. But like with any powerful tool, generative AI requires the appropriate skills to be used effectively. The key difference between developers who succeed with these tools and those who struggle is not technical skill. It's about knowing how to communicate with AI, when to trust its suggestions, and how to integrate generated code into real projects.

The first part of the book will guide you through your initial steps with AI-assisted development. It will lay the groundwork for how you use these tools to build Python applications. Chapter 1 introduces the landscape of generative AI tools and the core concepts you need to know. Chapter 2 puts these tools into action; you'll dive into hands-on development and build your first AI-assisted Python project.

By the end of this part, you'll understand not just what these tools can do, but how to make them work for you as a productive member of your development team.

Introducing generative AI

Robots are not going to replace humans, they are going to make their jobs much more humane. Difficult, demeaning, demanding, dangerous, dull— these are the jobs robots will be taking.

—Sabine Hauert, Co-founder of Robohub.org

What if you could use your existing Python expertise alongside AI that understands your code context, anticipates patterns, and generates implementation details while you focus on architecture and design? That's the power of generative AI tools for experienced developers. When I first encountered these tools, I approached them with healthy skepticism. But after integrating them into real production projects over the past year, I've reduced implementation time by approximately 30%, while improving code quality and test coverage.

It's likely you've already used ChatGPT or Claude for coding. You've probably seen GitHub Copilot suggestions pop up in your editor. Or maybe you're just curious about all the AI buzz. If you're interested in learning how to use these tools to make yourself super productive, you're in the right place. This book is your practical guide to using AI tools to supercharge your coding, and no AI expertise is required.

This book will show you exactly how to use these tools to write code faster, catch bugs earlier, create better documentation, create design diagrams (UML, flowcharts, etc.), and test your code more thoroughly. The best part? You don't need a PhD in math, data science, or a background in AI to benefit. I've traveled this road extensively and discovered valuable tricks along the way. Consider this your field guide to generative AI coding tools. I'll help you navigate the potholes I've encountered.

This book approaches generative AI from a developer's perspective, examining both programming-specific tools and general text generators that belong in your toolkit. We'll look at how these revolutionary tools work and how to use them efficiently. Coding will never be the same from now on.

By sharing my insights and experiences, I aim to cut through the hype and sales pitches to focus on what matters—making you a more productive Python developer. These techniques extend to many languages, empowering you to use AI as a tool for innovation and growth, and adding both fun and productivity to your daily work.

This book provides an overview of several popular tools. It includes step-by-step instructions on installing and using these tools to your advantage. You'll also learn techniques for crafting effective prompts to get the best results.

1.1 Generative AI for coders

Generative AI can benefit you, the coder, in various ways, from code generation and bug detection to documentation and testing. Let's take a look at the ways generative AI can assist you in your everyday development work.

1.1.1 Code generation and autocompletion

Autocompletion of code by software is nothing new. We've been using that for years. Smart autocompletion and code generation, however, are much newer concepts. Large language models (LLMs) can be trained to understand programming languages in depth and generate code snippets in a smart way. What do I mean by smart? They can utilize context and evaluate the code around it. They can generate code based on user inputs or requirements. By employing AI tools, developers can quickly prototype ideas or even generate entire applications. Many AI-powered tools predict and suggest the next lines of code, as you type. This makes the development process much faster. Let's take a look at a simple example comparing traditional Python development with an AI-assisted approach.

You need to parse a CSV file, filter rows based on certain criteria, perform calculations, and output the results. In a traditional approach, you might

- Search for the Python CSV module documentation
- Write boilerplate for file opening and error handling
- Implement the parsing logic line by line
- Debug edge cases manually

In an AI-assisted approach,

- You comment, "# Parse the CSV file at `data.csv`, filter rows where the `status` column equals `active`, calculate the average of the `value` column, and write results to `output.csv`."
- The AI generates a complete implementation, including error handling.
- You review the response, adjust for specific requirements, and test it.

1.1.2 Bug detection and automated fixes

Generative AI analyzes existing code to identify potential bugs, security vulnerabilities, and performance problems. AI tools can evaluate context while generating suggestions for the code you're working on. Many of these tools learn as they go. Since they're based on trained models, they are refined over time to get even better. They detect problems and suggest appropriate fixes, saving you heaps of time.

1.1.3 Documentation generation

Writing clear, concise, and accurate documentation is crucial for a successful software project to thrive. Without good documentation, your users or other developers will suffer. The greatest software written can be useless without good documentation. But documentation can be boring to write. Generative AI helps with this by automatically generating human-like documentation for your software. It can provide well-structured and contextually relevant explanations for your code. Not only does it generate documentation for you, but it can help you understand your own code better as well.

1.1.4 Code refactoring and optimization

It's always good to take a second or third look through your code to ensure there aren't any errors and that it is optimized. AI tools make this process much easier as they can analyze your code and make suggestions. They can identify redundant code, inefficient algorithms, and more. By suggesting improvements, they make refactoring easier and more effective.

1.1.5   Test case generation and mock data creation

I'm one of those strange developers who loves testing and building mocking tools. Creating good tests is imperative, and I've found that many generative AI tools produce great tests and uncover things I haven't thought of. They can be used to generate test cases and create mock data for your application that meets your needs. This improves your testing systems significantly.

What generative AI tools am I talking about? Let's take a look.

1.2   Developer tools landscape

Generative AI is still new, yet AI developer tools are already making their mark on the industry. These tools utilize LLMs to generate code, provide suggestions, and automate tasks. We're going to take a look at two types of tools:

- *Integrated tools*—Tools that work within Visual Studio Code or other IDEs and function within them
- *Standalone tools*—Tools with their own interface, usually a website, that don't interact with an integrated development environment (IDE)

1.2.1   Integrated developer tools

Generally, standalone tools are meant for many types of general text generation and chat. Think of ChatGPT or Gemini, which have a web interface and are meant for general help. Integrated tools are designed for software development. They can often generate code specific to your problem within your code, using your code as context, which we'll examine in this book. Standalone tools such as ChatGPT are better for abstraction and design.

The integrated tools we'll be using are all powered by generative AI to assist you as you're writing code, boosting your productivity and revealing easier, smarter coding techniques. Your software can become more efficient, accurate, and performant with the use of AI tools. Although each tool is different, many of them operate similarly. In this book, we are going to examine their differences. And using the tools properly will make you a better developer.

GITHUB COPILOT

GitHub is a well-known name in the developer ecosphere. Most developers today have at least some of their code on GitHub. Microsoft released GitHub Copilot in October 2021. It's an AI-powered code completion tool developed by Microsoft and OpenAI. It uses the OpenAI Codex model. Copilot integrates with popular editors such as Visual Studio Code. It suggests code improvements, completions, comments, and even functions as you type. Copilot is context aware and provides relevant suggestions in a variety of programming languages and frameworks.

TABNINE

Tabnine is another popular AI-powered code assistant. Tabnine utilizes many popular LLM models to provide context-aware code suggestions. It integrates with popular code editors such as Visual Studio Code and IntelliJ. It has a local version for offline use, as well as a cloud-based version for faster, more accurate suggestions. Its feature, called "Deep Completion," uses deep learning to provide more accurate suggestions. Tabnine is also contextually aware of your code as you write and will attempt to auto-suggest code in the style you use.

BLACKBOX AI

Blackbox AI is an AI-powered code assistant that works within Visual Studio Code and Jupyter Notebook. It is available for over 20 programming languages, including Python, JavaScript, TypeScript, Go, and Ruby. Blackbox AI is an integrated tool, but it also has a web interface and the ability to ask questions and interact with the backend model from your IDE.

1.2.2 *Standalone tools*

In addition to integrated developer tools, there are several standalone tools and platforms that employ generative AI for code generation and assistance. These tools operate outside of traditional integrated development environments (IDEs) and usually have a web interface.

CHATGPT

Surely, you've heard of ChatGPT by now. It's an awesome tool that can help software developers with developing software outlines, code generation, testing, documentation, and more. Its ability to understand and generate text specific to programming languages and frameworks is striking. The GP4x models used by ChatGPT are impressive.

ChatGPT uses a web interface for communication—you can enter a question and get an answer. Most importantly, you can have a full discussion with ChatGPT, and it keeps context in the threads. There is also a CLI (command line interface) and a full API for ChatGPT, which gives you many options for interacting with it, including the ability to build plugins.

GOOGLE GEMINI

Google Gemini is similar to ChatGPT from an interface standpoint. You can ask questions and receive answers. It generates software outlines, code, and so on, just like ChatGPT. Functionally, they are very similar; however, in my experience, Gemini isn't quite as sophisticated as ChatGPT yet. It will eventually get better and become a great contender.

One advantage to Google Gemini is the potential to integrate with other Google Services in their ecosystem, which I consider a great future advantage. Also, Google as a company has access to a lot of source code for training. This could help the model improve over time.

COPILOT CHAT

Copilot Chat has a similar interface to ChatGPT and Gemini. It uses several different models from OpenAI and Anthropic on the backend. However, there are some differences. Although Copilot has a familiar web-based question-and-answer format, it's also integrated into Microsoft software. Both desktop and mobile versions are available.

Another difference is that the results focus more on simple requests than complex conversations. When you put in requests, it does a "search," which may perform differently than other text prediction functionality. It also has an "agent" mode so you can give it a list of tasks, and it will go through the list and attempt to perform them step by step.

1.3   *How does generative AI work?*

Generative AI is a kind of statistical mimicry of the real world, where algorithms learn patterns and try to create things. If we replace the child with a generative AI model, we must "train" it to create a dog. We need to show it thousands of photos of dogs as examples. The patterns gathered from these pictures help the model learn more about dogs. What shape is a dog? How many legs does it have? What are the odds it has a tail? These are all possibilities with a probability attached to them. These parameters and many more would be used for the model. The tool can use this model to assemble what it thinks a dog will most likely look like.

Similarly, when musicians learn to play an instrument, they aren't just memorizing notes. They learn the patterns, rhythms, and structures of songs. They'll listen to a particular song enough to train themselves on what it's supposed to sound like. They'll listen to so many songs that they grasp exactly what a song in general should sound like. Eventually, they can play the songs others have written until they sound like the original. Then, of course, they move on to improvisation and creating songs of their own based on this training.

Let's add another layer to this analogy: feedback. Musicians seldom work in a vacuum. How do they know they're playing the song correctly? By sharing it with others and looking for feedback. If the music teacher nods, they're doing it right. If the audience applauds, the musician knows the song is successful. If the audience throw tomatoes, they know something has gone wrong and it needs to be fixed. This is the evaluation and feedback process that contributes to their ongoing training.

Generative AI used for coding is very similar. The model evaluates hundreds of thousands of lines of code or more. It parses the code and looks for patterns used to create working software. With enough training, it develops an idea (this is what software looks like) of what new, original code should be.

First, training data is created by taking existing source code in many languages and feeding it into a model. This model is evaluated and has layers that look for specific things. One layer checks the type of syntax. Another checks for keywords and how they're used. The final layer determines whether "this is most likely to be correct and functional source code."

There is a vast array of machine learning algorithms that use the model to run through these layers and draw conclusions. Then, the AI produces output that is a prediction of what the new software should look like. The tool says, "based on what I know, this is the most statistically likely code you're looking for." Then you, the programmer, reach the evaluation point. If you give it a thumbs up, the feedback returns to the model (in many cases, not always) as a correct prediction. If you give it a thumbs down and reject it, that is also tracked. With this continuous feedback, the tool learns what good code should look like.

Figure 1.1 illustrates the feedback loop between developer and AI that powers generative coding tools. Unlike traditional code completion, which operates on predefined rules, generative AI creates a continuous improvement cycle, which includes the following five basic steps:

1. *Developer input*—You provide source code, comments, or natural language requirements.
2. *Context analysis*—The model analyzes patterns in your existing code and requirements.
3. *Prediction*—Based on training data and your specific context, the model generates probable code.
4. *Developer feedback*—You accept, modify, or reject suggestions.
5. *Model adaptation*—The system incorporates your feedback to improve future suggestions.

This cycle creates a powerful symbiotic relationship—the AI learns your coding patterns and preferences, while you gain implementation speed and exposure to new patterns and techniques that might not have been in your toolkit.

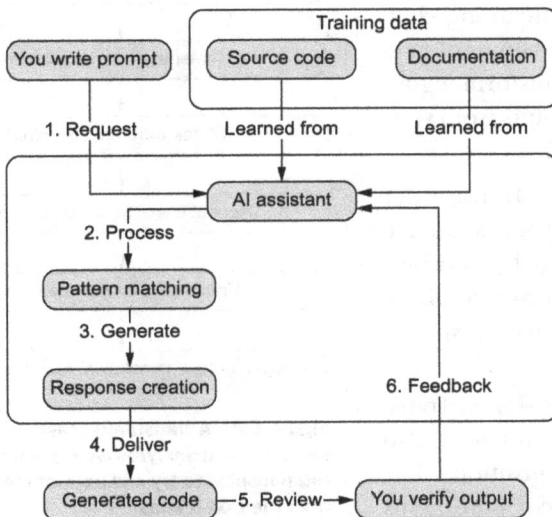

Figure 1.1   Integrated tools use a sophisticated system to generate code. The process starts with your prompt, and the assistant gathers up documentation and source code to see whether your answer can come from these sources. It makes a best guess at what you're looking for and generates a response. Your acceptance of these responses helps train the assistant in the future (unless you've blocked feedback).

This is a very high-level explanation of generative AI. It's the science of predicting what is most likely to be a correct example of something new, based on the data it was trained on. There are features in the algorithms that make things probabilistic instead of deterministic. A deterministic system will always produce the same output if given the same input—it follows fixed rules with no randomness or variation. For example, a traditional calculator always gives exactly 4 when you input 2 + 2. Generative AI models are not deterministic by design. You rarely get the same answer twice. This is intentionally done to create originality in the output. In other words, AI models strive to generate something *new* rather than regurgitate a copy of something already written.

1.4   What is an LLM, and why should I care?

Generative AI for coding and language tools is based on the LLM concept. A large language model is a type of neural network that processes and generates text in a human-like way. It does this by being trained on a massive dataset of text, which allows it to learn human language patterns, as described previously. It lets LLMs translate, write, and answer questions with text. LLMs can contain natural language, source code, and more.

An LLM is a deep learning architecture based on the Transformer model—a significant architectural advancement over previous RNNs (Recurrent Neural Networks) and LSTMs (Long Term–Short Memory Networks) for sequence processing. Transformers employ multiple layers of self-attention mechanisms that process entire sequences in parallel rather than sequentially, vastly improving training efficiency and enabling the scaling to billions of parameters.

Imagine you have a smart system that reads sentences and tries to understand and generate text; this is what a Transformer does. It's a powerful technology that underpins many advanced applications today, including chatbots, automatic translation, and content generation. Here are the steps a transformer goes through, from input data to results from your prompts, as shown in figure 1.2:

- *Starting with words*—A Transformer begins by looking at your sentence word-by-word, turning each word into numbers that it can understand. Think of each word as getting its own special ID tag.
- *Remembering word order*—The Transformer doesn't just see words; it also pays attention to their positions. For example, in the sentence "Jane helps

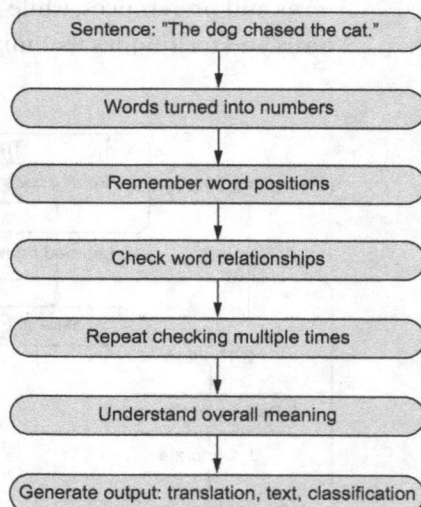

Figure 1.2   **A transformer takes a sentence and analyzes word positions and relationships to try and extract meaning from the text it sees.**

Joe," it knows "Jane" comes first and "Joe" comes last. It tracks this position information so it can better understand the meaning of your sentence.

- *Understanding context and meaning*—Now, the Transformer examines how words relate to each other. It checks each word against all the other words in the sentence. Imagine each word asking every other word, "Hey, how relevant are you to me?" Words that are closely related have stronger relationships, helping the Transformer understand context. For example, in the sentence "The dog chased the cat," the Transformer understands "dog" and "chased" have a strong connection.

- *Repeating this analysis multiple times*—The Transformer doesn't just do this once. It repeats this "checking relationships" step many times, each time learning something deeper about how words in the sentence connect. With each round, the system gains a clearer understanding of the sentence's overall meaning.

- *Producing the output*—After understanding the sentence, the Transformer can now use its knowledge to do different tasks:
  - *Translation*—It can convert text from English to another language.
  - *Text generation*—It can predict what words might naturally come next.
  - *Code generation (what we care about)*—It can predict the chunk of code that might come next.
  - *Classification*—It can recognize the overall meaning or sentiment behind a sentence.

Transformers excel at grasping relationships between words and concepts in sentences and documents. They greatly enhance tasks that were once challenging, such as natural language translation and understanding complex human questions.

When applied to code, these models use attention mechanisms. This feature helps them assess the importance of various parts of the existing codebase when generating suggestions. Attention mechanisms act like a spotlight, helping AI focus on what matters.

Picture yourself in a crowded room. You listen to one conversation while ignoring the noise around you. In coding, when an AI assistant suggests code, it doesn't see every line as equal. It uses attention to identify which parts are most relevant to its task.

For instance, if you're writing a function to calculate taxes, the AI will focus more on your tax rate variables. It will pay less attention to unrelated code, such as your login system. This way, it makes suggestions tailored to your project instead of generic ones.

This ability to zero in on important code is why modern AI coding assistants can offer meaningful suggestions for your specific needs. It's similar to how skilled developers know which code sections affect a new implementation the most. Each transformer layer learns about various code patterns, ranging from syntax validation to understanding the relationships among functions, classes, and modules.

The LLM is trained on vast amounts of text from sources such as books, articles, and websites. For example, GitHub Copilot learns from GitHub's public code base, which allows it to understand the semantic structures of both human language and code.

Once deployed, the LLM uses language patterns and context to create human-like text based on a prompt. It generates text and completes sentences to simulate conversation. For code tools, it aims to produce the most likely correct source code based on your input.

By adjusting parameters such as temperature (which controls randomness) and top k (which affects diversity), developers can tailor the model's output for different needs. This approach ensures the output is high quality and closely resembles human language.

1.5   Why do these tools sometimes get it wrong?

Generative AI tools for coding are sometimes inaccurate. They can produce results that look good but are wrong. This is common with LLMs. They can write code or chat like a person. And sometimes, they share information that's just plain wrong. Not just a bit off, but totally backwards or nonsense. And they say it so confidently! We call this "hallucinating," which is a funny term, but it makes sense.

So, why does this happen? Many people imagine the AI as a giant library, like the Library of Congress in a chip. You ask a question, it zooms to the right shelf, pulls out a book, and reads you the answer. That's not how it works at all. If it did, it wouldn't make things up; it would just say, "I don't know" if the book wasn't there.

So, what is it doing? Think about finishing a sentence. If I say, "The cat sat on the...," what word comes to mind? Probably "mat," right? Or maybe "chair" or "sofa." You're not looking it up; your brain just knows those words fit. You've heard them, read them, and seen them used.

LLMs do something similar, but on a huge scale. They've read a lot of the internet, tons of books, and millions of lines of code. They haven't "understood" it like we understand it, but they've learned the patterns. They know which words usually follow others and which bits of code often appear together.

When you give a prompt, the AI is not looking up the answer. It's predicting it, piece by piece. It thinks, "Okay, based on the prompt and what I've generated so far, what's the most likely next word? And the next? And the next?" It's like a super-powered prediction machine, always guessing the most statistically probable continuation based on learned patterns.

Now you see where the trouble can start. Sometimes, the most probable sequence of words, the one that fits best according to statistics, isn't true. The pattern it learned might come from faulty information online, or maybe your question was tricky. It could latch onto a pattern that seems right but leads to a wrong answer. It's just following statistical likelihood, not checking facts against a truth-database (because there isn't one!).

That's the key. It's a pattern-matching predictor, not a knowledge retriever. It's great at what it does, but since it works by prediction, it can predict nonsense just as confidently as it predicts facts. So, when you use these tools, be curious and skeptical! Don't just accept what it gives you. Ask, "Is this just a likely sounding pattern, or is it actually right?" Understanding how generative AI works helps you know when to trust it and when to double-check. Keeping this skepticism in mind is crucial when working with these tools to produce code.

For most of us, the new concept of text *prediction* to generate answers is vague or even confusing. But we're getting the hang of it, and it's now a part of daily life.

1.5.1 How LLMs differ from databases

Another problem that can be confusing is that LLMs seldom put out the same thing twice. When starting out, many folks confuse ChatGPT and other LLMs with a large, all-knowing database. Instead, ChatGPT, and the tools we'll work with LLMs to generate new text based on mathematical probability.

Traditional databases are straightforward—you ask for something specific, and you get back exactly what was stored. Search engines work similarly, finding existing information.

LLMs work differently. They analyze massive amounts of text data to understand statistical patterns in language. The model processes information through multiple layers, each capturing different aspects—from simple word patterns to complex relationships between ideas.

When you input a question, the LLM goes through a series of steps to create a response:

- Processes your text through its mathematical model
- Calculates the relationships between different parts of your input
- Generates new text by predicting the most probable next word or character
- Repeats this process using both your input and what it just generated

The process of text prediction explains why:

- The same question can get different answers.
- Responses can be confidently incorrect.
- The model can create new combinations it hasn't seen before.

It's essentially a sophisticated prediction system. Instead of looking up stored answers, an LLM calculates probabilities to determine what text should come next. While these predictions are often accurate, they're still *predictions*—which is why it's crucial to verify any code or factual claims the model generates.

This probabilistic nature makes LLMs powerful tools for generating text and code but also means they can make mistakes, even when seeming very confident. Understanding this helps set realistic expectations about what these tools can and cannot do reliably.

1.5.2 Training phase problems

In machine learning, "training" is when we teach models to understand language and code by analyzing massive amounts of data. During training, the model learns statistical patterns—how often certain words appear together, what code structures are common, and how different parts of text relate to each other.

The quality of training data directly affects how well the model performs. If the training data contains errors, incorrect code, or misleading information, the model will learn these flaws. Unlike humans, the model can't independently judge whether information is correct—it simply learns from everything it sees, treating all training data as equally valid.

When generating responses, the model uses probability calculations based on its training data to predict what text should come next. If it learned from flawed data during training, it may confidently generate incorrect or nonsensical output—called hallucinations—when the model produces convincing but incorrect information.

Think of it like teaching someone to code using both good and bad examples without telling them which is which. They'll learn patterns from both and might later write code that looks correct but contains hidden problems. This is why it's crucial to verify AI-generated code and not assume it's correct just because it looks good or because the model seems confident.

These training data problems are different from simple mistakes—they're systematic problems baked into the model during its learning phase. This is one reason why even advanced AI models need human oversight and verification.

For Python developers specifically, these training biases might manifest as

- A preference for common but suboptimal patterns (e.g., using lists where sets would be more efficient)
- Overuse of popular libraries even when simpler solutions exist
- Generating code that works for common cases but fails with edge cases
- Replicating outdated Python patterns from pre-3.6 codebases that don't use newer language features

This is why your expertise remains crucial. You can recognize when the AI is suggesting patterns that don't align with Python best practices or your project's architectural standards.

1.5.3   *Misinterpreting context*

Context is crucial for how language models understand and generate code. The model processes your input by analyzing relationships between different parts of the code and documentation to determine meaning and intent.

Common interpretation challenges in code generation are

- Variable names with multiple potential meanings
- Function overloading where context determines behavior
- API calls that could be valid but incorrect for the use case
- Syntactically correct code that violates semantic conventions
- Ambiguous requirements that could lead to different implementations

The model evaluates context by calculating mathematical relationships between elements in your input. However, it may miss important domain knowledge, coding standards, or architectural patterns that experienced developers understand implicitly.

While model training is fixed, you can improve code generation by

- Providing detailed specifications and constraints
- Including relevant code context (imports, dependencies, related functions)
- Specifying error handling requirements
- Declaring expected inputs and outputs
- Breaking complex features into smaller, focused components

The tools themselves do a great job of pulling in other parts of application into consideration, creating "context" for you. Later chapters will explore specific techniques you can apply to improve context and get more accurate and maintainable code from AI models.

1.6 The potential of LLMs

LLMs and development tools have been increasingly improving, and tens of thousands (or maybe more) of brilliant people are working every day to improve these models. They're making incredible progress, and the pace of improvement is staggering. The potential is enormous.

LLMs and development tools that derive from them greatly enhance productivity and software quality. By understanding the fundamental principles of language and communication, LLMs can provide intelligent assistance in tasks such as code generation, code analysis, and documentation. They will become a mandatory part of your toolbox. You can use these tools to assist you from the abstract design process down to the code syntax. When things break, you can find the reason faster and get assistance for fixing it.

We will write better quality software much faster. We'll test it better and provide better documentation. These tools can turn you into a super developer, and this book will help you set yourself up to reap these benefits.

1.7 Generative AI vs. code completion

It is likely that you have already encountered generative AI technologies as a software developer. When I discuss generative AI tools with other developers, they frequently mention IntelliSense, which was created by Microsoft for Visual Studio. They sometimes say "So, GitHub CoPilot is just another version of IntelliSense, right?" Having spent many years in the trenches as a C# developer with IntelliSense, I agree and disagree simultaneously. Let me explain.

IntelliSense is a code completion tool, very similar to tools in NetBeans, Eclipse, XCode, PyCharm, and many others that proliferated before AI. Generative AI is far more prescriptive. They're similar but not identical. Table 1.1. lists some of the differences.

Table 1.1   The differences between traditional code completion tools and generative AI

Function	Code completion	Generative AI
Input	Relies on predefined rules, syntax information, and available libraries	Utilizes machine learning models (LLMs) to analyze vast amounts of code from the internet and other sources
Output	Context-aware suggestions based on keywords, functions, and libraries	Suggestions based on patterns and relationships in code, and your coding style or patterns
Learning	Rule-based approach that relies on pre-defined knowledge of the language	Deep learning techniques from neural networks; the tool learns from the data it processes.
Scope	Limited to keywords, functions, and libraries available to the language; limited context of surrounding code	Code files, code blocks, functions, and libraries, as well as previously written code publicly available from the internet

Both types of tools are intended to help the developer be more productive in a similar way. How they work under the covers is different. Let's dig deeper into what makes generative AI the next stage of developer productivity tools.

1.7.1   *Other types of generative AI*

As discussed, generative AI is a type of artificial intelligence that can create new content. You've seen it sprouting up all over the place. AI-generated text, images, videos, music, and more can be produced to varying degrees of success. Each field is at a different level of maturity. For instance, text, music, and images are generally more mature than video and voice generation. All this content is generated by learning from existing data or training.

For example, with images, think of generative AI as a super-intelligent artist that has studied and memorized the works of thousands of painters over time, and watched them paint while gathering tips about their technique and composition. It keeps track of how each of these painters did what they did. So, when you ask the tool to create a cyberpunk image of Mona Lisa riding a skateboard in the desert, it can do it easily (figure 1.3).

Figure 1.3   Mona Lisa riding a skateboard in the desert. Generated with Midjourney, a generative AI image-building tool.

Generative AI differs from traditional AI systems, which focus on analyzing and processing data. Instead, generative AI learns patterns and relationships within the data and uses this knowledge to create something new and unique.

1.7.2 Why coders care about generative AI

You picked up this book to boost your productivity as a Python developer with generative AI coding tools. Let's explore the key AI features we'll master together and how they'll help you write better code faster:

- *Code completion and suggestion*—Tools such as GitHub Copilot, Tabnine, and Blackbox AI use generative AI to analyze your code and suggest snippets. Here, you'll learn how to use these tools effectively. This not only saves time but also lets you focus on complex problems while AI manages routine tasks, speeding up your development.

- *Automated testing*—Generative AI can create a variety of test cases to cover edge cases. You'll learn to use AI for generating test suites quickly. This improves your code's reliability and catches bugs early, a crucial skill we'll practice. Better testing leads to much stronger software.

- *Documentation generation*—Generative AI analyzes your code and comments to automate documentation. This book will show you how to simplify this often-boring task, ensuring your projects are well-documented with less effort. This makes your software easier to maintain and user-friendly.

- *Natural language processing*—Chatbots and virtual assistants, such as ChatGPT, utilize generative AI to understand and produce human-like text. While our focus is on coding, knowing how these tools process language is important. The skills you gain here can help you build better prompts and have better experiences with generative AI tools in general.

- *Vibe coding*—At the far end of the AI-assisted development spectrum lies an emerging approach called "vibe coding," a conversational programming style where developers guide AI with natural language rather than detailed specifications. While this book focuses on structured, production-ready AI integration, we'll explore how tools such as Cursor enable rapid prototyping through simple conversation in chapter 10. This is a new and different way of interacting with AI tools, and it has become popular. Vibe coding is great for "just for fun" projects and rapid prototyping, where ideas can become working demos in minutes rather than hours.

1.8 Project workflow with AI assistance

Incorporating AI assistance into your software development workflow can significantly improve productivity, reduce repetitive tasks, and elevate the overall quality of your projects. So long as you verify the output, you can speed up the development process and build better products faster.

Let's outline a typical project workflow that leverages the generative AI tools mentioned above to enhance various aspects of the software development process (figure 1.4).

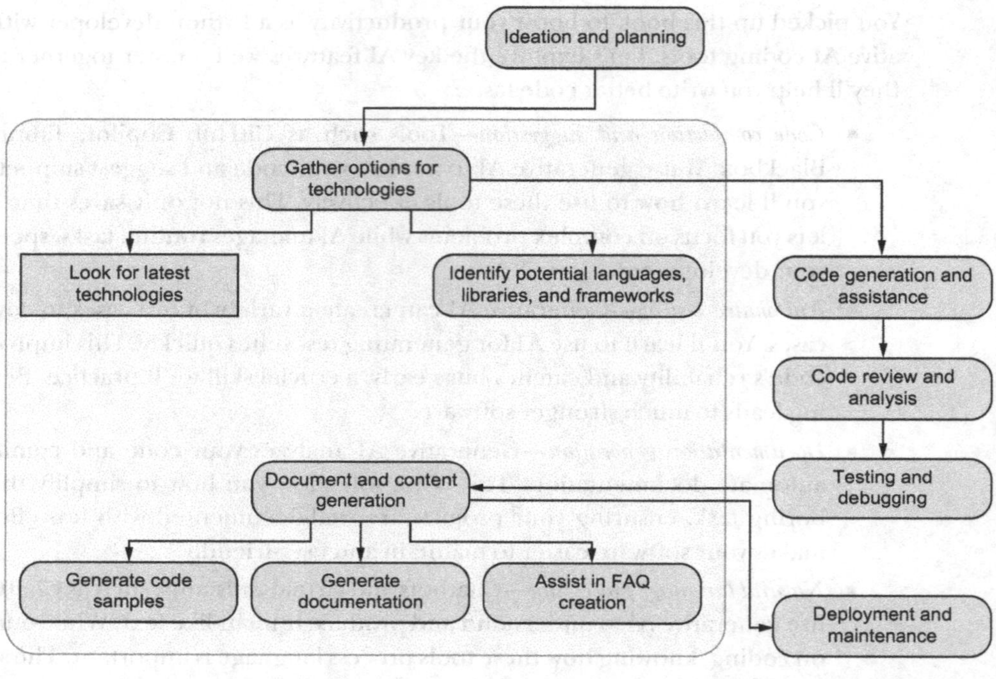

Ideation and planning

Gather options for technologies

Look for latest technologies

Identify potential languages, libraries, and frameworks

Code generation and assistance

Code review and analysis

Testing and debugging

Document and content generation

Generate code samples

Generate documentation

Assist in FAQ creation

Deployment and maintenance

Figure 1.4 Generative AI tools play a big role in the planning process—from ideation and planning, to choosing a technology, and finally to building the software and deploying it. Each of these steps can be enhanced with AI tooling.

1.8.1 Ideation and planning

At this stage of the process, something chat-based such as Chat GPT, Gemini, or Bing is best to start with. Use plain English to describe what you want to do and send the tool prompts to get started, such as

> Act as a software architect skilled in software design and development. I would like to create a TODO application where I can add a list of tasks to complete, and then mark them as completed. What tech stack should I use for a web-based version of this software?

Tools such as ChatGPT will give you a list of options for the frontend, backend, and database. Maybe you have a tech stack in mind. You could modify the prompt to say something like

Act as a software architect skilled in software design and development. I would like to create a TODO application where I can add a list of tasks to complete and then mark them as completed. I would like to build this with MariaDB, Flask, and Vue. How can I get started?

When sending this query to ChatGPT 4, I got this result:

Great! Here's a high-level overview of the steps you can take to build your TODO application using MariaDB, Flask, and Vue:

Database Design: First, you'll need to design the database schema for your TODO application. This will include creating a table to store the tasks, along with any relevant columns such as task name, description, due date, and completion status.

Set up MariaDB: Install MariaDB and set up a new database instance. Then, create the necessary tables and columns based on your database design.

Set up Flask: Install Flask, a popular Python-based web framework. Create a new Flask app and set up routes to handle CRUD (create, read, update, delete) operations on the task data.

Set up Vue: Install Vue.js, a popular JavaScript-based frontend framework. Create a new Vue.js app and set up components to display the task data and handle user interactions, such as adding a new task or marking a task as completed.

Connect Flask and Vue: Use Flask's REST API to expose the task data to your Vue.js app. You can use libraries such as Axios to make HTTP requests to the Flask API and retrieve the data.

Test and Deploy: Once you have the basic functionality working, test your application thoroughly to ensure it works as expected. Then, deploy your application to a web server or a cloud-based hosting service.

Some additional tips:

You can use SQLAlchemy, a popular Python-based ORM, to interact with the MariaDB database in Flask.

You may want to consider adding user authentication to your application to prevent unauthorized access to task data.

You can use Vue.js libraries such as Vuex and Vue Router to manage state and handle routing within your application.

Don't forget to add error handling and validation to your application to ensure it is robust and secure.

Overall, building a TODO application with MariaDB, Flask, and Vue.js should be a fun and rewarding project! Good luck!

You can use this conversational style to generate ideas and start an outline for your project to plan things out before getting into the code. This is also a good point to start documentation, such as a project proposal, feature descriptions, application requirements, and more, which will allow you to focus on high-level objectives.

1.8.2   Code generation and assistance

As you begin writing code, the integrated developer tools we mentioned earlier provide AI-powered code completions and suggestions. You can also use external tools to start "scaffolding" this code.

Scaffolding an application is generating a basic structure or framework for an application. This is similar to "create react app" with Node or "dotnet new" with C# applications. It involves automatically generating code, files, and directories that provide a starting point for development. This operation gives you a basic skeleton of an application you can complete and make whole.

I asked ChatGPT:

> JM   Please scaffold the routes of the backend API of this application in Python

As a result, it generated a full Python script with routes, a model, and methods automatically.

NOTE   While this prompt generates code that may be thorough and functional, do not blindly copy and paste it into your product, especially if you don't understand it. The code generated can be functional but not optimal and even dangerous if you do not fully understand it.

At this point, you want to write out your code and use the integrated tools to help you on your way.

1.8.3   Code review and analysis

External tools can be great for code review. You can use prompts such as

> JM   Evaluate the following code for performance, and identify any possible bottlenecks: (insert source code)

We will be doing this frequently later in the book.

External tools such as ChatGPT, Gemini, and Bing will evaluate your code and give you feedback. I have recently found that Gemini is very good at identifying bottlenecks and suggesting code improvements and rewrites. While ChatGPT is somewhat better for outlining and design, when I've dumped my own code into both, I've received some surprisingly good suggestions from Gemini, with little context. Figure 1.5 shows how you can drop in a function and request evaluation. Gemini doesn't know anything about how the code will be used but can still make suggestions.

You can perform similar actions for security as well. This is one of my favorite things to do with software. Use a prompt such as

> JM   Evaluate the following code for security issues, and identify any possible vulnerabilities:

```
(insert source code)
```

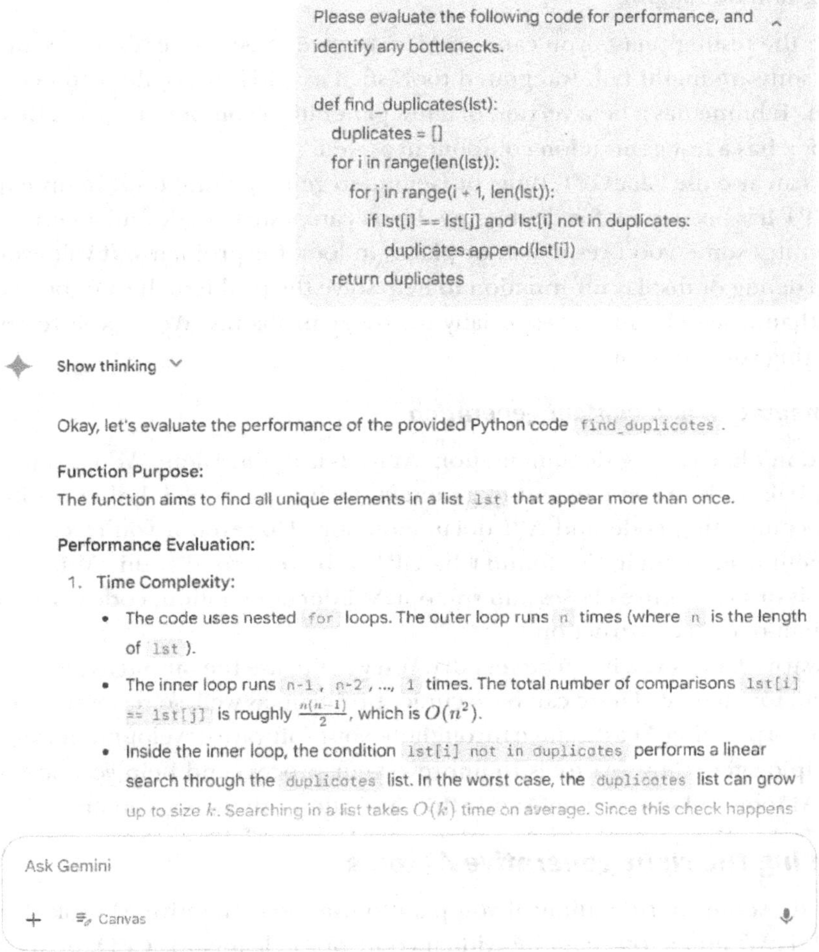

Please evaluate the following code for performance, and
identify any bottlenecks.

```
def find_duplicates(lst):
    duplicates = []
    for i in range(len(lst)):
        for j in range(i + 1, len(lst)):
            if lst[i] == lst[j] and lst[i] not in duplicates:
                duplicates.append(lst[i])
    return duplicates
```

Show thinking ∨

Okay, let's evaluate the performance of the provided Python code `find_duplicates`.

Function Purpose:
The function aims to find all unique elements in a list `lst` that appear more than once.

Performance Evaluation:

1. Time Complexity:

- The code uses nested `for` loops. The outer loop runs `n` times (where `n` is the length of `lst`).

- The inner loop runs `n-1`, `n-2`, ..., `1` times. The total number of comparisons `lst[i] == lst[j]` is roughly $\frac{n(n-1)}{2}$, which is $O(n^2)$.

- Inside the inner loop, the condition `lst[i] not in duplicates` performs a linear search through the `duplicates` list. In the worst case, the `duplicates` list can grow up to size k. Searching in a list takes $O(k)$ time on average. Since this check happens

Ask Gemini

＋ ☰ Canvas   🎤

Figure 1.5 Even with a few lines of code, Gemini can analyze it and make suggestions to improve it.

In my experience, it has found glaring errors or provided suggestions to put you into a more security-focused mindset.

With Gemini, I've received replies that look like this:

◆   The code is well-written and easy to understand. It does not contain any obvious security vulnerabilities. However, there are a few things that could be improved to make it more secure.

ChatGPT gives similar results. These tips are crucial to changing the way you write software. It can give you tips you didn't know about or offer different ways of doing things you haven't thought about. We'll see that as we move through this book.

1.8.4   Testing and debugging

During the testing phase, you can use AI assistance to generate test cases and identify where software might fail. Integrated tools such as GitHub Copilot can generate tests for you. Tabnine has a beta version of a test generation component (as of this writing). Blackbox has a test generation component as well.

You can also use ChatGPT, Bing, or Gemini to generate unit tests. In my experience, ChatGPT has been great for debugging. If you can paste in code and an error message, it generates some good responses or places to look for problems. It will even tell you ways to debug or display information to help solve the problem. It's not perfect, but it's faster than a search engine, especially for tricky problems. We'll explore testing and debugging your code later.

1.8.5   Documentation and content generation

If you don't like writing documentation, AI tools are your friend. You can use the integrated IDE tools to some extent to generate documentation. Tabnine works very well at autocompleting code and API documentation. However, if you're creating a new document from scratch, I've found ChatGPT to be very good at this. You can dump in methods or even entire classes and spit out API documentation, code documentation, or human-readable instructions.

Be warned, however, it can be very dry. You want to use the output as *guidance* and put a human touch on it. There can be accuracy problems as well, so review it thoroughly.

By incorporating AI assistance throughout your software development workflow, you can employ generative AI tools to improve your process and help you develop faster. Using AI tools will save you time and effort and allow you to focus on more fun stuff.

1.9   Choosing the right generative AI tools

There are some considerations if you plan to use the generative AI tools discussed in this book. Whether you're an individual contributor, leader, or CEO, if you decide to utilize these tools, many of these factors apply to you.

1.9.1   Data quality and availability

As the old saying goes, "Garbage in, garbage out." Generative AI tools are only as good as the data they're trained on. They need high-quality, diverse, and extensive datasets to create great code as output. Unfortunately, you have no control over this input. You must trust the creators behind the product are using the best code possible for the *corpus*, or data used for training. Researching the tools lets you learn how each tool gathers data and decide based on that.

You must decide how much you value open source software for training versus proprietary software. Most tools use a combination of the two. Software trained on mostly open source software is a safe bet. A corpus derived from proprietary code can be more creative or meet a specific need. You must decide which one you value more.

The source code used to train these models provides unique challenges when it comes to licensing. If the tool is trained on licensed software and it generates something close enough to the original, there are some legal and copyright matters to think about. I'm no lawyer, so I can't help you much, and it's still a hotly debated topic in the field right now.

1.9.2 Integration with development workflows

Whether you're working solo or in an enterprise team with rigorous processes, as an experienced Python developer, you have likely established workflows. Integrating AI tools requires thoughtful consideration. If you are a solo developer,

- Evaluate how these tools interact with your existing IDE extensions and configurations
- Consider how to maintain consistency between AI-generated code and your personal coding style
- Develop strategies for validating AI suggestions against your domain-specific knowledge

For team environments,

- Establish team conventions for documenting which parts of the codebase used AI assistance (for future maintenance).
- Consider how AI tools interact with code review processes and standards.
- Address potential security concerns when AI tools process proprietary code.
- Ensure consistent access to these tools across your development team.

The learning curve varies across tools. While simple code completion might become intuitive within days, mastering more advanced capabilities such as architectural pattern generation could take weeks. Throughout this book, I highlight integration strategies that minimize disruption, while maximizing productivity gains.

1.9.3 Quality assurance

AI-generated code must function correctly and adhere to your organization's quality standards. Ideally you won't be using large amounts of AI generated code you don't understand, but it's still a consideration. These tools can speed up development and complicate code review and QA testing. You should always be transparent about your use of the tools and ensure they adhere to the standards expected of human-written code.

1.9.4 Keeping up with evolving tools

I don't have to tell you how fast these tools are evolving—you already know. You must stay abreast of the latest advancements in the tools and need to be familiar with advancements and new techniques. You must discern which of these tools and features are useful and not just a trend. And once again, it's a balancing act. You must determine if the long-term benefits are worth the churn of learning and re-learning the tool.

1.9.5   *Shift in focus*

In my career as a software engineer, I had to change my thinking from the day-to-day mechanics of writing code to more abstract skills. The shift from writing code to designing systems and architecture is a natural path for software developers. The AI tools accelerate that. and as you use the tools, you'll transition to thinking more like a designer than a coder much faster. Can you adapt to this rapid change? Can your team members?

1.10   *Don't fear the rise of AI*

A big concern among developers is the fear that AI will replace their jobs and render their skills obsolete. I agree that things will change, and some jobs will disappear. It's hard to deny that reality. Accenture (2023) estimates that language AI will support 40% of work hours as generative AI adoption grows (see https://mng.bz/pZo5). That same report says AI will spark creativity and innovation and "usher in an era of enterprise intelligence." Changes are coming.

While the concern is valid, it's sometimes overhyped. Software developer jobs won't disappear overnight. Things will change fast, and we're already seeing that. I don't have the psychic abilities to tell you what the future looks like, but nobody can deny that our industry will permanently change with generative AI. As a forward-looking developer learning about it, you're positioning yourself to stay ahead of the game.

Generative AI is a powerful ally rather than a threat. It's not a tool to replace you but a tool to make you more effective. By understanding and embracing generative AI now, you can harness its capabilities to augment your own skills. You *can* use it to streamline your workflow and create more innovative solutions. Consider generative AI as a smart assistant that can help you do what you do faster and more efficiently.

Generative AI is not a replacement for software developers. Here's why:

- *It handles the boring stuff.* Do you love writing boilerplate code? While it's not the worst part of the job, it's not fun. Writing repetitive code to do unexciting things is part of the job. It's more fun to create features, solve problems, and improve performance. Generative AI tools can generate repetitive code quickly, so you can focus on more interesting work. This interesting work is exactly what humans are good at, and AI (currently) isn't.

- *Humans still play the main role in problem solving.* AI driven tools will automate mundane tasks, write boring plumbing code, and even generate comments and documentation. AI can also generate tests very well. However, producing meaningful results still requires knowledge, intuition, and creativity. AI tools can generate code and make helpful suggestions. They don't fully understand all the context or your business. Critical decisions should still be made by the people involved.

- *Adaptability is required.* Nobody needs to tell you how fast this industry moves. It constantly evolves at an ever-increasing rate. Your challenges might be brand new, while your AI tool's knowledge may have stopped a year and a half ago.

Trends and best practices can easily change between the tool's deployment and when you're using it. Your ability to think critically, learn, and innovate is still better than that of AI. Having a good, experienced developer to gut-check the result from these tools is extremely valuable.

- *Ethical and moral considerations hold significance.* Generative AI is designed to be neutral. It has no opinions and no human sense of right or wrong. It's your job to ensure technology is used responsibly and ethically.

- *The human touch is still important.* Generative AI can produce impressive results. Folks in tech are using ChatGPT to build entire applications. However, remember your favorite AI tool isn't a person but clever automated assistant. It doesn't possess emotional intelligence or empathy. It doesn't understand context or experiences the same way you do. Your ability to connect with users and see things from their perspective is important. Your creativity and gut feelings are still needed in this space.

Some say the tools can encourage laziness and usher unchecked code into products. Or they can help people write software they don't understand. There is an element of truth to these possible side effects of code generation and the abstraction of code in general. However, like any tool, it depends on how you use it and how experienced developers influence the new folks. This is a larger problem we'll address later.

1.11 Go forth and code!

While we've covered the fundamentals, the true power of these tools emerges when you master advanced techniques explored in upcoming chapters:

- *Context management*—You'll learn how to structure your codebase and prompts to provide optimal context for AI tools, resulting in more accurate and relevant suggestions.

- *Prompt engineering*—We'll develop sophisticated prompting techniques that guide AI tools to generate precisely the code patterns your project requires.

- *Testing integration*—You'll discover how to generate comprehensive test suites that cover edge cases you might not have considered.

- *Architectural guidance*—Beyond just code completion, you'll learn how to use AI for higher-level design decisions and architecture validation.

Each of these techniques builds on the fundamentals covered in this chapter, transforming generative AI from a useful assistant into an indispensable development partner.

This book takes a hands-on approach to mastering generative AI tools. Each chapter builds on a core project—creating a full-featured web application—while introducing new AI tools and techniques. You'll start with basic code generation and progress to testing, documentation, and advanced features.

Rather than just reading about concepts, you'll learn by doing: writing prompts, evaluating AI responses, and integrating generated code into real applications.

By the end of this book, you'll be able to

- Use AI to speed up your coding workflow by 30%–50%.
- Generate and validate high-quality code and documentation.
- Choose the right generative AI tool for different coding tasks.
- Build complete applications using AI assistance.
- Debug and optimize AI-generated code.

You'll see practical examples, clear diagrams, and step-by-step instructions suitable for both beginners and experienced developers. Each chapter includes exercises to reinforce your learning and real-world scenarios you're likely to encounter in your development work. Later in the book we'll explore "vibe coding" where we use plain language to create software.

Join me in the next chapter as we roll our sleeves and build software with generative AI tools.

Summary

- Generative AI tools are changing software development. They boost productivity by generating code, finding bugs, and automating documentation.
- Modern AI tools come in two types: integrated tools such as GitHub Copilot and Tabnine, which work in your IDE, and standalone solutions such as ChatGPT and Gemini for bigger tasks.
- Large language models (LLMs) drive these tools. They learn patterns from massive code datasets, which help them create relevant code based on probabilities.
- It's important to know that AI tools make predictions and not certain outcomes. This understanding sets realistic expectations and shows why checking results is key.
- The AI-assisted development workflow includes ideation, planning, coding, testing, and documentation. Each phase gains unique benefits from AI support.
- To adopt AI tools effectively, consider training data quality, how they fit into workflows, quality assurance processes, and the need to adapt to new tools quickly.
- AI tools do not replace developers. Instead, they take care of routine tasks, letting humans focus on problem-solving, design, and creativity.
- As you read this book, you'll discover ways to use these tools, seeing them as valuable partners in your Python development process.

First steps with AI-assisted coding 2

This chapter covers

- The fundamentals of GitHub Copilot
- Creating a Python environment for a Python project
- Building a project using generated code
- Using code completion to generate snippets
- Using the Copilot Chat interface

Getting started with generative AI tools can be daunting. Many people frequently ask me, "How do I get started? Which model do I choose?" Fortunately, the easiest way to start is to pick a tool and experiment. Once you do, you'll find the learning curve surprisingly small.

We begin by using GitHub Copilot. To learn the basics, we'll jump in headfirst to solve a programming problem. Next, we'll build a useful application in Python with assistance from Copilot. By the end of this chapter, you'll be comfortable using Copilot when writing code.

2.1   *What is GitHub Copilot?*

Do you remember the "rubber duck" debugging method? You visualize a rubber duck on your desk and explain the problem to it. You can use a real rubber duck or, like me, a toy wizard. I've confided in that wizard many times, working through problems. The key is to verbalize the matter to an imaginary helper. Once you articulate the problem clearly, by shifting focus, you might find solutions you didn't see before.

Imagine having an intelligent assistant that helps you with coding, like the rubber duck method, but one that can respond and suggest solutions. The tool will suggest word completions as you type, help you find and fix mistakes, and even make whole functions when asked. This is GitHub Copilot.

Launched in October 2021, GitHub Copilot is an AI coding tool powered by OpenAI's Codex algorithm. It employs extensive GitHub training data to offer context-aware code suggestions in multiple programming languages. It's an incredible tool that will surprise you with its usefulness. Copilot aims to boost your productivity and cut down on repetitive coding tasks. It's like having your own pair programmer or intelligent rubber duck providing suggestions as you work.

At the time of this writing, GitHub Copilot is available for Visual Studio, Visual Studio Code, Vim, NeoVim, JetBrains IDEs, and Azure Data Studio.

NOTE GitHub Copilot is not a free tool. There is a monthly fee for this tool. You can find more information on the GitHub Copilot information page (https://github.com/features/copilot). It is free for verified students, teachers, and maintainers of popular open source projects.

GitHub Copilot is trained on public source code using the OpenAI Codex model. Training involves providing a model with a large dataset of text and code to enable it to learn patterns and generate similar content. The model then uses machine learning to teach itself how to generate text and code that is like what it was trained on. GitHub's model was trained on billions of lines of code from GitHub repositories and other publicly available code. The Copilot service connects to and utilizes this model.

When you write code in the editor, it is sent to the Copilot service. The *context* is the code in your project that Copilot can view. The Copilot uses this context to gather information for queries. The code is sent to the model, and suggestions are returned to your editor. Then, when you accept the changes, this feedback is sent to the Copilot service. The model then uses this feedback to determine whether you liked what was sent, which forms a loop that gradually improves the suggestions over time. Figure 2.1 shows an overview of this process.

2.1.1   *How GitHub Copilot works*

Figure 2.1 is a good high-level example, but let's dig deeper into the process of how Copilot creates results. We can step through the entire process and understand how queries turn into code suggestions.

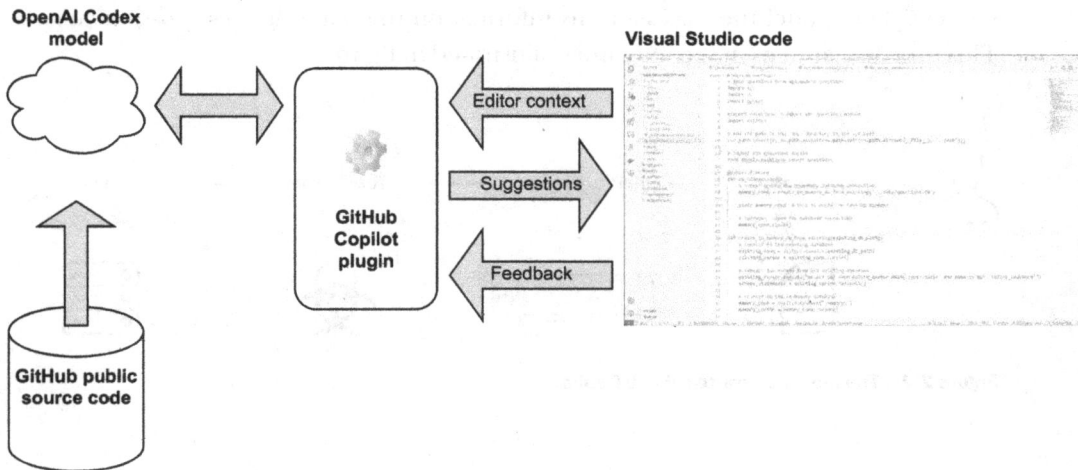

Figure 2.1   GitHub Copilot takes the code from your editor and analyzes it. It then sends suggestions back from the Codex model. Your decision to accept those suggestions or reject them is fed back into the model to refine the future suggestions.

INBOUND FLOW

Here's the process your prompt goes through as it's sent to GitHub Copilot. Understanding this process helps you generate better results by taking better control of the tool.

The process begins in your code editor, either as a comment or chat message. The prompt itself is sent with important context, such as

- Code before and after the cursor
- Code and information in open tabs
- Filename and file type
- Project structure and paths
- Programming language and frameworks used

Fill-in-the-middle (FIM) refers to a technique where Copilot analyzes both the code preceding the segment selected or asked about and the segment that follows it. FIM allows Copilot to understand a greater amount of code.

This code is then sent to a proxy server, which acts as a filter. This filter prevents attempts to hack the LLM or manipulate the system in a harmful way. The next step is a toxicity filter, which looks for hate speech and inappropriate content. Anything that could be harmful or offensive is blocked at this point. It also filters out personal information such as names, addresses, or identifiable information.

Finally, the prompt is prepared and shipped to the LLM model to generate code suggestions. These suggestions are based on the prompt, but also on the surrounding context. The model then uses all this information to create the best possible answer. This process happens in seconds and is illustrated in figure 2.2.

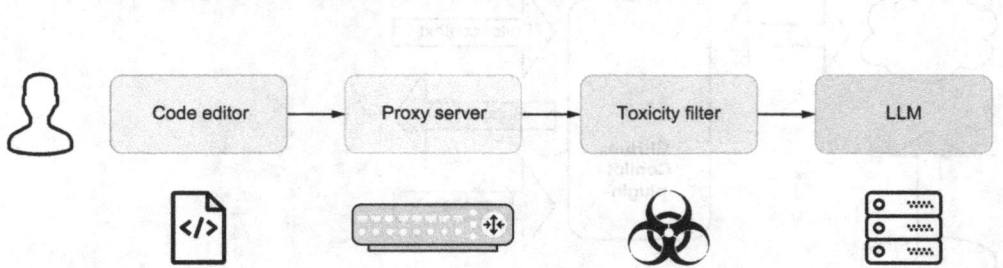

Figure 2.2   The inbound flow to GitHub Copilot

OUTBOUND FLOW

The outbound flow is in the reverse direction. First, the result is passed through a toxicity filter to ensure no hate speech, inappropriate, or private material is sent from the LLM. Then, the proxy server runs a final check for

- *Code quality*—Checks for common bugs and bad patterns.
- *Security*—Checks for known vulnerabilities and insecure patterns.
- *Matching public code* (optional)—Checks whether the content is original and how closely it matches public code. This code can then be removed or truncated if the Copilot administrator wants to do so.

This process is illustrated in figure 2.3, as the suggestions travel back to the IDE.

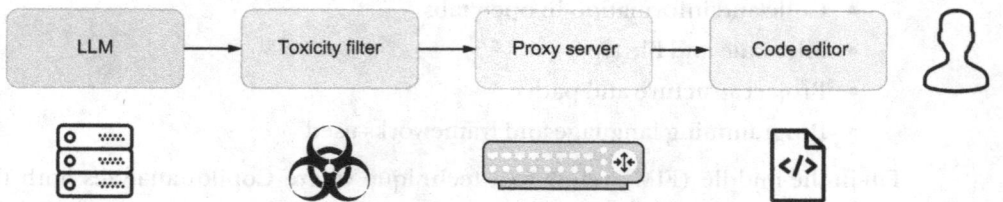

Figure 2.3   Outbound flow from the LLM back to the code editor

This process is ongoing as you use the GitHub Copilot application in your IDE. This continuous loop ensures your code suggestions are appropriate and useful for your project. This is one of the key distinctions between GitHub Copilot and ChatGPT when handling code suggestions. The context and filtering can make a big difference in the quality of work.

2.1.2 Interacting with GitHub Copilot

There are several ways to interact with Copilot. You can work from the editor with assistance or open a separate Copilot chat window. Here are the ways Copilot can work for you as a developer.

CODE COMPLETION

Copilot can suggest code completions as you type in the editor. It analyzes the current context of your code and provides real-time suggestions to complete statements or functions. This can speed up coding and reduce syntax errors (figure 2.4).

```
       return response
10
11  @app.route('/delete-cookie', methods=['GET'])
12         ⊙ route
13         ⊙ run
14         ⦿ secret_key
15         ⊙ select_jinja_autoescape
16  @app. ⊙ send_static_file              ', methods=['GET', 'POST'])
17  def q ⦿ session_interface
18      o ⊙ shell_context_processor      ')
19      t ⦿ shell_context_processors
```

Figure 2.4 Copilot can suggest code completions as you type by analyzing comments or surrounding code for context.

In the previous example, we were building an API. GitHub Copilot knows a lot about APIs and how to create them. You can describe API endpoints and structure, and Copilot will generate appropriate data classes and request handling code automatically, saving you time.

CODE GENERATION

Copilot can generate full segments of code based on statements, comments, or partial code snippets. You can enter a comment describing a function, and Copilot will attempt to complete the code. This feature is great for repetitive tasks and when looking for different ways to solve a problem (figure 2.5).

```
## function to add your current question data to a cookie
def add_question_to_cookie(question_id, question_number):
    question_data = {
        'question_id': question_id,
        'question_number': question_number
    }
    response = make_response(render_template('quiz.html', question=thisquestion, questi
    response.set_cookie('question_data', json.dumps(question_data))
    return response
```

Figure 2.5 Copilot can generate entire functions or segments of code based on comments or partial code snippets.

TRANSLATION

You can translate code from one language to another by highlighting the code and invoking Copilot. This feature allows you to convert legacy codebases into newer or modern languages. It can also help you understand what a function is doing by translating it into a language you're more familiar with (figure 2.6).

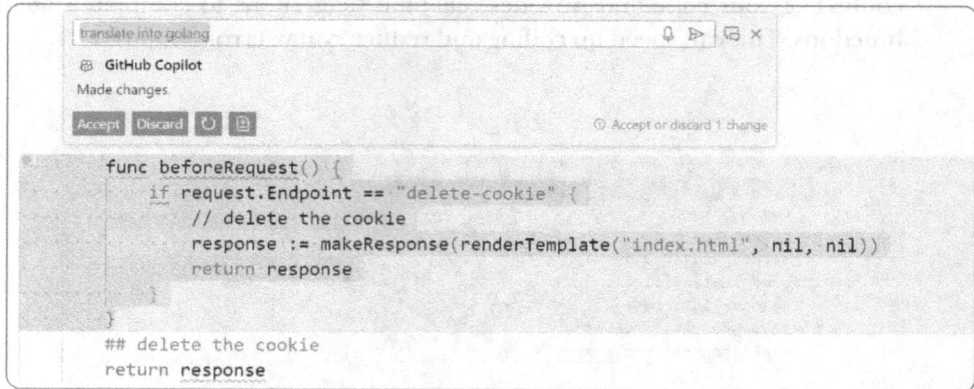

```
translate into golang                                    🎤 ▷  🗔 ✕
🐙 GitHub Copilot
Made changes.
 Accept   Discard  ↺  ▤                        ⓘ Accept or discard 1 change

func beforeRequest() {
    if request.Endpoint == "delete-cookie" {
        // delete the cookie
        response := makeResponse(renderTemplate("index.html", nil, nil))
        return response
    }
}
## delete the cookie
return response
```

Figure 2.6   You can use Copilot to translate code from one language to another. Here, I have highlighted a section of Python code and asked Copilot to translate it into Go.

DEBUGGING

You can highlight a problematic piece of code and ask Copilot to debug it. It can provide suggestions to fix syntax errors, logical errors, or performance problems, which lets you quickly identify and resolve bugs and speed up your debugging process (figure 2.7).

```
def before_request():
    if request.endpoint == 'delete-cookie':
        response = make_response(render_template('index.html', data=None, session_id=None))
        ## delete the cookie
        /fix                                              🎤 ▷  🗔 ✕
        🐙 GitHub Copilot
        The problem is that the response.delete_cookie() method is missing the cookie name as an argument. To
        fix this, you need to provide the name of the cookie to be deleted.
         Accept   Discard  ↺  ▤                    ⓘ Accept or discard 1 change
        response.delete_cookie('session_id')
        return response
```

Figure 2.7   You can highlight a problematic section of code and get suggestions on how to fix it. You can either accept the answer and have the code inserted or discard it and attempt a fix of your own.

DOCUMENTATION GENERATION

You can ask Copilot to generate documentation for you. This is handled either in the editor window or through the chat window. You can use the chat window to have conversations with Copilot and ask questions or get ideas (figure 2.8).

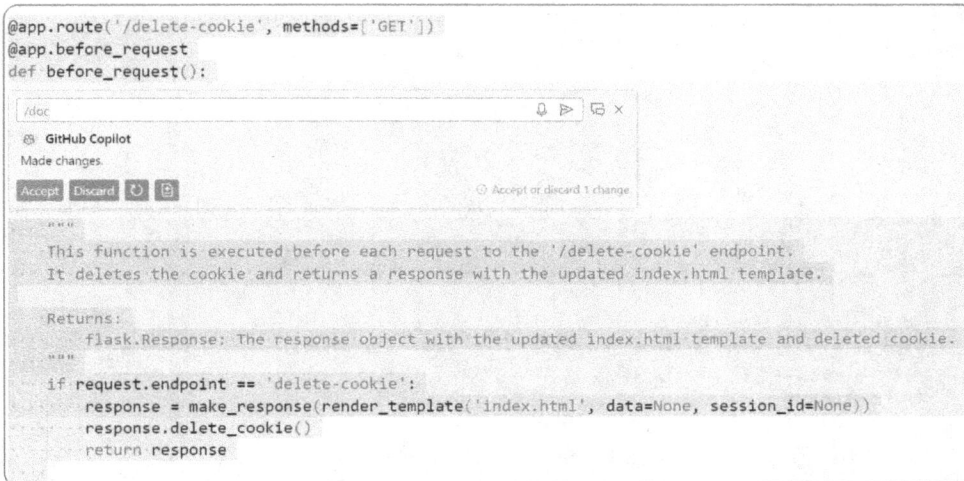

```
@app.route('/delete-cookie', methods=['GET'])
@app.before_request
def before_request():
```

```
/doc                                                    🎤  ▷  📋  ✕
```

```
⊚  GitHub Copilot
Made changes.
[Accept] [Discard]  ↻  📋                          ⊙ Accept or discard 1 change
```

```
    """
    This function is executed before each request to the '/delete-cookie' endpoint.
    It deletes the cookie and returns a response with the updated index.html template.

    Returns:
        flask.Response: The response object with the updated index.html template and deleted cookie.
    """

    if request.endpoint == 'delete-cookie':
        response = make_response(render_template('index.html', data=None, session_id=None))
        response.delete_cookie()
        return response
```

Figure 2.8 You can automatically generate comments and other code documentation using Copilot. This is one of my favorite features of the tool, as it saves a tremendous amount of time.

RIGHT-CLICK TOOL WINDOWS

It is possible to interact with Copilot in many ways inside your IDE window. There are some shortcuts for the features mentioned before. For example, you can click in the IDE near the code and ask it to document it, explain it, fix it, or generate tests, as shown in figure 2.9.

```
def before_request():
    if requ___ _____   '_____ _____'
        res  /                          🎤  ▷     ('index html', data=None, session_id=None))
        ## de    /doc            Add documentation comment for this symbol
        retur    /explain        Explain how the code in your active editor works
                 /fix            Propose a fix for the problems in the selected code
                 /tests          Generate unit tests for the selected code
```

Figure 2.9 GitHub Copilot can perform many actions from a right-click menu within your IDE.

CHAT WINDOW

You can interact with GitHub Copilot in a chat window as well, and it has a familiar dialog interface like ChatGPT and other models. The difference is that this chat window is fully aware of the code in your project. In fact, some commands in the IDE will send you to a chat window so you can ask more questions or attempt to regenerate the results (figure 2.10).

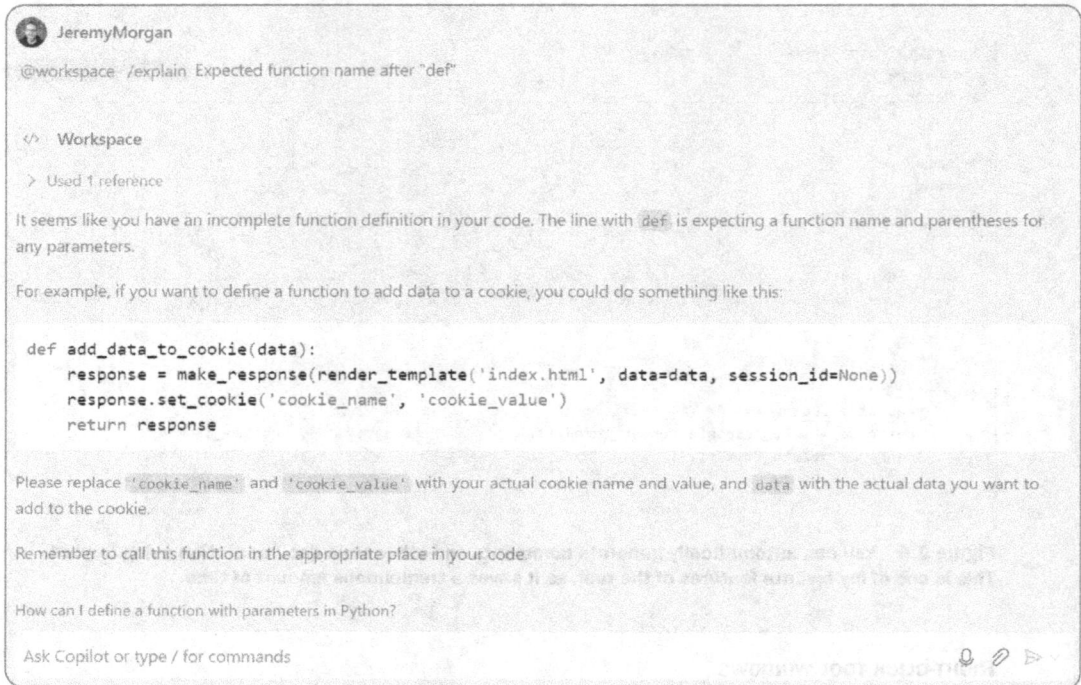

JeremyMorgan

@workspace /explain Expected function name after "def"

</> Workspace

> Used 1 reference

It seems like you have an incomplete function definition in your code. The line with `def` is expecting a function name and parentheses for any parameters.

For example, if you want to define a function to add data to a cookie, you could do something like this:

```python
def add_data_to_cookie(data):
    response = make_response(render_template('index.html', data=data, session_id=None))
    response.set_cookie('cookie_name', 'cookie_value')
    return response
```

Please replace `'cookie_name'` and `'cookie_value'` with your actual cookie name and value, and `data` with the actual data you want to add to the cookie.

Remember to call this function in the appropriate place in your code

How can I define a function with parameters in Python?

Ask Copilot or type / for commands

Figure 2.10 Copilot has a traditional chat window interface within Visual Studio, making it easy to ask for help or suggestions.

We're going to explore this tool through practical, hands-on activities. You'll learn how Copilot can assist in auto-generating Python code as we build an application to analyze text. We'll explore how Copilot understands context from comments and function names. With Copilot's help, we can put together a working script quickly.

> **TIP** You can use "hints" to guide Copilot to generate exactly what you're looking for. For instance, if you want an asynchronous function, you can type in "async def," and that will tell Copilot you want a coroutine instead of a normal function.

By the end of this chapter, you'll be ready to bring this AI coding sidekick into your own projects. Copilot may not yet write flawless code, but it can make you a more productive programmer. Let's dive in and see what this tool can do. We'll build an app that does some primitive natural language processing (NLP), which is appropriate since we use tools that utilize it.

2.2   Common patterns

As you continue working with generative AI coding tools, you'll develop patterns when working with chat windows. These patterns will become second nature to you after a while, and you can use this approach for many different tools. Here are some common phrases you can ask in chat to get better results:

- *Find the error in the selected code.* You highlight a code snipped and ask it to diagnose bugs or problems with syntax. This phrase works especially well with tools that keep your application in context and consider that context for the result.
- *Refactor this code to make it better.* While this can be highly subjective, there are times when Copilot and other tools can suggest a better pattern or algorithm for what you're trying to do. You can ask it to optimize for security, speed, or resource usage.
- *Generate code for {specific task}.* This is a common way to generate boilerplate code for things you've done countless times but don't want to write out by hand. Things such as connecting to databases, reading from files, and sending HTTP commands are great examples of code that can be generated this way.
- *Explain how this code works.* This pattern is invaluable when working with legacy code or anything you didn't build. It can quickly get you up to speed on what the code is designed to do, and all the tools we'll talk about do a great job at it.
- *Add tests for this code.* This pattern can sometimes feel like cheating. The tools we discuss are great at generating tests. This feature gives you a clear time advantage, as it generates tests for you rather than writing them out by hand. It provides a quality advantage as well, because it can find cases you haven't considered or forgot to add. This is a valuable pattern you'll use repeatedly.
- *Suggest improvements for readability and maintainability.* This is another helpful pattern for refactoring or working with legacy code. Admit it, all of us have put something together just to make it pass tests and fix a problem. It wasn't the clearest or simplest way to do it, and this is a way to root out code like that and improve it.
- *Compare tradeoffs for {option a} and {option b}.* Sometimes, our first idea isn't the best approach. Sometimes we're tired, burned out, or just can't think of the best way to do something. This is where our AI powered assistants can really shine by generating different ways to approach a problem and weighing out the best choice.

2.3   Context is everything

Coding assistants seem to just know what you're trying to do, and it's not magic. Tools such as GitHub Copilot, Tabnine, and BlackboxAI use context to generate smarter, more relevant suggestions. They don't just analyze a single line of code, but they pull in information from the entire workspace, the files you've got open, and even the structure of your project. This means that when you're writing a function, Copilot isn't just guessing—it's making an educated suggestion based on your existing code. Generative tools in IDE integration draw insights by analyzing

- Code from the current file being edited
- Content from neighboring tabs in the IDE
- The entire workspace or solution structure
- Code before and after the cursor position (Github Copilot)

As for project understanding, the insights come from

- Repository-level context
- Pull requests and open problems
- Project documentation and configuration files

The level of product you're using makes a difference here. Often, the enterprise or professional level products give a deeper dive than individual licenses. However, all three IDE-based tools we'll use look at the file being edited and files in your project.

One of the biggest tricks up Copilot's sleeve is something called "fill-in-the-middle" (FIM). Instead of only looking at what you've typed so far, it scans the surrounding code before and after your cursor to generate more accurate completions.

This is a game-changer because it allows AI to suggest code that fits seamlessly within your existing logic. The result? Better suggestions for your project instead of generic solutions.

Now let's jump right into using GitHub Copilot for a project. We will build an application that uses NLP to analyze and count words in a document. But first, let's look at what NLP is. It's important for the project and for our understanding of generative AI tools.

2.4   *What Is NLP?*

Have you ever wondered how virtual assistants such as Siri or Alexa understand what you're saying? It can seem like magic, but it's natural language processing, or NLP. NLP combines linguistics, computer science, and artificial intelligence to allow computers understand, interpret, and generate human language.

NLP systems aim to take text input, process it, interpret the words, and produce meaningful output. These applications perform sentiment analysis, machine translation, and text summarization. NLP isn't just for virtual assistants. It's also used in fields from customer service to healthcare by allowing computers to communicate with humans effectively.

A core concept of NLP is tokenization, which breaks down text into smaller units called tokens. These are usually words, punctuation, or phrases. Tokenization helps computers understand the structure and attempt to evaluate the meaning of text by breaking it into smaller chunks (figure 2.11).

The words and punctuation are broken into chunks, as shown in figure 2.11, and given an identifier. NLP systems look for patterns in words, such as

Hi, how are you today?

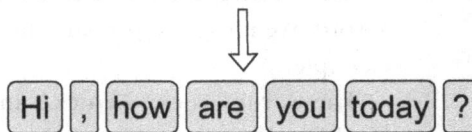

Hi , how are you today ?

Figure 2.11 Word-based tokenization breaks whole words and punctuation into chunks that can be processed and analyzed.

- *Word frequency*—What words are used the most? Which are used the least? Is this an indicator of what the subject is about?
- *Word types*—NLP distinguishes between the types of words used: nouns, verbs, adjectives, and similar. This helps with assembling sentences and extracting meanings.
- *Word co-occurrence*—NLP analyzes which words are frequently found together in text. This can reveal semantic relationships between these words.
- *Text classification*—Words are analyzed and fit into predefined categories. They're then analyzed for tasks such as spam detection, document categorization, and sentiment analysis.

Word-based tokenization is core to NLP, but it's just one of the many ways NLP analyzes text. This is a high-level overview of NLP and not the focus of this book. However, this is what our next project is about, and NLP is used extensively with our tools, so if it interests you, it's a great subject to learn more about.

2.5 A simple Python project

As our first Copilot-assisted program, we will perform some crude NLP. We'll take a text file from Project Gutenberg and count the word frequency. Then, we will rank the words and see which ones were used the most. Finally, we'll build and view a bar chart of the results. All of this will be done with a simple Python script that we build, and we'll use GitHub Copilot as our smart assistant.

For this example, we'll use GitHub Copilot in Visual Studio Code. We'll use Copilot to create the code for our program based on small descriptions and a conversation with Copilot Chat. Copilot Chat is an extension for Visual Studio code with a chat-like interface. You can ask the tool questions, and it will produce answers.

In addition, we'll use a combination of Visual Studio Code, Python, and the GitHub Copilot extensions. If you're following along, you'll need all three of these installed on your machine.

For this project, we need a big text file with a lot of words. I selected a file from Project Gutenberg and analyzed it. The text is one of my favorite books on that site, *Free Air* by Sinclair Lewis. The full-text version of this novel is available at https://www.gutenberg.org/cache/epub/26732/pg26732.txt.

I want to know which words are used the most frequently in this novel. I will count all the words in this text file and rank them by frequency to learn this.

Next, I need to load up the text and parse it. I need to identify a "word" by anything enclosed with spaces. If there is a space before or after a set of characters, we assume it's a word. We must also prepare the text to ensure our word count is accurate. Here's an example.

The words "truck," "Truck," and "truck!" are considered three distinct words. The resulting data will be scattered everywhere if we look at how many times a truck is mentioned in different ways. We can solve this problem by making all the letters lowercase and removing punctuation. This way, data will show the word "truck" being mentioned three times, which is what we're looking for.

We need to tokenize the text. This is what we just learned about in the previous section, so let's put it into action. Consider the sentence "My name is Jeremy, and I like apples." After tokenization, it becomes

```
My
Name
is
Jeremy
,
and
I
like
apples
.
```

Each word and punctuation mark are treated as a separate token. The tokens become the building blocks the computer uses for text analysis and processing. By breaking the text into tokens, the computer can attempt to understand the content and meaning behind the words. The word itself and placement are important here. The process of splitting up text like this is called *tokenization*.

We will parse every token, count the unique tokens (words), and count the identical ones. We don't need to count punctuation as we're only concerned about word count here. Punctuation will provide irrelevant data. This will give us accurate data to find which words are used the most.

Let's review our primary objectives for this application:

- Open a text file and read it.
- Remove any punctuation and convert all text to lowercase.
- Tokenize the text into individual words.
- Count the frequency of each unique word as quickly as possible.
- Display the top N most frequent words in a bar chart.

Figure 2.12 shows what the flow looks like.

This first application is simple enough we can build it here. Let's do it!

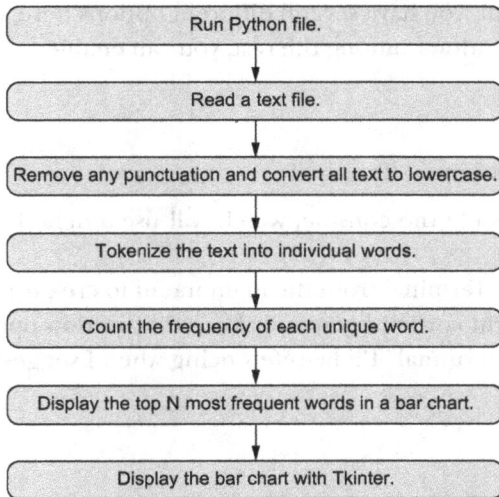

Figure 2.12   The workflow of
our sample application

2.5.1   Preparing your development environment

Let's familiarize ourselves with our environment. First, you'll want to create a folder for
the application to live in. Next, open that folder with Visual Code going to File and then
Open Folder. You'll see a blank VS Code project with the welcome page (figure 2.13).

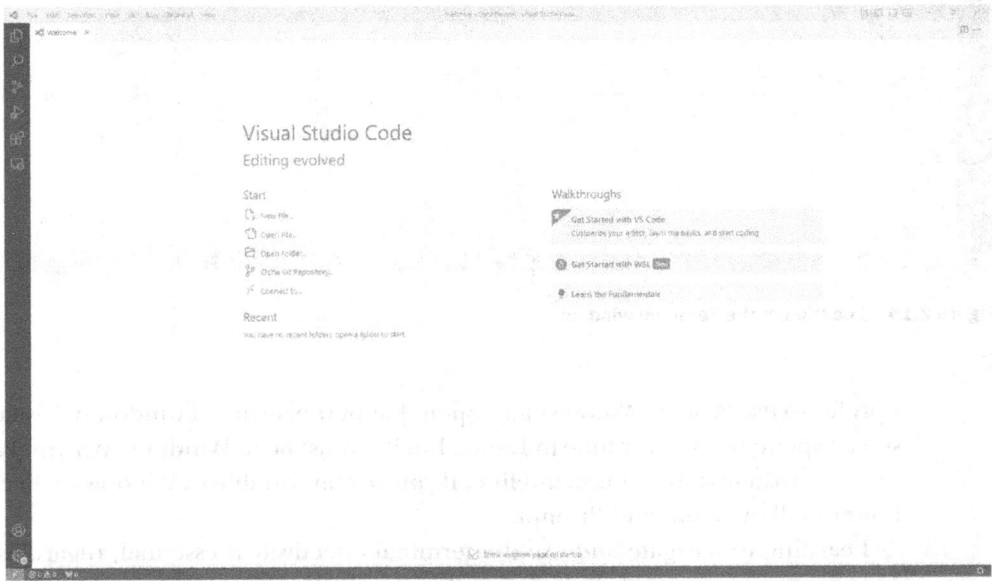

Figure 2.13   Visual Studio Code opened to a new folder

Next, we want to enable the terminal. You have several different options here, depending on your operating system. In Windows, among the rest, you can enable

- A PowerShell console
- Windows Terminal
- WSL (Windows Subsystem for Linux) Terminal

On a Mac or in Linux, you can enable the console, which will use a default OSX or Linux console.

Go to Terminal and then to New Terminal from the main menu to create a new terminal. You'll find it in the lower right corner. I generally keep this window open while developing. Figure 2.14 shows the "terminal" I'll be referencing when I suggest "entering something into the terminal."

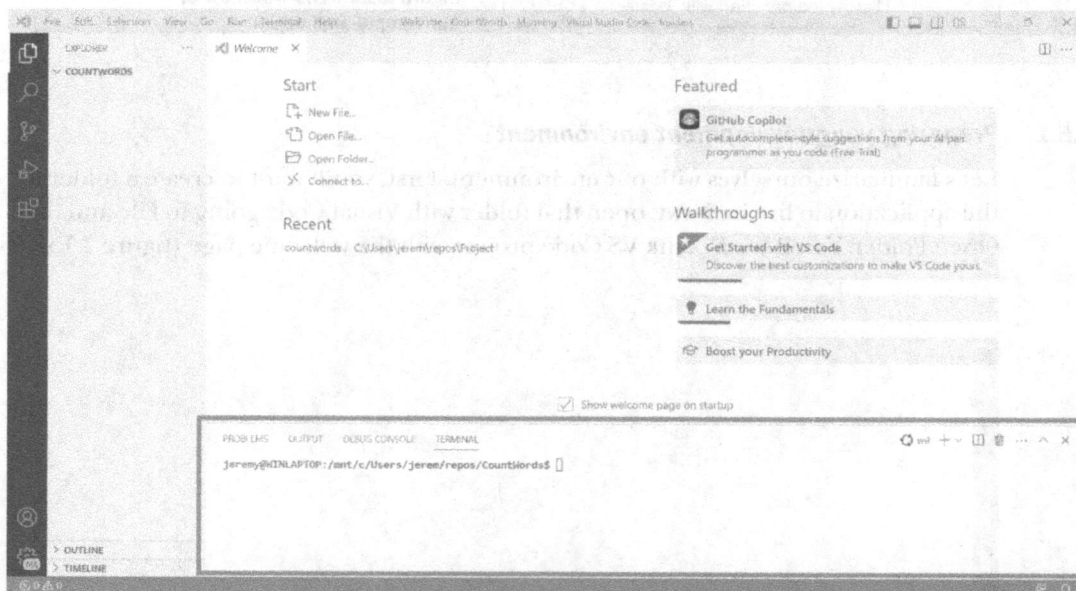

Figure 2.14   Location of the Terminal window

I prefer to use WSL in Windows and open that in the terminal window in Visual Studio since I spend most of my time in Linux. But if it must be in Windows, WSL makes everything consistent at the command line. If you're comfortable in Windows, you can use a PowerShell or Command Prompt.

Learning to navigate and use the terminal effectively is essential, regardless of the operating system you select. If you're already a Python developer, you're likely already familiar with the terminal. It makes creating and moving files around easy, while working with Python scripts. Figure 2.15 shows the layout of our Visual Studio Code Desktop.

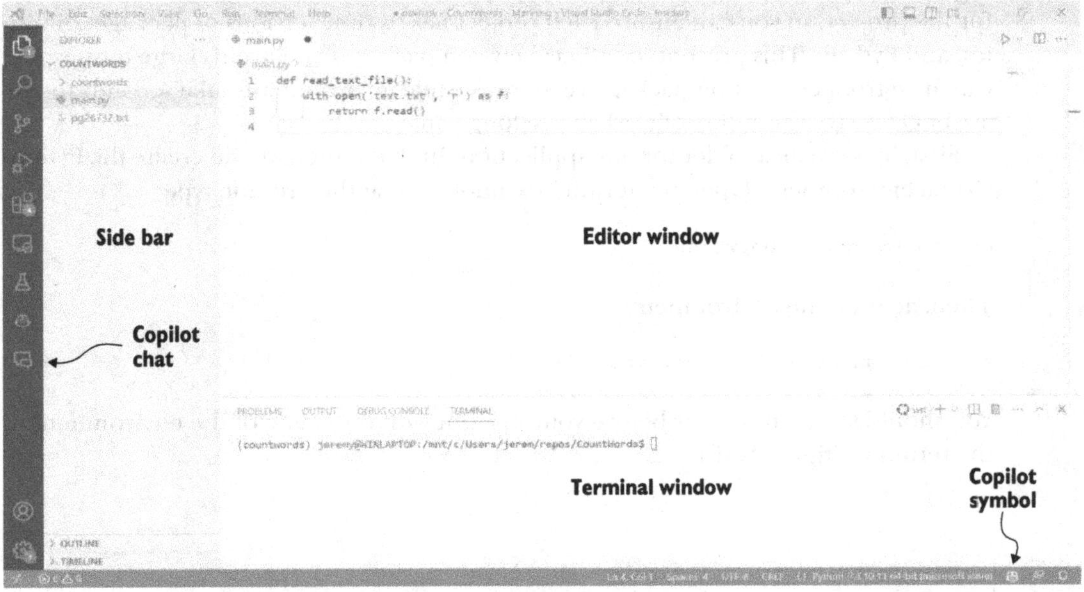

Figure 2.15   The Visual Studio Layout, showing Copilot is accessible in the activity bar, and the lower taskbar

I'll use the following terminology moving forward. These are the basic components of Visual Studio code:

- The *side bar* lists files so you can easily navigate between them.
- *Copilot Chat* is located to the left of the sidebar in the activity bar.
- The *terminal window* is where we'll enter terminal commands.
- The *editor window* is where we'll enter code.

We will utilize Copilot to generate and analyze code for us. As discussed earlier, you can interact with Copilot in the following ways:

- *Adding a comment to your code*—You can add a comment describing something you want to happen, and Copilot will attempt to generate a solution.
- *Code completion*—You start writing code, and Copilot will attempt to complete the statement or method you're trying to build.
- *Copilot Chat*—You can interact with Copilot Chat like a person. Ask questions, debug snippets, and more.

2.5.2   *Creating the application*

We will use a Python virtual environment for this application. Regardless of the project size, I create virtual environments for it. This is essential for maintaining clean and organized environments for Python development. It creates an isolated environment for the project, so you can ensure each project has its own versions of packages, libraries, and Python. This prevents conflicts between packages and avoids large messes that can arise from conflicting package versions. Virtual environments take seconds to create but can save you hours of work in the long run.

First, let's create a folder for our application. In that folder, we will create the Python virtual environment. Open the terminal window, and at the prompt, type

```
python -m venv countwords
```

Then, activate the environment:

```
source countwords/bin/activate
```

You should see an indicator before your prompt with the name of the environment in the terminal (figure 2.16):

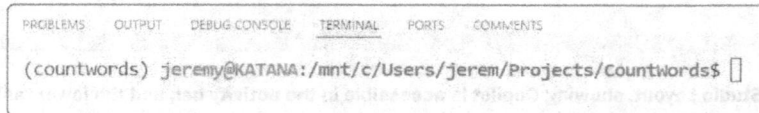

```
PROBLEMS    OUTPUT    DEBUG CONSOLE    TERMINAL    PORTS    COMMENTS

(countwords) jeremy@KATANA:/mnt/c/Users/jerem/Projects/CountWords$ []
```

Figure 2.16   A terminal window showing an active Python environment

I recommend using a Python virtual environment for all your projects. It helps decouple your Python installations. This approach makes your projects more portable and less reliant on globally available packages, which you may want to change. If you have multiple projects with multiple libraries, it's the best way to work. It's quick to set up, so it's worth getting into the habit of always creating them.

For instructions on how to create virtual environments, including in Windows, check out the guide at https://code.visualstudio.com/docs/python/environments.

Now that I have the environment created, I want the text file of *Free Air* to live on my hard drive. You can copy this text and save it to your drive, download it from the browser, or use a utility such as wget to download it:

```
wget https://www.gutenberg.org/cache/epub/26732/pg26732.txt
```

This utility is available on all three platforms (Windows, Linux, and Mac), so I highly recommend installing it. It will download pg26732.txt to your hard drive. So now that we have our text file, let's build our app.

STEP 1: READING A TEXT FILE

Our first objective is to open our text file so we can read it. Let's create a `main.py` file and create our first function. We'll use the code completion method to interact with Copilot here. This happens when you type in some code, and the Copilot attempts to autocomplete it for you.

As we type in the line

```
def read_text_file(file_path):
```

Copilot has a suggestion for us immediately (figure 2.17).

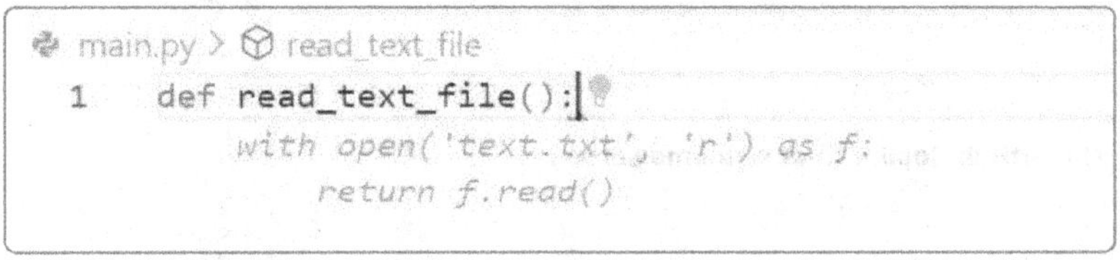

```
main.py >  read_text_file
1   def read_text_file():
        with open('text.txt', 'r') as f:
            return f.read()
```

Figure 2.17   A typical Copilot suggestion

Copilot assesses what I'm trying to do based on what I've named the function. It gives the following two options:

Option 1:

```
def read_text_file(file_path):
    with open(file_path, 'r') as f:
        return f.read()
```

Option 2:

```
def read_text_file(file_path):
    """Reads the text file and returns the text as a string"""
    with open(file_path, 'r') as file:
        text = file.read()
    return text
```

The two options are functionally identical. Both read a text file and return the text as a string. However, option 2 is more readable. It contains a docstring and uses `file` for the variable name instead of `f`. It also returns text as a variable instead of simply returning the output of the `read()` function.

But let's take a step back and do a little test. Let's write the function *inefficiently* and see how Copilot handles that. To do this, we'll use the Copilot Chat extension. Note that at the time of this writing, Chat is in beta, so it will likely look a little different (see figure 2.18).

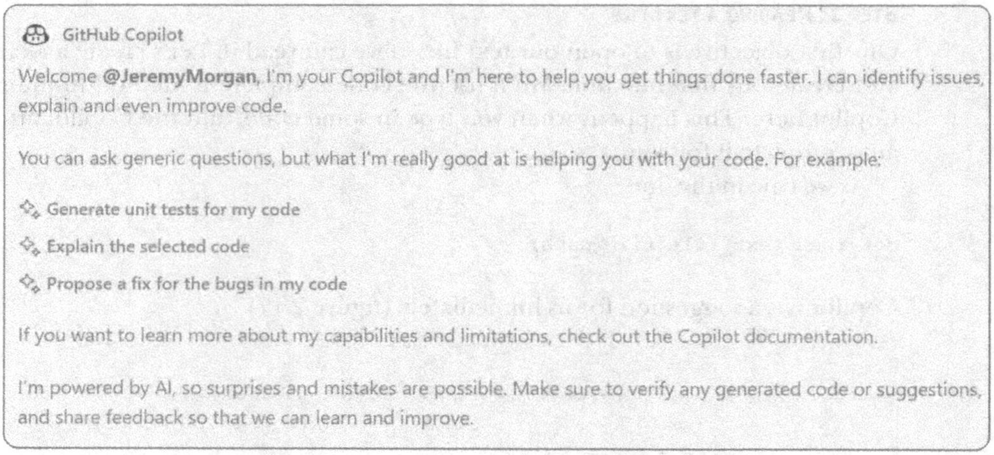

Figure 2.18   The GitHub Copilot Chat welcome screen

I have written some code that's not so great. It adds a list to the operation that isn't needed and doesn't automatically close the file. It's not horrible, but it can be improved:

```
def read_text_file(file_path):
    file = open(file_path, 'r')
    lines = []
    for line in file:
        lines.append(line)
    file.close()
    text = "".join(lines)
    return text
```

Let's ask GitHub Copilot Chat how it would improve this code. I open Copilot Chat and type in a question. I use a simple, plain-English prompt. With that prompt in the chat window, I paste the code to let Copilot know which code I'm referring to.

JM   How can I improve this code?

It's worth noting that my prompt was very simple. This is all you need for most cases; however, you can implement prompt engineering for more complex problems. Generally, you won't need to assign a role as you do with other tools, as Copilot is already set up for this. I press Enter to send my prompt (figure 2.19). As shown in figure 2.20, Copilot outputs a response with a cleaner, more efficient method.

These are two ways we can use Copilot to create this function. We can either name the function cleverly and get code automatically suggested, or write code ourselves and ask GitHub to refactor it.

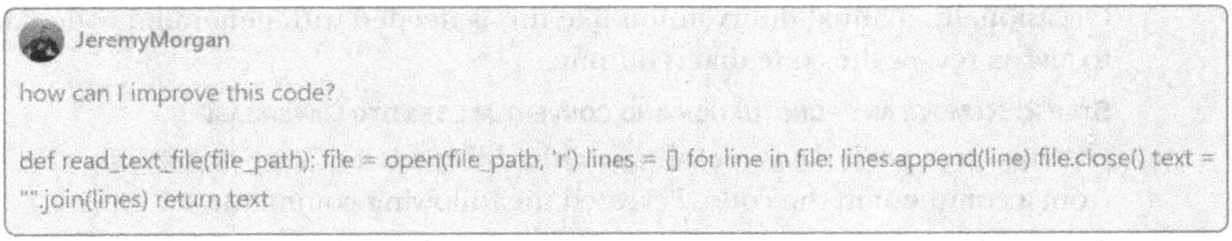

JeremyMorgan

how can I improve this code?

def read_text_file(file_path): file = open(file_path, 'r') lines = [] for line in file: lines.append(line) file.close() text = "".join(lines) return text

Figure 2.19 Prompt entered in Copilot Chat

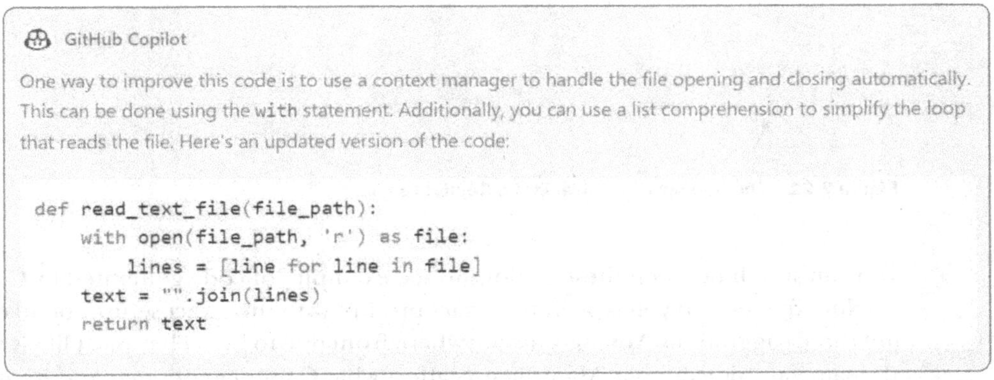

GitHub Copilot

One way to improve this code is to use a context manager to handle the file opening and closing automatically. This can be done using the `with` statement. Additionally, you can use a list comprehension to simplify the loop that reads the file. Here's an updated version of the code:

```python
def read_text_file(file_path):
    with open(file_path, 'r') as file:
        lines = [line for line in file]
    text = "".join(lines)
    return text
```

Figure 2.20 A response from Copilot Chat

Copilot's code generation capabilities are neat, but we don't want to rely on them too heavily. Don't assume this is optimized or that it's been tested or validated. Always evaluate the generated code and make sure you understand it.

In our case, let's take this code snippet from the Copilot Chat window and paste it into our editor window (which is the source code for our application):

```python
def read_text_file(file_path):
    """Reads the text file and returns the text as a string"""
    with open(file_path, 'r') as file:
        text = file.read()
    return text
```

Note that in this generated code, there is no encoding specified. This is an example of Copilot generating code that works but may not be optimal. The code runs fine on my Linux computer, but if you open it in Windows, you may have a problem. You can change the open function to include encoding if you want to make it safer to use. Try something like

```python
with open(file_path, 'r', encoding='utf8') as file:
```

Occasionally, manual intervention like this is needed with generated code. Make sure to always review the code that is output.

STEP 2: REMOVE ANY PUNCTUATION AND CONVERT ALL TEXT TO LOWERCASE

For this step, we'll do something a little different. Let's try generating this function from a comment in the code. I created the following comment:

> (JM)   # create a function to convert the text to lowercase and remove punctuation.

We're given three different options, as indicated in the toolbar that pops up (figure 2.21).

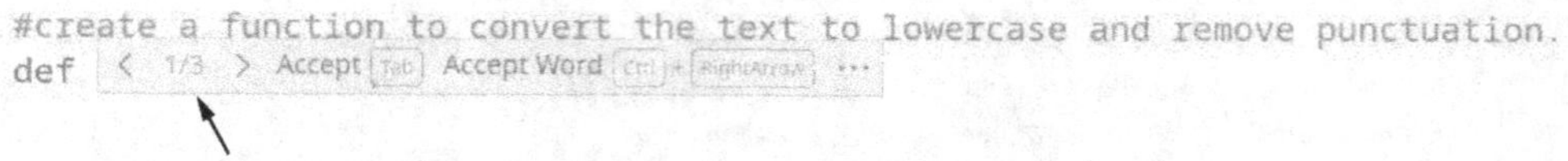

```
#create a function to convert the text to lowercase and remove punctuation.
def  < 1/3 > Accept [Tab]  Accept Word [Ctrl] + [RightArrow]  ···
```

Figure 2.21   The options are shown in the Copilot toolbar.

You can switch between these options to see examples of code generated by Copilot.

Note that even if you type in this exact prompt with this exact setup, you likely won't get three suggestions. You may see anywhere from one to five. They most likely won't be the same as this example. Many factors affect what Copilot generates, and it's dynamic. This is the nature of generative AI.

> **Why is the output different every time?**
>
> Most large language models (LLMs), including GitHub Copilot, are deterministic in operation, but the post-processing actions produce varied results. This means they can generate different outputs each time. Even under similar conditions, your output may differ with the same input. This variability is both a natural feature and a benefit of these models, allowing for more creative and diverse responses.

Let's examine the options given.

Option 1

```
def clean_text(text):
    """Converts the text to lowercase and removes punctuation"""
    text = text.lower()
    punctuation = '!"#$%&\'()*+,-./:;<=>?@[\\]^_`{|}~'
    for character in punctuation:
        text = text.replace(character, '')
    return text
```

This is a decent option, and I like it. It's clean and easy to understand what's happening. We have some big text replacement operations happening here that can take some time. We're parsing the entire document 30+ times, so that will add some time. However, this is something we'd reasonably expect. Let's look at option 2:

Option 2

```
def clean_text(text):
    """Converts the text to lowercase and removes punctuation"""
    text = text.lower()
    punctuation = '.,;:"!@#$%^&*()-_+=~`[]{}|\/<>?'
    for mark in punctuation:
        text = text.replace(mark, '')
    return text
```

This option isn't significantly different. Variable names are changed, and there are fewer punctuation marks. Finally, option 3 is

Option 3

```
def clean_text(text):
  """Converts the text to lowercase and removes punctuation"""
  # convert to lowercase
  text = text.lower()
  # remove punctuation
  punctuation = ['.', ',', ';', ':', '"', '\'', '!', '?', '-', '(', ')']
  for punc in punctuation:
      text = text.replace(punch, '')
  return text
```

This version is interesting because it treats each punctuation mark as individual items in a list instead of a string, which I suspect will be faster. Let's find out if that's true.

2.5.3   *Side quest: Testing the function speed*

Since this is a significant part of our application, we want to find out which of these functions are faster, if any. This is a great way to check the code that Copilot is producing. We're doing this for two reasons:

- We want to know which function is more performant.
- We want to review and check the code Copilot is giving us.

Remember that Copilot isn't producing perfect code that's ready to use. You need to check the code it outputs every time. Testing, profiling, and debugging are still needed. Having knowledge about the languages enough to smell when something isn't right is crucial—trust but verify. Let's verify which method is the most optimal from a performance standpoint as an example.

We'll break it into two options based on how the punctuation data is stored. We'll test options 1 and 3.

In our file, we create the following two functions:

```
def clean_text1(text):
    """Converts the text to lowercase and removes punctuation"""
    text = text.lower()
```

```
        punctuation = '!"#$%&\'()*+,-./:;<=>?@[\\]^_`{|}~'
        for character in punctuation:
            text = text.replace(character, '')
        return text
def clean_text2(text):
    """Converts the text to lowercase and removes punctuation"""
    # convert to lowercase
    text = text.lower()
    # remove punctuation
    punctuation = ['.', ',', ';', ':', '"', "'", '!', '?', '-', '(', ')']
    for punc in punctuation:
        text = text.replace(punc, '')
    return text
```

And we'll create the following code the functions to time them. I asked Copilot Chat:

> JM   How can I write code to call cleantext1 and cleantext2 on the text from read_text_file and time them to see which is faster?

It generated the following code, which looks like something I would have created.

```
text = read_text_file('pg26732.txt')

start_time = time.time()
clean_text1(text)
end_time = time.time()
print(f"clean_text1 took {end_time - start_time} seconds")

start_time = time.time()
clean_text2(text)
end_time = time.time()
print(f"clean_text2 took {end_time - start_time} seconds")
```

Awesome. So, I run it a few times (figure 2.22):

```
(countwords) jeremy@KATANA:/mnt/c/Users/jerem/Projects/CountWords$ python speedtest.py
clean_text1 took 0.005719661712646484 seconds
clean_text2 took 0.0026023387908935547 seconds
(countwords) jeremy@KATANA:/mnt/c/Users/jerem/Projects/CountWords$ python speedtest.py
clean_text1 took 0.005422830581665039 seconds
clean_text2 took 0.0026755332946777344 seconds
(countwords) jeremy@KATANA:/mnt/c/Users/jerem/Projects/CountWords$ python speedtest.py
clean_text1 took 0.0050449371337890625 seconds
clean_text2 took 0.002609491348266016 seconds
(countwords) jeremy@KATANA:/mnt/c/Users/jerem/Projects/CountWords$ python speedtest.py
clean_text1 took 0.00489354133605957 seconds
clean_text2 took 0.002547025680541992 seconds
(countwords) jeremy@KATANA:/mnt/c/Users/jerem/Projects/CountWords$ python speedtest.py
clean_text1 took 0.0053517818450927734 seconds
clean_text2 took 0.002520322799682617 seconds
(countwords) jeremy@KATANA:/mnt/c/Users/jerem/Projects/CountWords$ python speedtest.py
clean_text1 took 0.005056858062744141 seconds
clean_text2 took 0.002579927444458008 seconds
(countwords) jeremy@KATANA:/mnt/c/Users/jerem/Projects/CountWords$ []
```

Figure 2.22   Output from our program

Neither one is slow, but it appears `clean_text2` is the faster function here. We'll use that. I've added additional punctuation marks by asking Copilot Chat to generate a list of additional punctuation marks.

> 🅙🅜 # Please create a thorough list of punctuation marks to avoid, including brackets, braces, and slashes

The final function is

```
def clean_text(text):
  """Converts the text to lowercase and removes punctuation"""
  # convert to lowercase
  text = text.lower()
  # remove punctuation
  punctuation = ['.', ',', ';', ':', "'", '"', '!', '?', '-', '(', ')', '[',
      ']', '{', '}', '/', '\\', '|', '<', '>', '@', '#', '$', '%', '^', '&',
      '*', '_', '+', '=', '`', '~']
  # clean the text
  for punc in punctuation:
      text = text.replace(punc, '')
  return text
```

Now, we can move on with our application.

STEP 3: TOKENIZE THE TEXT INTO INDIVIDUAL WORDS

Next, we need to count individual words. This is simple to do in Python, and we can add this to our clean text function. Creating an entire function that only splits text is unnecessary. I'll add a line above `return text` and type the following comment:

> 🅙🅜 # tokenize the text into words

It generates the following line of code, and now we'll return `words[]` instead of text.

> 🐙 # tokenize the text into words
> words = text.split()
> return words

STEP 4: COUNT THE FREQUENCY OF EACH UNIQUE WORD

Now, we want to count the frequency of each unique word. Let's try a comment prompt for that.

> 🅙🅜 # count the frequency of each unique word in words

This prompt gives us a single option that looks fine. It could be improved by using `Defaultdict()` from the collections module. Again, Copilot usually generates code that works, but it may not be as good as code generated by an experienced developer. Your suggestion may also show something completely different from this example.

```
def count_words(words):
    """Counts the frequency of each unique word in words"""
    word_count = {}
    for word in words:
        if word in word_count:
            word_count[word] += 1
        else:
            word_count[word] = 1
    return word_count
```

Awesome. This program is coming along nicely. Now, we need to display our results in a human-readable format.

STEP 5: DISPLAY THE TOP N MOST FREQUENT WORDS IN A BAR CHART

Now for the fun stuff. Let's generate a function that builds a graph in Matplotlib. This tool produces clean and useful graphs with a few simple parameters and helps you display data in an interesting way. Here's the prompt we'll use:

> # create a function to plot out the top n words on a graph with matplotlib

This gave me a few options, but here's the one I chose. It's clear and easy to understand and includes comments.

```
def plot_word_count(word_count, n):
    """Plots the top n words in a word_count dictionary"""
    import matplotlib.pyplot as plt
    # sort the word_count dictionary by value
    word_count = sorted(word_count.items(), key=lambda x:
    x[1], reverse=True)
    # get the top n words
    top_words = word_count[:n]
    # create the plot
    plt.bar(range(n), [x[1] for x in top_words], align='center')
    plt.xticks(range(n), [x[0] for x in top_words])
    plt.xticks(rotation=70)
    plt.xlabel('Word')
    plt.ylabel('Frequency')
    plt.title('Top {} Words in the Text'.format(n))
    plt.show()
```

Now, we just need to tie these functions together. Can Copilot do this for us?

STEP 6: PUTTING IT ALL TOGETHER

Now it's time to put it all together into a main function. I want a single function that calls the functions we just built in the right order. I want this function to run first every time someone executes the Python file. Here's the comment prompt I used:

> # create a main function that runs when the Python file is run and execute the functions

I wasn't sure this would work out, but it did. Here's the generated function:

```
def main():
    """Main method that runs when the python file is run"""
    # read the text file
    text = read_text_file('data/hamlet.txt')
    # clean the text
    words = clean_text(text)
    # count the words
    word_count = count_words(words)
    # plot the top n words
    plot_word_count(word_count, 20)
```

I need to rename the file it calls to the name of my text file. I'll change `'data/hamlet.txt'` to the filename I downloaded:

```
text = read_text_file('pg26732.txt')
```

Now, assuming we don't know Python, if you run this file, nothing will happen. I'll create a comment in the code above the method to prompt Copilot. I want it to generate code to make this our "main method" executed when the file is run by itself.

I will give the following comment prompt:

execute the main method if this file is run

It generates

```
if __name__ == '__main__':
    main()
```

We're just about ready to go. We just need to install Matplotlib and Tkinter. Tkinter is a library that will show our Matplotlib graph in a GUI window, whether we're running Windows, Mac, or Linux. This way, we can reliably show the graph regardless of our environment:

```
pip install matplotlib tk
```

We also need to change the imports a bit. We need to tell Matplotlib to use Tkinter to display it, which can be done by specifying the library we'll use to display a window showing our Matplotlib plot. In addition, we can also ask Copilot for these imports:

show me the libraries I need to import to make this script functional

You should get an output like this. If you don't know the libraries needed, you can use trial and error until you get something like

```
import matplotlib
import matplotlib.pyplot as plt
matplotlib.use('TkAgg')
```

This way, we can specify Tkinter as our GUI library. Now it's time to run it!!

```
python main.py
```

And we did it! Here are the most used words in the novel *Free Air* presented in an easy-to-understand graph (figure 2.23).

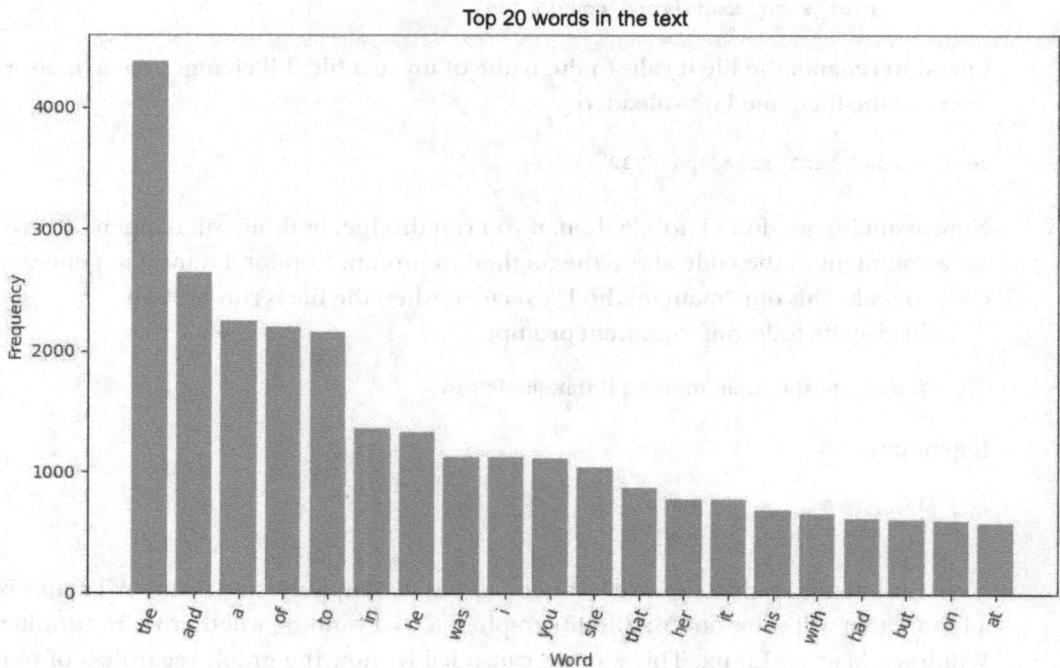

Figure 2.23   Our Matplotlib graph shows the top 20 words in the text file.

This isn't a complex application, but it shows how quickly you can use GitHub Copilot for your projects. From simple one-off scripts to large enterprise applications, I'm impressed with how well Copilot grasps context and contributes useful suggestions.

Getting started is easy with these tools. Building them into your workflow may take more time. Of course, there are many ways you can dig deeper with this tool, and we certainly will.

Summary

- Be as clear and as descriptive as possible. Copilot evaluates comments and function names for suggestions. For example, `connect_to_database` is better than `get_data`.
- Use complete sentences and clear directions. For example, "Convert the text to lowercase" is better than "make lowercase."
- Provide sufficient context when selecting code. You improve the results by selecting more than just the line of code with a problem. Surrounding text gives the request more context to work with.
- Don't create large prompts. The saying "Do one thing and do it well" applies to prompts. If they are too long and complex, they should be broken down to prevent errors.
- You can always try different prompts. If the prompt you use in the chat isn't giving you what you want, you can get creative and try different things. Make a note of the prompts that serve you well.
- Chat naturally with Copilot as if it were a human. If you get stuck, try explaining the problem like you would to another person in a real conversation. This is what the model was designed for, and it works well.
- Always review and test generated code. As demonstrated with the text cleaning functions, Copilot's first suggestion may not be the most efficient or secure solution.
- Use Copilot's different interaction methods appropriately. Code completion works well for simple tasks, while chat is better for refactoring or understanding complex code.
- Remember that context matters. Copilot analyzes your entire workspace, so keeping related files open and organized can improve its suggestions.
- Don't be afraid to iterate. As shown in the text-cleaning example, you can generate multiple solutions and test them to find the best one.
- Consider performance implications. While Copilot generates working code, you may need to profile and optimize it for your specific needs, as demonstrated in the punctuation-removal comparison.
- Include proper error-handling and edge cases. Our example showed how adding UTF-8 encoding support could make the file reading more robust across different operating systems.

## Part 2

Building applications with AI assistance

Great planning and initial setup are crucial for a successful project. Having an idea and immediately cracking open an IDE is rarely a good approach. Many developers find the planning process boring and tiresome. Generative AI tools make these tasks more efficient, accurate, and enjoyable. If you don't like planning and setup, they can make the process smoother and faster. If you enjoy planning, you may find these tools make it even more fun. Modern AI assistants such as ChatGPT, GitHub Copilot, and Tabnine can change how you handle everything from project architecture to complex functions.

These tools have evolved to understand software projects well. They can streamline your planning process, helping you with checklists and reminding you of tasks you may otherwise have forgotten about. They assist by suggesting good design patterns and maintaining best practices. When used the right way, these tools can help you build scalable robust systems faster. They can generate project scaffolding, suggest optimal file structures, create stub methods that follow design principles, and help debug tricky problems. However, knowing how to prompt these tools effectively matters. You need to know when to trust their suggestions and when to rely on your own judgment. The next few chapters will help you understand how to create that balance.

This part of the book will guide you through building a real Flask web application with AI tools as your development partners. You'll learn to use AI for rapid prototyping, while keeping control over architectural choices. Chapter 3 covers planning and requirement gathering with AI help. Chapter 4 shows how to set up project structure and create your first working application. Chapter 5 dives into advanced development techniques using tools such as Tabnine and BlackboxAI. Finally, chapter 6 focuses on building strong user interfaces and managing sessions with AI-generated code.

Design and discovery

3

Design is key in software development, yet programmers often rush it. I've done this, too. Taking time to plan an app's architecture leads to happy users and lower maintenance costs. How can generative AI speed up the design process?

Our goal here is to design a web application that solves a common problem: studying for a certification exam. The app will provide randomized practice tests for exam preparation. First, we'll analyze the problem and create a design document with ChatGPT's help. Then, we'll use ChatGPT to improve the document and develop user stories to guide development.

By collaborating with ChatGPT in the design phase, we can quickly outline architecture for our app. We'll also ask ChatGPT-targeted questions to uncover ideas and details we may not have considered on our own. The result is a solid foundation to build and iterate upon as we progress through the project.

Let's learn how AI can boost creativity and productivity, even early in the software life cycle. We'll set ourselves up for easier development by using these generative tools.

3.1   Getting to know ChatGPT

ChatGPT is an advanced large language model (LLM) from OpenAI. It aims to be useful, safe, and truthful. It has been trained on a wide range of texts, such as internet content and books. This training gives ChatGPT a broad knowledge base. However, there are some limitations to this AI system:

- ChatGPT cannot independently authenticate or validate information. Its responses are generated stochastically. It's a "best guess" by the model and can contain inaccuracies. You should always verify the output.
- While ChatGPT's responses can seem convincing, they may lack depth. The model doesn't have a genuine comprehension of the topics it discusses.
- ChatGPT has no personal identity, opinions, or memory. This limits its ability to engage in prolonged conversations or exhibit a consistent personality.
- ChatGPT doesn't understand real-world context. For this reason, always review its output carefully, especially for sensitive or critical tasks.
- ChatGPT's skill set is more restricted than the broad intelligence of humans. It is particularly adept at tasks such as text generation, but it doesn't match the overall versatility of human cognition. Don't be fooled! It's not a super-intelligent human.

Even with these limitations, ChatGPT is an invaluable asset for developers. It enables you to generate high-quality text and code. It also fosters creativity and aids in idea development.

The key to using ChatGPT effectively is crafting thoughtful prompts and evaluating responses. We'll explore some techniques to maximize the benefits of using ChatGPT for software development, focusing on design and documentation.

3.2   The problem

As software developers, we love building cool stuff. We overhear someone say, "I'd love to have an app for that," and our ears perk up. Instantly, we want to crack open the IDE and get to work. When starting a new project, one of my favorite questions is glaringly simple but often overlooked: What problem are we trying to solve?

It's a question you should ask first and continue to ask throughout the process. There should be only one answer at the beginning. Let's look at a problem and then build a web application to solve it.

Imagine you want to get a HAM radio license. With this license, you can communicate with other radio operators around the world. To get the license, you must pass a test that assesses your knowledge of radio theory, electronics, and rules and regulations related to radio communication. The test consists of 35 multiple-choice questions. So, rather than finding out how well you know the material by taking the test for the first time, you want to try some practice tests to see how well you do.

The application should use a pool of questions, similar to those on the test, and randomly select 35 to display on the screen. This way, you can practice and see how well you are doing and what areas you need to study.

This application needs to be implemented as a web-based interface for seamless use on any computer. You don't want to download and install software on each of your devices. We will write it in Python because we're Python developers and have built many applications with it. It's familiar. This approach will allow us to focus on the problem rather than learning a new language or platform.

We now have enough information to open the IDE and get started. But let's be smart about this. What if you want to expand the application to all three levels of HAM radio testing? What if you want to make it public? There are things to shake out in the design process before we start.

Our problem so far is simple. We want to

- Study for the test by taking practice tests
- Have questions similar to those on the test
- Have those questions randomly delivered in 35-question sessions

We need to

- Build a web application
- Have a set of test questions with answers
- Store them somewhere
- Have an interface to view them
- Select 35 of them for a test randomly

This is an excellent start. Let's see if we can use ChatGPT to break down this problem. It will help us reveal any blind spots or alternative solutions worth pursuing. We can't run blindly into ChatGPT and hope for the best results. We need to craft our prompt to get exactly what we need. Here are some prompts to help you understand the problem domain:

- "What are common edge cases when building {type of application}?"
- "What regulatory considerations exist for {domain}?"
- "What nonfunctional requirements are typically important for {application type}?"

3.3 Creating the right prompt

Let's talk about prompt engineering. It's a complex topic, but it becomes intuitive after a while. There are some important things to think about when creating prompts. We'll start with a *role prompt*. A role prompt instructs the model to act as someone performing a role. The resulting text is (hopefully) what someone in that role might say. A prompt includes the following components:

- *Introduction*—Give ChatGPT a role to fill: "Act as a software design expert."
- *Task*—Give it something to do: "Help me break down a problem."
- *Contextual information*—"I want it to be a web app written in Python."
- *Instructions*—"Include details about structure and outline some potential pitfalls."
- *Closing*—"Craft the output in the form of a software design document."

Your prompt isn't required to have all these components, but if you aren't getting the desired results, including these things is helpful.

Using this example, our prompt will look as follows:

> Act as a software design expert. Help me break down a problem. I want to create practice tests to study for a HAM radio license. I will take a pool of questions from the test. I want to draw 35 questions randomly from that pool. I want to show the possible answers and select an answer. At the end of the test, I would like to grade it with a percentage. Include details about the structure and outline some potential pitfalls. Craft the output in the form of a software design document

This type of prompt—often referred to as a *persona prompt* or a *role prompt*—helps shape the response style, and it should be effective in getting us started.

In addition to the role prompt, other basic prompt types include

- *Chain of thought prompting*—Ask the AI to "think step by step" when breaking down complex design problems.
- *Few-shot prompting*—Show examples of what good output looks like before asking for your own.
- *Persona prompting*—Beyond just "Act as a software design expert," try "Act as a software architect with 15 years of experience in scalable systems" for more specific expertise.

Now, let's learn more about these techniques and how to refine them for our workflow.

3.4   Measuring the effect on the design process

To understand the real benefits of using ChatGPT in the design process, let's look at how much time you can save. Your results may vary, but overall, it's almost always a net gain. As table 3.1 shows, we save significant amounts of time generating documents, while they still retain our original intent.

Table 3.1   Time saved by using ChatGPT

Documentation task	Traditional method	ChatGPT-assisted	Time savings
System overview	90–120 minutes	15 minutes	~83%
Technical stack	60 minutes	10 minutes	83%
User stories	120 minutes	25 minutes	79%
Complete design document	6–8 hours	1–2 hours	~75%

The biggest gains come from not starting with a blank page. While traditional methods require drafting all content from scratch, ChatGPT generates a comprehensive first draft in seconds. This draft then needs refinement. The shift from creation to curation dramatically accelerates the documentation process.

In my experience, a team of developers can spend up to 70% less time in design meetings, with no reduction in documentation quality. We've never just generated a document and run with it. The documents always require editing and revisions; however, that overhead is still present in any documentation project, and the brainstorming and initial assembly costs are now gone.

ChatGPT and other LLMs are great for "removing the boring stuff" so you can work on more creative endeavors. This principle is a recurring theme throughout this book. The biggest reason to adopt this approach is to save valuable time for more interesting work.

3.5 *A design document created with ChatGPT*

The software development life cycle (SDLC) is a framework that defines the stages software goes through, from initial planning to deployment and maintenance. The SDLC brings structure to an otherwise chaotic process. You are likely already familiar with this framework, so we only cover it briefly here.

Understanding the SDLC can help us align our workflow to industry best practices. It can also show the types of documents we need to create for each step of the way. I don't want to get buried in documentation here, but a simple guide will help us stay on track and know what to expect.

We will use ChatGPT to create that guide with a simple design document. The term "design document" is intentionally abstract. This won't be a complex set of documents you would create for a large enterprise project. I aim to draft a simple outline document to structure my ideas for this application. We'll create it with the SDLC in mind. Remember, this model varies depending on the organization or person creating it. This is my best understanding of the model.

The SDLC process usually follows these steps:

1 Planning
2 Analysis
3 Design
4 Implementation
5 Testing
6 Deployment
7 Maintenance

Each stage builds on the last, with some overlap and iteration as needed. Knowing what is expected to happen at each phase sets expectations and helps surface any gaps early on (figure 3.1).

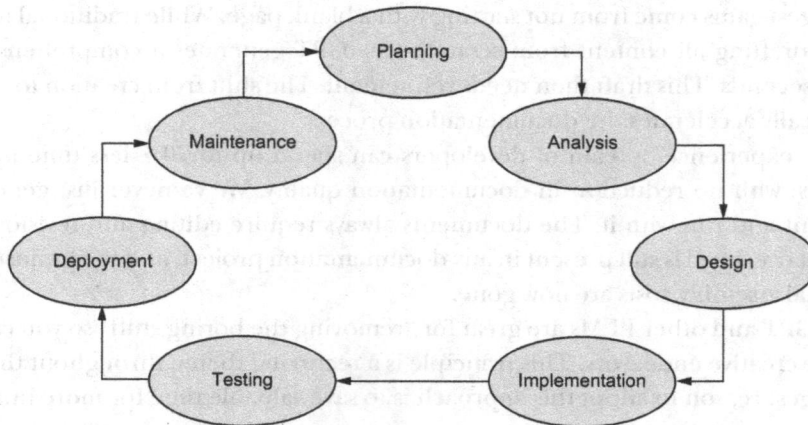

Figure 3.1   An example of the software development life cycle

As we work with ChatGPT to design our app, we'll try to address the key elements presented here and plan for them. Our goal is to produce documentation that captures requirements and gives us guidance.

We start this process with a prompt and then work within a single context to refine and build on the document. As we've discussed, the ChatGPT *context* is like a real-life conversation. The thread of conversation you have with ChatGPT lives in the side panel. Figure 3.2 shows the section where your conversations are stored, as indicated by the arrow.

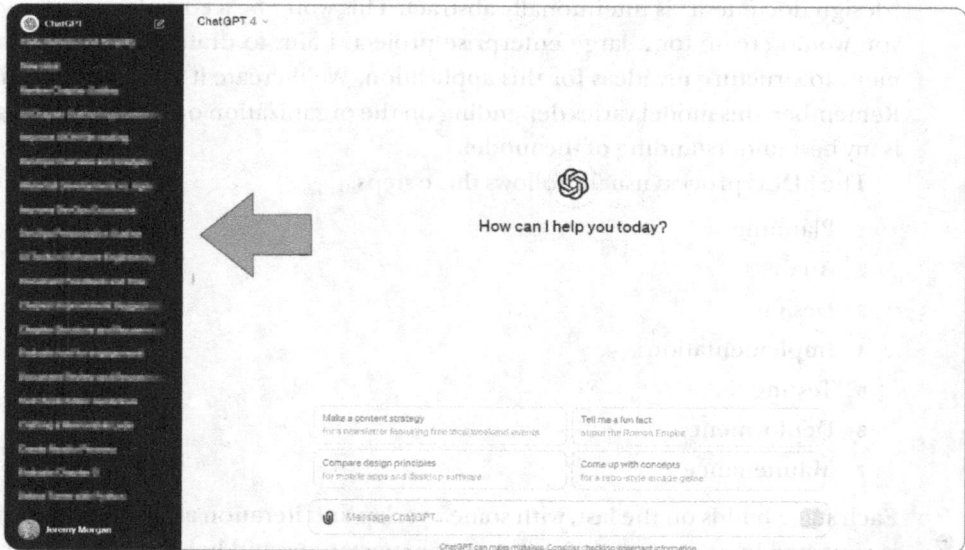

Figure 3.2   The arrow shows where to find conversations in ChatGPT.

This is important to remember because information you've provided is the context, and ChatGPT uses it for future generations. It includes the current conversation history, specific instructions given, and some assumptions based on the dialogue.

To start out our conversation, we'll use the prompt we've just created:

> (JM) Act as a software design expert. Help me break down a problem. I want to create practice tests to study for the HAM radio license. I will take a pool of questions from the test. I want to draw 35 questions randomly from that pool. I want to show the possible answers and select an answer. At the end of the test, I would like to grade it with a percentage. Include details about structure and outline some potential pitfalls. Craft the output in the form of a software design document.

Note that I asked for a software design document to keep the output abstract. Had I wanted to be more specific, I would have asked for process documentation, budget, or planning documents. But I just want a single, simple document to start out. I want to keep the goal in mind when crafting a prompt.

Red flags in AI-generated design documents

There are things to watch out for with AI-generated design documents, such as

- Overly generic architectural patterns without justification
- Technology recommendations without considering your specific constraints
- Missing error handling or security considerations
- Ignoring cross-platform compatibility when it's critical for your app

---

I sent the prompt we crafted to ChatGPT 4.0, and the next section contains the output. It's the direct result of my query in ChatGPT. Note that at the time of this writing, ChatGPT 4.0 is only available with a premium account. The free account only allows ChatGPT 3.5; however, if you're following along, ChatGPT 3.5 will work for this, too. Just remember that the output will be different from what you see here, regardless of the version you use. Next, we'll see what ChatGPT produced.

3.6   *Software design document: HAM radio license practice test application*

Let's jump in and see what ChatGPT produced. We will examine each section of the document in turn, beginning with the introduction.

(⑤) 1. Introduction

The purpose of this document is to provide a detailed and structured plan for the creation of a HAM radio license practice test application. The primary function of this application will be to generate randomized 35-question tests from a predetermined question pool, present possible answers for each question, and finally provide a score percentage at the end of each test.

The introduction dives right into the purpose of the document. It's mostly rewording the input we gave it and writing it in a formal way. It immediately describes the problem and the application's function. It could use a little more detail about what the program should do, but we'll address that.

2. System Overview

The system can be broken down into several main components:

Question Pool Database: This is where all potential questions and corresponding answers will be stored.

Question Selector: This component will handle the random selection of questions from the question pool.

User Interface: This is where the user will interact with the system to take the practice tests and view their results.

Grading Component: This will grade the test upon completion and provide a score.

The system overview gives us a general idea of the parts of the application. ChatGPT breaks it down into four main components. These abstract components help us think about the problem a layer deeper. While this may seem obvious to even beginner developers, these suggestions help create a model in your mind about how this system should work.

The next section digs into the details. This is the next layer to think about. One thing to notice is the inclusion of pitfalls, which we asked for in our prompt.

3. Detailed System Design
3.1 Question Pool Database

The question pool database will store all the possible questions, along with their multiple-choice options and correct answers. This could be implemented using a SQL database or a NoSQL database like MongoDB, depending upon the structure and volume of data.

Structure

A basic structure would have a table/collection with the following fields:

`question_id`: A unique identifier for each question.

`question_text`: The question text.

`options`: The possible answers for each question. This could be an array of strings.

`correct_option`: The correct answer for the question.

Pitfalls

- If the questions, options or answers change over time, there needs to be a system for updating the question pool database to ensure accuracy.
- Considerations for data validation and cleansing are also needed to ensure that incorrect or poorly formed data do not enter the system.

3.2 Question Selector

The question selector module will use a randomizing algorithm to select 35 questions from the question pool database for each test.

Pitfalls

- Care should be taken to ensure true randomness in question selection.
- The same question should not appear more than once in a single test.

Even a quick glimpse of our description tells you the database for this application is simple. The document outlines a data structure and gives us some suggestions for a database server. We have a single table that contains some basic fields. In the pitfalls, we have a couple of considerations for scaling and maintaining the system.

3.3 User Interface

The User Interface (UI) will present the questions and answer choices to the user, accept their answers, and present their score at the end of the test. The UI could be implemented as a web application, a desktop application, or a mobile app, depending on requirements.

Pitfalls

- The UI needs to be intuitive and user-friendly. A poor UI could frustrate users and hinder the effectiveness of their study sessions.
- The design should also consider accessibility needs to cater to a wider audience.

This section is sparse. We need a UI, and it suggests a simple workflow. It also tells us we can implement it as a web, desktop, or mobile application, which is fairly obvious but good to note.

3.4 Grading Component

The grading component will compare the user's answers with the correct answers from the question pool database to calculate a final score, which will be expressed as a percentage.

Pitfalls

- This component must handle cases where the user doesn't answer some questions. Those should be marked as incorrect for scoring purposes.
- Potential inconsistencies or inaccuracies in grading due to any discrepancies in the database need to be handled.

This section is also sparse, and there isn't much to discuss. We need something that will compare the user's answers to the correct ones and calculate a score. The pitfalls are helpful. ChatGPT mentions things to think about, such as the user not answering questions. What should we do about that? Furthermore, it also includes a reminder about potential database discrepancies.

4. Future Considerations

The initial system design as outlined above is minimal and function specific. However, there are several additional features that could be added over time to increase its utility:

- Tracking user performance over time and providing performance analytics

- Allowing users to focus on specific areas or question types
- Integrating with a larger learning platform

By breaking down the application into these components and understanding potential challenges, we can ensure a robust and efficient design that provides a user-friendly tool to help users prepare for their HAM radio license test.

ChatGPT suggests a few features that might be useful. I'm always leery of these types of things in software documentation. Thinking too far ahead leads to stubbing out things we'll never build or falling into the YAGNI (you aren't gonna need it) trap. However, there's no harm in looking at the suggestions.

Tracking user performance over time is a great idea. This helps us as well as the students. It mentions allowing users to focus on specific areas or question types, which is also handy. These are good things to think about, so I'll leave this section in the document.

5. Technical stack

Based on the functionality and design considerations, the following technical stack could be utilized:

Backend: A Node.js server running Express.js for handling API requests and server-side operations.

It recommends a Node.js backend for our project. We've already decided we're using Python for this because that's where our expertise lies. We will change this by altering our context with additional prompts soon. Here's what it recommends. Though we won't use it, I'm happy with the fact that ChatGPT suggested a tech solution with great potential like Node.

The technical stack is where most developers get excited. We don't want to exclude this section, although we will make some changes to it.

Database: MongoDB or a SQL database like PostgreSQL for storing and managing the question pool.

Again, we have some great choices. MongoDB and PostgreSQL are solid products. In my opinion, we don't need a database that complex. This is a very small dataset that doesn't require complex operations or data safety, so I'll use SQLite instead. However, MongoDB and PostgreSQL are excellent alternatives.

Frontend: A React.js application for the user interface would allow for a dynamic, user-friendly experience.

ChatGPT suggests React.js for the frontend—a solid choice and one likely influenced by the number of people using it. However, we're going to use Flask. Using Flask on the frontend allows for easy integration with the Python backend. We don't have the overhead of introducing and setting up a React system for a small, simple UI. Instead, we can stick with Python.

Hosting/Deployment: The application could be hosted on AWS or any other cloud platform, providing flexibility and scalability.

I'm relieved to see ChatGPT isn't suggesting building out some server. It suggests AWS or another cloud platform, which is the best choice for an application like this. It doesn't provide great detail, but we can work with it.

6. Development Plan

6.1 Requirements Gathering

Conduct a detailed study to gather all possible features, requirements, and constraints for the application. Define user roles and permissions if needed.

6.2 Database Design and Setup

Set up the database as per the design mentioned in section 3.1. Import the initial set of questions into the database.

6.3 Backend Development

Implement the server-side functionality, such as the random question selector and grading system. Set up appropriate API endpoints for fetching questions, submitting answers, and receiving grades.

6.4 Frontend Development

Develop the user interface following the best practices for UX/UI. Ensure it is easy to navigate, aesthetically pleasing, and functional across different device types.

6.5 Testing

Carry out rigorous testing to identify and fix any bugs or issues. Both unit testing and end-to-end testing should be included.

6.6 Deployment

After testing, deploy the application to the chosen cloud platform.

In this section, ChatGPT lays out what you need to do once you've started the process. It goes through a familiar SDLC process.

7. Possible Challenges

7.1 Data Security

Ensure that appropriate security measures are in place to protect user data and to prevent unauthorized access to the question pool.

7.2 Scalability

The system should be designed to handle an increasing number of users and questions. This could involve planning for database sharding and considering horizontal scaling of the server setup.

7.3 Accessibility

Ensure that the software complies with accessibility standards and best practices, so that it can be used by as wide an audience as possible.

8. Conclusion

By following the above detailed design and development plan, it would be feasible to develop an efficient and user-friendly HAM radio license practice test application. This application would help users prepare for their exams and potentially enhance their chance of success.

However, the design and development of software applications require careful attention to detail, thorough testing, and continuous refinement based on user feedback. These factors, along with a solid foundational design as provided in this document, will guide the successful development and deployment of the application.

Overall, I'm satisfied with the document that ChatGPT produced so far. It's thorough and provides some real-world suggestions that pass the sniff test. Let's see if we can get some additional details from ChatGPT.

To conclude the document, we have some possible challenges, which include data security, scalability, and accessibility. There's nothing new or groundbreaking here. But it's good to see it's included for us.

3.7   *Digging deeper*

The document we produced is a good start to our project's journey. We could work from this document and improvise or modify the plan as we go. This is how most of my software projects have gone in the past. We work on a plan, agree on it, and then spend the rest of the time building and modifying it. We can prevent this excessive churn in this process by deciding on some key details upfront. Let's examine some sections of our document in more depth and try to bring more clarity.

3.7.1   *System overview (section 2)*

Let's look at our system overview section. For now, we have the following:

2. System Overview

The system can be broken down into several main components:

Question Pool Database: This is where all potential questions and corresponding answers will be stored.

Question Selector: This component will handle the random selection of questions from the question pool.

User Interface: This is where the user will interact with the system to take the practice tests and view their results.

Grading Component: This will grade the test upon completion and provide a score.

This is a reasonable overview of the system. It's not too long or detailed. It outlines the main system components. But we'd like just a bit more detail here. If we present this document to executives, it will work. If we send it to engineers, they'll want far more detail. Let's see if ChatGPT can help with this. I'll add the following prompt to the same chat instance as before.

> Give more details in "2. System Overview." Elaborate on the key subjects.

With this prompt, I'm keeping it simple. I asked for more details in the specified section. Then, I mentioned elaborating on key subjects. This is to direct the prompt to the exact detail I want. I run this script, and this is what ChatGPT came up with.

2. System Overview (Detailed)

The system for the HAM radio license practice test application can be divided into several key components, each playing a crucial role in achieving the desired functionality. These components interact with each other to form a cohesive system. Here are the elaborations on each one:

Question Pool Database: This database serves as the primary store of information from which the system operates. It houses all potential questions that can be asked on the HAM radio license test, their corresponding answers, and the multiple-choice options that will be presented to users. The database will be set up to facilitate efficient retrieval of question sets, and secure updating of question-answer pairs as required. The system's efficiency and effectiveness will heavily rely on the organization and structuring of this database.

Question Selector: Once the question pool is established, the question selector component becomes the key element in generating each practice test. This module will use algorithms to select 35 questions at random from the question pool for each test a user takes. The randomness is an essential factor in mimicking the unpredictability of the actual test, thus better preparing the user. The complexity of these algorithms can range from simple random sampling to more complex methods to avoid question repetition and to ensure an even coverage of topics.

User Interface: This is the point of interaction between the users and the system. The user interface needs to be well-designed, not just aesthetically, but also functionally, to facilitate ease of use. It will present the randomly selected questions and corresponding answer choices to the user, collect their responses, and finally present their score upon test completion. It also needs to handle and display system or user-generated errors appropriately.

Grading Component: The grading component is integral to providing feedback to users. After a user completes a test, this module will take the user's responses, compare them against the correct answers from the question pool database, and calculate the user's score. This score will then be converted into a percentage for easy understanding and standardization. This immediate feedback mechanism is crucial for effective learning and preparation.

These components work together to provide the full functionality of the system. The database acts as the primary information source, the question selector uses this information to generate unique tests, the user interface presents these tests to users and collects their responses, and the grading component uses these responses to provide immediate feedback to the user. The careful design and interaction of these components will determine the overall success and utility of the HAM radio license practice test application.

This section is now far more detailed, with important information added. Rather than a single sentence describing each component, we now have a paragraph. There's more detail and more to consider when thinking about our application. The value here isn't in the ready-to-go text it generates. Sure, we have a nice full document, but it could be loaded with inaccuracies. We must review and double-check all the information. Don't rely on implied accuracy!

The primary advantage of using ChatGPT in this case is outlining concepts and exploring ideas you may not have thought about. It helps you start the documentation process and assists you in writing documentation.

3.7.2   *Technical stack (section 5)*

Let's dive into another section and extract more details. Again, we're doing this to get a general outline and suggestions. Because LLMs are trained on vast sets of similar texts, the structure they come up with will likely resemble formats you've encountered or created yourself. It can also bring up topics and ideas you haven't thought of yet.

I want to get additional details from the technical stack section. I also want to influence the model a bit. I don't want to use React, Node.js, or Mongo. We're Python developers! One of the most popular web frameworks for Python is Flask, and it will allow us to use Python to build a web application.

We can steer the model for different results by adding to the existing context. We can do that with a single prompt.

> JM   This web-based application will be a typical Flask application.

Now, the context of our chat will involve Flask and the technologies around it. This helps the model know our intentions clearly.

To get the additional details, I decided to use a very simple and concise prompt. Here's the prompt I used:

> JM   Give more details for section "5. Technical stack."

Notice that this time, I gave a very terse prompt. No need to add "Elaborate on the key subjects" because we're still in the same chat context. ChatGPT will know I'm looking for the same thing as before, but with a different section. Let's see what the model created for us.

> ### 5. Technical Stack (Detailed)
>
> This section describes the selection of tools and technologies (referred to as the "tech stack") for our HAM Radio License Practice Test Application.
>
> **Backend:** A server-side web framework is necessary to handle HTTP requests and serve web pages. In our case, we'll be using Flask. Flask is a lightweight Python web framework that is easy to use and provides a lot of flexibility for developers. It doesn't include many of the tools that heavier frameworks like Django come with, but this means that developers have more freedom to choose the tools they want to use.

Database: Given the structure of our data (questions, multiple-choice options, and correct answers), both SQL and NoSQL databases could be used. PostgreSQL or MySQL could be appropriate choices if we choose SQL. Both are robust, reliable, and widely used, offering strong performance, powerful features, and good support for various data types and index strategies. If we go with NoSQL, MongoDB could be a good choice due to its flexibility, scalability, and performance. MongoDB is a document-oriented database that stores data in flexible, JSON-like documents.

Frontend: For the user interface, we will use React.js, a JavaScript library for building user interfaces. React allows for the creation of reusable UI components, which can greatly speed up development and result in code that's easier to maintain. React is maintained by Facebook and is widely used, so it has a large community and a lot of resources for developers.

Hosting/Deployment: Deployment and hosting could be done on Amazon Web Services (AWS). AWS offers a robust, secure, and scalable environment for deploying web applications. With AWS, you can leverage various services like EC2 for running your application, RDS for database management, and S3 for storage. AWS also offers excellent scalability, which is beneficial for the future growth of the application.

Version Control: We will use Git for version control, which allows us to track changes in our code over time and collaborate effectively. GitHub can be used to host our Git repositories.

Testing: Python's unittest module can be used for back-end testing, while Jest and React Testing Library can test React components on the front end.

Containerization: We could use Docker for creating a container for our application. This helps to eliminate issues related to differences in local development environments.

Continuous Integration/Continuous Deployment (CI/CD): We could use tools like Jenkins or GitHub Actions for setting up a CI/CD pipeline. This would enable us to automatically build, test, and deploy our application whenever we push changes to our codebase.

This proposed tech stack is designed to provide a balance between performance, development speed, and ease of use. However, the exact tools and technologies used may vary depending on specific project requirements, developer familiarity, and other factors.

This result generates some additional details that seem accurate. The document lays out our application very nicely. I will modify many of these details for the final document and trim some things. ChatGPT has saved me a considerable amount of time here. While I won't just copy and print this text, I have an outline and guidance to help me. ChatGPT provides tremendous value for outlining sample ideas.

Why is ChatGPT suggesting React.js?

ChatGPT suggests React.js instead of Flask for the frontend, even though we've specified using Flask for the frontend. There's a good reason for this, and it's not a mistake. Developers frequently use React.js as a frontend in addition to Flask and the Flask API. It's likely that the model has seen this combination so many times it assumes we

(continued)

will do the same. There's nothing wrong with this pairing. I would certainly consider it if we were to build a larger, more complex application. However, the simplicity of this application will allow us to use Flask for the frontend as well. This will save us time since we won't have to configure React.js and set it up. We'll just use HTML templates.

So far, ChatGPT has acted as a software design expert and created a basic document outlining the architecture for our Python web application. The document includes important sections such as

- System overview
- Technical considerations
- Development roadmap

This is a good rough draft for our initial design. However, this documentation doesn't cover something very important—the user's point of view.

We can expand the design by having ChatGPT take on another role—that of the product owner. The product owner is the person who represents the user of the application and ensures their needs are met. By asking ChatGPT to act as one, we can generate user stories to capture requirements for the application from the user's point of view. Let's see what ChatGPT comes up with.

> **Using AI to help your tech stack**
>
> Here are some additional techniques to help you evaluate tech choices:
>
> - Pros/cons analysis of different frameworks for your specific use case
> - Specifying questions to determine if the proposed technology is appropriate
> - Prompts for getting migration paths if technologies need to be changed later

3.8   *Generating user stories for our project*

Organizing tasks in an optimal way is an art. This isn't a book about project management, so we won't explore all the possibilities here. We will, however, see what ChatGPT can do to help us organize our project. We'll start by having it generate some user stories for our project.

I want to go down a level deeper into the project. The projects I've been working on for many years have had a product owner involved. Product owners manage the project and control the backlog of tasks. They try to assign tasks in an orderly manner to fit the flow of the project. It's a tough job, and ChatGPT can help with it.

ChatGPT will change from a *software design expert* to *an experienced product owner*. We'll still be in the same context (chat) we used to generate the previous documentation. ChatGPT is aware of the project, so we won't have to add additional background information to our prompt.

The next prompt I send is

> (JM) Act as an experienced product owner. Create user stories for this software project.

This is the prompt I used with GPT-4, and we'll look at the output. I intentionally kept it short and sweet, so the request was clear.

3.8.1 Defining roles in prompts

ChatGPT generates content based on what it thinks someone in that role will say. By providing a role such as "software designer" or "product owner," we set the context for the information we want to generate.

Roles give ChatGPT a persona, guiding the output's style and substance. As a software designer, it will provide technical details. As a product owner, it will focus on user needs. Roles such as marketer or CEO would yield different perspectives.

Clearly defining a role provides a lens through which ChatGPT views the problem. This role-playing mirrors real life. The CEO of the company will see software problems differently from a developer. They will also have entirely different conversations, and using roles helps ChatGPT emulate that. You're creating a persona to discuss the problem with. You wouldn't ask a person in finance which database provider to consider. We can interact with ChatGPT just like a real person in that role.

Specifying roles in prompts is a great way to steer the output of ChatGPT. It saves guesswork and optimizes your time. Otherwise, the model may present less information that you don't care about. Also, this approach allows you to problem-solve from different angles and can uncover things you haven't thought about. Let's see what this prompt from a new role gives us.

3.8.2 The output: User stories document

The following is the output from ChatGPT, unedited, that builds user stories based on our previous prompt and the context of the overall conversation. ChatGPT knows as much about our project as we do, based on our conversation so far. Here's what it generated for my user stories:

> (⑨) **User Stories for HAM Radio License Practice Test Application**
> **1. User Registration and Authentication**
> 1.1 As a new user, I want to be able to register an account so that I can have a personalized test-taking experience.
> 1.2 As a registered user, I want to log in to access my personal test dashboard and track my progress.
> 1.3 As a registered user, I want to reset my password in case I forget it.
> **2. Accessing the Test**
> 2.1 As a user, I want to start a new practice test so that I can test my knowledge on HAM radio topics.

2.2 As a user, I want to see a clear indication of how many questions are in each test so that I can manage my time effectively.

3. Taking the Test

3.1 As a user, I want to be presented with one question at a time to focus on answering each question without distraction.

3.2 As a user, I want to see multiple-choice options for each question so that I can select the best answer.

3.3 As a user, I want the ability to skip questions and return to them later before submitting the test.

3.4 As a user, I want a timer that shows me how much time I have left for the test to manage my pace.

4. Submitting and Grading

4.1 As a user, once I've answered all questions or the time is up, I want to submit my test for grading.

4.2 As a user, after submission, I want to see my test score as a percentage to understand how well I performed.

4.3 As a user, I'd like to see which questions I got wrong, and what the correct answers are so that I can learn from my mistakes.

5. Tracking Progress

5.1 As a registered user, I want to see a history of my past test scores so that I can track my progress over time.

5.2 As a registered user, I want insights on areas/topics where I need improvement based on my test results.

6. User Interface and Experience

6.1 As a user, I want an intuitive and friendly interface so that I can navigate the application easily.

6.2 As a user, I want to see helpful feedback messages or alerts if I forget to answer a question or if there's an error in the system.

7. Accessibility and Usability

7.1 As a user, I want the application to be accessible, catering to users with disabilities, ensuring everyone can use it without hindrance.

7.2 As a user with a slow internet connection, I want the application to load efficiently without much waiting time.

8. Additional Resources

8.1 As a user, I'd like to have access to additional study materials or resources related to HAM radio to aid my preparation.

8.2 As a user, I'd like a frequently asked questions (FAQ) section in case I have common queries about the test or the platform.

9. Feedback and Support

9.1 As a user, I want the ability to provide feedback about the questions, user interface, or any bugs so that the system can be improved.

9.2 As a user, I want a support or help section where I can get assistance if I face any challenges.

These user stories outline the primary interactions and expectations users might have with the system. As development progresses, new stories might emerge, and existing ones may need to be refined based on user feedback and changing project requirements.

3.8.3   Analyzing the output

Now that we have ChatGPT's initial draft of our user stories, we will scrutinize the content. As I've said before, you must perform due diligence and review all the output from ChatGPT. Don't blindly copy and paste code, and make sure you understand the output. Generative AI provides great value in rapidly producing frameworks and outlines. However, they must be reviewed.

Before diving into the details, we'll take a high-level view. Do the user stories follow a logical progression that mirrors the user's journey? Does it seem accurate? Does the language resonate, or does it need to be tweaked a bit? This critical step allows us to shape the output into documentation that fits our needs. With good reviews, we use ChatGPT's speed without compromising accuracy.

The next section reviews the stories individually to extract the useful parts and determine what needs adjustment. The goal is to retain ChatGPT's framework, while fine-tuning the content to our specifications. With thoughtful examination and editing, we can craft documentation that clearly captures user and technical requirements.

Additional prompts that help with document generation include

- "Create a technical specification template for a REST API."
- "Generate a database schema design document outline."
- "Create an architecture decision record template."

3.8.4   User stories document in detail

This output looks great at a quick glance. I can see areas where I'll likely make changes to our application, but it's a great start. Let's look at each section and see whether it meets our needs.

User Registration and Authentication

This section walks us through the first steps in the process. We can generate tasks from these high-level items: registering an account, a personal dashboard, and resetting the password. It also includes why we'd like to do this. So, the user can have a personalized test-taking experience, track their progress, and reset their password.

Accessing the Test

This section sheds little light on content and should be rolled into another section. It outlines a story for starting a new test and another step to see how many questions are in each test. These are simple requirements but still need to be added to our backlog.

Taking the Test

Section three digs deeper into the process. It shows a workflow of the user being presented one question at a time, with multiple options for each. It also outlines a feature for skipping questions and returning to them later and a timer. These are things I hadn't yet considered for my application. I appreciate the idea generation ChatGPT has provided us.

Submitting and Grading

This section is crucial to letting the student know what their score was. It outlines the process of submitting the test for a grade, converting it to a percentage, and showing what answers were wrong. All great features we can think about adding to our application.

Tracking Progress

This section digs deeper into the process and suggests adding more features.

Namely a history of past scores and areas for improvement. These are a bit complex for an MVP, but we may implement them later.

User Interface and Experience

In section six, we have interface concerns addressed, however they're abstract. It outlines creating an intuitive interface with helpful feedback. These are implied functions regardless, so we should give more detail to this section for our project.

Accessibility and Usability

This section is very important. If we want everyone possible to use this application, we need to accommodate as many people as possible. As a personal note on re-wording: I don't like the phrase "cater to users with disabilities." It has a negative connotation so that I wouldn't add this phrase to a user document. I will find another way to say I want my software to be inclusive of others. This is an example of using the tools to outline your ideas while adding your own voice. You should absolutely reword text when needed.

Additional Resources

This section outlines the addition of additional resources. It also outlines a new feature, the FAQ section. Again, this is an idea I hadn't thought much about, but thanks to GPT-4, it's here. This is certainly something I will consider in the plan.

Feedback and Support

Section nine is the final section and adds some features to our application. We're adding the ability for users to provide feedback about the questions or the application itself. And it suggests creating a help section for the application.

This follows our software's "user journey" from start to finish. It's a decent start to our collection of user stories. Remember, generative AI should assist you in your task rather than do the task for you. This applies to documentation just as much as code. The documentation we've generated so far is decent. We will use this as a guide to building our application. In some ways, we'll follow it closely. Most software design documents aren't set in stone, and this document is no exception. We'll follow it closely in some areas and stray from it in others, depending on the problem. In the next chapter, we'll dig into coding the first version of our application.

Summary

- Precise prompts boost AI effectiveness. Well-crafted prompts state the task, context, and specific instructions clearly. Vague prompts lead to guesswork and poor results. Detailed prompts yield more accurate and useful code.

- AI collaboration improves through refinement. Treat AI interaction as a conversation. This means refining prompts based on your initial results. This dialogue helps you guide the AI toward better outputs.

- Evaluate multiple responses for quality. Creating and comparing various AI responses helps find the best solution. This method ensures we don't accept poor initial results. It also boosts code quality.

- Technical verification is key for AI content. While AI tools offer valuable help, all generated code and suggestions need human validation. You must use your expertise to fill knowledge gaps and ensure accuracy.

- Strategic AI integration balances help with independence. Using AI tools well means using them for brainstorming, drafting, and everyday tasks. However, it's important to retain critical thinking and technical judgment. The goal is to enhance human abilities, not replace crucial developer decisions.

Coding the first version of our application

This chapter covers

- Extracting software requirements from a design document
- Setting up a Python virtual environment
- Creating code stubs to lay out the application structure
- Organizing a Flask web application
- Running a simple Flask app for the first time

In this chapter, we're diving headfirst into the wild world of developing software with AI. By now, you've gotten a taste of what AI can do, and we're just getting started. We will use AI extensively in this chapter, and by the end, you'll be even more comfortable with integrating these tools into your workflow.

We begin our journey by building a useful application for HAM radio test preparation. We'll explore ChatGPT and Gemini and show how each can assist us as we build our project. In the following chapters, we'll use these and other new tools. As you progress, you'll develop a clearer sense of how and when to use the tools.

Creating software is like building a house. The foundation is the first step; you can't start without it. Building the rest of the house will be a struggle if the foundation doesn't meet the requirements (figure 4.1). If you don't have the time to be thoughtful and do it right, you won't have the time to fix it later.

Figure 4.1   The foundation is the most crucial part of your project. Generated with Midjourney, a generative AI image-building tool.

We will use generative AI to build a solid foundation for our application. We'll turn abstract design concepts into code. We're also going to focus on stubbing parts of our application. *Stubbing* is when you create a simplified piece of code, known as a "stub," that acts as a stand-in for functional code. Once you've built several stubs, you can connect them and run the application. Then, you fill in functionality to make each piece functional.

You've probably done this countless times in your career, but now there is the power of generative AI to help speed things along. Once you're comfortable using these tools for assistance, it will become a part of your application creation routine. Let's load up our tools and get started.

4.1   *Stubbing: Building the skeleton of your application*

Stubbing is a fundamental technique in software development where simplified placeholder versions of code components are created before implementing the full functionality. It is like building the frame of a house before adding the walls, plumbing, and electrical systems. The stubs provide a way to test the overall structure and flow of an application early on, without getting bogged down in the details of individual components. Some of the benefits of stubbing are

- *Early integration*—Stubbing allows you to integrate different parts of your application sooner, identifying potential compatibility problems early in the development process.
- *Parallel development*—Team members can work on different components simultaneously, using stubs to simulate dependencies.
- *Testability*—Stubs provide a controlled environment for testing, where specific components can be isolated and evaluated for functionality.
- *Faster iteration*—By focusing on the overall structure first, it is possible to iterate faster and make significant changes without rewriting large portions of code.

4.1.1   A simple code example

Let's say we're building an application that needs to connect to a database. Instead of immediately writing the complex database connection code, we can create a stub:

```
class DatabaseManager:
    def __init__(self):
        pass

    def connect_to_database(self):
        # TODO: Implement this method to connect to the database.
        print("Connecting to the database...") # Placeholder
        return True # Simulate successful connection

    def fetch_data(self, query):
        # TODO: Implement this method to fetch data from the database.
        print("Fetching data...") # Placeholder
        return [] # Simulate empty result set
```

In this example, `connect_to_database()` and `fetch_data()` are stubs. They don't actually connect to a database or fetch data. Instead, they print placeholder messages and return dummy values. This feature allows us to test the parts of our application that use the `DatabaseManager`, even without an active, fully functional database connection.

As we develop the application, we can gradually replace these stubs with real implementations. Such an iterative approach makes a development process more manageable and less prone to errors.

By starting with stubs, you create a working skeleton of your application, which enables you to test, refine, and build on a solid foundation. This is where generative AI tools can be incredibly helpful, quickly generating these initial stubs based on your specifications. Let's gather our requirements and build stubs from them.

Stubbing strategically

Effective stubbing creates a solid foundation:

- Create stubs for a feature before implementing it.
- Use generative AI to suggest method signatures and class structures.

- Start with empty functions to establish interfaces between components.
- Consider implementing one feature at a time rather than creating all stubs upfront.
- Use TODOs to document intent for each stub.
- Ensure that your stubbed application runs before adding functionality.
- Remember YAGNI (you aren't gonna need it): don't create stubs for features you might not implement.

4.2 *Extracting requirements from the design*

When building new software, the clarity and precision of project requirements are pivotal. Getting the requirements right is critical as they often determine whether a software project meets its deadlines or faces significant delays. Requirements always change. Also, they're frequently misinterpreted because we tend to grab the requirements and get to work. There is a lot of room for error here, so if we rush, we can get in trouble. Because generative AI tools make the requirements gathering process easier and faster, we can spend more time working on those requirements and getting them right.

The process of extracting requirements is not merely listing what the software should do, but it is about understanding and interpreting all stakeholders' goals, needs, and constraints. With generative AI, this is even more critical. Although adaptive, these models require a nuanced understanding of the desired outcomes to function optimally. Without precise, well-defined requirements, the tools will help you build a bad project faster.

Let's use generative AI to turn this design document into a set of requirements. The approach is straightforward, and it is helpful to go through it step by step. To extract the requirements using tools, I decided to use ChatGPT and Gemini.

Prompt engineering for requirements extraction

When using AI to extract requirements

- Start with clear, specific prompts that define the scope.
- Ask for structured output (e.g., numbered requirements, categorized lists).
- Request identification of potential pitfalls for each requirement.
- Use follow-up prompts to drill deeper into specific areas.
- Always validate the output with stakeholders or domain experts.
- Remember that AI can hallucinate requirements that seem plausible but aren't really needed.

Here is a three-step process that works well:

1. Ask for key requirements.
2. Convert to user stories.
3. Create stubs based on those stories.

4.2.1   *Step 1: Extract the requirements using ChatGPT*

Our design document is brief, so we could easily review it and extract the main requirements visually. It would only take a few minutes to complete. But what if the project and documents were larger and more complex? We're using ChatGPT to do this to save time. Moreover, ChatGPT helps with accuracy as it can catch errors or surface something you've missed.

Let's see how ChatGPT handles reviewing our document and narrowing the requirements. Not only is ChatGPT good at generating text, but it also can interpret and analyze it. It's likely seen tens of thousands of software design documents. It's also seen as many requirement lists. So, it should be able to come up with something reasonably good.

I copied everything from our design document as text. Then, I used the following prompt:

> What are the key requirements we can obtain from this software design document?
> {Contents of document}

Granted, it's a basic prompt that's straight to the point. Will it produce something decent or steer us wrong? Here's the output:

> From the provided software design document, the following key requirements can be inferred:
>
> 1 Question Pool Database
>
>   a Requirement 1.1: Develop a database, SQL or NoSQL, to store questions, options, and correct answers.
>
>   b Requirement 1.2: The database should contain fields for `question_id`, `question_text`, `options`, and `correct_option`.
>
>   c Requirement 1.3: Implement a system to update the database to ensure accuracy over time.
>
>   d Requirement 1.4: Ensure data validation and cleansing to prevent incorrect or poorly formed data from entering the system.
>
> 2 Question Selector
>
>   a Requirement 2.1: Develop a module to select 35 questions randomly from the database for each test.
>
>   b Requirement 2.2: Implement an algorithm to ensure true randomness in question selection.
>
>   c Requirement 2.3: Ensure that the same question does not appear more than once in a single test.
>
> 3 User Interface
>
>   a Requirement 3.1: Develop a user interface, which could be a web, desktop, or mobile application.
>
>   b Requirement 3.2: The UI should be intuitive, user-friendly, and accessible to cater to a wider audience.

c Requirement 3.3: The UI should present questions and answer choices, accept users' answers, and present the score at the end of the test.

4 Grading Component

a Requirement 4.1: Develop a component to compare user's answers with the correct answers from the database and calculate the final score in percentage.

b Requirement 4.2: Handle cases where the user doesn't answer some questions, considering them as incorrect for scoring purposes.

c Requirement 4.3: Handle any inconsistencies or inaccuracies in grading due to discrepancies in the database.

5 Future Considerations

a Requirement 5.1: Consider adding functionality for tracking user performance over time and providing performance analytics.

b Requirement 5.2: Consider adding features allowing users to focus on specific areas or question types.

c Requirement 5.3: Explore the possibility of integrating the application with a larger learning platform.

6 General Requirements

a Requirement 6.1: The application should be robust and efficient in design, providing a user-friendly tool to help users prepare for their HAM radio license test.

b Requirement 6.2: Consider accessibility needs in all components to ensure the widest possible audience can use the application.

c Requirement 6.3: Ensure the effectiveness of study sessions by avoiding frustrations related to poor UI or inaccuracies in question/answer data.

This list might not be exhaustive, and additional requirements may arise as the design and development process progresses. However, these are the identifiable key requirements based on the provided document.

This looks great, and I'm pleased with the result. It provides enough detail to assign tasks to some of these requirements. These are high-level requirements, and they represent our intention well. At this point, it's good practice to bring these back to your stakeholders and validate the data. A quick meeting to make sure you're on the right track will save you time in the long run. There is a chance a generative AI tool hallucinates and produces a result that looks good to you but is complete nonsense. Human reviews are key.

In this case, I'm the stakeholder. Although I am happy with this output, I'd like to get a second opinion. This is a big project, so exploring more options is worth the time. I turn to Google's Gemini for comparison.

4.2.2 *Step 2: Gathering requirements from Gemini*

I sent the same prompt to Gemini to see how it would interpret our design document.

JM What are the key requirements we can obtain from this software design document? {Contents of document}

The results were unexpected. While ChatGPT and Gemini often produce the same output output, there are times when it's drastically different. This is the nature of generative AI. Each model will interpret input or prompts differently. How they generate output also varies wildly.

You will often encounter similar output across tasks. It even happens with code generation. Why? This is likely because many folks have published code with similar patterns. The model determines the right answer based on how often it has seen it. Whether we admit it or not, we get echoes of the same output because so many developers solve these problems in nearly identical ways. There are only so many ways you can connect to a database!

Don't be thrown off by highly similar outputs from separate tools. It's common. Also, be prepared for things to be far different between tools, which is good. This is what Gemini put out as a response:

From the software design document, the following key requirements can be obtained:

- The application should generate randomized 35-question tests from a predetermined question pool.
- The application should present possible answers to each question.
- The application should provide a score percentage at the end of each test.
- The question pool database should be able to store all the possible questions, along with their multiple-choice options and correct answers.
- The question selector module should be able to use a randomizing algorithm to select 35 questions from the question pool database for each test.
- The User Interface (UI) should be intuitive and user-friendly and should present the questions and answer choices to the user, accept their answers, and present their score at the end of the test.
- The grading component should be able to compare the user's answers with the correct answers from the question pool database to calculate a final score, which will be expressed as a percentage.

Additionally, the software design document also mentions some potential future considerations, such as

1 Tracking user performance over time and providing performance analytics.
2 Allowing users to focus on specific areas or question types.
3 Integrating with a larger learning platform.

These future considerations are not essential requirements for the initial version of the application but could be added over time to increase its utility.

This response looks drastically different from what ChatGPT produced, which is to be expected. Each flavor of GPT has its own personality. Generative tools often produce divergent outputs because the methodology used to generate results differs. Gemini's results are shorter in length, omitting details. It's a level of abstraction higher than the ChatGPT results.

So, I used another source to evaluate our design documents and get a second opinion. If you have multiple tools at your disposal, it helps to cross-check them, even if the output from the first tool is good. A second tool can reveal things you haven't thought of. It can also help validate the core parts of a design. If both models create the same topic or idea, it's more likely that it should be included. That extra bit of research adds value, and it justified the time spent to investigate.

Verifying AI-generated requirements

Critical steps when reviewing AI-generated requirements are

- Cross-reference with original project documentation.
- Validate with stakeholders, especially for technical requirements.
- Look for hallucinated features (things that seem plausible but weren't in your original plan).
- Check for consistency across different sections.
- Ensure all requirements are testable and specific.
- Be wary of overly generic requirements that don't add value.
- Consider how each requirement affects your development timeline.

ALWAYS GET A SECOND OPINION

For crucial generative AI tasks, I duplicate my efforts across tools. We tested model divergence by inserting a similar input into two separate models and obtained different results. This process is a checking mechanism. It seems more likely to be true if you see the same result twice. If the results contradict each other, you can investigate why. Some models will bring up things the other model "didn't think of." These are some reasons why running another tool is worth the time spent.

WHICH ONE SHOULD WE CHOOSE?

If we wanted to, we could dig deep into the details and gather two large lists. We could merge the results from ChatGPT and Gemini just like we do with source code. It's best at this point to go back to the stakeholder(s) and do a quick review. Have them help refine and distill a single set of requirements. This is a small, basic project, and I'm the only stakeholder. We're all set to move forward from here.

After careful consideration, I think the ChatGPT-generated list will be easier to work with. It's far more detailed and includes concrete requirements. The document outlines our overall goal well. With enough work, we could have squeezed more detail from Gemini to little benefit.

We'll use this document as a checklist for things our application must do, so the extra information from the ChatGPT output will be helpful. Now that we have requirements in our hands, we're ready to build some stuff.

The power of multiple AI tools

When working with generative AI, using multiple tools can provide significant advantages:

- Different models interpret prompts differently, offering unique perspectives.
- Seeing the same concept repeated across tools increases confidence in its importance.
- Contrasting outputs helps identify gaps or inconsistencies.
- Some tools excel at specific tasks (code generation, analysis, etc.).
- The extra time spent is often worth the additional insights.

Remember that each model has its own personality and strengths. What seems like an inconsistency between tools is in fact an opportunity to get a more well-rounded view of your problem.

4.3   Setting up our development environment

If you want to follow along with this book and create the application (you should), here is how we'll set it up. One great thing about developing in the Python world is the cross-platform functionality. You can run this on Windows, Mac, or Linux, and the setup won't be drastically different. For our demo, I'm using

- Windows 11
- Python 3.11.5
- Visual Studio Code
- GitHub Copilot

You'll need a dedicated directory on your hard drive to serve as the home for our project. I'm naming mine HAM-Radio-Practice-Web, but you can name yours whatever you like.

In Visual Studio Code, open the folder as a new project. You can do this by navigating to File > Open Folder or by clicking the Open Folder button in your Explorer panel (figure 4.2).

It's just an empty folder for now, but we'll need to open a command prompt or terminal for this folder. You can open a new command prompt in Windows or use a terminal in Linux or Mac. Visual Studio Code can also include a nice terminal window in the editor, which I prefer. To open a terminal window, in the top menu, select Terminal, then New Window. You can also use Ctrl + Shift + ' to open it. When developing in Windows, I prefer using WSL (Windows Subsystem for Linux), with Ubuntu in a VS Code terminal (figure 4.3). This approach allows me to run the powerful Linux commands I prefer and work efficiently using Windows as my desktop.

If you're more comfortable with Windows, you can also use a PowerShell or Command line terminal in VS Code. The commands and usage are very similar. Use whatever works best for you.

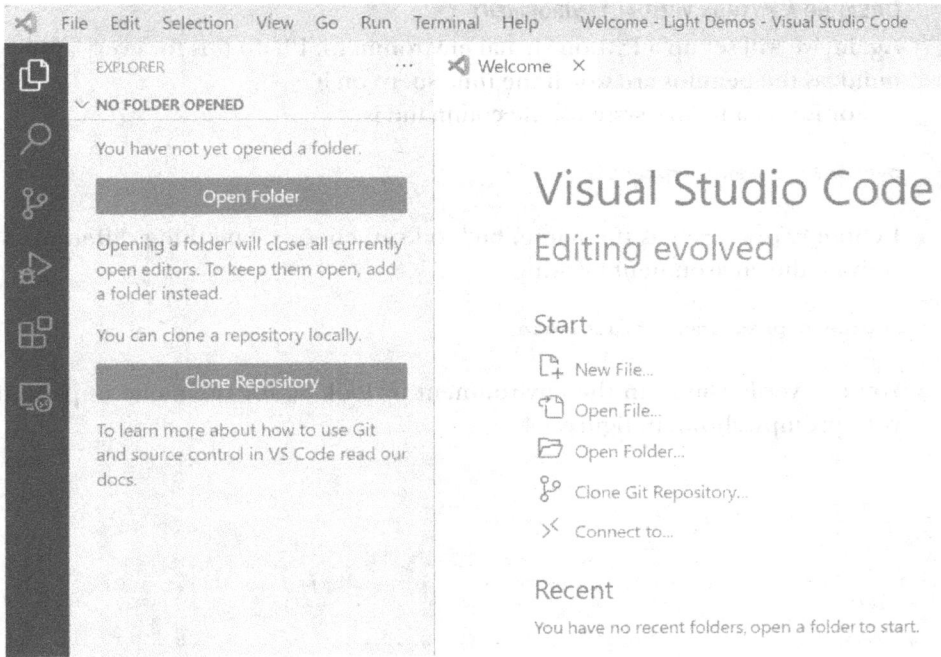

Figure 4.2   Opening a new folder in Visual Studio Code

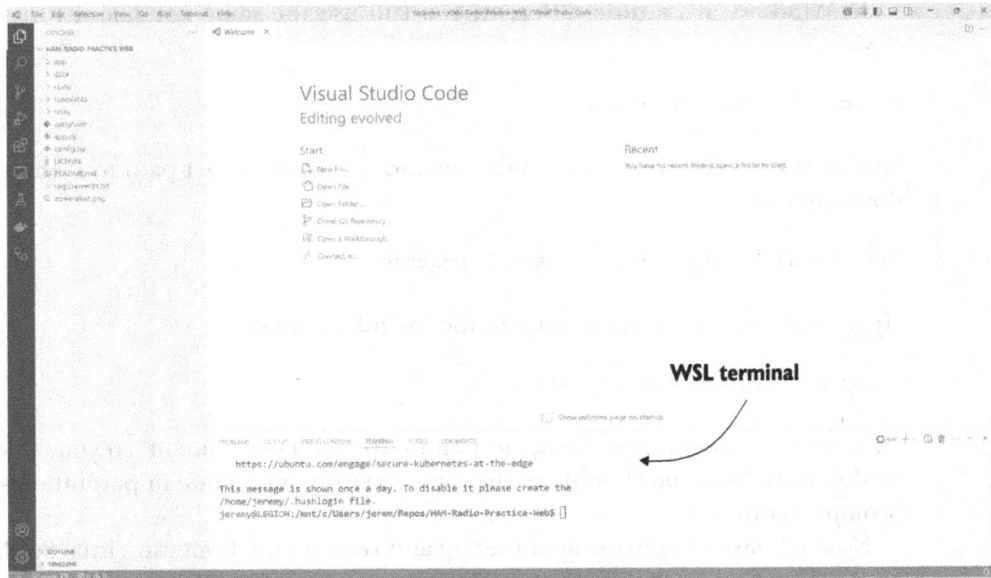

WSL terminal

Figure 4.3   A WSL terminal running in Visual Studio Code

CREATING A PYTHON VIRTUAL ENVIRONMENT

Again, we will set up a Python virtual environment. I'll do this for every application we build, as the benefits are worth the time spent on it.

For Linux and Mac systems, the command is

```
python3 -m venv hrpractice
```

I chose `hrpractice` as the name, but you can choose something different. Then, we activate the environment by using

```
source hrpractice/bin/activate
```

You can verify you're in the environment by looking for the name in parentheses in your prompt, shown in figure 4.4.

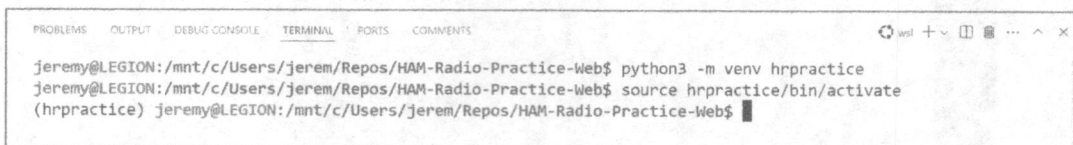

```
PROBLEMS   OUTPUT   DEBUG CONSOLE   TERMINAL   PORTS   COMMENTS
jeremy@LEGION:/mnt/c/Users/jerem/Repos/HAM-Radio-Practice-Web$ python3 -m venv hrpractice
jeremy@LEGION:/mnt/c/Users/jerem/Repos/HAM-Radio-Practice-Web$ source hrpractice/bin/activate
(hrpractice) jeremy@LEGION:/mnt/c/Users/jerem/Repos/HAM-Radio-Practice-Web$
```

Figure 4.4   Prompt showing the environment is active in Linux/Mac

This prompt shows your environment is active.

In Windows, it's a little different. You still use the same command to create the environment:

```
python -m venv hrpractice
```

Note that on some systems, you may need to specify the exact path to Python in Windows, such as

```
C:\Python311\python.exe -m venv hrpractice
```

To activate, call the activate script in the Includes folder:

```
.\hrpractice\Scripts\activate
```

Of course, `hrpractice` is the name I chose for the environment, so your folder may be different. Now you should see the same environment name in parentheses at your prompt (figure 4.5).

Now, we have our environment set up and ready to go. I will use Visual Studio Code and GitHub Copilot in this chapter. The instructions for installing Copilot can be found at https://mng.bz/OwXK. Now, let's start organizing our Flask application.

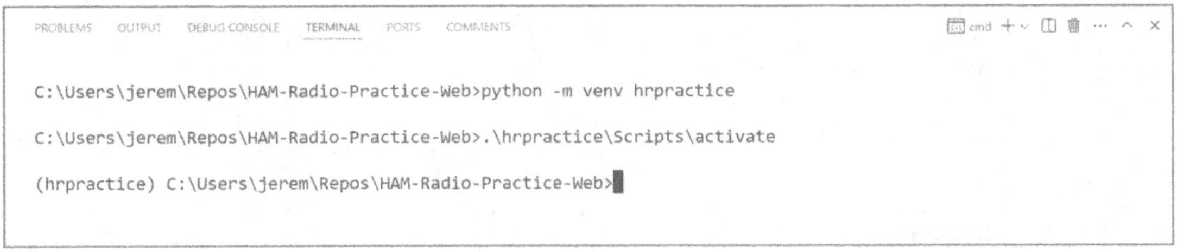

```
PROBLEMS   OUTPUT   DEBUG CONSOLE   TERMINAL   PORTS   COMMENTS                          cmd  + ∨  □  🗑  …  ∧  ×

C:\Users\jerem\Repos\HAM-Radio-Practice-Web>python -m venv hrpractice

C:\Users\jerem\Repos\HAM-Radio-Practice-Web>.\hrpractice\Scripts\activate

(hrpractice) C:\Users\jerem\Repos\HAM-Radio-Practice-Web>█
```

Figure 4.5   Prompt showing the environment is active in Windows

4.4   *Flask application structure*

I have chosen Flask as the framework for our application. We could easily install Flask, create a single Python file, and be up and running. As we add functionality, we just put more code in the file, save, and restart it. This is fine for small applications built in a hurry. However, if you ever want to expand the application later, it quickly becomes a mess.

How can we structure this application in a nice, organized way? Let's ask ChatGPT. I'll ask my question in the same context (thread) that I used to generate the software documentation. It's important to keep these threads open in ChatGPT if you want it to remember the details of your conversation.

Here is the prompt I entered:

> JM This will be a Flask application. Show the best folder structure and file name suggestions for this application.

In this case, the model already has the context of our application, so it should be able to layout a decent structure. Let's see what it generates.

OUTPUT FROM CHATGPT

Assuming you are building a relatively standard Flask application, the folder structure presented in figure 4.6 could be used:

Here's a brief overview of what each part does:

- `app/_init_.py`—This file initializes your Flask application.
- `app/routes.py`—This file defines the routes (URLs) for your application and the logic associated with them.
- `app/templates/`—This folder contains HTML templates that your application will render, which in this case is an index (landing) page, a test page for taking tests, and a results page for showing the scores.
- `app/static/`—This folder contains static files such as CSS for styling, JavaScript for interactivity, and any images your application might use.
- `app/models/questions.py`—This file defines the structure of your question model and interacts with your database.

```
arduino                        Copy    Edit
HAMRadioPracticeTest/
|
├── app/
|    ├── __init__.py
|    ├── routes.py
|    ├── templates/
|    |    ├── index.html
|    |    ├── test.html
|    |    └── results.html
|    ├── static/
|    |    ├── css/
|    |    ├── js/
|    |    └── img/
|    ├── models/
|    |    └── questions.py
|    └── utils/
|         └── question_selector.py
|
├── tests/
|    ├── __init__.py
|    └── test_routes.py
|
├── config.py
├── run.py
└── requirements.txt
```

Figure 4.6   File structure as suggested by ChatGPT

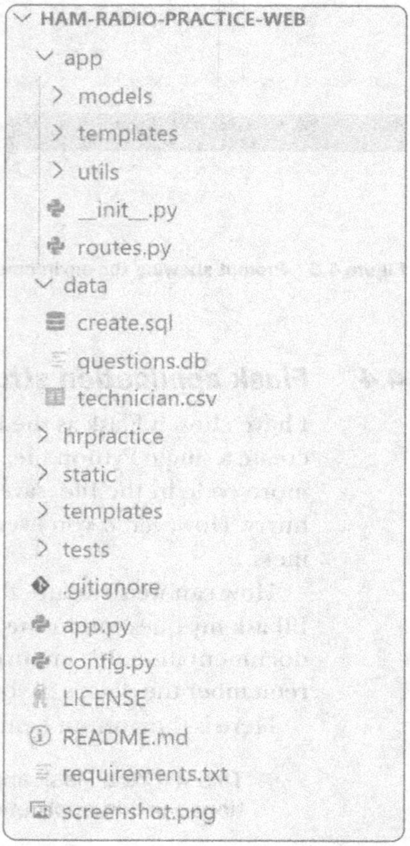

```
∨ HAM-RADIO-PRACTICE-WEB
  ∨ app
    > models
    > templates
    > utils
    🐍 __init__.py
    🐍 routes.py
  ∨ data
    🗄 create.sql
    🗄 questions.db
    🗒 technician.csv
    > hrpractice
    > static
    > templates
    > tests
    🔷 .gitignore
    🐍 app.py
    🐍 config.py
    📄 LICENSE
    ⓘ README.md
    📄 requirements.txt
    🖼 screenshot.png
```

Figure 4.7   Our application in Visual Studio Code

- app/utils/question_selector.py—This file contains the logic for selecting the random questions for each test.
- tests/—This folder contains all test files, such as tests for your routes, question selection logic, grading logic, and similar.
- config.py—This file contains configuration variables for your Flask application (e.g., database URIs, secret keys).
- run.py—This file is used to run the application.
- requirements.txt—This file lists all Python dependencies that your Flask application needs to run.

This setup offers a good starting point and can be further expanded or refined based on your specific needs. It's a solid approach, and there's every reason to explore it further. Let's follow the outline by creating the folders and then use text files in place of working scripts. Figure 4.7 shows our project.

Our project is laid out and ready for code implementation. Now that we have established a file structure, we need to create a code structure to match it. Generative AI can help us with this as well. You can ask ChatGPT to generate a Python script to create this folder structure:

JM Create a Python script to create this structure. Create the folders and blank files in each folder where they are stored.

It saves you the hassle of making it all yourself.

> **Using generative AI for application structure**
>
> Remember, when using AI for application architecture
>
> - AI tools excel at suggesting standard project structures.
> - Request different options to compare approaches.
> - Always question AI's suggestions against your specific needs.
> - Use AI suggestions as a starting point, not a final decision.
> - Ask for reasoning behind structural decisions.
>
> For Flask applications specifically, AI can help organize
>
> - Routes and controllers
> - Templates and static assets
> - Database models and migrations
> - Testing structure

4.5 Stubbing out our application

We're ready to stub out our application. We talked about stubbing earlier in the chapter. Now let's put it into action.

For example, our `DatabaseManager` class could look like this:

```python
class DatabaseManager:
    def __init__(self):
        pass
    def connect_to_database(self):
        # TODO: Implement this method to connect to the database.
        pass
    def update_database(self, data):
        # TODO: Update the database with the given data.
        pass
    def validate_and_cleanse_data(self, data):
        # TODO: Validate and cleanse the given data.
        pass
    def fetch_questions(self):
        # TODO: Fetch questions from the database.
        pass
```

These stubs can be organized in your files, and those files are placed in appropriate folders. This way, you can preemptively organize your code. Here is how I've chosen to generate stubs for this application, outlined in figure 4.8. I do this in three steps:

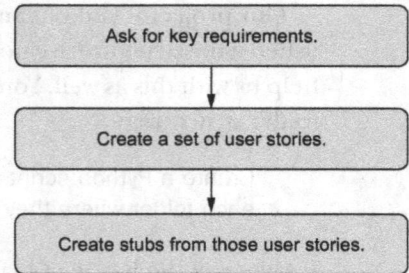

Figure 4.8   The three-step prompt process

1 *Requirements extraction*—Ask AI to identify key requirements from your design document.

2 *User story creation*—Have AI convert those requirements into user stories with roles and objectives.

3 *Stub generation*—Request that the AI create class and method stubs organized by feature.

This methodical approach helps

- Ensure alignment between design and implementation
- Create a logical organization for your code
- Identify missing components early
- Establish clear interfaces between system components
- Produce documentation that maps to your actual code

Although the process involves several steps, it's a technique that's worked well for me. I won't show the output of the first two steps here for brevity and as we've already reviewed the requirements. So, I'll show you the three prompts I used, and we can look at our final output.

JM   What are the key requirements we can obtain from our software design document?

JM   Rewrite this as a set of user stories in SCRUM. Each headline will serve as a story, and the requirements will become tasks for the appropriate story.

JM   Rewrite this as a set of features organized in groups. Create a list of stubs and the classes they would go in to design the application.

I discovered these steps through experimentation and found that if you can distill the requirements and put them in stories, it makes it easier for ChatGPT to create useful stubs. After running these prompts in the same order, we'll come up with a decent start for stubbing. Here is the output from ChatGPT:

Features:

Database Management Feature

- Manage Question Pool Database.

- Update, validate, and cleanse data.

Question Selection Feature
- Randomly select 35 questions for each test.
- Ensure true randomness and no repetition within a single test.

User Interface Feature
- Present questions and answer choices to users.
- Display final score at the end of the test.
- Be user-friendly and accessible.

Grading Feature
- Compare selected answers with correct answers.
- Calculate and display the final score as a percentage.
- Handle unanswered questions.

Enhancement Feature
- Performance analytics.
- Focused study on specific areas or question types.
- Integration with a larger learning platform.

Robustness and Efficiency Feature
- Ensure robustness and efficiency in all components.
- Address accessibility needs.
- Collect and address user feedback.

Stubs and Classes:
1 Class: `DatabaseManager`
   a Stub: `connect_to_database()`
   b Stub: `update_database()`
   c Stub: `validate_and_cleanse_data()`
   d Stub: `fetch_questions()`

2 Class: `QuestionSelector`
   a Stub: `randomize_questions()`
   b Stub: `fetch_single_test()`

3 Class: `UserInterface`
   a Stub: `display_questions()`
   b Stub: `display_final_score()`
   c Stub: `receive_user_input()`
   d Stub: `validate_user_input()`

4 Class: `Grader`
   a Stub: `compare_answers()`

    b Stub: `calculate_final_score()`

    c Stub: `handle_unanswered_questions()`

5 Class: `EnhancementManager`

    a Stub: `track_user_performance()`

    b Stub: `focus_study_area()`

    c Stub: `integrate_learning_platform()`

6 Class: `ApplicationManager`

    a Stub: `ensure_robustness()`

    b Stub: `ensure_efficiency()`

    c Stub: `address_user_feedback()`

    d Stub: `ensure_accessibility()`

This setup organizes the features and associated stubs within appropriate classes, laying the foundation for a structured and modular development approach. The classes and stubs can be further refined and detailed during the actual implementation phase.

When looking at the output, we can see things are organized well. But how can we fit these stubs into our application with the structure we asked for earlier? Here's the prompt I used:

> JM Consider the file structure you provided for this application. Arrange these stubs into the appropriate files and merge them in with the existing structure. Provide the output.

This prompt takes advantage of our conversational history, which is important because it's treated like a human conversation. This allows ChatGPT to act as if it remembers the file structure it suggested. And it works well. Figure 4.9 shows the new file structure.

This structure is more useful than the previous one. It shows files and folders; some of our stub methods can be included in different files. What we need to do now is build this structure out. It should be noted that this will be a *suggestion* for our application. We are not forced to use this suggestion by any means. Remember, this isn't a source of truth but *a representation of what the model thinks a software file structure looks like.* I don't want to build an application manager or enhancement manager, so I'll take some liberties with this design and remove them. Figure 4.10 shows the final folder structure.

Now that we have our file structure established, I'll fill in the methods in the classes as placeholders. Here's an example of `questions.py`:

```
class Questions:
    def connect_to_database(self):
        pass

    def update_database(self):
        pass
```

```
def validate_and_cleanse_data(self):
    pass

def fetch_questions(self):
    pass
```

```php
php                                                    Copy    Edit

HAMRadioPracticeTest/
|
├── app/
|   ├── __init__.py      # Initialization code for the app.
|   ├── routes.py        # Define routes for handling user requests and responses.
|   ├── templates/
|   |   ├── index.html   # Main page (possibly for starting a test or seeing options).
|   |   ├── test.html    # Page for showing the randomized test questions.
|   |   └── results.html # Page to display the score/results after the test.
|   ├── static/
|   |   ├── css/
|   |   ├── js/
|   |   └── img/
|   ├── models/
|   |   └── questions.py # Store the structure and logic related to questions and database.
|   |       - connect_to_database()
|   |       - update_database()
|   |       - validate_and_cleanse_data()
|   |       - fetch_questions()
|   ├── utils/
|   |   ├── question_selector.py # Logic for randomizing and fetching questions for a test.
|   |   |   - randomize_questions()
|   |   |   - fetch_single_test()
|   |   ├── grader.py           # Logic for grading the test.
|   |   |   - compare_answers()
|   |   |   - calculate_final_score()
|   |   |   - handle_unanswered_questions()
|   |   ├── enhancement_manager.py # Logic for future enhancements like focused study or inte
|   |   |   - track_user_performance()
|   |   |   - focus_study_area()
|   |   |   - integrate_learning_platform()
|   |   └── application_manager.py # Logic to ensure the app's robustness, efficiency, and ac
|   |       - ensure_robustness()
|   |       - ensure_efficiency()
|   |       - address_user_feedback()
|   |       - ensure_accessibility()
|
├── tests/
|   ├── __init__.py
|   └── test_routes.py # For testing the routes.
|
├── config.py # Configuration settings for the app.
├── run.py     # Script to start the application.
└── requirements.txt # List of required libraries/packages.
```

Figure 4.9 The suggested file and stubbing structure from ChatGPT

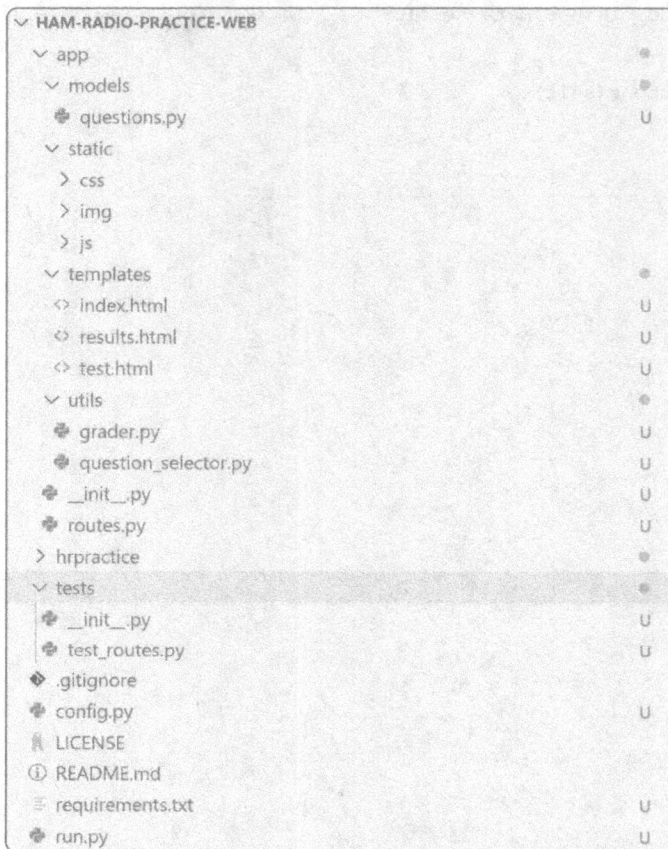

```
∨ HAM-RADIO-PRACTICE-WEB
  ∨ app                                    ⊕
    ∨ models                               ⊕
      🐍 questions.py                       U
    ∨ static
      > css
      > img
      > js
    ∨ templates                            ⊕
      <> index.html                        U
      <> results.html                      U
      <> test.html                         U
    ∨ utils                                ⊕
      🐍 grader.py                          U
      🐍 question_selector.py               U
    🐍 __init__.py                          U
    🐍 routes.py                            U
  > hrpractice                             ⊕
  ∨ tests                                  ⊕
    🐍 __init__.py                          U
    🐍 test_routes.py                       U
  ◆ .gitignore
  🐍 config.py                              U
  ▌ LICENSE
  ① README.md
  ≡ requirements.txt                       U
  🐍 run.py                                 U
```

Figure 4.10   Our application file structure

Once the methods are stubbed out, I can define classes and flesh out each method's implementation as I go. This helps with iterative development styles by creating a structure and adding small pieces as we go.

We'll add the empty functions to our other files, too. In Figure 4.9, ChatGPT suggested stub functions for each file, so we'll implement its recommendation. Remember, this isn't set in stone, and we'll change things as we go. After all, we're using generative AI to *assist* us with writing an application, not having it write an application for us.

`models/questions.py`

- `connect_to_database()`
- `update_database()`
- `validate_and_cleanse_data()`
- `fetch_questions()`

`utils/question_selector.py`

- `randomize_questions()`
- `fetch_single_test()`

`utils/grader.py`

- `compare_answers()`
- `calculate_final_score()`
- `handle_unanswered_questions()`

We have an initial version of our application created. We have generated a folder structure, inserted some empty files named accordingly, and added stubs for our classes. This will be the foundation or "the bones" of our application. Now, we're ready to initiate the setup process.

Understanding AI limitations in software design

Be aware of these AI limitations when using it for software design:

- AI may suggest popular but inappropriate technologies (like the React example in the chapter).
- Models tend to recommend what they've seen most often, not necessarily what's best.
- Technical suggestions require your critical evaluation.
- AI doesn't understand your specific team's skills or constraints.
- Models can be overconfident in their recommendations.
- Always validate AI suggestions against your actual requirements.
- Remember that *you* are the designer—AI is merely a tool.

4.6 Running our application

We have a file structure and know everything is organized for a Flask application. It's also far from a real application since we can't run it yet. Where can we start? For this problem, I turned to GitHub Copilot chat. I have the project open, and I can ask how to get started.

Here is the prompt I used:

> This project will be a Flask application. How can I build an invokable Flask application? What must I include in `run.py` so that a basic flask application will run?

I am pretending to know nothing about Flask to see whether it will provide code to get the application running. The results are presented in figure 4.11.

The result looks great. It gives you sample code to put in the application. Then, the code is explained line by line. This is useful if this is a topic or technique you aren't familiar with. As we've discussed many times, it's not advisable to paste in generated

---

GitHub Copilot

To create a basic Flask application, you need to import the Flask module and create an instance of the Flask web server from your main project file. Here's a simple example of what your run.py file could look like:

```python
from flask import Flask

app = Flask(__name__)

@app.route('/')
def home():
    return "Hello, World!"

if __name__ == "__main__":
    app.run(debug=True)
```

In this code:

- Flask(__name__) creates an instance of a Flask web server.
- @app.route('/') is a Python decorator that Flask provides to assign URLs in our app to functions easily. In this case, it's linking the main URL to the home() function.
- def home(): is a function that returns "Hello, World!" when called.
- if __name__ == "__main__": makes sure the server only runs if the script is executed directly from the Python interpreter and not used as an imported module.
- app.run(debug=True) runs the application on the local development server. The debug=True argument enables debug mode, providing detailed error pages if something goes wrong.

You can run the Flask application by running the run.py script with Python.

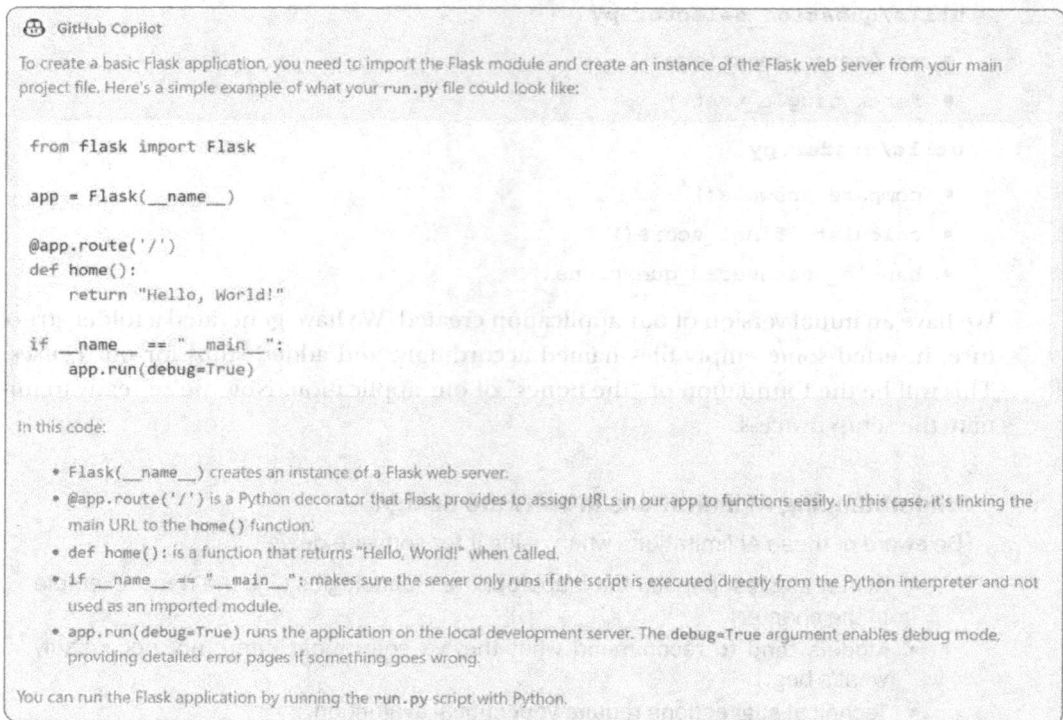

Figure 4.11   A response to our prompt with GitHub Copilot chat

source code you don't understand. It's crucial to understand the code you're working with. I'll paste this into my run.py and follow the instructions.

Here's the exact code I added to run.py:

```python
from flask import Flask

app = Flask(__name__)

@app.route('/')
def home():
    return "Hello, World!"

if __name__ == "__main__":
    app.run(debug=True)
```

NOTE   The instructions do not include installing Flask. You can do this by typing pip install flask at your terminal.

I then type python run.py, as instructed in the Copilot chat. Figure 4.12 shows the outcome.

```
* Serving Flask app 'run'
* Debug mode: on
WARNING: This is a development server. Do not use it in a production deployment. Use a production WSGI server instead.
* Running on http://127.0.0.1:5000
Press CTRL+C to quit
* Restarting with stat
* Debugger is active!
* Debugger PIN: 820-232-364
[]
```

Figure 4.12   A terminal window showing Flask running with no errors

We have a Flask application up and running. Let's go to the URL displayed and check it. We should see a working web page that displays our message, shown in figure 4.13.

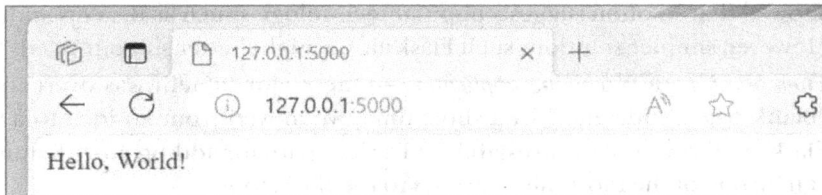

Figure 4.13   A successful "Hello, World!" display from our Flask application

This is exactly what we expect to see from our Flask application. This is our basic "Hello, World!" application. While we're still far from an actual application, this is a great start. We've made a lot of progress in a short amount of time.

AI as an idea generator, not a decision maker

Remember these principles when using AI for software design:

- AI tools are brainstorming partners, not architects.
- The best use is to augment your creativity, not replace it.
- Always apply your domain knowledge and experience.
- Use AI to speed up routine parts of design, freeing time for complex problems.
- Choose what to keep from AI suggestions based on your project's specific needs.
- Combine ideas from multiple AI sessions for optimal results.
- Remember that you make the final decisions—AI is just one input.

In this chapter, we've taken our first practical steps into developing with AI assistance, transforming abstract design concepts into a functional application skeleton. We explored how generative AI tools can accelerate the software development life cycle, while still preserving developer control and creativity. The journey from requirements to running code demonstrated several key principles:

- *AI as a collaborative partner*—Using multiple AI tools such as ChatGPT and Gemini helped us gather and refine requirements. This approach provided different perspectives, improving our grasp of the problem space. Each tool offered unique insights. AI collaboration shines when seen as a conversation, not just a one-time query.
- *Structure before function*—The AI-suggested file structure and code stubs gave us a strong start. They helped us organize our thoughts before writing any functional code. This stubbing method creates clear interfaces between components. It also prevents the chaos that can happen in quickly developed apps.
- *Human judgment remains essential*—We carefully choose which AI suggestions to use and which to change or ignore. The technical stack recommendations showed that AI often suggests popular technologies such as React.js and Node.js. However, simpler solutions such Flask alone might better suit our needs.
- *From blank page to working application*—One major benefit was overcoming the "blank page syndrome." In a short time, we moved from an idea to a working Flask application. We also established a clear path for adding more features. This can be one of the most valuable ways to use these tools.

As we progress, we'll explore how AI tools can improve various parts of the development process. The skills you've learned in this chapter—creating effective prompts, critically assessing AI outputs, and blending suggestions—set the stage for better AI–human collaboration.

Keep in mind that AI tools are great helpers at many stages of application development. However, you decide how to use their suggestions. Your judgment, creativity, and expertise are key to successful software development. In the next chapter, we'll dig in and start building our application, with our new AI assistants helping us along the way.

Summary

- We can extract requirements from our design by sending the right prompts to ChatGPT.
- ChatGPT can suggest a file structure for our application.
- It is possible to generate stubs and classes with generative AI to structure our application.
- GitHub Copilot will create a starting point for our Flask application.
- You can use multiple AI tools at once for the same process.
- AI tools provide suggestions, but programmers still make key decisions on how to use the output.

Using Blackbox AI to
generate base code

5

This chapter covers

- Establishing and managing persistent user sessions in Flask-based applications
- Implementing database functionality to track question sets
- Crafting effective prompts for troubleshooting technical errors
- Applying separation of concerns to improve application architecture
- Building a session-based user interface for practice tests

Let's continue our exploration of generative AI tools by building a real web application. Learning to use these tools effectively is an art, and finding the right balance between AI-generated code and human judgment and logic is key to purposeful development.

We will walk through developing our HAM radio practice exam web app. I'll focus on using Blackbox AI to generate code and accelerate development. However, I will also intervene at key points to refine the architecture, ensure separation of concerns, inject our own code, and override AI suggestions when needed.

The goal is to demonstrate effective cooperation between human expertise and AI. We use the tools to accelerate development through suggestions, while providing context, direction, and corrections. This approach will produce code that surpasses what AI could achieve alone, while also accelerating development compared to human-only workflow. Let's continue our journey!

AI tools as programming partners

When using generative AI for coding

- Bear in mind that each tool has its strengths—Blackbox AI, GitHub Copilot, and Tabnine offer unique features.
- Let AI create scaffolding and boilerplate code to save time.
- Think of AI as your junior pair programmer, not a replacement.
- Be ready to refactor AI-generated code to fit your project's needs.
- Keep a critical eye—these tools are strong, but they miss context that you understand.
- This is a collaborative process: you set the vision, and AI speeds up the work.
- Try different prompting styles to see what fits your workflow best.

Remember: Your skill in recognizing good code architecture is still essential as AI tools change.

5.1 Application development with generative AI tools

We will work on a beta version of our application. In the beginning, we will use Blackbox AI aggressively. Instead of the smart assistant role, the tool will be the lead programmer. Typically, I wouldn't suggest this approach. However, I want to demonstrate the techniques you can use and the full capability of the tools. We'll generate most of the initial code directly from the tool.

If you're an experienced Python developer, you might say, "I would never do it this way." This is perfectly reasonable. In real life, you'll use some suggestions and reject others. You are the final reviewer in your IDE, and that's how it should be. Let's see how far generative AI can take us. After we get things set up, we will do some heavy refactoring to make this work. Overall, it should be a faster pace of development than it would be without the tools.

If you're following along with and coding this project step by step, these tools cost money. I can understand why you wouldn't want to purchase all three. The good news is you don't have to. In my experience, any of the main tools we've talked about (GitHub Copilot, Tabnine, and Blackbox AI) can do this project individually, from start to finish, using the same techniques. You can still follow along if you prefer using a different tool.

5.2 Setting up the development environment

Here is the development environment I'll use to build this application:

- Visual Studio Code, available at https://code.visualstudio.com/download (free)
- DB Browser for SQLite, available at https://sqlitebrowser.org/dl/ (free)
- Python 3.10.12 (The latest version should work fine.)
- Windows 11
- The GitHub Copilot Extension, available at https://github.com/features/copilot (Pro Version, $10 per month)
- The Blackbox.AI Extension, available at https://mng.bz/DwBn ($1.99 per week)
- The Tabnine Pro Extension, available at https://www.tabnine.com/install/vscode ($12 per month)
- WSL running Ubuntu 22.04 LTS

One of the things I love about Python development is its cross-platform capabilities. I'm using Windows 11. If you're following along, you can use Linux or Mac instead, and the instructions are the same. I chose the SQLite browser to work with our database because it works equally well on all three platforms.

The GitHub repository for this code is available at https://mng.bz/1Z86 if you want to download the code and check it out. Now that we're all set up, let's jump right into developing this application.

5.3 Developing core features

Here, we develop the core of the application. We'll get a rough version of our HAM radio practice test app working by the end of this chapter. I start with the database. A dataset is available for download from the following GitHub repository: https://mng.bz/Bz80.

A note about the HAM radio test: Unlike tech certifications, the questions *and answers* to the test are publicly available. So, we will take this database of questions for the technician exam and use it for our application.

5.3.1 Creating the database

In this step, there isn't much for generative AI to do. We will download a CSV from the GitHub repo and place it in a /data folder. Here is the direct link to the file: https://mng.bz/dWYN .

You can download the file with your browser or use a tool such as CURL or wget to download it directly. The file is separated by commas, and its format is shown in table 5.1.

Table 5.1 Format of our questions data. It maps directly to a database table with this information.

id	correct	question	a	b	c	d
T1A01	2	Question?	possible answer	possible answer	possible answer	possible answer

We create a new database and a table in that database for these questions. We can start by opening the DB Browser for SQLite. Click on New Database (figure 5.1).

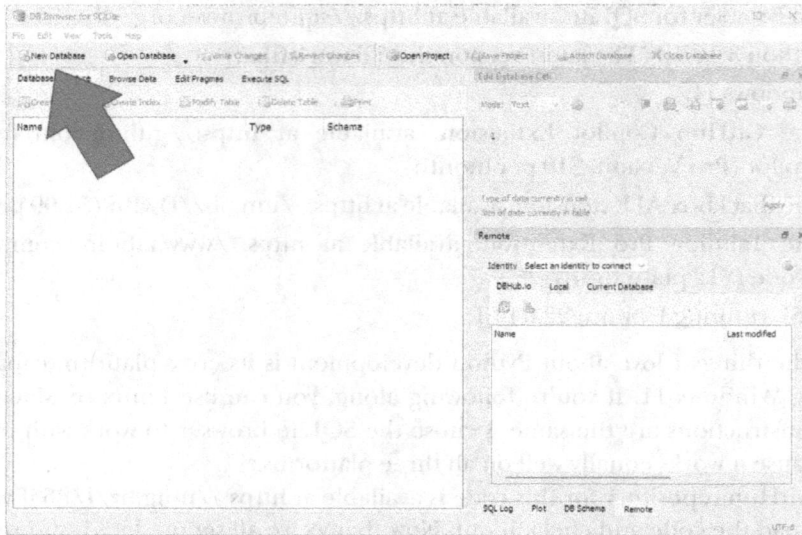

Figure 5.1   **The DB Browser main screen. We'll create a new SQLite database here.**

In the next screen (figure 5.2), we can specify our file name and click Save.

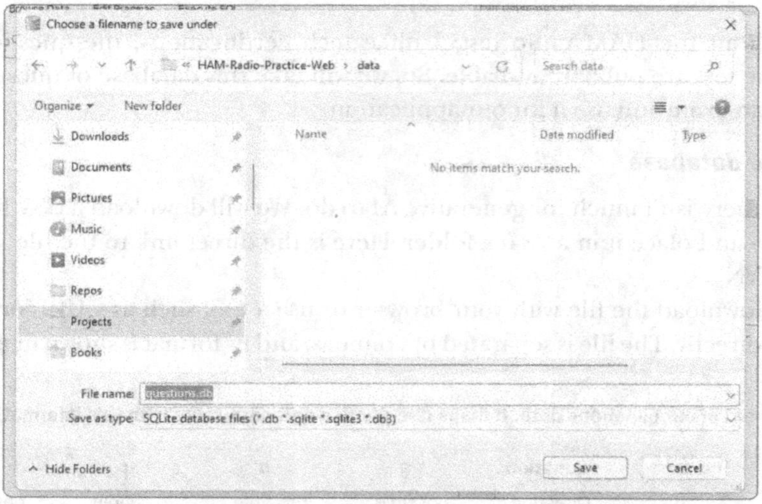

Figure 5.2   **Saving a new database as the** `questions.db` **file**

You will see a screen pop up that says, "Edit table definition." We will skip that, so click Cancel in that window.

Next, go to File -> Import -> Table from the CSV file (figure 5.3).

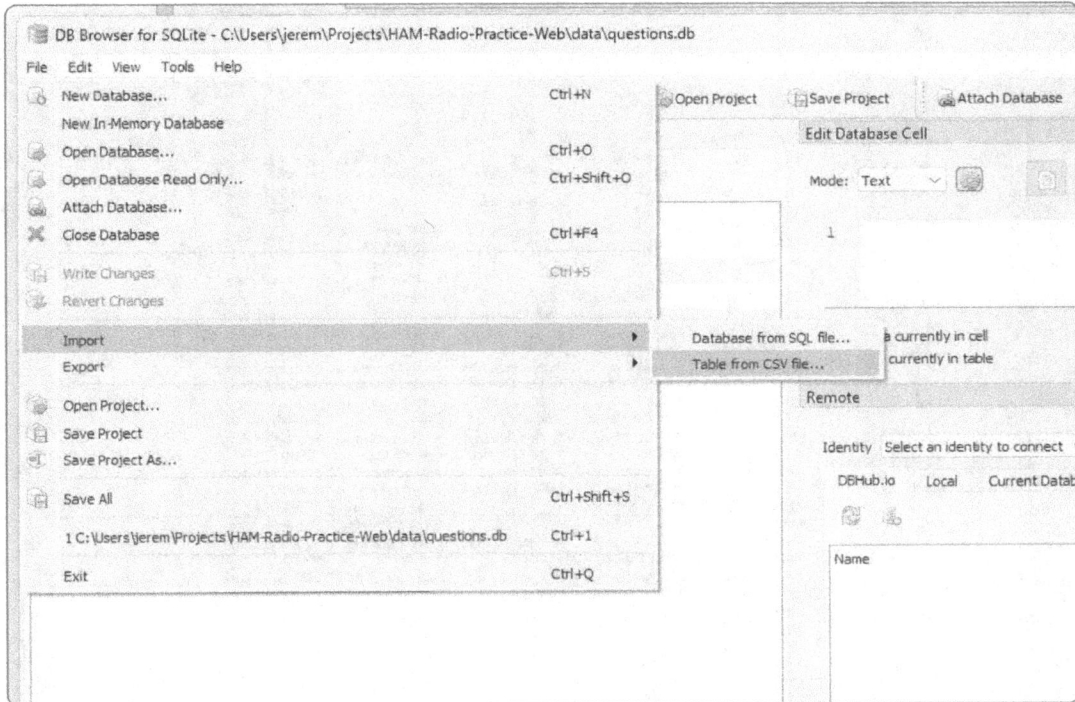

Figure 5.3 Importing a CSV file into the database. We'll create a table from a CSV file.

We select the file we downloaded from the repository, and you will get an Import CSV file window on the screen. Make sure the following options are selected (figure 5.4).

- Change "Table name" to questions.
- Check "Column names" in the first line.
- Enter , as "Field separator."
- Enter " as "Quote character."
- Select UTF-8 for "Encoding."
- Check "Trim fields."

This dialog will import the CSV file into our SQLite database. Click the "Write changes" button to ensure the database is created with this data. Next, we want to modify the table. Right click on the questions table and select "Modify table." Then, in the "Edit

	id	correct	question	a	b	c	d
1	T1A01	2	Which of the following is a ...	Providing personal radio	Providing communications f...	Advancing skills in the technical and ...	All of these choices are correct
2	T1A02	2	Which agency regulates and ...	FEMA	Homeland Security	The FCC	All of these choices are correct
3	T1A03	3	What are the FCC rules regarding t ...	It is required when transmitting ...	It is prohibited	It is required when in contact with ...	It is encouraged
4	T1A04	0	How many operator/primary ...	One	No more than two	One for each band on which the ...	One for each permanent statio...
5	T1A05	2	What is proof of possession of an ...	A printed operator/ primary station ...	The control operator must ...	The control operator's ...	All of these choices are correct
6	T1A06	2	What is the FCC Part 97 definition ...	A government transmitter marki...	A bulletin sent by the FCC to ...	An amateur station transmitting ...	A continuous transmission of ...
7	T1A07	2	What is the FCC Part 97 definition ...	Any satellite orbiting the earth	A manned satellite orbiting the earth	An amateur station located more tha...	An amateur station using amateur ...
8	T1A08	1	Which of the following entities ...	Frequency Spectrum Manag...	Volunteer Frequency	FCC Regional Field Office	International Telecommunicati...
9	T1A09	2	Who selects a Frequency ...	The FCC Office of Spectrum ...	The local chapter of the Office of ...	Amateur operators in a local or ...	FCC Regional Field Office
10	T1A10	3	Which of the following describ...	A radio service using amateur	A radio service using amateur	An emergency service using ...	All of these choices are correct
11	T1A11	1	When is willful interference to ...	To stop another amateur station ...	At no time	When making short test transmissions	At any time, stations in the ...
12	T1B01	1	What is the International ...	An agency of the United States ...	A United Nations agency for ...	An independent frequency ...	A department of the FCC
13	T1B02	1	Which amateur radio stations ma ...	Only members of amateur radio ...	Any amateur holding a ...	Only the astronaut's famil...	Contacts with the ISS are not ...
14	T1B03	1	Which frequency is within the 6 mete...	49.00 MHz	52.525 MHz	28.50 MHz	222.15 MHz
15	T1B04	0	Which amateur band are you usi...	2 meter band	20 meter band	14 meter band	6 meter band

Figure 5.4   This dialog allows you to visually verify the CSV is read properly and the data is formatted the way you expect it.

table" definition screen, make sure PK and U are selected for ID. This selection will ensure that our ID key is treated as a unique and primary key, which will help with indexing and tying this to other tables later (figure 5.5).

Now your database should be up and running, and you can browse the database and see our question data (figure 5.6).

With our database set up, we now need to build the functionality to connect to it. We're going to do this with one of the generative AI tools in our toolbox.

5.3.2   Connecting to our database

Now that we have a working database preloaded with data, we need to connect to it. We can build something that will open the database and connect to it, then send a

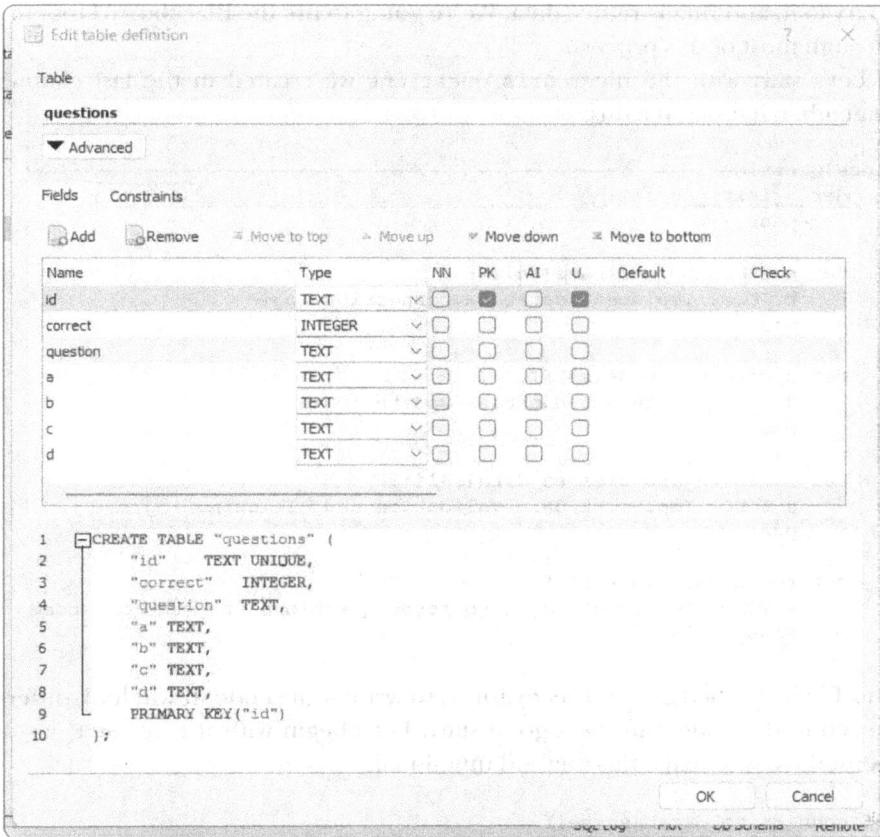

Figure 5.5 In this screen, ensure that the PK and U fields are selected for ID.

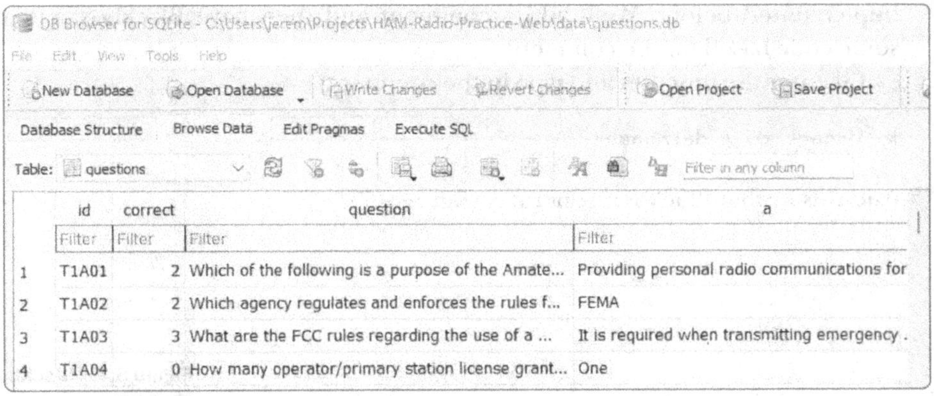

Figure 5.6 In DB Browser, you can visually inspect your tables by clicking Browse Data.

query to it, and finally return data. We're going to use the Blackbox AI tool to guide us through most of this process.

Let's start with the file models/questions we created in the last chapter. If you remember, it looks like this:

```
class Questions:
    def __init__(self):
        pass

    def connect_to_database(self):
        # TODO: Implement database connection logic
        pass

    def update_database(self):
        # TODO: Implement database update logic
        pass

    def validate_and_cleanse_data(self):
        # TODO: Implement data validation and cleansing logic
        pass

    def fetch_questions(self):
        # TODO: Implement logic to fetch questions from the database
        Pass
```

This file is stubbed out and ready for us to write some code. It will look different after we refine the code, but it's a good start. Let's begin with the connect_to_database method. We will make this method functional:

```
def connect_to_database(self):
# TODO: Implement database connection logic
    Pass
```

Let's pretend we've never done this before and ask Blackbox to complete the function. Will it work? There are a few approaches we can try. The first approach is one we've implemented before. We'll add a comment and then have Blackbox auto-generate some code based on the comment.

I'll enter the function and type in the comment:

```
# Connect to a database
```

And this is what Blackbox generates (figure 5.7).

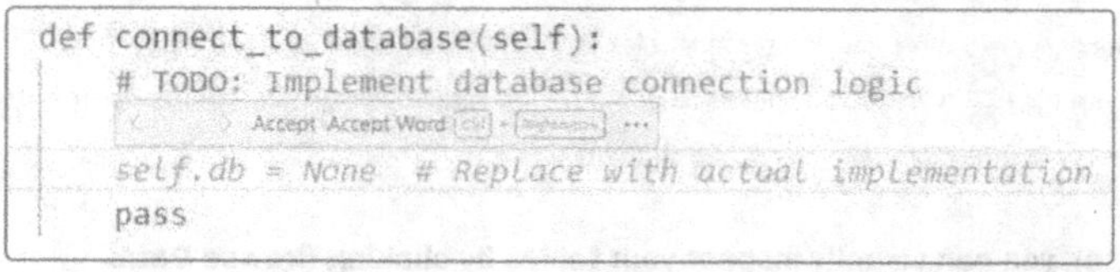

```
def connect_to_database(self):
    # TODO: Implement database connection logic
    <  > Accept Accept Word [ctrl] · [Refresh] ...
    self.db = None   # Replace with actual implementation
    pass
```

Figure 5.7 Blackbox showing a vague result from our prompt

The response isn't very helpful. And if you're this far into the book, you likely already know why. In previous chapters, we learned about context and input. Let's take a look at our code and check what Blackbox sees. By the way, this is pure speculation and an assumption of what the tool looks for. But I do know we're sending the following for context:

- This is written in Python and is part of a class.
- It has four empty functions in the file.
- It seems to have something to do with databases.
- The user wants me to connect it to a database.

We aren't sending Blackbox nearly enough information about what we want. Treat the comment as a prompt. Provide it with clear directions, concise and simple. We can't expect any tool to read our minds (yet). Instead, let's improve our prompt:

connect to a SQLite database. The file name is data/questions.db.

This prompt will tell Blackbox what we want it to do and give specificity. It now knows we have a SQLite database file and want to connect to it. Figure 5.8 shows the outcome.

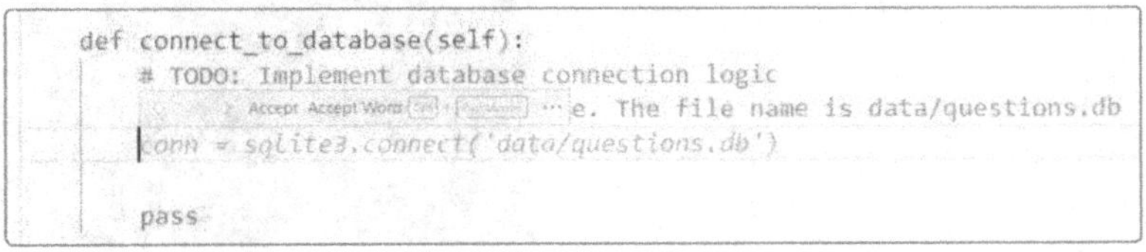

Figure 5.8 Code suggestion with more information in the prompt

This result is much better. Blackbox attempts to write code for connecting to an SQLite database. The code looks like it could be correct, so we accept it. Additional code is needed, and we have a couple of options:

- *Go through and fix errors and generate code step by step.*
  We can walk through the code and generate lines. I can see errors pop up that give me a clue what to do, as shown in figure 5.9.

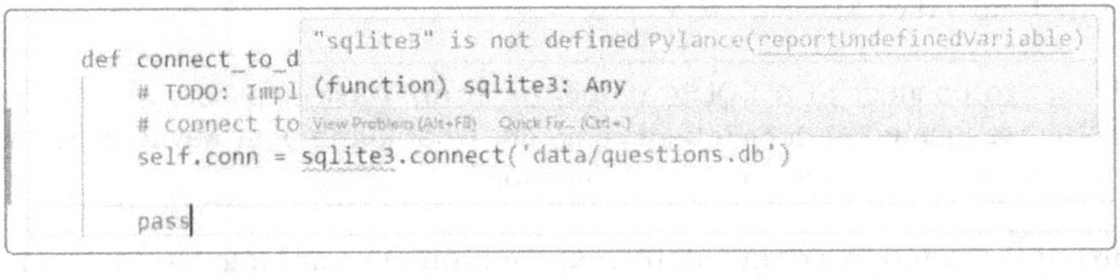

Figure 5.9 Error suggesting we need to install the SQlite3 library

This method works fine but takes a bit more time. It can be slower than coding by hand. But we have another option that will work better—the Blackbox AI chat.

- *Start a chat in the Blackbox AI chat window.*

Since we are generating more than a few lines of code, it may be easier to have a dialog with the tool in the chat window. This way, we can add lots of context to our prompts and get exactly what we want.

You can open the chat window by clicking the Blackbox icon. It will bring up the window and take up around 50% of your IDE space (figure 5.10).

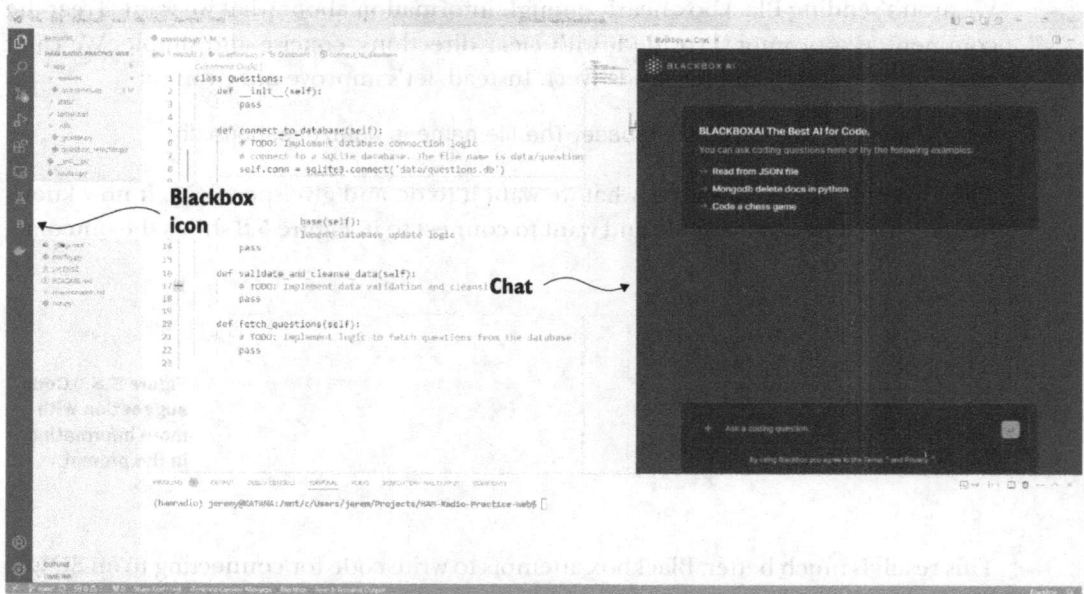

Figure 5.10   The Blackbox AI chat window

This is the approach I like to take when generating larger chunks of code. Later in the chapter, we'll use the comment approach again. For now, let's try to come up with the best prompt to get code to connect to the database. Here is the first one I started with:

> I want to connect to a SQLite database in my Flask application. I have a SQLite database located at data/questions.db. What is the best way to write this out for my connect_to_database(self) function?

This prompt resulted in a detailed, full explanation of what I needed to do. However, it suggests using SQLAlchemy to connect (figure 5.11).

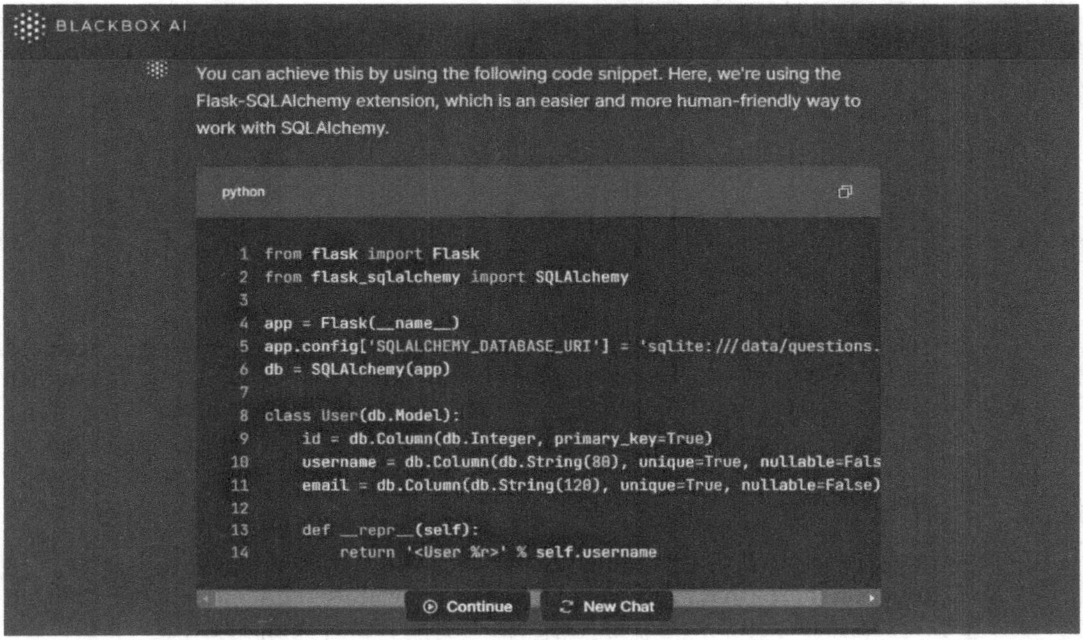

Figure 5.11 Blackbox AI's first suggestion from our prompt

There's nothing inherently wrong with this suggestion. In fact, it's quite good. And I don't want to use SQLAlchemy in this project. Since this is a dialog with the tool, I can make a simple adjustment and send the following prompt:

JM   How can I do this without using SQLAlchemy and connect directly instead?

This will let Blackbox know my intentions. Expressing intent clearly is a good technique for getting better results quickly. Here is how Blackbox responded:

Sure, you can achieve the same result without using SQLAlchemy by connecting to the SQLite database directly using Python's sqlite3 module. Here's how you can do it:

Python code:

```python
import sqlite3

# Establish a connection to the SQLite database
conn = sqlite3.connect('data/questions.db')

# Create a cursor object
cur = conn.cursor()

# Define your query
query = "SELECT * FROM users WHERE id=1"
```

```
# Execute the query
cur.execute(query)

# Fetch the results
results = cur.fetchall()

# Close the connection
conn.close()

# Print the results
for row in results:
    print(row)
```

This code connects to the SQLite database file `'data/questions.db'`, executes the query to retrieve all rows from the `'users'` table where the `'id'` is 1, and then fetches and prints the results. Finally, it closes the connection to the database.

You can customize the `'query'` variable to fetch data based on your requirements. For example, you can change the condition in the `where` clause, or use different SQL functions.

This output is great. It's exactly what we need to connect to our database. It even has a fetch function there (that we won't use). Let's do one more refinement in this chat and see if we can make it fit into our existing class. Here is the prompt I used:

Take this code and make it integrate into our questions class. This method will be `connect_to_database` and its only purpose is to create a connection with the database.

With this prompt, we get specific about what we want to do with this code. Blackbox then produced the following response:

To integrate this code into our questions class, you can add a method called `connect_to_database` to the class. Here's how you can do it:
Python Code:

```python
import sqlite3

class Questions:
    def __init__(self):
        # Connect to the database
        self.connect_to_database()

    def connect_to_database(self):
        # TODO: Implement database connection logic
        # connect to a SQLite database. The file name is data/questions.db
        conn = sqlite3.connect('data/questions.db')

        # Create a cursor object
        cur = conn.cursor()

        # Define your query
        query = "SELECT * FROM users WHERE id=1"
```

```
# Execute the query
cur.execute(query)

# Fetch the results
results = cur.fetchall()

# Close the connection
conn.close()

# Print the results
for row in results:
    print(row)

# Other methods for the class
```

This looks like another great solution that will integrate into our class quite nicely. So, let's add this to our file, and we can focus on testing it next.

5.3.3 Calling our database from the frontend

We can assume our database function works, but we'll need to test it out. We can ask Blackbox how to do this. There is one way to ask: by clicking on the plus sign near a line of code, you can open a chat about it, or you can use a chat window (figure 5.12).

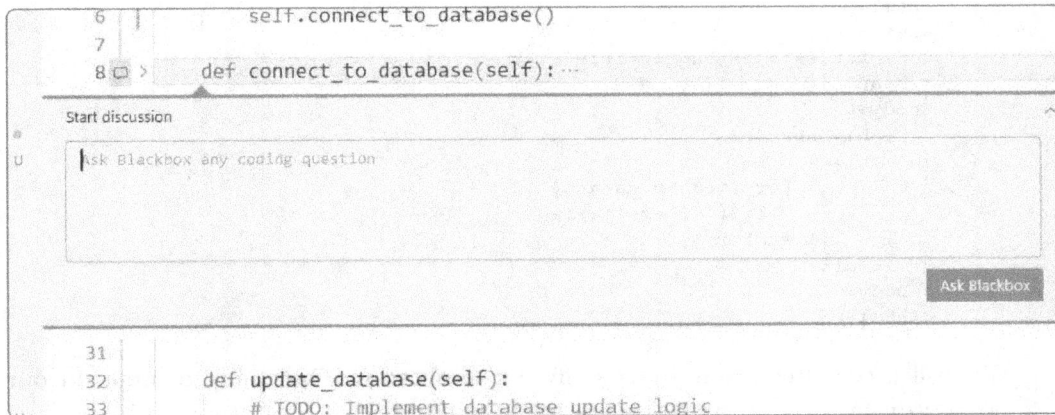

```
6  |        self.connect_to_database()
7  |
8  ⊙ >   def connect_to_database(self): ⋯

Start discussion
⊕
U    Ask Blackbox any coding question


                                                        Ask Blackbox

31 |
32 |        def update_database(self):
33 |            # TODO: Implement database update logic
```

Figure 5.12 You can ask questions directly from the editor window by clicking a plus sign next to a line of code.

I then type in the following prompt:

> 🔵 How can I extract the data from this function and display it on the html index page in Flask?

What follows is the answer I received. It gives us clear steps to run this query and display the results on our front page. Here is the full Blackbox AI output:

To extract the data from the function and display it on the HTML index page in Flask, you can follow these steps:

Create a route in your Flask application for the HTML index page.

In the view function for the HTML index page, import the function that contains the data you want to extract.

Call the function and store the returned data in a variable.

In the HTML template for the index page, use Jinja2 templating to access the data in the variable and display it on the page.

Here is an example of how you could implement these steps:

```python
# Import the function that contains the data you want to extract
from my_module import get_data

# Create a route for the HTML index page
@app.route('/')
def index():
    # Call the function and store the returned data in a variable
    data = get_data()

    # Return the HTML template for the index page
    return render_template('index.html', data=data)
```
```html
<!-- HTML template for the index page -->
<!DOCTYPE html>
<html>
<head>
    <title>Index Page</title>
</head>
<body>
    <h1>Data</h1>
    <ul>
        {% for item in data %}
            <li>{{ item }}</li>
        {% endfor %}
    </ul>
</body>
</html>
```

We will accept this result and modify our application. One thing to note. In our `models/questions.py`, we have a query that won't work:

```python
# Define your query
query = "SELECT * FROM users WHERE id=1"
```

This query is set to look at the `users` table, which doesn't exist. Our table is named `questions`. Let's change this query to our table name. We know that SELECT * is bad. It causes performance problems (e.g., selecting too many fields) and can expose sensitive information. But for now, we'll use SELECT * to query our table and refine it later:

```python
# Define your query
query = "SELECT * FROM questions"
```

We also need to change the return type of this function:

```
# Print the results
for row in results:
print(row)
```

As it sits, we are printing the query results to our console. This won't mean much to Flask. Delete the previous lines above and replace them with

```
return results
```

This way, it will pull all the question records from our table when executed and send them to Flask. We can refine the query later.

MODIFYING THE INDEX PAGE

In our query, we got a recommendation for importing our data, but it's a little vague:

```
from my_module import get_data
```

It shows example code rather than the specific names we're working with. It happens sometimes with this tool. I have seen it scan the context of the application and generate specific code, and I have seen it generate code that looks like boilerplate or example code. In this case, we can clarify the code with the name of our class and file. We add this to the top of run.py:

```
from app.models.questions import Questions
```

This change will bring in the data class we've just created.

Now, we will add the following code to app.py as suggested by Blackbox:

```
@app.route('/')
def index():
    # Call the function and store the returned data in a variable
    data = get_data()

    # Return the HTML template for the index page
    return render_template('index.html', data=data)
```

This code will call a function into the data variable and then display it within a template. We know the data = get_data() line of code will not work. Because it doesn't match anything we have in that class, I will change it to what it should be. I'll create an instance of our Questions class and call the connect_to_database method:

```
my_questions = Questions()
data = my_questions.connect_to_database()
```

Next, I need to create our template. We were given the following HTML code, and I'm going to place it in templates/index.html:

```
<!-- HTML template for the index page -->
<!DOCTYPE html>
<html>
<head>
    <title>Index Page</title>
</head>
<body>
    <h1>Data</h1>
    <ul>
        {% for item in data %}
            <li>{{ item }}</li>
        {% endfor %}
    </ul>
</body>
</html>
```

I know this project isn't ready to run yet. Figure 5.13 shows an error for the Flask template generation.

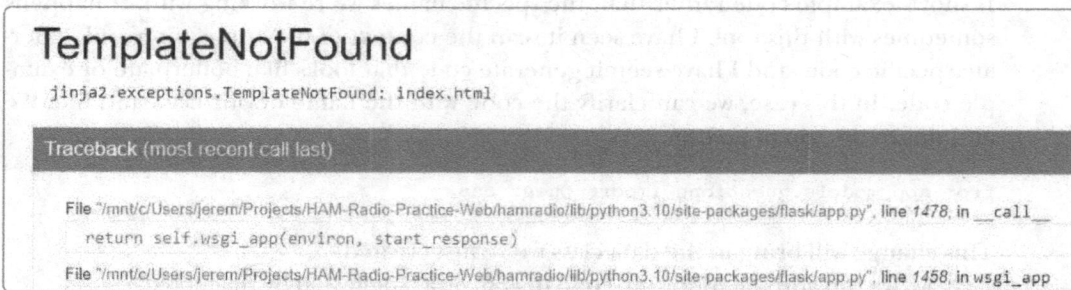

TemplateNotFound

jinja2.exceptions.TemplateNotFound: index.html

Traceback (most recent call last)

File "/mnt/c/Users/jerem/Projects/HAM-Radio-Practice-Web/hamradio/lib/python3.10/site-packages/flask/app.py", line *1478*, in __call__
    return self.wsgi_app(environ, start_response)

File "/mnt/c/Users/jerem/Projects/HAM-Radio-Practice-Web/hamradio/lib/python3.10/site-packages/flask/app.py", line *1458*, in wsgi_app

Figure 5.13   We're getting an error with the `render_template` **function not being found.**

Let's ask Blackbox AI chat what to do:

> JM   How can I use the `render_template` function in this file so it resolves?

This response I received suggested adding the following to our import statement:

> ✦   from flask import Flask, `render_template`

I will add this to our file and see if the application runs. There aren't any errors in our IDE, so let's try it out. I now execute `run.py` and see the error shown in figure 5.14.

What's happening here? This error goes back to the last chapter when we laid out our file structure. According to the Flask documentation, it looks for templates in the `/templates` folder. Yet our templates are in `app/templates` because that's what ChatGPT suggested previously (figure 5.15).

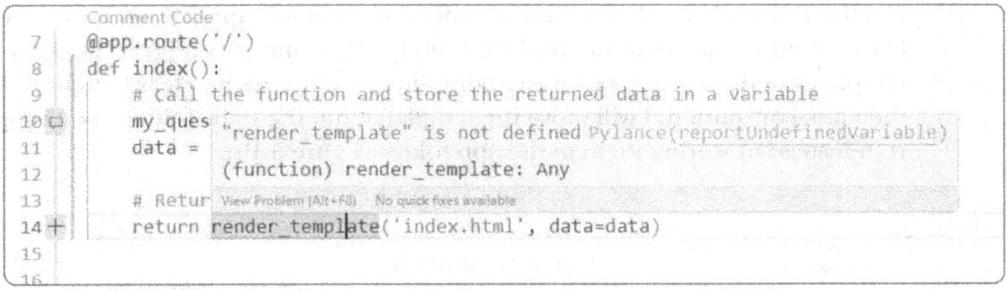

```
      Comment Code
7     @app.route('/')
8     def index():
9         # Call the function and store the returned data in a variable
10        my_ques  "render_template" is not defined Pylance(reportUndefinedVariable)
11        data =
12                 (function) render_template: Any
13        # Retur  View Problem (Alt+F8)   No quick fixes available
14        return render_template('index.html', data=data)
15
16
```

Figure 5.14 Jinja is Flask's templating system. It's showing an error with finding our template.

```
arduino                                                          ⎙ Copy    ✐ Edit

HAMRadioPracticeTest/
|
├── app/
|   ├── __init__.py
|   ├── routes.py
|   ├── templates/
|   |   ├── index.html
|   |   ├── test.html
|   |   └── results.html
|   ├── static/
|   |   ├── css/
|   |   ├── js/
|   |   └── img/
|   ├── models/
|   |   └── questions.py
|   └── utils/
|       └── question_selector.py
|
├── tests/
|   ├── __init__.py
|   └── test_routes.py
|
├── config.py
├── run.py
└── requirements.txt
```

Figure 5.15 The file structure ChatGPT suggested for us earlier. It is incorrect according to the common Flask file structure.

ChatGPT is likely displaying best practices or common application layouts. However, Flask applications are structured differently. We could reconfigure Flask to look for templates in the /app/templates folder; however, there's no clear benefit to breaking the Flask convention. I will move the templates and the static folder to our application root instead of storing them in the app folder (figure 5.16).

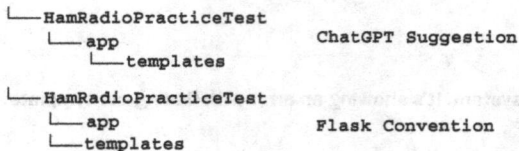

```
└──HamRadioPracticeTest
    └──app                        ChatGPT Suggestion
        └──templates

└──HamRadioPracticeTest
    └──app                        Flask Convention
    └──templates
```

Figure 5.16   We're moving the templates folder to the application root because Flask expects the templates folder at the root by default.

Figure 5.17 shows the new file structure.

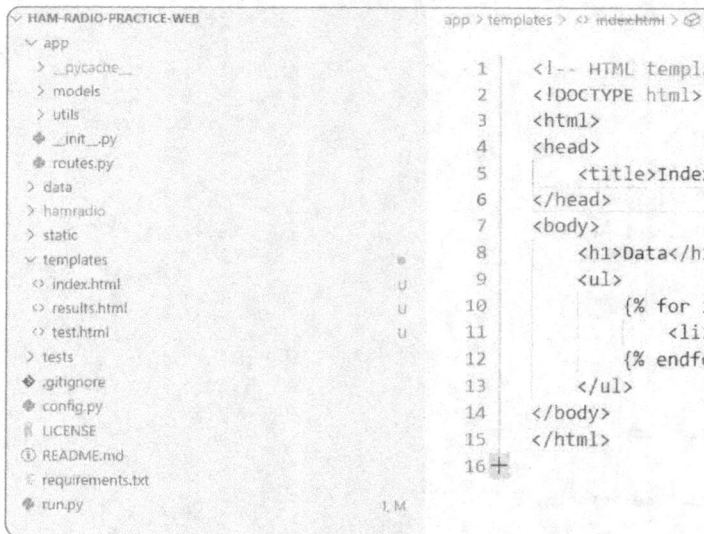

Figure 5.17   Our new file structure based on Flask documentation recommendations

With our new file structure in place, I'll re-run the application. Figure 5.18 shows what I see at this stage.

This is the output I'm expecting. The page shows us a few things:

- We can connect to the database.
- We can run a query.
- We can display that data on a page.

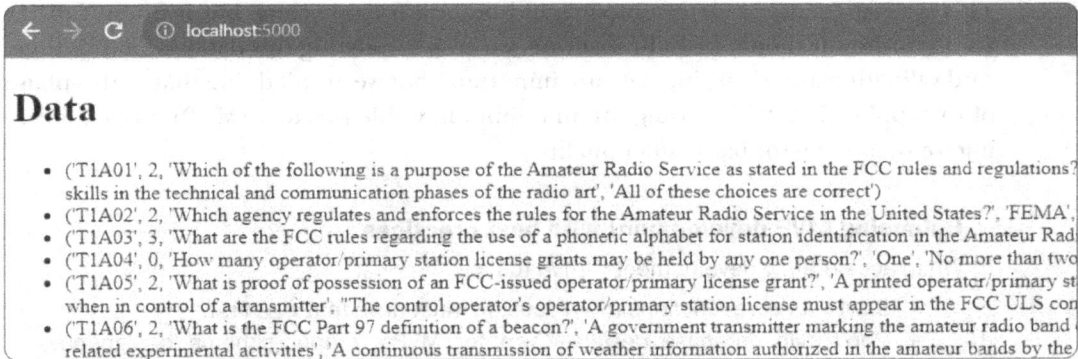

Figure 5.18 The index page showing the results from `connect_to_database()` function, rendered on the screen

This is awesome and a big step forward. We built this to ensure we can connect to a database and display data. But now we need to turn it into something useful for the final product. We will refactor the `connect_to_database()` function to do only one thing—connect to the database.

There's a principle in software development that comes from the original developers of the Unix operating system: *"Do one thing and do it well."* When a method or software module tries to do too many different things, its complexity increases as it becomes difficult to understand, test, and most importantly maintain. By making your components as simple and lean as possible, you avoid future problems. Code should be easy to understand and work with—especially for future readers, including yourself. Moreover, it should be easy to test.

We'll take that approach with this method. It will connect to the database and pass the cursor back. Nothing more, nothing less. That way, we can quickly connect to the database, perform some actions, and close it.

5.3.4 Refactoring our Questions class

Now, we're going to step back into the hands-on experiences that shaped our understanding. You should never blindly have these tools write an entire application for you. Experience and knowledge still matter. They matter even more in the world of generative AI. You must know what you're building. Here's an example of how we'll tweak things beyond what's generated.

Right now, our `Questions` class has four methods:

- `connect_to_database()`
- `update_database()`
- `validate_and_cleanse_data()`
- `fetch_questions()`

This is what ChatGPT determined would be best for our class, but it doesn't fit my vision for how it should be built. For one, we aren't updating this database at this time. And validating and cleansing data are important, but we aren't doing that in this phase of the application. We're going for an minimum viable product (MVP) model, meaning we're looking for basic functionality.

> ### Balancing MVP development with best practices
> When accelerating development with AI tools
> - *Start with core functionality*—Focus on must-have features first.
> - *Don't skip database design*—Even for MVPs, proper schema design pays dividends.
> - *Defer optimization*—Aim for working code first and performance improvements later.
> - *Simplify where possible*—Resist feature creep and overengineering.
> - *Maintain separation of concerns*—Even fast development benefits from clean architecture.
> - *Keep security in mind*—Some best practices shouldn't be compromised even for speed.
> - *Document as you go*—Leave breadcrumbs for your future self in comments.
> - *Test critical paths*—Ensure core functionality works as expected.
>
> The sweet spot is creating maintainable code quickly without introducing technical debt that will slow future development.

In the spirit of building a good MVP, here are the methods I'm thinking of:
- `connect_to_database()`
- `close_database()`
- `fetch_questions()`

With these methods fleshed out, we can get the functionality we need to deliver questions to the student.

Here is the `connect_to_database()` function I'll build:

```
def connect_to_database(self):
    # connect to a SQLite database. The file name is data/questions.db
    conn = sqlite3.connect('data/questions.db')
    # Create a cursor object
    cur = conn.cursor()
    # return the cursor
    return cur
```

This is a bare minimum connection to our database. We know that we need some correction and error handling here. It's likely you can code this up in your sleep, but let's ask Blackbox for help. For this step, I use Blackbox differently and select the code I'm asking about. This gives the tool context to work with and avoids generic answers. The selected code becomes part of the prompt.

I'll select the code and ask in Blackbox chat:

(JM) What error correction should be placed in this function?

I will make sure to check Include Code in Active File, as shown in figure 5.19

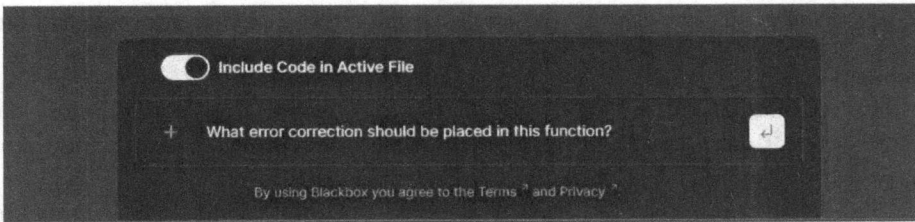

Figure 5.19 Asking a question in Blackbox chat and making sure it's looking at our code

Here is the response from Blackbox. First, it included a suggested code snippet of the entire file:

```python
import sqlite3

class DatabaseConnection:

    def __init__(self):
        self.conn = None
        self.cur = None

    def connect_to_database(self):
        # connect to a SQLite database. The file name is data/questions.db
        try:
            self.conn = sqlite3.connect('data/questions.db')
            # Create a cursor object
            self.cur = self.conn.cursor()
        except sqlite3.Error as e:
            print(f"An error '{e.args[0]}' occurred while connecting
to the database.")
        finally:
            if self.conn:
                return self.cur
            else:
                return None

    def close_connection(self):
        if self.conn:
            self.conn.close()
            self.conn = None
            self.cur = None
```

This is exactly what I had in mind when I asked the question. Then, Blackbox follows up with an explanation of the code generated:

> The above code implements the `DatabaseConnection` class with the `connect_to_database` and `close_connection` methods. It includes error handling, and the cursor is stored as an instance variable for later use.
>
> When using the `connect_to_database` method, if there is an error while connecting to the database, it will be printed out. Additionally, if the connection was successful, the cursor will be returned.
>
> When using the `close_connection` method, it will close the connection to the database if it exists.

This is great, and it's what I asked for. You may have noticed something in the generated code, though. In `Questions.py`, the class is named `Questions:`, and in the generated code, we now have class `DatabaseConnection:`. Why?

Looking at this change prompts a great question. Should we be connecting to the database in the `Questions` class at all?

Crafting effective AI prompts for code generation

To get better code from AI tools:

- Be specific about language, frameworks, and versions.
- Include context about your existing code structure and patterns.
- Specify exactly what the function should do and return.
- Mention error handling expectations.
- Include file paths and database details when relevant.
- Break complex requests into smaller, focused prompts.
- Use code comments as inline prompts when working in your IDE.
- For more complex tasks, use the chat interface to maintain conversation context.

Let's compare the flowing prompts:

Weak—"Connect to a database."

Better—"Connect to a SQLite database. The file name is `data/questions.db`."

Best—"Create a method that connects to a SQLite database at `data/questions.db`, handles connection errors, and returns a cursor object."

HUMAN INTERVENTION IS REQUIRED

It's once again time to override the suggestions given by generative AI. ChatGPT and Blackbox did as we asked, but the suggestions still lack the context and ability to read my mind thoroughly. I need to make some design decisions of my own here.

We can reuse this code because there's no reason to put the database open and close functions in every class we create. In fact, our `Questions` class should have *no database connections in it all*.

This follows the basic computer science principle called "separation of concerns." According to this principle, functions or units of software should be focused on their given task and not overlap or attempt to do too many things. It's very similar to "Do one thing and do it well." The `Questions` class should focus on delivering questions, and we should have a separate class to handle database connections.

When to override AI suggestions

Trust your judgment over AI when

- The generated code doesn't follow separation of concerns principles.
- AI suggests a complex solution when a simpler one would suffice.
- The suggested architecture doesn't align with your project's patterns.
- Performance considerations aren't being addressed (e.g., `SELECT *`).
- The best security practices are being ignored.
- The AI is making assumptions about your project that aren't accurate.
- The code works but isn't maintainable long-term.
- You see library or dependency choices that don't match your stack.

Remember: AI tools can create correct code, but they don't understand your project's needs, limits, and future goals. Your ability to detect design flaws early on, before they lead to implementation problems, is your greatest asset.

I'll create a new file with the code that Blackbox generated for us. Now we're using a separate class to connect to the database. When we mix the database connection functionality into each of our classes, we risk repeating code. More importantly, we'll create more code that we must update if we decide to use another database engine, for instance. It's best to abstract this into its own class for simplicity and avoid these problems.

The database connection pattern

A robust database connection pattern should

- *Isolate connection logic*—Keep database-specific code in one place.
- *Manage resources properly*—Ensure connections are always closed.
- *Support transactions*—Allow for atomic operations.
- *Handle errors gracefully*—Provide meaningful error messages.
- *Be configurable*—Make database paths and credentials configurable.
- *Be thread-safe*—Consider connection pooling for web applications.
- *Follow the single responsibility principle*—Database connection code should do one thing well.

We'll use this for every database connection we make. Let's create a new file named `DatabaseConnection.py` in our Models directory, and we'll use it to handle our database connections:

```
import sqlite3

class DatabaseConnection:
    def __init__(self, db_path):
        self.db_path = db_path

    def __enter__(self):
        self.connection = sqlite3.connect(self.db_path)
        return self.connection.cursor()

    def __exit__(self):
        self.connection.commit()
        self.connection.close()
```

This will be our way of connecting to the database, and we can reuse this code in other parts of our application. Let's break it down to understand it completely.

This code defines a context manager for managing database connections using the SQLite3 module in Python:

```
import sqlite3
```

SQLite3 is a database engine that is part of the standard Python library. The following line imports the SQLite3 module:

```
class DatabaseConnection:
```

This line defines a new class named `DatabaseConnection`:

```
def __init__(self, db_path):
    self.db_path = db_path
```

The following method is the class constructor. It takes a single argument `db_path`, which is the path to the SQLite database file:

```
def __enter__(self):
    self.connection = sqlite3.connect(self.db_path)
    return self.connection.cursor()
```

The next method is a special method in Python, called when the `with` statement is used. The `with` statement in Python is employed to wrap the execution of a block of code that uses methods requiring setup and cleanup steps. The `with` statement allows you to perform a task and have setup and cleanup performed automatically. That way, you don't have to manually allocate and deallocate resources. We'll design this class to use the methodology. When this class is used as a context manager, `__enter__` will be called first if we use the with statement.

In this method, a connection to the SQLite database is established using the `sqlite3.connect()` function. The connection object is stored in the `self.connection` attribute. Then, a cursor object is created by calling the `cursor()` method on the connection object. This cursor object is returned by this method, allowing it to be used inside the `with` block:

```
def __exit__(self):
    self.connection.commit()
    self.connection.close()
```

This is another special Python method triggered by the `with` statement. When the class is used as a context manager, this method is called last.

The changes made to the database during the `with` block are committed by calling the `commit()` method on the connection object. Then, the connection to the database is closed by calling the `close()` method on the connection object.

To use this class as a context manager, you can do the following:

```
with DatabaseConnection('path/to/database.db') as cursor:
    cursor.execute('SELECT * FROM some_table')
    results = cursor.fetchall()
```

The `DatabaseConnection` class is used as a context manager in a `with` statement. When the `with` block is exited, the `__exit__()` method of the `DatabaseConnection` class will be called automatically, ensuring that the database changes are committed and the connection is closed properly.

Here is how I refactor the `questions.py` file to use the `database_connection.py` file:

```
class Questions:
    def __init__(self, cursor):
        self.cursor = cursor

    def fetch_data(self):
        self.cursor.execute("SELECT * FROM questions")  # Adjust SQL query as needed
        return self.cursor.fetchall()
```

We'll return to `fetch_questions` soon, but now our `Questions` class can utilize a separate database connection and focus on doing its primary job, which is delivering questions.

The art of refactoring AI-generated code

Common refactoring needs for AI-generated code are

- Separating concerns (database access, business logic, presentation)
- Removing hardcoded values and adding configuration
- Improving error handling and edge cases
- Making code more testable through dependency injection
- Ensuring code follows project-specific patterns and standards
- Removing unused or redundant code sections
- Improving variable and function naming for clarity

(continued)

Remember that AI tools often generate happy-path code, which works in ideal conditions but may need hardening for production. The most valuable refactoring typically focuses on

- Exception handling
- Resource management (connections, file handles)
- Configurability
- Testability

5.3.5 *Modifying our entry point (App.py)*

Now that we've changed how our questions are generated and separated, the `Questions` class from the database connection, our entry point needs to change as well. We need to add some imports. We will import Flask, as well as the files we've created so far. They're named explicitly so `app.py` knows where to find them:

```
from flask import Flask, render_template
from app.models.database_connection import DatabaseConnection
from app.models.questions import Questions
```

Then, we need to change our `index()` function to point to our database and then call the database connection class into our cursor:

```
def index():
    db_path = 'data/questions.db'
    # Call the function and store the returned data in a variable
    with DatabaseConnection(db_path) as cursor:
```

Next, we pass the cursor into our `questions` class and use `questions.fetch_data` to populate the `data` variable we use for displaying our data. This is the same data variable that our page rendering will use:

```
questions = Questions(cursor)
data = questions.fetch_data()
```

Here is what our modified `App.py` looks like in its final form:

```
from flask import Flask, render_template
from app.models.database_connection import DatabaseConnection
from app.models.questions import Questions

app = Flask(__name__)

@app.route('/')
def index():
    db_path = 'data/questions.db'
```

```
    # Call the function and store the returned data in a variable
    with DatabaseConnection(db_path) as cursor:
        questions = Questions(cursor)
        data = questions.fetch_data()
    # Return the HTML template for the index page
    return render_template('index.html', data=data)

if __name__ == "__main__":
    app.run(debug=True)
```

Let's break this down and explain what's happening. This file sets up a single route to serve the root path (`'/'`) of the application. First, we need to import the necessary modules and initialize the Flask application:

```
from flask import Flask, render_template
from app.models.database_connection import DatabaseConnection
from app.models.questions import Questions

app = Flask(__name__)
```

Then we need to set up a route and a handler for the root path. The `@app.route()` is the route the app takes when the root path is requested. Then the `index()` function is called as a route handler for the path:

```
@app.route('/')
def index():
```

Next, we set the path to the SQLite database file (`db_path`) and create a connection to the database using the `DatabaseConnection` class we just created. The connection is managed by a context manager (`with` statement), which ensures that the connection is properly closed after the data has been fetched:

```
    db_path = 'data/questions.db'
    # Call the function and store the returned data in a variable
    with DatabaseConnection(db_path) as cursor:
```

Then, we create an instance of the `questions` class and call its `fetch_data` method to retrieve data from the database. This data is stored in the `data` variable:

```
        questions = Questions(cursor)
        data = questions.fetch_data()
```

Finally, we render the `'index.html'` template using the `render_template` function and pass the fetched data to the template:

```
    # Return the HTML template for the index page
    return render_template('index.html', data=data)
```

In this block, we run the Flask application if the script is being executed directly (not imported as a module). The debug=True argument tells Flask to enable debugging features, such as displaying detailed error messages in the browser:

```
if __name__ == "__main__":
    app.run(debug=True)
```

This is our new entry point, and when we run this application, this is what we'll see in the browser (figure 5.20).

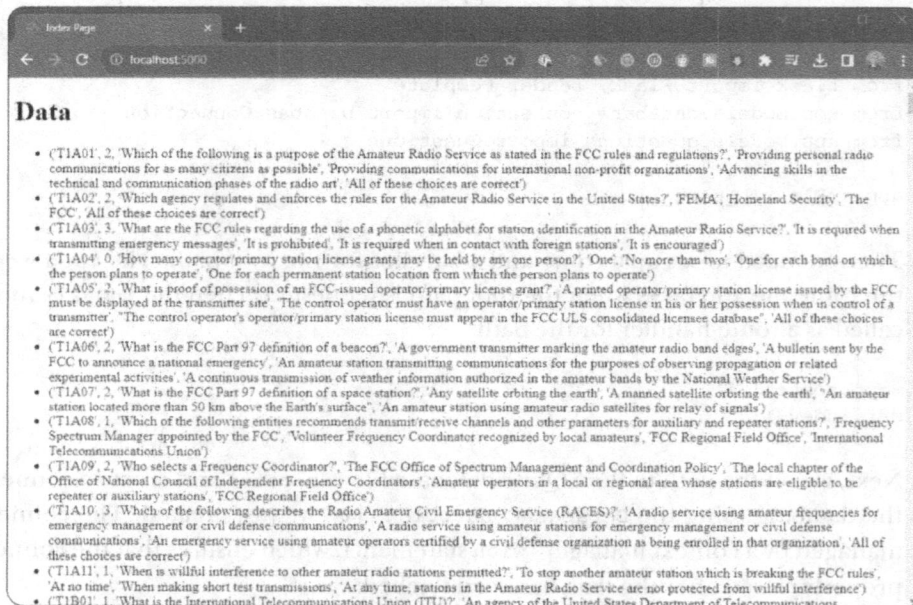

Figure 5.20   The web page displayed at the root of our application. It shows a raw printout of the data returned from our database.

This is a working page, a dump of our questions straight from the database. To the user, this is exactly what we had before, but under the hood, we have more reusable and extensible code that's easier to test. These changes will help us move forward.

Now we'll need to do some refinement to get it closer to our objectives for the application. We'll need to show one question at a time randomly for the student to see and provide an answer for. Let's build out some of that functionality.

5.3.6   *Pulling a set of questions*

Currently, our application is only showing a dump of questions. We need to extract questions one by one to simulate the test-taking experience. The HAM radio technician test has 35 questions, so we need to extract 35 questions at random for this test. Then, we'll have our students go through these questions to simulate a test. Let's focus on the function of selecting the questions. We'll start by making it simple.

Our requirements are as follows:

- Pick 35 questions from the database.
- Questions must be unique.
- Attempt to randomize the selection.

We'll attempt to use Blackbox to help us out with this task. The first thing we'll do is open `questions.py` and create a new function:

```python
def get_question_set(self):
```

Next, we will highlight this line of code and click `BlackboxAI Code Chat`, as shown in figure 5.21.

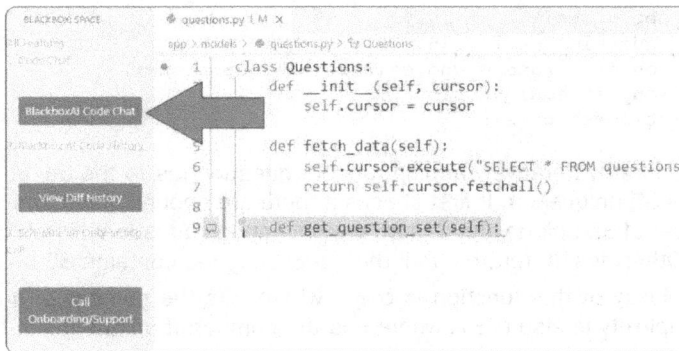

Figure 5.21   The Blackbox AI code chat button

We also make sure the Include Code in Active View button is selected and enter our prompt (figure 5.22).

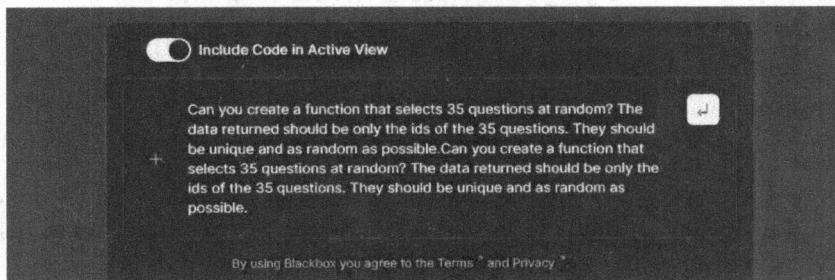

Figure 5.22   The prompt we'll send to Blackbox AI. It is enclosed in the chat window.

Our next prompt is

> (JM) Can you create a function that selects 35 questions at random? The data returned should be only the ids of the 35 questions. They should be unique and as random as possible.

And here is what Blackbox returns:

> Sure! Here's an alternative approach to solving this problem using a different data structure called a set. The set data structure allows us to efficiently perform set operations such as unions, intersections, and differences. It also guarantees uniqueness, which is a desirable property for our problem.
>
> Here's a function that achieves the desired result:

```
import random

def get_question_set(self):
    all_questions = self.get_all_questions()
    if len(all_questions) < 35:
        return "There are not enough questions to generate a set."
    question_set = set()
    while len(question_set) < 35:
        question_id = random.choice(list(all_questions))
        question_set.add(question_id)
    return list(question_set)
```

> This function works by iteratively adding random question ids to the `question_set` until it contains 35 unique ids. It first checks if there are enough questions available to generate a set of 35 unique ids. If there are not enough questions, it returns an error message. Otherwise, it iterates until the `question_set` contains 35 unique ids.
>
> The time complexity of this function is $O(n)$, where n is the number of questions. The space complexity is also $O(n)$, where n is the number of unique ids in the set.
>
> Note: The function assumes that the `get_all_questions` method returns a set of unique question ids. If the `get_all_questions` method returns a list or any other data structure, you will need to convert it to a set before using it in the `get_question_set` function.

I'll add in the suggested code to our `get_question_set` function. This requires adding in a new function called `get_all_questions()`. However, our `fetch_data` function already provides this service:

```
def get_all_questions(self):
    self.cursor.execute("SELECT * FROM questions")
    return self.cursor.fetchall()
```

This should provide us with what we need. Let's modify our run.py file to use our new method. Ideally we can modify this and it should provide us with a set of ids for the "random" questions. Change:

```
data = questions.fetch_data()
```

So, we'll rename it to

```
data = questions.get_question_set()
```

This adjustment should update our application to get the IDs of the 35 questions we need. Let's load it in our browser (figure 5.23).

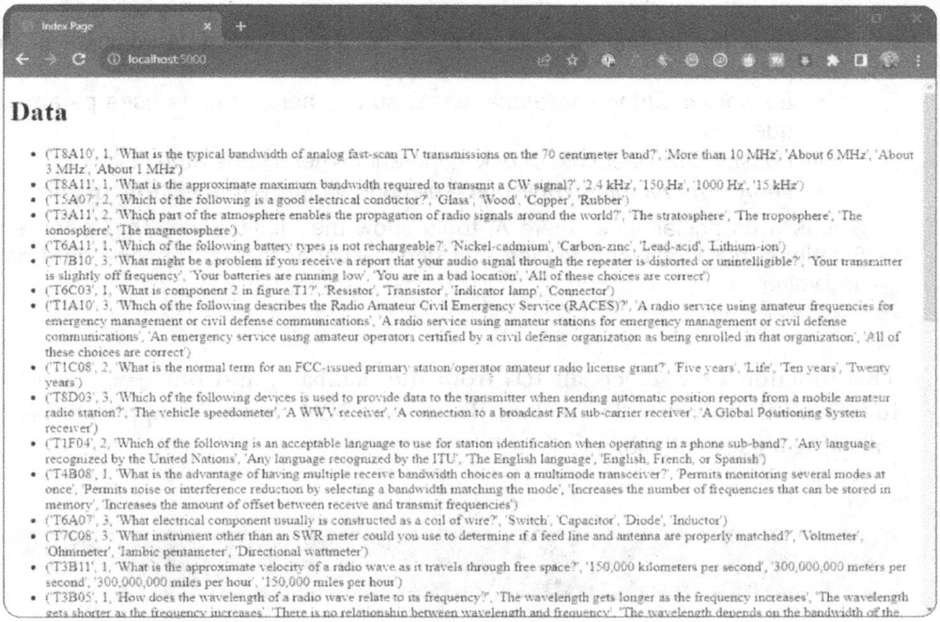

Figure 5.23 Our results from creating a function to randomly grab 35 questions

After loading this up, we can see that it is pulling 35 questions at random. However, we are seeing the full record here, and we only need the ID of each question. The idea here is we can store a set of IDs in a new table and then retrieve the question data from that ID as the student is taking the test. Let's look closer at our questions class. I can see that our function get_all_questions() is what is pulling the full record:

```
def get_all_questions(self):
    self.cursor.execute("SELECT * FROM questions")
    return self.cursor.fetchall()
```

So, we can change that to only pull IDs. Then we can get a list of IDs and use them as a reference set. We will change this line to

```
self.cursor.execute("SELECT id FROM questions")
```

I like this better because it serves our purpose, but also we never want to SELECT * from a table anyway. It can lead to a host of problems and security vulnerabilities.

Effective SQL practices with generative AI

When generating SQL code with AI tools

- *Always review queries.* AI-generated SQL may work but be suboptimal.
- *Avoid* SELECT *. Specify exact columns needed to improve performance.
- *Check* where *clauses.* Ensure proper filtering to avoid table scans.
- *Look for missing indexes.* AI might not know your data volumes or access patterns.
- *Be wary of string concatenation.* Ensure generated code uses parameterized queries.
- *Consider transactions.* Check if operations need to be atomic.
- *Verify error handling.* How does the code handle database exceptions?

SQL is a particular area where AI tools show their limitations. They often suggest functional but inefficient queries that don't account for your specific data patterns and volumes.

This function now selects all IDs from the database, and our get_question_set() function will only pull 35 random IDs. Figure 5.24 shows the application's response following a page refresh.

Figure 5.24   Our index page now only shows IDs as output from our query.

This is a step in the right direction. And it completes the functionality I was looking for:

- Pick 35 questions from the database.
- Questions must be unique.
- Attempt to randomize the selection.

Now I just need to create a table that will store these IDs and some session data for our students.

5.3.7 Creating a test session in the database

Now that we can pull 35 random questions from the database, we need to establish a test session. Here is what I have in mind. I'd like a table that can store a state for the test session as it's running. This session will run as the students take the test. Here are the high-level requirements:

- Create a session.
- Keep track of the 35 questions.
- Keep track of the correct answer for each.
- Track the answer the student has entered.
- Track the number of correct answers.

We need to create three tables:

- *Sessions*—This table will be instances of tests that a user creates. As they create a test session, it will keep track of the answers answered correctly and incorrectly.
- *Question sets*—For the purposes of a practice test, we need a table of questions grouped together from the main question pool. This will be 35 randomly selected questions.
- *Questions*—This is the table we've already created, the one that contains all the questions from the HAM radio test.

Figure 5.25 shows the database design I'm considering using.

I need to create a `sessions` table that looks like this:

```
"session" (
      "session_id"    INTEGER,
      "questions_correct"    INTEGER,
      "questions_incorrect"  INTEGER,
  )
```

We'll open DB Browser for SQLite and click Create Table (figure 5.26).

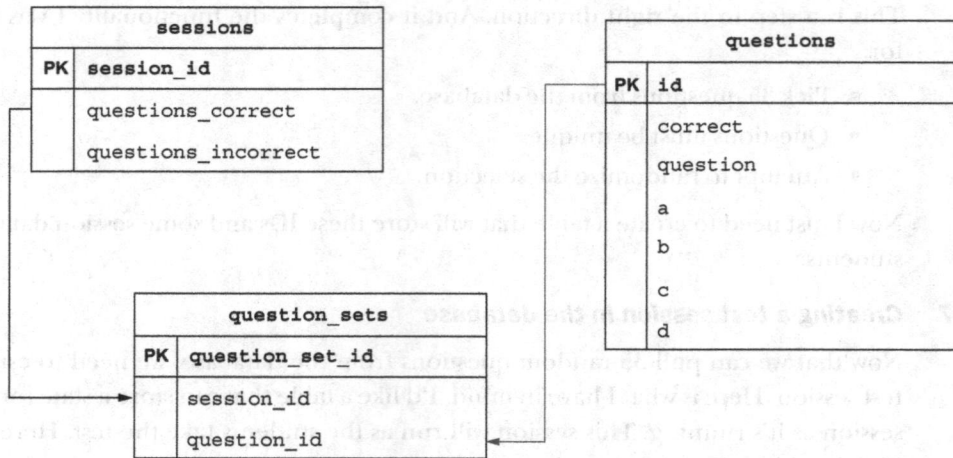

Figure 5.25   **Our proposed database design that contains our sessions, question sets, and questions from the test**

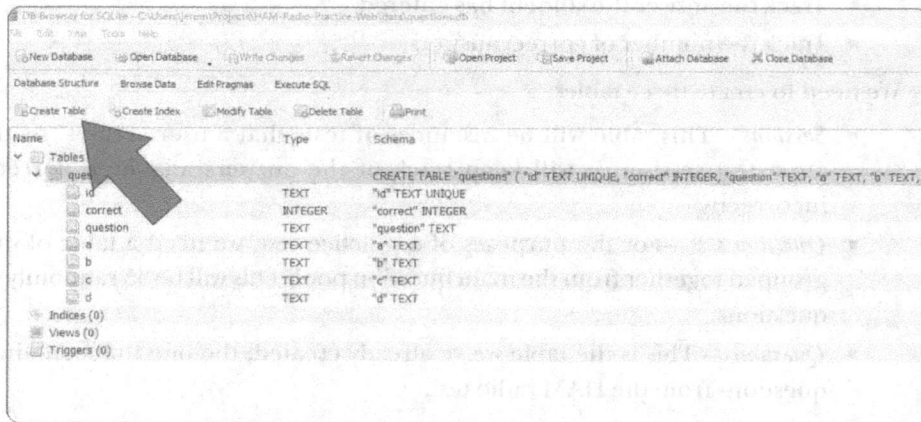

Figure 5.26   **DB Browser for SQLite main screen**

Then, we'll configure our session table using the dialog box in figure 5.26. We want to create each field, and in this case, they're all integer types. The `session_id` field is a primary key that's auto incremented, so we'll check the PK and AI boxes for that field (figure 5.27).

Next, we create a question set table that looks like the table in figure 5.27. This is also a set of integer fields, with `question_set_id` being a primary key that's auto incremented. The `session_id` field will link to our session ID, and the `question_id` will link to a question in the main question pool (figure 5.28).

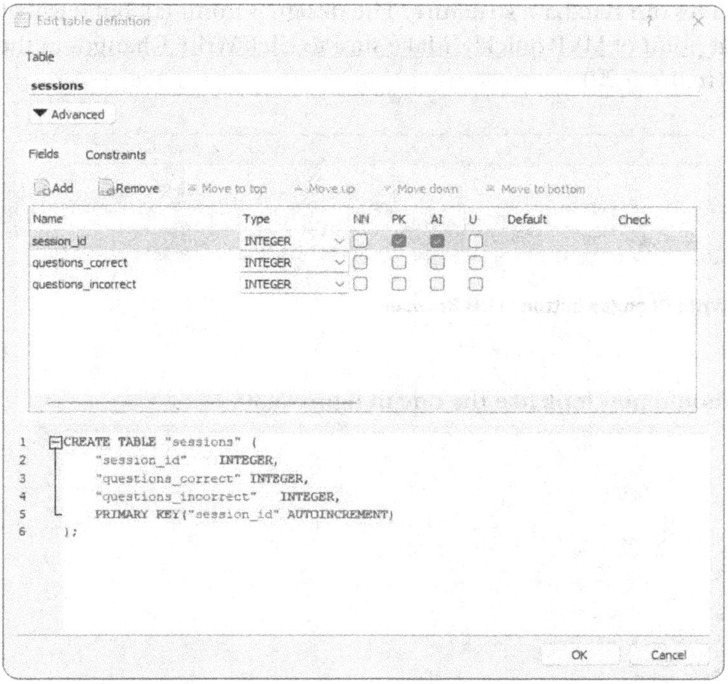

Figure 5.27 Creating table dialog box for session table

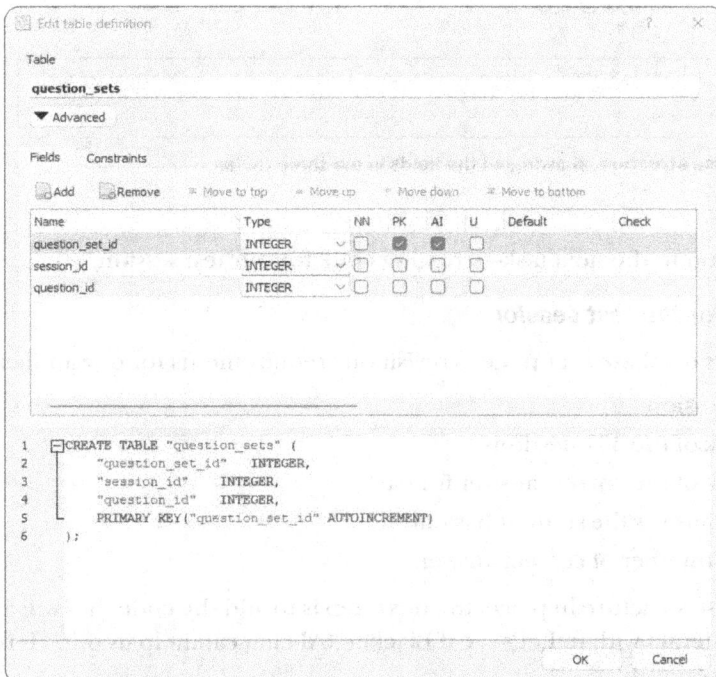

Figure 5.28 Our question set table in SQLite. We'll enter the fields you see in the top window and save them as the question_ sets table.

This step completes our database structure. The design is minimal, but it will efficiently propel us to that point of MVP quickly. Make sure to click Write Changes in the top bar of DB Browser (figure 5.29).

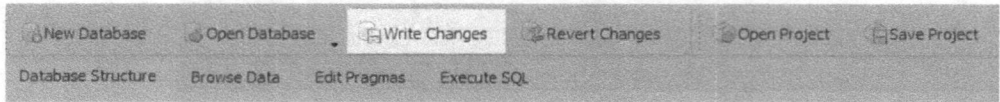

Figure 5.29   The Write Changes button in DB Browser

Your database should now look like the one in figure 5.30.

Figure 5.30   The final database structure, showing all the fields in our three tables

Now, let's move on to the next task—creating code for our test session.

5.3.8   Creating code for the test session

Now we have our database set up. Let's revisit our requirements for our application:

- Create a session.
- Keep track of the 35 questions.
- Keep track of the correct answer for each.
- Track the answer the student has entered.
- Track the number of correct answers.

With our database structure in place, the next step is to add the code that will allow our application to interact with it. Let's see if BlackboxAI chat can help us out. Here is what I'll type in for a prompt:

I need to create a class that creates a new session. Here is the SQL used to create the table:

```
CREATE TABLE "sessions" (
    "session_id"   INTEGER,
    "questions_correct"   INTEGER,
    "questions_incorrect" INTEGER,
    PRIMARY KEY("session_id" AUTOINCREMENT)
)
```

Please create a class that will create a new session record, and session_id is the primary key, so it must be unique and increment from the last id. Insert zero for the questions_correct and questions_incorrect fields upon creation.

And here is what it returns—a class named session.py that looks like this:

```python
import sqlite3

class Session:
    def __init__(self):
        self.session_id = self.create_session()
        self.questions_correct = 0
        self.questions_incorrect = 0

    def create_session(self):
        connection = sqlite3.connect('database.db')
        cursor = connection.cursor()
        cursor.execute("SELECT MAX(session_id) FROM sessions")
        result = cursor.fetchone()
        if result[0] is None:
            session_id = 1
        else:
            session_id = result[0] + 1
        cursor.execute("INSERT INTO sessions
VALUES (?, ?, ?)", (session_id, 0, 0))
        connection.commit()
        connection.close()
        return session_id
```

This code looks pretty good, except that it has database connection functionality in it. We have a DatabaseConnection class to handle that for us. I will create a session.py in the /models folder and save it. Then I will use this file as context and ask it to use our database class. Let's go back to Blackbox AI chat again. I open session.py and ask the following:

How can I make this class utilize my DatabaseConnection class located at /models/ database_connection.py?

Here is the Blackbox AI response:

You can import the `DatabaseConnection` class in your `Session` class and use it to execute your SQL commands. Here's how you can do it:

Import the `DatabaseConnection` class at the beginning of your `Session` class file:

```
from models.database_connection import DatabaseConnection
```

Modify your `create_session` method to use the `DatabaseConnection` class instead of directly creating a SQLite connection:

```
def create_session(self):
    connection = DatabaseConnection()
    cursor = connection.cursor()
    cursor.execute("SELECT MAX(session_id) FROM sessions")
    result = cursor.fetchone()
    if result[0] is None:
        session_id = 1
    else:
        session_id = result[0] + 1
    cursor.execute("INSERT INTO sessions
VALUES (?, ?, ?)"(session_id, 0, 0))
    connection.commit()
    connection.close()
    return session_id
```

Here's the complete code for your `Session` class:

```
import sqlite3
from models.database_connection import DatabaseConnection

class Session:
    def __init__(self):
        self.session_id = self.create_session()
        self.questions_correct = 0
        self.questions_incorrect = 0

    def create_session(self):
        connection = DatabaseConnection()
        cursor = connection.cursor()
        cursor.execute("SELECT MAX(session_id) FROM sessions")
        result = cursor.fetchone()
        if result[0] is None:
            session_id = 1
        else:
            session_id = result[0] + 1
        cursor.execute("INSERT INTO sessions
VALUES (?, ?, ?)", (session_id, 0, 0))
        connection.commit()
        connection.close()
        return session_id
```

Make sure that your `database_connection.py` file is located in the `/models` directory and contains the necessary code to establish a SQLite database connection.

With this advice, I should be able to utilize my existing database connection, so I'll give it a shot. I updated the code in `session.py`, and now I need to invoke it to test it. I ask Blackbox AI how to do that:

> **JM** How can I invoke this from `APP.py` to create a new session?

Sometimes it's good to keep the prompts short and sweet. I only add additional information when it's needed to clarify something. The results it generated are helpful.

> To invoke this from your `APP.py` file, you can simply import the `Session` class and create a new instance of it. Here's how you can do it.
>
> Import the `Session` class at the beginning of your `APP.py` file:
>
> ```
> from models.session import Session
> ```
>
> Create a new instance of the `Session` class:
>
> ```
> session = Session()
> ```
>
> Use the session object to interact with the session. For example, you can print the session ID like this:
>
> ```
> print("Session ID:", session.session_id)
> ```
>
> Here's the complete code for your `APP.py` file:
>
> ```
> from models.session import Session
>
> session = Session()
> print("Session ID:", session.session_id)
> ```
>
> By following these steps, you can invoke the `Session` class from your `APP.py` file and create a new session.

This looks good, and I can give it a shot. However, we do have one problem here. There is more functionality required to create our session. If we remember from our original database design, we have to build a question set and tie it to our session. The question set is unique and tied to each session. The relationship is shown in figure 5.31.

We will add this implementation code; however, we still have work to do to create a session.

5.3.9 Generating a question set

According to our requirements, we need to pull a set of 35 random questions and insert

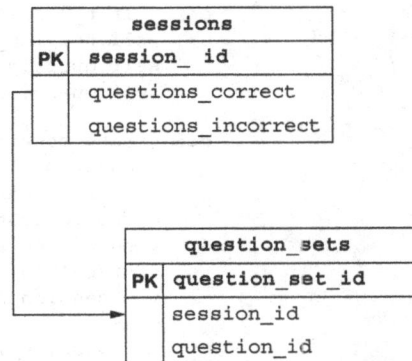

Figure 5.31 The relationship between sessions and questions sets in our database

them into our `question_sets` table. It needs to be tied to our session, so we know those 35 random questions are associated with the test the student is taking. I have an idea of how this should work, but let's run it with Blackbox AI to see how it thinks we should accomplish this. The next prompt is longer and more detailed:

> In our `create_session()` method, I need to pull 35 random questions from our database. I can do that with the `get_question_set()` method from `questions.py`. I need to take these questions and insert them into the `question_sets` table. Here is the SQL used to create that table:
>
> ```
> CREATE TABLE "question_sets" (
> "question_set_id" INTEGER,
> "session_id"      INTEGER,
> "question_id"     INTEGER,
> PRIMARY KEY("question_set_id" AUTOINCREMENT)
> )
> ```
>
> In the `create_session()` method, I need to
>
> - Create a new session and store the ID generated
> - Create a new `question_set_id`
> - Pull 35 questions from `get_question_set()`
> - Insert the ID of each question into the `question_sets` table with the `session_id` stored in the same record.
>
> How can I refactor the `create_session` method to accomplish this?

At times, you'll find a longer more detailed prompt can get you closer the right answer faster.

> Here is a refactored version of the `create_session` method that accomplishes the task:
>
> ```python
> class Session:
>     def __init__(self):
>         self.session_id = self.create_session()
>         self.questions_correct = 0
>         self.questions_incorrect = 0
>
>     def create_session(self):
>         connection = DatabaseConnection()
>         cursor = connection.cursor()
>         cursor.execute("SELECT MAX(session_id) FROM sessions")
>         result = cursor.fetchone()
>         if result[0] is None:
>             session_id = 1
>         else:
>             session_id = result[0] + 1
>         cursor.execute("INSERT INTO sessions
> VALUES (?, ?, ?)", (session_id, 0, 0))
>         connection.commit()
>
>         question_set_id =
> ```

```
            self.create_question_set(session_id, connection, cursor)
            connection.close()
            return session_id

    def create_question_set(self, session_id, connection, cursor):
        question_set_id = 1
        question_set = get_question_set(35)
        for question in question_set:
            cursor.execute("INSERT INTO question_sets
VALUES (?, ?, ?)", (question_set_id, session_id, question.id))
            question_set_id += 1
        connection.commit()
        return question_set_id
```

In this refactored version, I have added a new method called `create_question_set`
that handles the creation of the question set and insertion of the questions into the
`question_sets` table.

  This method takes the `session_id`, `connection`, and `cursor` as parameters. It creates
a new `question_set_id`, pulls 35 random questions from the `get_question_set()`
method, and inserts the ID of each question into the `question_sets` table with the
`session_id` stored in the same record.

  The `create_question_set` method is then called within the `create_session`
method, after the new session has been created and stored in the sessions table. This is
a lot of code to digest at once. I copied and pasted this code, and right away, I noticed I
must fix some import statements. In `app.py`, change

```
from app.models.questions import Questions
```

to explicitly call our method:

```
from app.models.questions import get_question_set
```

Now, it should be ready to run. I'll start up my application. At this point, the page load
will create a new session (we'll fix that soon). I type `python run.py` at the prompt, and
it quickly returns this error:

```
Traceback (most recent call last):
  File "/mnt/c/Users/jerem/Projects/HAM-Radio-Practice-Web/run.py", line 4,
in <module>
    from app.models.session import Session
  File "/mnt/c/Users/jerem/Projects/HAM-Radio-Practice-Web/app/models/
session.py", line 2, in <module>
    from .questions import get_question_set
ImportError: cannot import name 'get_question_set' from 'app.models.
questions' (/mnt/c/Users/jerem/Projects/HAM-Radio-Practice-Web/app/models/
questions.py)
```

The problem stems from the code not creating a new instance of questions. If we look
at the `create_question_set` method, it's not creating a new instance:

```
def create_question_set(self, session_id, connection, cursor):
question_set_id = 1
question_set = get_question_set(35)
for question in question_set:
cursor.execute("INSERT INTO question_sets
VALUES (?, ?, ?)", (question_set_id, session_id, question.id))
    question_set_id += 1
connection.commit()
return question_set_id
```

I need to add the following import:

```
from .questions import Questions
```

The new method should look like this:

```
def create_question_set(self, session_id, connection, cursor):
questions = Questions()
question_set_id = 1
question_set = questions.get_question_set(35)
for question in question_set:
cursor.execute("INSERT INTO question_sets
VALUES (?, ?, ?)", (question_set_id, session_id, question.id))
    question_set_id += 1
connection.commit()
return question_set_id
```

Now I will try to run `python run.py` again, and it loads successfully (figure 5.32).

```
WARNING: This is a development server. Do not use it in a production deployment. Use a production WSGI server instead.
 * Running on http://127.0.0.1:5000
Press CTRL+C to quit
 * Restarting with stat
 * Debugger is active!
 * Debugger PIN: 402-123-914
```

Figure 5.32 A successful load of our Flask application

However, once we load up a page in the browser (figure 5.33), I get a `TypeError`.
I know why this has gone wrong, and if you're paying close attention, you do as well. Our generated code in `create_session` looks like this:

```
connection = DatabaseConnection()
```

The class requires a `db` path to be injected into it. We could easily write

```
connection = DatabaseConnection('data/questions.db')
```

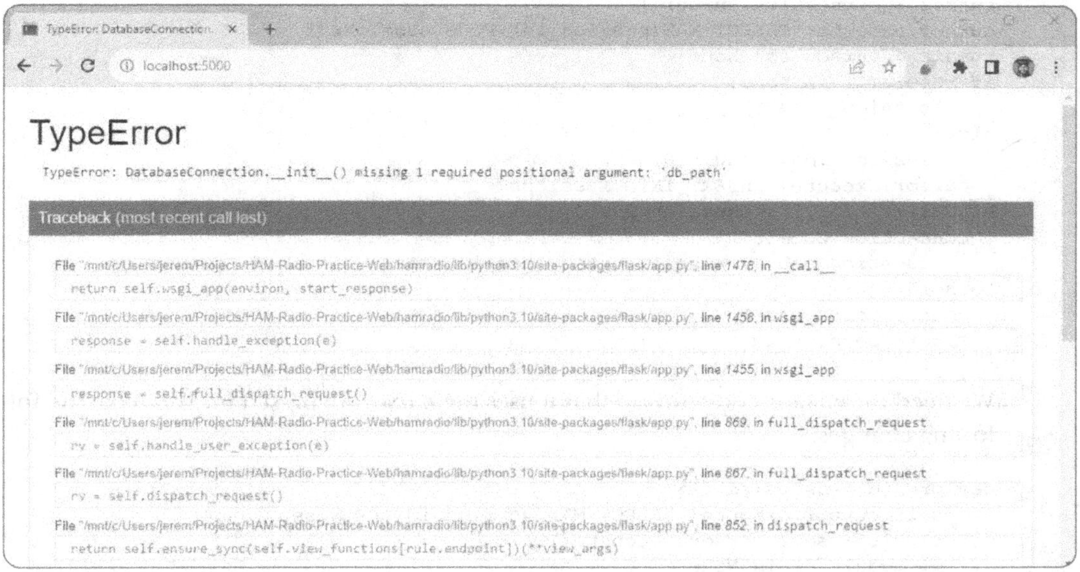

Figure 5.33 `TypeError` **from our application.**

This code would likely work. However, it is bad practice. If we set the pathname location of our database in multiple places, when the name changes, we must update it multiple times in several files. Let's inject this pathname into the `Session` class instead. That way, we only specify the pathname in one place. Let's open `session.py` and make some small changes.

Change this line of code

```
class Session:
def __init__(self):
```

to

```
class Session:
def __init__(self, cursor):
```

Next, add the following under the definition:

```
self.cursor = cursor
```

This line will pass in the cursor when you initialize the session. In this manner, we can use the existing database connection throughout each step of the process. Right now, the `create_session` method looks like this:

```
def create_session(self):
connection = DatabaseConnection()
cursor = connection.cursor()
cursor.execute("SELECT MAX(session_id) FROM sessions")
result = cursor.fetchone()
if result[0] is None:
    session_id = 1
else:
    session_id = result[0] + 1
  cursor.execute("INSERT INTO sessions
VALUES (?, ?, ?)", (session_id, 0, 0))
  connection.commit()
    question_set_id = self.create_question_set(session_id, connection,
cursor)
  connection.close()
  return session_id
```

We need to refactor code now so that it uses the cursor we passed in. We make the following changes:

```
def create_session(self):
    self.cursor.execute("SELECT MAX(session_id) FROM sessions")
    result = self.cursor.fetchone()
    if result[0] is None:
        session_id = 1
    else:
        session_id = result[0] + 1
    self.cursor.execute("INSERT INTO sessions
VALUES (?, ?, ?)", (session_id, 0, 0))

    question_set_id = self.create_question_set(session_id)
    return session_id
```

This refactored code will use `self.cursor` instead of creating a new `Database-Connection` and cursor. We need to refactor `create_question_set` in the same way. Here is what it looks like now:

```
def create_question_set(self, session_id, connection, cursor):
    questions = Questions()
    question_set_id = 1
    question_set = questions.get_question_set()
    for question in question_set:
        cursor.execute("INSERT INTO question_sets
VALUES (?, ?, ?)", (question_set_id, session_id, question.id))
        question_set_id += 1
    connection.commit()
    return question_set_id
```

Here is the new method, using our cursor:

```
def create_question_set(self, session_id):
questions = Questions(self.cursor)
question_set_id = 1
```

```
question_set = questions.get_question_set(35)
for question in question_set:
    self.cursor.execute("INSERT INTO question_sets
VALUES (?, ?, ?)", (question_set_id, session_id, question[0]))
    question_set_id += 1
return question_set_id
```

Now we're ready to load up the page. Once again, we'll start up our application:

```
python run.py
```

I can see immediately there are no errors in my console, which is a good first sign (figure 5.34). We've done a lot of refactoring here!

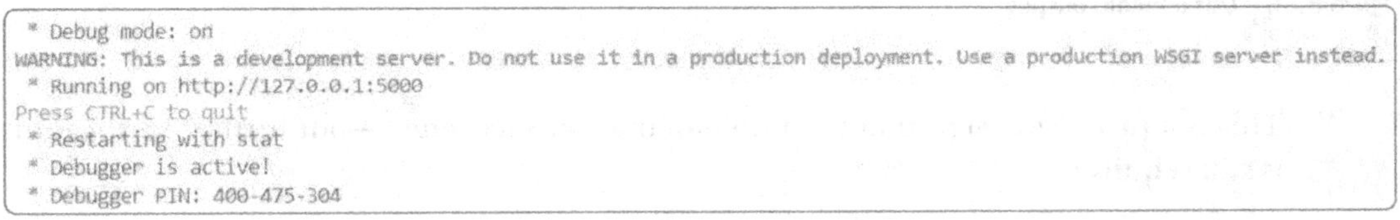

```
* Debug mode: on
WARNING: This is a development server. Do not use it in a production deployment. Use a production WSGI server instead.
 * Running on http://127.0.0.1:5000
Press CTRL+C to quit
 * Restarting with stat
 * Debugger is active!
 * Debugger PIN: 400-475-304
```

Figure 5.34   There are no errors present in the console, which means our application started properly.

And now I load up the web page at http://localhost:5000 and see a list of question IDs (figure 5.35). This is exactly what we want.

Figure 5.35   Our web browser screen showing IDs

Why are we excited about seeing question IDs? Because this verifies that we've pulled a set of random questions using the following line of code:

```
data = questions.get_question_set()
```

We can assume it worked because we didn't see an error. In fact, we also print out the data variable to our console and can see the same set there, as well as our session ID (figure 5.36).

```
Session ID: 1
[('T6A08',), ('T0A07',), ('T5D06',), ('T6D05',), ('T1F03',), ('T3A06',), ('T5B06',), ('T8A02',), ('T9B01',), ('T8D13',), ('T7D02',), ('T2C09',), ('T7D10',),
 ('T7A09',), ('T3A07',), ('T4A05',), ('T0C10',), ('T1F02',), ('T5C12',), ('T1E08',), ('T4B04',), ('T8D03',), ('T6D10',), ('T2B02',), ('T0B12',), ('T8A05',),
 ('T5C02',), ('T7C11',), ('T7C04',), ('T0A02',), ('T1A09',), ('T4B05',), ('T6C10',), ('T2B06',), ('T8A04',)]
127.0.0.1 - - [13/Dec/2023 16:35:48] "GET / HTTP/1.1" 200 -
```

Figure 5.36   Our console output

This is a promising sign that the implementation succeeded—but further verification is still required.

5.3.10   *Verifying our test session was created*

As a recap, here are our primary objectives for our MVP. We've been working on the first objective so far:

- Create a session.
- Keep track of the 35 questions.
- Keep track of the correct answer for each.
- Track the answer the student has entered.
- Track the number of correct answers.

In our session creation, we aimed to

- Create a session with an ID
- Pull 35 random questions
- Attach them to our session

We can verify that by looking at our database. First, let's check out the session table. It should have a `session_id` of 1, since it's our first session, and we should have neither correct nor incorrect answers yet because the student hasn't answered any questions. We look at our sessions table (figure 5.37) and see that it's true.

Next, we need to see whether we indeed inserted 35 questions at random into our `question_sets` table. It appears we did. As shown in figure 5.38, I have 35 questions associated with `session_id` 1.

Our initial setup is complete and is working as expected. We can create a new session with a set of questions. We're on the right track, but there's still more to build before the

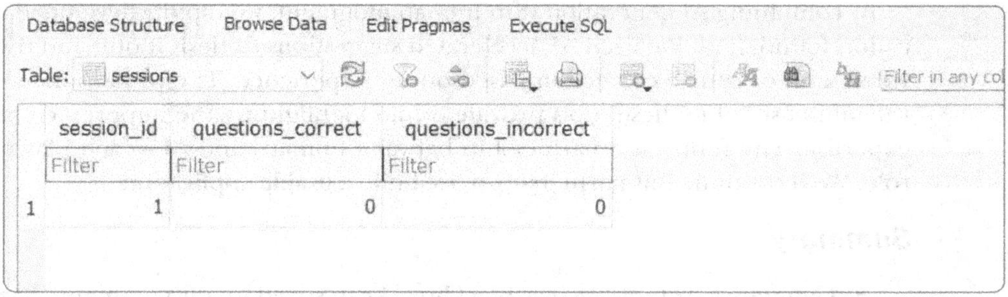

Figure 5.37 A view of our sessions table showing our first ID and no questions answered

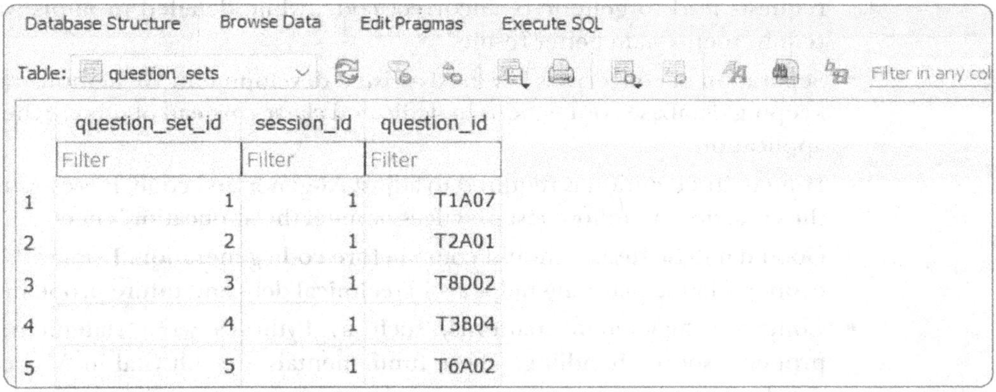

Figure 5.38 A view of our `question_sets` table showing random questions associated with our `session_id`

application is fully functional. In the next chapter, we're going to run into a bug in the application we've just built. We will use Tabnine as our tool this time to tackle the bug and add more functionality to our application.

5.3.11 Conclusion

We collaborated with Blackbox AI to successfully develop a functioning web application. We used the tool to quickly generate the initial code and advance development. Next, we intervened to refine the architecture for maintainability, ensured proper separation of concerns, added our own code, and overrode AI suggestions when beneficial. This is common practice.

The resulting application meets our core requirements, with a suitable database schema and Python code to manage test sessions. Our application is generating random question sets, creating test sessions, and tracking test state. However, it still needs additional work to be usable.

By combining AI generation with human judgment, we rapidly developed an application foundation. We used AI accelerated suggestions to flesh it out, and then I provided a bit of course correction based on my experience. The process demonstrated the immense value these tools provide, while highlighting the importance of human expertise. The future is a partnership between humans and AI—each playing a vital role. We'll continue this partnership as we build a usable application.

Summary

- Generative AI tools such as BlackboxAI can speed up development. They generate initial code, letting developers focus on refining architecture and improving quality.

- Clear and specific context in prompts is key when using AI coding tools. Vague requests lead to generic or incorrect code, while detailed prompts with clear requirements yield better results.

- Separation of concerns is key in AI-assisted development. We demonstrated it by keeping database connections in dedicated classes instead of mixing them in the application.

- Human intervention is required to adjust AI-generated code. It is essential when the code doesn't follow best practices or meet the application's needs.

- Good database design should come before code generation. Even with AI help, proper schema planning helps avoid technical debt and future problems.

- Context management patterns, such as Python's `with` statement, ensure proper resource handling. These fundamentals are still vital in AI-accelerated development.

- Rather than replacing us, AI should serve as an intelligent partner in our work. It speeds up implementation but requires human judgment for design and architecture choices.

- Testing and checking the database are key with AI-generated code. This aspect helps find problems that might be missed in code reviews alone.

6

Generating a software backend with Tabnine

This chapter covers

- Creating and maintaining persistent sessions
  for test-takers
- Implementing backend functionality in Flask with
  database integration
- Using Tabnine to generate code solutions and
  fix errors
- Crafting effective prompts to troubleshoot
  technical challenges
- Building an interactive interface that maintains
  user state

In chapter 5, we set up our practice test application using Blackbox AI for the database and question selection. In this chapter, we'll create a user-friendly experience—the session management and user interface components—which will make our question database interactive.

We'll use Tabnine as our AI coding assistant. It will help us fix bugs, add new features, and simplify the development process. But before we move on, let's review our progress with the user stories:

- *User Story 1*—As a developer, I want to create a question pool database:
  - *Task 1.1*—Choose an appropriate database technology (SQL or NoSQL) based on the structure and volume of data
  - *Task 1.2*—Design a table/collection with fields `question_id`, `question_text`, `options`, and `correct_option`
- *User Story 2*—As a developer, I want to implement a question selector:
  - *Task 2.1*—Develop a module to randomly select 35 questions from the question pool database for each test
  - *Task 2.2*—Implement an algorithm to ensure true randomness in question selection and prevent the same question from appearing more than once in a single test
  - *Task 2.3*—Test the module for randomness and verify it doesn't repeat questions within a single test

With these basics covered, we can focus on key user experience needs: managing sessions well, ensuring questions persist, and making a user-friendly interface for test-takers. By the end of this chapter, we'll have an application that maintains state across browser sessions and gives users smooth testing experience.

Before creating a cohesive UI, we need to complete some work on the backend. We have the following objectives to think about:

- We must verify whether a session is created on the first visit to the web page.
- We must ensure that a set of questions is added to the pool, that the session persists, and that we can step through the test with the same set of questions.
- Our application should keep the session in the browser in case the user closes it.
- The user should be able to destroy the session at any time and restart the test.

We'll tackle these problems by using Tabnine as our guide to improve our application and get it closer to our requirements. We'll create a session that persists in the application and assign our question set to it. By doing so, we can ensure that the questions persist as the student goes through them. The session will also remain active if the user closes the browser window by accident.

6.1   Creating a session and our first bug

In the last chapter, we launched our application and loaded it into a web browser. This initiated a test session, creating a unique ID and pulling a set of 35 random questions. We wrapped up the chapter upon verifying that the process was successful. However, if we open the application a second time, here's what we'll see (figure 6.1).

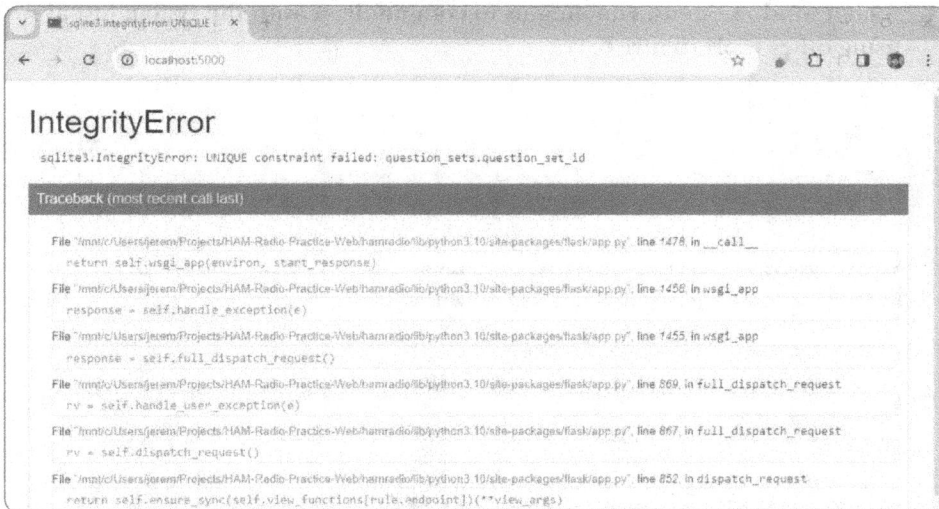

Figure 6.1   A SQLite error that comes up when we load the application a second time

We know the application worked the first time we loaded it. Now we see an error, and it's clear that it has something to do with creating a new session. Because we closed the browser and restarted, the application should start a new session. Let's see if Tabnine can help us with this problem. We'll load up Tabnine chat in Visual Studio Code by clicking on the Tabnine icon in the activity bar, as shown in figure 6.2.

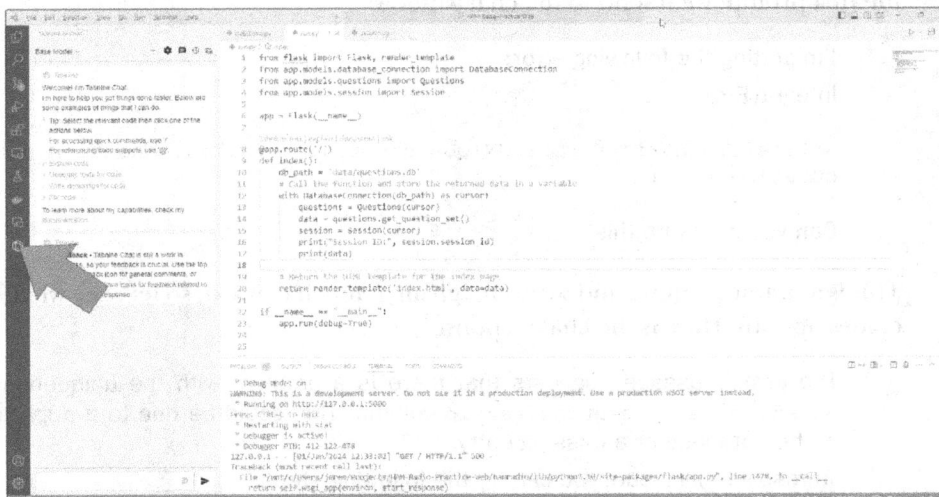

Figure 6.2   Opening Tabnine chat in our activity bar. The chat window opens to the left of the main IDE window.

A chat window opens, enabling us to communicate with the system just as we've done using other tools (figure 6.3).

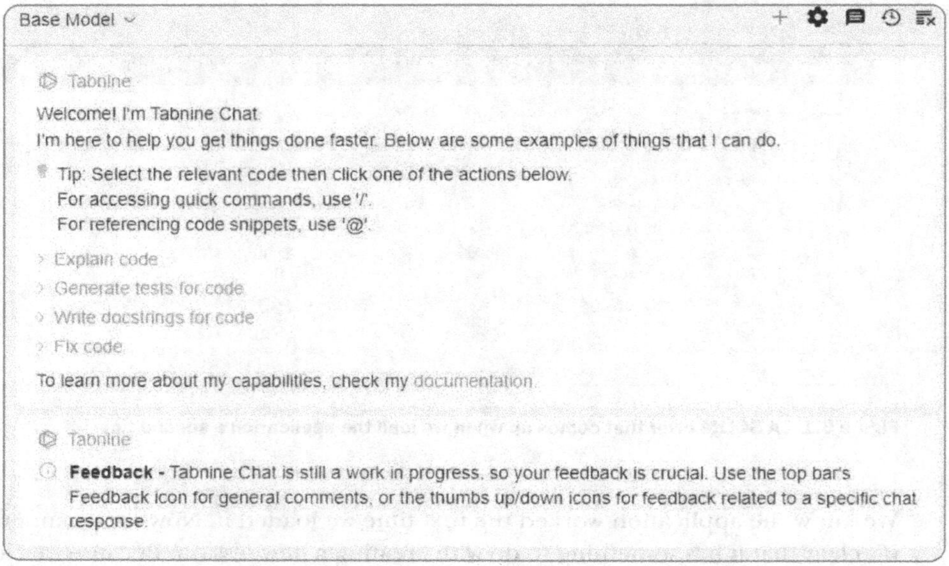

Figure 6.3   The Tabnine Chat window supporting simple conversational interaction

Let's copy the error from our browser and ask Tabnine chat if it can assist us. Here's the first prompt we'll send to the chat window:

> I'm getting the following error:
> IntegrityError
>
> ```
> sqlite3.IntegrityError: UNIQUE constraint failed: question_sets.
> question_set_id
> ```
>
> Can you help with this?

This is a simple prompt, and we aren't giving it much context, so let's see what Tabnine comes up with. Here is the chat response:

> The error message suggests that there is a problem with the uniqueness of the `question_sets.question_set_id` column. This could be due to a duplicate entry in the database or a missing entry.
>
> To resolve this issue, you can try the following steps:
>
> 1 Check the database for any duplicate entries in the `question_sets` table. You can use a SQL query to do this.

2 If there are no duplicate entries, you can add the missing entry to the table.

3 If the problem persists, you may need to investigate further and try other solutions.

Let me know if these steps help resolve the issue.

Thie response gives us a good start for troubleshooting. One thing to note: if I refresh the page, a new session is created every time. Things are working as expected for that part of the process (figure 6.4).

Database Structure   Browse Data   Edit Pragmas   Execute SQL

SQL 1

```
SELECT * FROM sessions
```

	session_id	questions_correct	questions_incorrect
1	1	0	0
2	2	0	0
3	3	0	0
4	4	0	0

Figure 6.4   The sessions table shows a valid session created every time we refresh the page. The session_id is incremented properly so we know this is correct.

We know the session is being created, but Tabnine is suggesting that there is a problem with the uniqueness of the `question_sets.question_set_id` column. We can confirm this with a query. If it's working properly, we'll see sets of questions with `session_ids` of 1, 2, 3, and 4 (figure 6.5).

SQL 1

```
SELECT COUNT(*) total, session_id FROM question_sets
GROUP BY session_id
```

	total	session_id
1	35	1

Figure 6.5   We only have one set of 35 questions for session_id 1. New question sets are not being created in this table.

Tabnine is right in suggesting the problem lies in the `question_sets` table, and it's caused by a unique constraint on the `question_sets.question_set_id`. When we create a new session, it's trying to insert a new set, starting with a `question_set_id` of

1 instead of starting where the last `question_set_id` left off. We can verify that with another query (figure 6.6).

```
SQL 1
1  SELECT question_set_id, session_id, question_id FROM question_sets
2  ORDER BY question_set_id DESC
3
```

question_set_id	session_id	question_id
1	35	1 T6C10
2	34	1 T1E10
3	33	1 T0C05
4	32	1 T8A05
5	31	1 T6D08
6	30	1 T2B01
7	29	1 T5D10
8	28	1 T8D04

Figure 6.6 Our numbering ends at 35 in the question sets table, indicating we had one successful set of questions inserted, and no new sets can be created.

Now we have a theory about our root cause. The `question_set_id` column is supposed to be unique, and we're trying to insert numbers into it, rather than let it auto-increment on its own. Let's see if Tabnine can help us. Here's the next question I'll ask Tabnine Chat:

> 🔵 I have a unique constraint on the `question_sets.question_set_id` column. It is also an auto-incrementing column. How can I modify the code in the `create_question_set` function so that it does not insert a new id and instead relies on the auto incrementing feature of the database?

This should give Tabnine enough context to assume what I'm looking for, which is a way to keep auto-incrementing the ID. Tabnine returns with a bunch of new code to attempt to solve our problem. The results are shown in figure 6.7. But I'm hesitant to copy and paste a giant chunk of code into my file. If it breaks something, trying to find out which change caused the breakage could be a cat and mouse game. So instead, I'll use a cool Tabnine feature—the "Show diff" feature—to display which portions of code have changed. In figure 6.7, you can also see the button at the bottom of the code window returned in the chat.

The term "diff" refers to a tool used to compare two sets of data. It's usually two text files. If you have two documents and want to compare them, you can quickly see what changed. A diff highlights both additions and subtractions of text and displays those changes on the screen. This is useful for things such as tracking modifications to code and merging conflicts.

By only showing the differences (diff) of the changes, we can get a better idea of what needs to change. This is a personal preference. If you've ever copied and pasted a large amount of code you don't fully understand, you've likely run into problems later when something breaks. I would rather understand the changes exactly and implement them myself, and this feature makes it much easier to do so (figure 6.8).

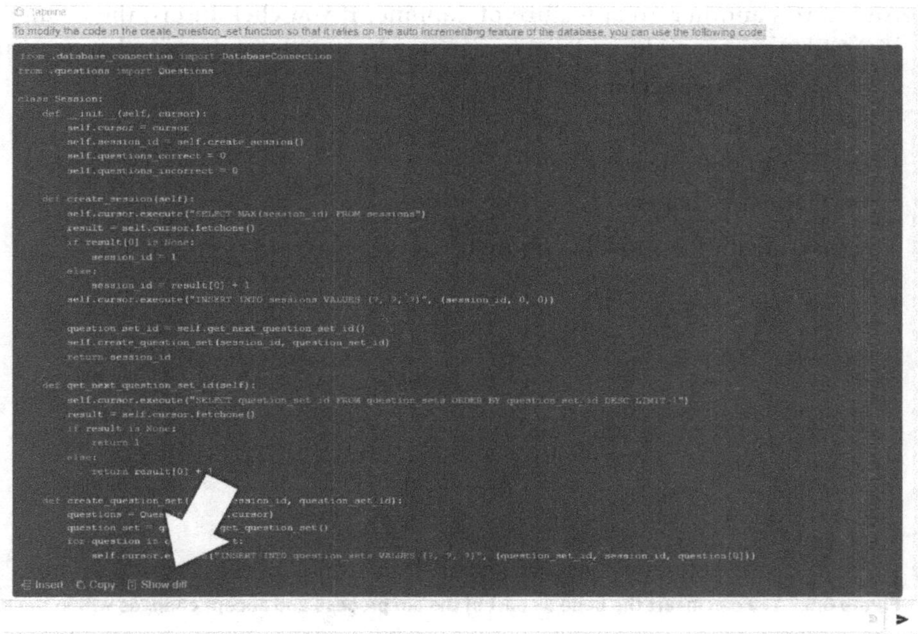

Figure 6.7 This is the code Tabnine has generated to fix our problem. Rather than copy and paste everything in the window, I'll use "Show diff" to see which code is changed.

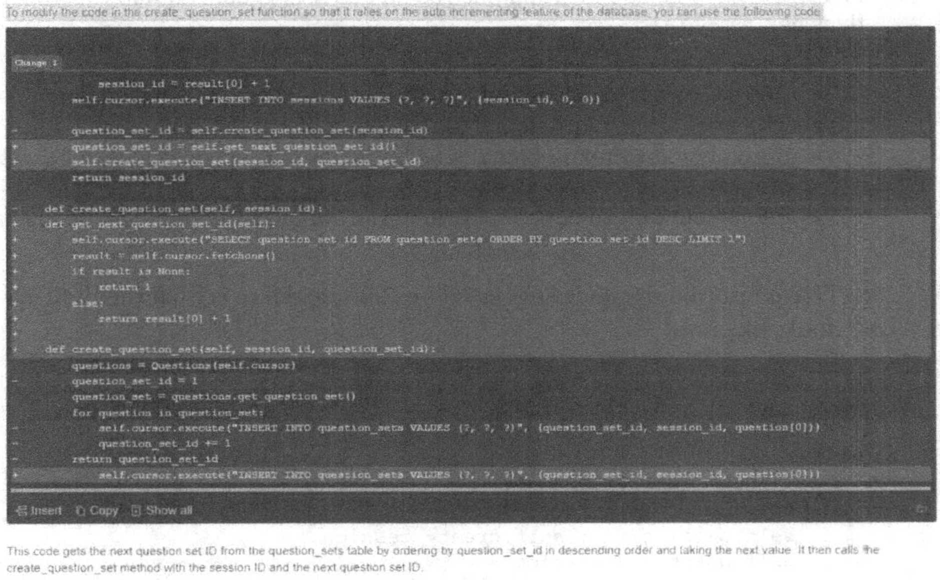

Figure 6.8 The diff view of the proposed changes showing exactly which lines of code need to be modified to implement Tabnine's suggestions

And here's another great feature of Tabnine. If you click Insert, the changes will be inserted into your code, and you can go step by step through each change. You can

- Accept current change
- Accept incoming change
- Accept both changes
- Compare changes

The Insert feature is shown in figure 6.9.

```
Accept Current Change | Accept Incoming Change | Accept Both Changes | Compare Changes
<<<<<<< Current (Current Change)
    def create_question_set(self, session_id):
=======
    tabnine: test | explain | document | ask
    def get_next_question_set_id(self):
        self.cursor.execute("SELECT question_set_id FROM question_sets ORDER BY question_set_id DESC LIMIT 1")
        result = self.cursor.fetchone()
        if result is None:
            return 1
        else:
            return result[0] + 1
```

Figure 6.9   You can insert the code as part of the diff process and accept changes within the IDE.

Debugging with AI tools

While AI coding assistants can offer solutions to bugs, remember that they're not infallible. The most effective approach combines AI suggestions with your own critical thinking:

- Show errors directly to AI tools for targeted help.
- Use diff views to understand exactly what changes are being proposed.
- Implement changes incrementally and test after each change.
- Be prepared to refine prompts when initial suggestions don't fully solve the problem.
- Remember that sometimes the AI will fix symptoms rather than root causes.

Now I have inserted the code suggested by Tabnine. Here is what the final `session.py` code looks like now:

```python
from .database_connection import DatabaseConnection
from .questions import Questions

class Session:
    def __init__(self, cursor):
        self.cursor = cursor
        self.session_id = self.create_session()
        self.questions_correct = 0
        self.questions_incorrect = 0

    def create_session(self):
```

```
        self.cursor.execute("SELECT MAX(session_id) FROM sessions")
        result = self.cursor.fetchone()
        if result[0] is None:
            session_id = 1
        else:
            session_id = result[0] + 1
        self.cursor.execute("INSERT INTO sessions VALUES
(?, ?, ?)", (session_id, 0, 0))

        question_set_id = self.get_next_question_set_id()
        self.create_question_set(session_id, question_set_id)
        return session_id

    def get_next_question_set_id(self):
        self.cursor.execute("SELECT question_set_id
FROM question_sets ORDER BY question_set_id DESC LIMIT 1")
        result = self.cursor.fetchone()
        if result is None:
            return 1
        else:
            return result[0] + 1

    def create_question_set(self, session_id, question_set_id):
        questions = Questions(self.cursor)
        question_set = questions.get_question_set()
        for question in question_set:
            self.cursor.execute("INSERT INTO question_sets
VALUES (?, ?, ?)", (question_set_id, session_id, question[0]))
```

We're now creating a new session_set_id based on the last ID value. I will refresh the page. If this fix is valid, we should see a new session created and no errors. However, after refreshing the window, I see the same error again (figure 6.10).

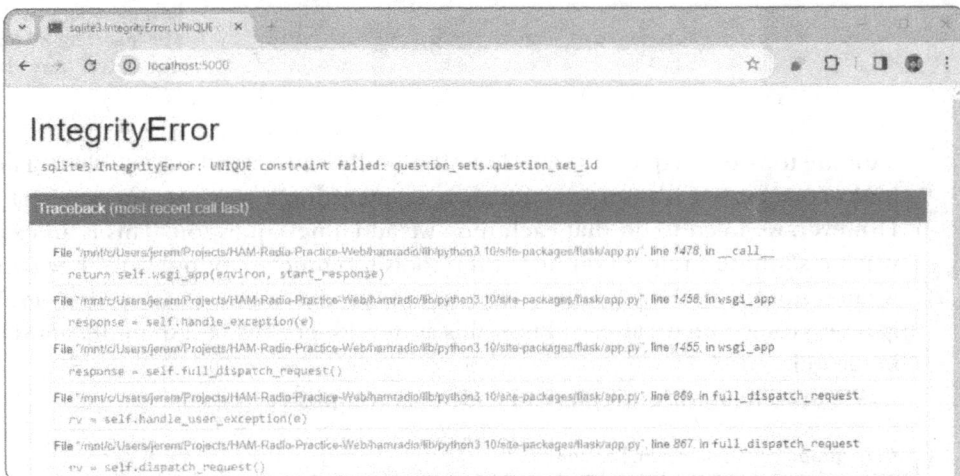

Figure 6.10 The same error as before—a unique constraint violation in the same field

We're getting the same error, but why? I can take a guess at it. You may have caught this error as well if you looked closely at the code above. Let's examine our code in the `create_session` function:

```
question_set_id = self.get_next_question_set_id()
self.create_question_set(session_id, question_set_id)
```

This code was modified to get the next ID in the series and then create a question set with that. However, remember that the question set is 35 questions, which means that in our `create_question_set` method, we attempt to insert that new ID 35 times!

```
def create_question_set(self, session_id, question_set_id):
        questions = Questions(self.cursor)
        question_set = questions.get_question_set()
        for question in question_set:
            self.cursor.execute("INSERT INTO question_sets
VALUES (?, ?, ?)", (question_set_id, session_id, question[0]))
```

This is certainly not going to work, meaning we can only use that new ID value one single time—then it's going to break again. To verify this, let's do a quick check of the database. Sure enough, there's only one record inserted with a `question_set_id` of 36, and a `session_id` of 6. On the next insert, we violated the constraint by trying to insert 36 as the next `question_set_id` value (figure 6.11).

Figure 6.11 Our method inserted record 36 correctly. However, as we iterate through the question set to add new questions, we're still inserting 36 for the `question_set_id` value.

Tabnine took our request literally but didn't fully understand the problem. The output looks correct, but it's not functional. It's generating a new incremented ID *one time*. However, we need to do that each time we add a new question. This is an example of why we shouldn't rely on output of the tools too much. Not only are they fallible, but we may not frame the prompt to express exactly what we need. Code that "looks right" can be wrong, and we already know this as developers. It's best to understand the code being generated.

We need to modify this piece of code to accomplish our goal:

```
for question in question_set:
            self.cursor.execute("INSERT INTO question_sets
VALUES (?, ?, ?)", (question_set_id, session_id, question[0]))
```

We can easily make that happen, but let's ask Tabnine for help. This time, we'll craft our idea into a query for the chat to interpret. Here's my next prompt for Tabnine:

> (JM) In our `create_question_set` function, we have an error. It is attempting to add new records into `question_sets`; however, `question_set_id` is an auto-incremented field. How do we modify the code within the `create_question_set` method so that we utilize the auto-increment functionality?

This should provide additional detail and context to solve our problem. Here is the answer I received:

> To modify the code within the `create_question_set` method so that it utilizes the auto increment functionality, you can modify the code as follows:

```
def create_question_set(self, session_id):
    questions = Questions(self.cursor)
    question_set = questions.get_question_set()
    for question in question_set:
        self.cursor.execute("INSERT INTO question_sets
VALUES (DEFAULT, ?, ?)", (question_set_id, session_id, question[0]))
```

> In this modified code, we are using the DEFAULT keyword in the SQL statement to let the database automatically assign a value to the `question_set_id` column.

I'll save you some time—this method did not work. That's because, as far as I know, the DEFAULT keyword doesn't work in SQLite. It's once again time for human intervention. I know how the auto-increment flag is supposed to work, and I am familiar enough with SQLite databases to know that if you insert a null value into an auto-incremented field, it will generate a new value. I'll give Tabnine an informal, conversational prompt:

> (JM) Default doesn't work here, can I just insert a null value into the database?

It immediately returns an answer that will work for me (figure 6.12).

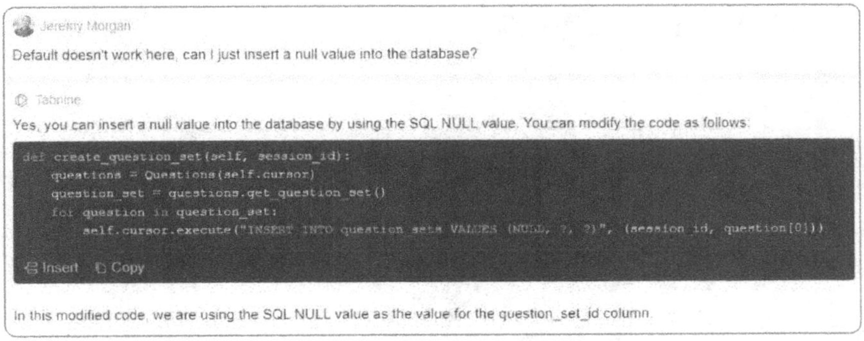

Figure 6.12 I asked Tabnine an informal question and suggested a solution. It responded with a solution that will work.

Crafting effective code prompts

The quality of AI code assistance depends heavily on your prompting approach:

- Start with clear, specific descriptions of what you want to accomplish.
- Include relevant context about your codebase and frameworks.
- For complex problems, try conversational, informal prompts.
- When you have a potential solution in mind, don't be afraid to steer the AI by suggesting an approach.
- Follow up with clarifying questions when suggestions aren't working.

Now let's change our insert line from this:

```
self.cursor.execute("INSERT INTO question_sets VALUES
(DEFAULT, ?, ?)", (question_set_id, session_id, question[0]))
```

to the following line of code, which simply uses "None" as the datatype to insert. By inserting a null value, SQLite will automatically create the question_set_id and increment it properly:

```
self.cursor.execute("INSERT INTO question_sets VALUES
(null,?,?)", (session_id, question[0]))
```

I'm sure Tabnine would have generated a similar solution first, with enough attempts. Sometimes, if you know the answer or feel strongly about an idea, it's good to steer the AI into a certain direction. We refresh the page and see the window displayed in figure 6.13.

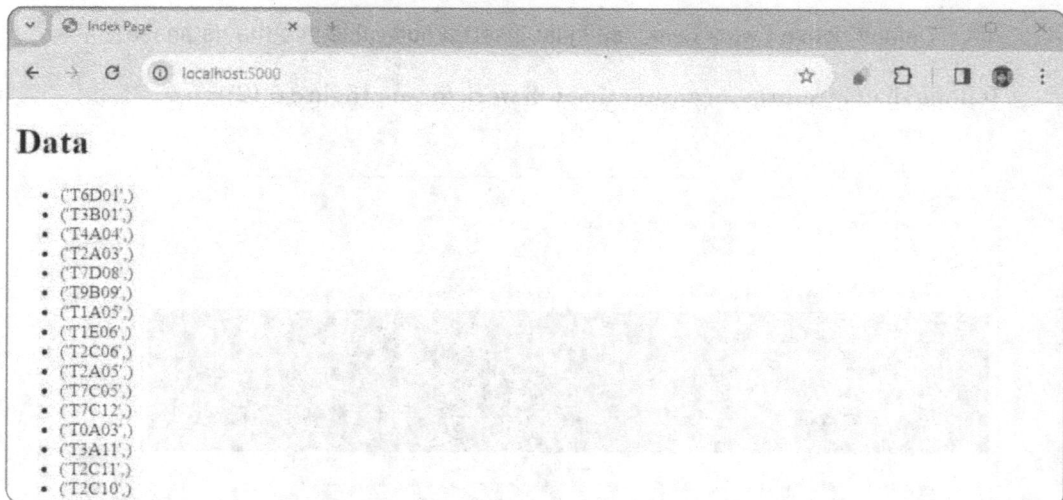

Figure 6.13   This is our makeshift success screen. It shows the IDs of the 35 questions inserted into our database.

With this screen, we know we're inserting records in our table again without an error. I'll refresh it a few times and create multiple sessions. We can then validate it by looking at our database again. We can count the number of questions and group them by `session_id`. There should be 35 questions in each set, except for the session that failed (figure 6.14).

```
Show Sessions ⊠
1  SELECT COUNT(*) total, session_id from question_sets
2  GROUP BY session_id
3
```

	total	session_id
1	35	1
2	1	6
3	35	20
4	35	29
5	35	30
6	35	31
7	35	32
8	35	33

Figure 6.14 We can see a list of sessions here with 35 questions each. Session 6 failed on insert, so there is only one question available.

Now that we have that bug squashed, we need to move on to a better way to create our sessions. Right now, just loading the website up creates a new session. Let's put a user interface on it so the user can create the session. Then, we'll add functionality to handle the questions.

6.2 Creating an index page

So far, our application can start a session, from a technical standpoint, but it's a little rough. We must reload the page to start a session, and we can't do anything after that except view a few `QuestionIDs` in a list. Let's change that.

In our `run.py`, we have a line of code that produces our index page:

```
return render_template('index.html', data=data)
```

This loads up a file located in `/templates`, and it looks like this:

```
<!-- HTML template for the index page -->
<!DOCTYPE html>
<html>
<head>
    <title>Index Page</title>
</head>
<body>
    <h1>Data</h1>
    <ul>
        {% for item in data %}
```

```
            <li>{{ item }}</li>
         {% endfor %}
      </ul>
   </body>
</html>
```

This file doesn't do much more than list every item in our data array. As it's not incredibly useful, let's create a function to start a new session with the click of a button. This gives the user control over when to start a session. Then we can store that session, and the user can go on to answer questions. Let's ask Tabnine to help us out with that. Here is the prompt I sent:

> How can I add a button to this page that will start our session for us? In `run.py`, our question session is started with `"data = questions.get_question_set()"`. I would like to add a form with a button to call that function. How would I code this?

In this prompt, I'm attempting to be as specific as possible about what I want to do, without revealing too much about how it's done. I don't want to give the solution away but ask for one. Here is the output:

> To add a button to the `index.html` page that starts the question session, you can add the following code to the `index.html` file:

```
<form action="/" method="POST">
    <input type="submit" value="Start Question Session">
</form>
```

> This code adds a form with a submit button to the index.html page. When the user clicks the submit button, the form will submit to the root URL (/), which is where the `index.py` file is located.

> In the `index.py` file, you can add the following code to handle the form submission:

```
@app.route('/', methods=['POST','GET'])
def index():
    # Check if the form has been submitted
    if request.method == 'POST':
        # Start the question session
        # ...

    # Return the HTML template for the index page
    return render_template('index.html', data=data)
```

> This code checks if the request is a POST request. If it is, it starts the question session. Otherwise, it returns the `index.html` template with the data variable.

> You can replace the code in the `index.py` file that retrieves the question data with the following code:

```
def index():
    # Start the question session
```

```
with DatabaseConnection(db_path) as cursor:
    questions = Questions(cursor)
    data = questions.get_question_set()
    session = Session(cursor)
    print("Session ID:", session.session_id)

# Return the HTML template for the index page
return render_template('index.html', data=data)
```

This code starts the question session before retrieving the data, which ensures that the session ID is generated before the data is retrieved.

Let's put this suggestion to test. I'll follow the instructions precisely, and we'll see how the result turns out.

In `index.html`, below this line

```
<h1>Data</h1>
```

add

```
<form action="/" method="POST">
  <input type="submit" value="Start Question Session">
</form>
```

In the `run.py` file, change

```
@app.route('/')
```

to the suggested line

```
@app.route('/', methods=['POST','GET'])
```

Under this line of code, within the function

```
def index():
```

add the following:

```
# Check if the form has been submitted
    if request.method == 'POST':
        # Start the question session
        # ...
```

Then we can indent the rest of the code, as shown in figure 6.15.

Now we know that a session will only be created if we ask for it. This is a great suggestion; however, I have a feeling it's not quite complete. If you are following along, you'll notice Tabnine catches a small problem here, as shown in figure 6.16.

```
# Check if the form has been submitted
if request.method == 'POST':
    # Start the question session
    # ...
    db_path = 'data/questions.db'
    # Call the function and store the returned data in a variable
    with DatabaseConnection(db_path) as cursor:
        questions = Questions(cursor)
        data = questions.get_question_set()
        session = Session(cursor)
        print("Session ID:", session.session_id)
        print(data)

# Return the HTML template for the index page
return render_template('index.html', data=data)
```

Figure 6.15   The remainder of the question creation code should be indented so it is only executed if this is a POST command.

```
 9    def index():
10        # Check if the form has been submitted
11        if request.method == 'POST':
12    Quick Fix
13      Add "from urllib import request"
14      Add "from socketserver import _RequestType"
15      Add "from http.client import REQUEST_ENTITY_TOO_LARGE"      urned data in a variable
16      Add "from http.client import REQUEST_HEADER_FIELDS_TOO_LARGE"  ursor:
17      Add "from http.client import REQUEST_TIMEOUT"
18      Add "from http.client import REQUEST_URI_TOO_LONG"           ()
19      Add "from http.client import REQUESTED_RANGE_NOT_SATISFIABLE"
20      Add "from urllib.request import Request"                    ion_id)
21      Add "from urllib.robotparser import RequestRate"
22      Add "from wsgiref.util import request_uri"
23      Fix with Tabnine                                            page
24        return render_template('index.html', data=data)
25
```

Figure 6.16   Tabnine catches an error and proposes several changes.

I'll select the "Fix with Tabnine," and it suggests changing this line of code

```
from flask import Flask, render_template
```

to

```
from flask import Flask, render_template, request
```

That way, we can import the request method from Flask. Since you're a Python developer, you've probably already spotted our next problem, where data isn't yet defined, in this line of code:

```
return render_template('index.html', data=data)
```

The code will return a "referenced before assignment" error with Python. So, let's add the following line of code above it:

```
else:
    data = None
```

This way, if a POST is sent, it will create a new session and populate data; if it's a GET (simply loading the web page), nothing will be sent. Let's open `index.html` and modify it to handle an empty variable.

Say we don't know anything about Flask. How do we check for empty strings? Let's find out.

In index.html, highlight the following code:

```
<ul>
    {% for item in data %}
        <li>{{ item }}</li>
    {% endfor %}
</ul>
```

And then, we'll ask Tabnine for some help. Here's the prompt I sent:

> In the selected code, I want to check to see if data is empty. If it is, render nothing. If it's not empty, render the selected code.

Tabnine understood my request and produced the following solution:

```
{% if data %}
    <ul>
    {% for item in data %}
        <li>{{ item }}</li>
    {% endfor %}
    </ul>
{% endif %}
```

Tabnine suggests some template code that will render if data is populated and do nothing if it isn't. Perfect. Let's run the application again. As you can see in figure 6.17, we have what we're expecting, which is a title and a button to create a new session.

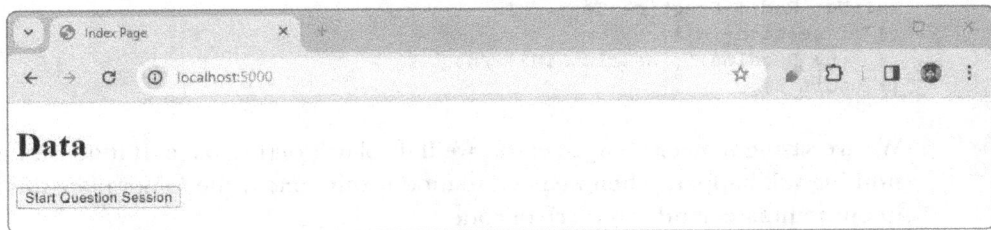

Figure 6.17 Our screen successfully loaded with our new button.

Now that the screen is loaded up, let's click the button! It should load up our question set (figure 6.18).

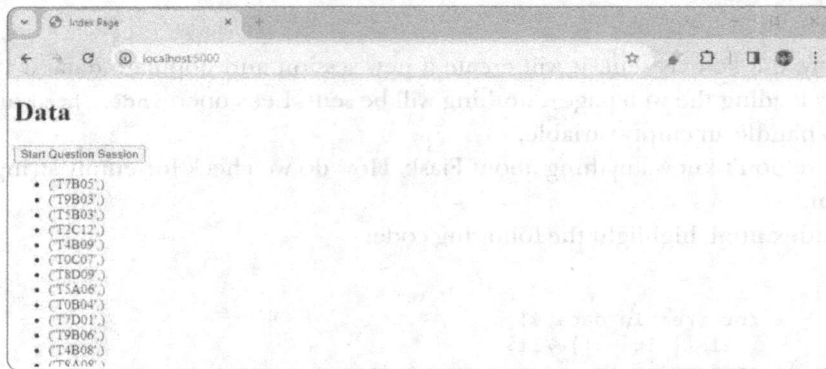

Figure 6.18   Our page loaded correctly with a new question set.

Awesome. We can now start a session. However, this session is only active if the browser window is open. We need to find a way to create a session for each user so that the application maintains state for them.

6.2.1   *Persisting the session*

We want to persist this session for a user so that if they close the browser by accident, the session will still be available. The first thing we'll do is display the session ID in the browser so we can make sure that we're working with the same session.

In `templates/index.html`, let's change the following code. We have an `h1` tag displaying "Data," and we're going to add a title and then add a display of our session ID. Let's change

```
<h1>Data</h1>
```

to look like this:

```
<h1>Ham Radio Practice Test</h1>
{% if session_id %}
    <h3>Session: {{session_id}}</h3>
{% endif %}
```

We are saying if a `session_id` exists, we'll display it on the page. If it doesn't exist yet, nothing will happen. Then we need to modify our `run.py` file to populate this variable in our template. Find this piece of code:

```
return render_template('index.html', data=data)
```

Let's change that to pass in our session ID:

```
return render_template('index.html', data=data, session_id=session.session_id)
```

By adding this additional para-
meter, it will pass that data to
our template, and we should
see it displayed as shown in figure 6.19.

Let's use Tabnine to learn
how to do that. I'll ask a brief, yet
direct question as my prompt.
I'm deliberately using a conversational approach here as it
works well with Tabnine.

Here's my first prompt:

Ham Radio Practice Test

Session: 42

Start Question Session

- ('T2C05',)
- ('T8C07',)
- ('T1B11',)
- ('T1F02',)

**Figure 6.19 Our index page after creating a new session.
Here, session 42 is shown so we can see which session
we're working with.**

> I want to store a session id in a cookie. I want flask to create this cookie based on
> the session id from the database. How can I build that?

Although it's basic, this prompt clearly states what I would like Tabnine to do. Tabnine
gives a detailed response to the question with a full code example (figure 6.20).

**Figure 6.20 The detailed response for our prompt. Tabnine explains exactly how to create and store a
cookie based on our request.**

Let's follow Tabnine's advice here. It suggests that we use the `Session` object and call
the `session.sid` object, then store it as a cookie. We can use the "Show diff" feature to
see what needs to change (figure 6.21).

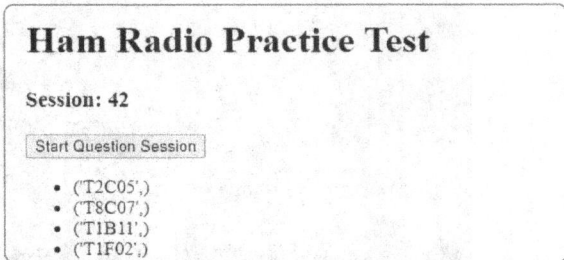

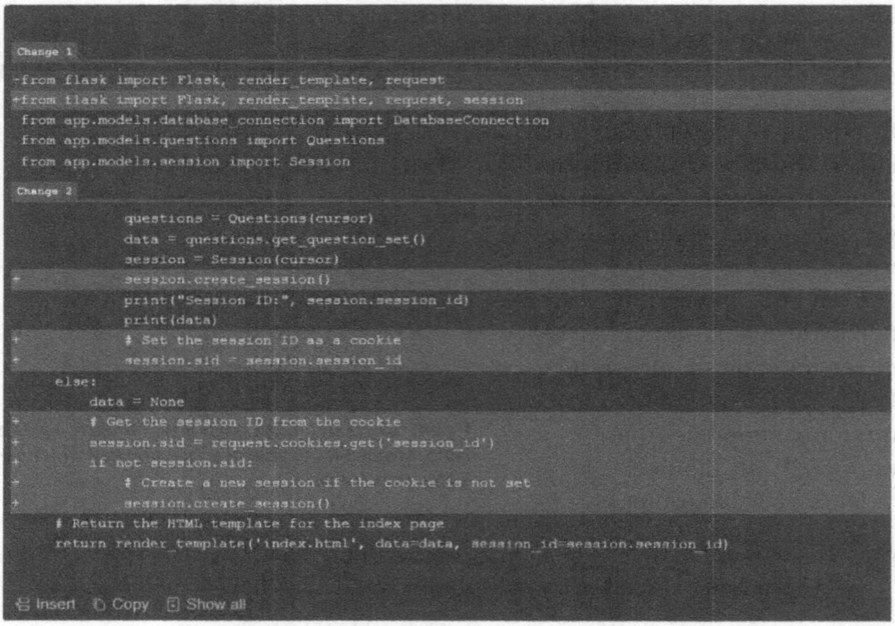

Figure 6.21   The "Show diff" feature does a diff on the file, highlighting which lines of code we need to add to our project.

Find this section of code in `run.py`:

```python
session = Session(cursor)
print("Session ID:", session.session_id)
        print(data)
```

Let's remove the print statements. We no longer need to print out the session ID in the console. After, we create the session variable. Let's add

```python
session.create_session()
    # Set the session ID as a cookie
    session.sid = session.session_id
```

Then, in our `else` block, we can add the code to get the session ID. If it doesn't exist, we'll create a new session automatically. Now that we've added the changes, let's refresh our page. We see an error as shown in figure 6.22.

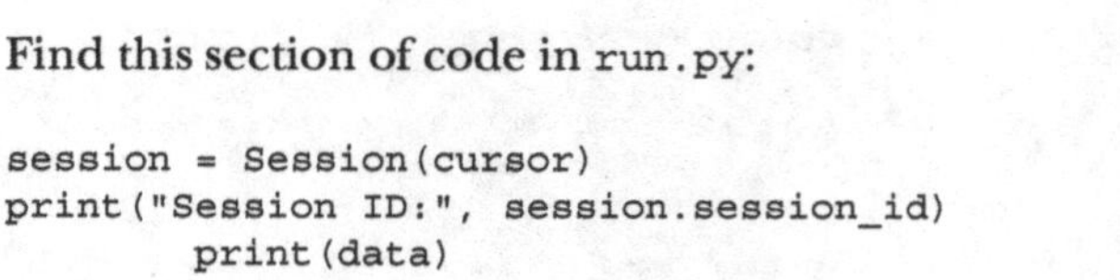

Figure 6.22   Our session variable cannot be accessed if it doesn't yet exist.

This error is another reminder that we can't blindly copy and paste code from these tools, and some bit of intervention is usually needed. We can't access session if it hasn't been created. We need to refactor this application anyway. Right now, it takes a POST to create a new session. It's an extra step that relies on the user clicking a button to start. We know the user wants to take a practice test, so there's no need for the extra step in creating it. Let's change the application to start a new test session when the user visits the page for the first time. Then we'll persist the session.

6.2.2 *Refactoring session creation*

At this time, we can only start a new question session by pressing a button and sending a POST to the application to create it. We can't access the session globally because the database connection is only made after that POST, as shown in our code:

```
# Check if the form has been submitted
    if request.method == 'POST':
        # Start the question session
        # ...
        db_path = 'data/questions.db'
        # Call the function and store the returned data in a variable
        with DatabaseConnection(db_path) as cursor:
```

Let's change this so the database connection is loaded every time our index page is called. And we'll create the session when we load it up. How can we do that? We'll remove the logic for handling a POST and put all the creation into our index method. This is what our index method looks like now:

```
@app.route('/', methods=['POST', 'GET'])
def index():
    db_path = 'data/questions.db'
    # Call the function and store the returned data in a variable
    with DatabaseConnection(db_path) as cursor:
        session = Session(cursor)
        questions = Questions(cursor)
        data = questions.get_question_set()
        session.sid = request.cookies.get('session_id')
        return render_template('index.html', data=data, session_id=session.
session_id)

if __name__ == "__main__":
    app.run(debug=True)
```

Now we open the database every time and create a session. However, we need to add logic around checking the cookie for an existing session. Right now, we have the following line of code that gets our session ID; still, it needs to be modified to create a session if none is found:

```
session.sid = request.cookies.get('session_id')
```

Let's instead look for this value and create a session if it doesn't exist. Here is our updated code:

```
with DatabaseConnection(db_path) as cursor:
        session = Session(cursor)
        our_session = request.cookies.get('session_id')
        if our_session is None:
            questions = Questions(cursor)
            data = questions.get_question_set()
session.session_id = session.create_session()
```

In the previous conversation with Tabnine, we didn't create a cookie. Let's do that and add it into a part of our session creation process. Let's ask Tabnine how to create a cookie value with Flask. Here is the prompt I used:

> How can I create a cookie with Flask and store our session id in a cookie. I want to do that after calling `session.session_id = session.create_session()` and store that generated id in a cookie with the value `session_id`.

Tabnine comes back with suggestion that changes how we respond to the request, so we need to remove this code:

```
return render_template('index.html',
    data=data, session_id=session.session_id)
```

It has to be replaced with code that will create a response based on our rendered template. We also need to set a cookie with the `response.set_cookie` method. Here is the new code:

```
# Set the session ID as a cookie
response = make_response(render_template
('index.html', data=data, session_id=session.session_id))
response.set_cookie('session_id', str(session.session_id))
return response
```

This change will set the cookie every time the page is loaded. Now we'll create an `else` block for what to do when the cookie value exists, and we just want to render the page from the existing session:

```
else:
# we have a cookie value and existing id
session.session_id = our_session
    questions = Questions(cursor)
    data = questions.get_question_set()
    response = make_response(render_template('index.html', data=data,
    session_id=session.session_id))
    return response
```

Now when we run the application, every time we refresh the page, it keeps the existing value of our session. However, with each refresh, we're getting a different set of questions in our questions set. But the ID we're displaying is the same. We know that the cookie is being set properly; however, our method is still generating more questions (figure 6.23).

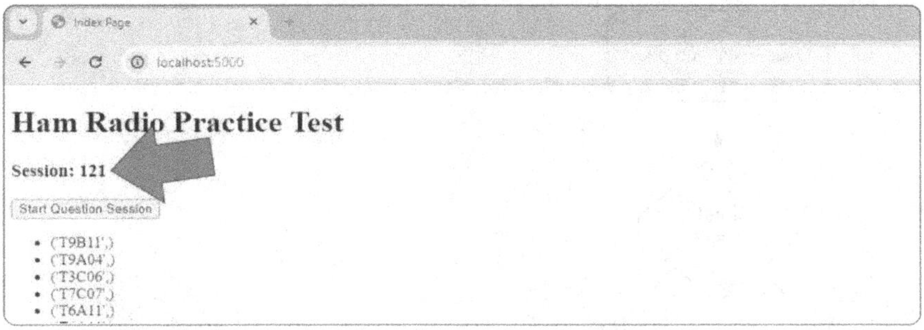

Figure 6.23 Our questions get refreshed, but the `session_id` stays the same.

We'll need to refactor that method so it works with an ID, and instead of generating a new question set every time, it will use an existing one that we've tied with an ID.

> **Verify, then trust**
>
> Always thoroughly test AI-generated code before considering it complete:
>
> - Test edge cases, not just the happy path.
> - Verify functionality after implementing each suggestion.
> - Look for unintended side effects in related functionality.
> - Database operations require extra scrutiny—check that database state is what you expect.
> - Remember: Code that looks right can still be functionally wrong.

6.2.3 Refactoring our question set method

What exactly is happening in our application right now? The first time you load up the web page, it checks whether a session ID is stored in a cookie. This is how the application determines if it's the user's first time visiting the page. If no session ID is present, the application creates a new session and a new question set from randomly selected questions. If there is an ID present, then it continues with that existing session. Per our design specification, we should then load the question set that is associated with that session ID. This flow is shown in figure 6.24.

In our case, we're still getting a random question set every time. This is because our method looks like this right now:

```
data = questions.get_question_set()
```

A random question set gets drawn every time the user visits the web page, essentially making the "first visit" check pass through and create a new session every time (figure 6.25).

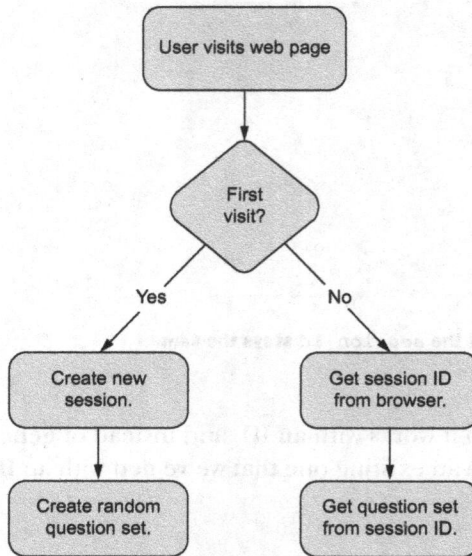

Figure 6.24   The initial flow of our website. The application looks for a cookie value and handles the session accordingly.

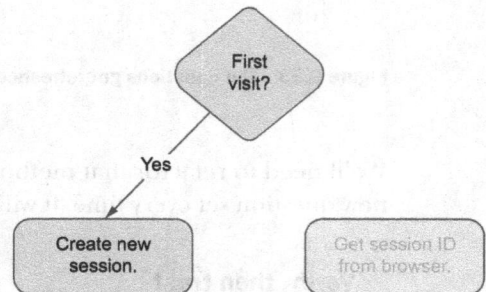

Figure 6.25   Because the method is being called without specifying our session ID, the first visit will always create a new session.

The method has no way of knowing whether we'll have an ID, but this is a simple fix. We can inject the session ID into the method, and if it exists, we'll use the existing question set instead of generating a new one.

Let's open `questions.py` and modify our method parameters. Change

```
def get_question_set(self):
```

to

```
def get_question_set(self, session_id=None):
```

We'll also change the logic of our method so that if a session ID is present, we'll query that instead. Our logic currently looks like this:

```
all_questions = self.get_all_questions()
if len(all_questions) < 35:
        return "There are not enough questions to generate a set."
```

```
    question_set = set()
    while len(question_set) < 35:
        question_id = random.choice(list(all_questions))
            question_set.add(question_id)
    return list(question_set)
```

We'll add in our logic to check. Since we aren't changing the return type, this in-place refactoring should be easy to test. We'll change the method to include logic to test for the ID, and if the session exists, we'll pull that set of questions for it.

Our method now looks like

```python
def get_question_set(self, session_id=None):

    if (session_id is None):
        all_questions = self.get_all_questions()
        if len(all_questions) < 35:
            return "There are not enough questions to generate a set."
        question_set = set()
        while len(question_set) < 35:
            question_id = random.choice(list(all_questions))
            question_set.add(question_id)
        return list(question_set)
    else:
        # Get a list of questionIDs
        self.cursor.execute("""WITH question_set_info AS (
                SELECT DISTINCT question_id
                FROM question_sets
                WHERE session_id = ?
                )
                SELECT
                questions.id,
                questions.correct,
                questions.question,
                questions.a,
                questions.b,
                questions.c,
                questions.d
                FROM questions
                JOIN question_set_info
                ON questions.id = question_set_info.question_id;"""
            ,(session_id,))
        result = self.cursor.fetchall()
        if result is None:
            return None
        else:
            return list(result)
```

We can now reload the browser and test the functionality. No matter how many times we refresh it, the values stay the same. I deleted the sessions table and restarted it. It now shows a single session and will not change the questions no matter how many times I refresh it (figure 6.26).

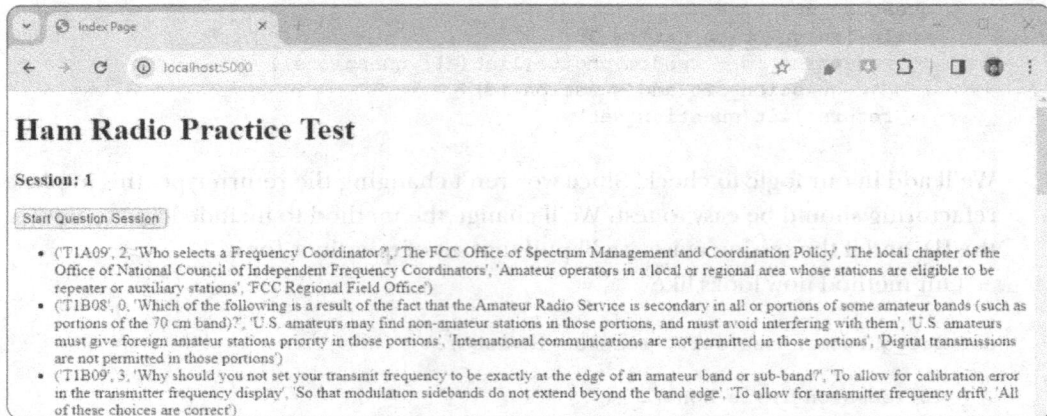

Figure 6.26   Upon the first visit, a session is created, and no matter how many times we refresh it, the session persists, and questions stay the same.

We refactored our method, and we're getting the functionality we were looking for in the design. Next, we need to remove the Start Question Session button because it's no longer needed. We'll also create a method to end the session.

6.2.4   *Creating an end session function that ends the test*

Let's create a button that will quickly get rid of our cookie, in case we want to end the test and start over. I want the solution to be as simple as possible. I'm thinking a simple JavaScript method can do it. We'll use a casual, conversational prompt to check this:

> I would like to add a button and delete the cookie and refresh the page. What's the best way to do that with JavaScript?

Here's the answer Tabnine came up with:

> To add a button in HTML, you can use the following code:

```
<button onclick="deleteCookieAndRefresh()">Delete Cookie and Refresh</button>
```

> To delete the cookie and refresh the page using JavaScript, you can use the following code:

```
function deleteCookieAndRefresh() {
  // Client-side JavaScript to delete the cookie and refresh
  document.cookie = "session_id=; expires=Thu, 01 Jan 1970 00:00:00 UTC; path=/;";
  window.location.reload();
}
```

> Make sure to add the JavaScript code inside the <script> tags.

This suggestion is perfect, so in `index.html`, I'll add it to the code (figure 6.27). I did change the wording of the button, however, to reflect its function. When I click the button, it refreshes with a new session and new questions.

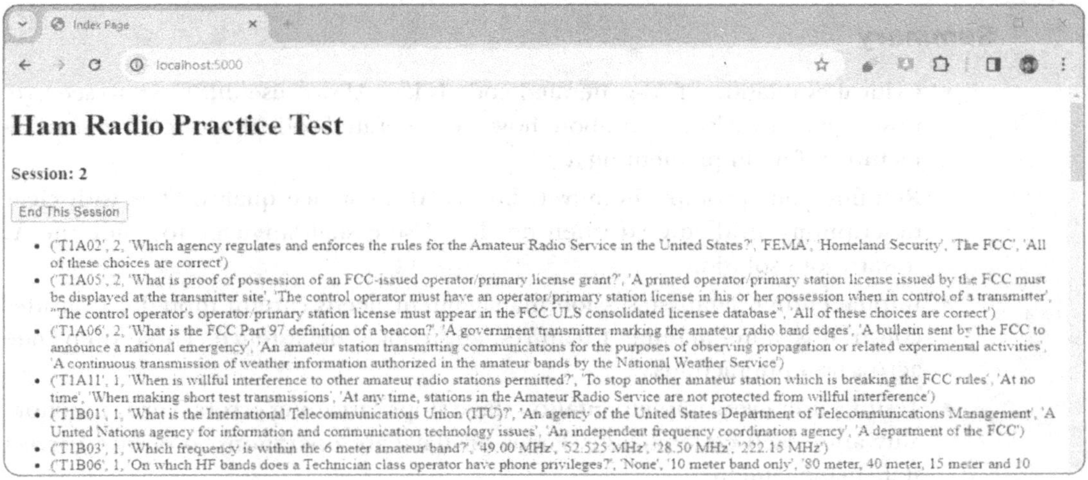

Figure 6.27　Clicking the End This Session button refreshes the page with a new session.

This is exactly what we intend for this application. Now comes the challenging part—taking this blob of questions and making a usable quiz from them.

> **AI as an accelerator, not an autopilot**
>
> The most productive use of AI coding tools balances automation with your own expertise:
>
> - Use AI to accelerate routine coding tasks and generate initial solutions.
> - Apply your domain knowledge to evaluate whether suggestions match your architectural goals.
> - Be ready to take manual control when the AI doesn't fully understand context.
> - Treat AI tools as collaborative assistants rather than autonomous developers.
> - Recognize that AI can help find solutions, but you're still responsible for understanding them. You can't hold AI accountable.

We built a strong backend for our app. It effectively manages random question selection and keeps user sessions active. During our development with Tabnine, we faced real coding challenges. We resolved these problems with Tabnine, showing how useful AI can be in development.

By combining AI suggestions with our development skills, we made a more reliable app that maintains state across user sessions. This is crucial for any web-based testing platform. We learned that generative AI tools can speed up development, while still requiring critical thinking and expertise. The key point is to find the right balance. Use AI to enhance your workflow, but don't rely on it completely. As we keep building our app in the next chapters, we'll refine this approach to using AI tools in various development situations.

Summary

- Critical evaluation of AI-generated code is key. Always use diff views to see proposed changes. Also, think about how the generated code fits your current architecture before implementing it.
- Refining your prompts iteratively boosts AI assistance quality. Start with clear descriptions. Add context when needed. Use casual language to guide the AI toward your solution.
- Implementing database session management needs careful thought. Consider constraints, auto-increment features, and cookie persistence. These keep state across user interactions.
- Testing after every implementation stage stops cascading errors. Verify functionality after each code change. Focus on database operations to ensure correct state management.
- Separation of concerns in web applications leads to cleaner architecture. For example, session creation, question retrieval, and user interface components can be separate, testable units.
- User experience considerations should guide development choices. For instance, automatically creating sessions is better than asking for user action when it fits the expected workflow.
- Error handling for edge cases makes applications more robust. Anticipate possible problems such as duplicate entries and set up fallback mechanisms.
- Using AI as a collaborative assistant boosts productivity. Pairing the AI's code generation with your domain knowledge gives the best results.

## Part 3

Advanced AI development techniques

As your applications become more complex, so do the challenges. Maintaining clean architecture, adding advanced features, and ensuring code quality all require attention. In rapid development environments, we can do the wrong things faster than ever. We now need to start thinking about how to use our own software development experience to guide AI assistance in the right direction. It includes managing templates, mastering prompt engineering, manipulating context, and using a new style of development.

Professional software developers must know how to use AI tools strategically. This involves mastering advanced prompting techniques and working with AI across various files and modules. We must also learn how to manage context wisely. This is a new concept for most, and it is vitally important with code generation. AI-generated code requires the same scrutiny and quality checks as any code written by humans.

The chapters in this section will take your AI-assisted development skill to an advanced level. Chapter 7 covers advanced templating and user interface development, helping you create polished, production-ready web applications. Chapter 8 dives into prompt engineering principles and techniques to enhance your AI interactions. Chapter 9 focuses on prompt manipulation strategies, including context control, output formatting, and iterative refinement. Chapter 10 introduces Cursor and other next-gen AI development environments that can build entire applications through conversational interfaces, showcasing the forefront of AI-assisted software development.

Let's dive into the world of advanced usage of these tools—how they can be strategically applied in real life enterprise development, as well as how to work on just-for-fun or prototype projects.

Building user interfaces with ChatGPT

7

This chapter covers

- Using generative AI tools to design effective user interfaces
- Creating structured prompts to get targeted UI guidance and code
- Visualizing application flow using AI-generated diagrams and flowcharts
- Transforming wireframes into functional Flask templates and components
- Implementing responsive design elements with AI-assisted HTML and CSS

Now that our backend is up and running, we are facing another challenge: we need to create an easy-to-use interface, which will turn our database engine into a full test preparation application. Even seasoned developers can find UI design tough, and generative AI tools help tremendously.

AI tools provide a big boost for developers who aren't great at UI. They draw from large collections of best practices, templates, and design patterns used by expert

Flask developers. This chapter shows how AI can connect functional backend code to polished user experiences—even if you don't see yourself as a design expert. By mixing AI suggestions with smart customization, you'll learn to build professional interfaces that boost user engagement, all without needing deep frontend knowledge.

To find a good strategy, we don't need as much existing code for context, so I'd like to start by using chat-based interfaces to ask for a general approach. We can give a bit of information about our application and get general guidance on how to build this frontend. I'm going to utilize several tools we're already familiar with for this task:

- ChatGPT
- Google Gemini (formerly Bard)
- Blackbox AI

Each of these has a web-based chat interface that can be used to work through this problem. It's not installed on our machine, so it has limited access to our code. However, they're also powered by large models that are very robust. Let's see which one comes up with a strategy we like. First, we need to build a great prompt for this.

7.1   *Getting our strategy from our AI tools*

Before we approach these tools, we should think carefully about our prompt. If we say "generate a frontend for my application" without enough information, the guidance will be too vague. There is a time and a place for brief prompts. In my experience, *brief prompts* are great for focused and specific advice, for problems such as "How do I query this table?" or "How do I debug this error message?" *Detailed prompts* are great for more abstract results, such as "How do I design this frontend?" or "What's a good approach for marshalling data?"

This will be the largest prompt we've used so far. I've given it a lot of thought and trial and error to come up with it. Here is how I want to structure it:

- *Role*—Role-based prompting is something we've done before here, and we want to establish that we want the model to act as a professional Python developer who specializes in Flask. Lately, I've found that establishing a role isn't as important as it used to be. ChatGPT for instance can infer what you want without it, and it's nearly the same. But just to make sure, we'll drop it in there.
- *Objective*—We want to clearly establish our objective. The clearer and more concrete we are, the better the results. We must describe exactly what we want here.
- *Details*—Here we can add some details that will be helpful. These are small but significant toward getting the right result.
- *Data*—I want to describe the data we're working with and what it means. This helps with code generation. If we get code specific to the data, we might not use it, but it will be helpful to give this direction.
- *Functionality requirements*—What do we want this to do? This is a good way to add detail to our objective.

- *Code production*—Here we are specific about what we want to generate. In my experience, this only helps marginally, but it's worth the effort to clarify it.

Here is the initial prompt that I've created and will send to our chat interfaces:

> Act as a professional Python Developer specializing in Flask. Create a solution based on this information.
>
> Objective: Develop a front end for a database-driven Flask application for a quiz system. The application will display questions and possible answers to the user, capture their selected answer, store the answer in a database, and then show the next question. Flask has been installed, and the backend is already functional.
>
> Details:
>
> Framework: Flask, with Flask templates for the frontend. The application is already created.
>
> Database: A SQLite Database that provides 35 questions with possible user responses. This database exists.
>
> Frontend: A simple and intuitive interface for users to interact with the quiz. This needs to be created.
>
> Data:
>
> This is an example of a question:
>
> ('T1A03', 3, 'What are the FCC rules regarding the use of a phonetic alphabet for station identification in the Amateur Radio Service?', 'It is required when transmitting emergency messages', 'It is prohibited', 'It is required when in contact with foreign stations', 'It is encouraged')
>
> Field 0 is the Question ID.
>
> Field 1 is the id of the correct answer.
>
> Field 2 is the question to be displayed.
>
> Field 3 is a possible answer.
>
> Field 4 is a possible answer.
>
> Field 5 is a possible answer.
>
> Field 6 is a possible answer.
>
> Functionality Requirements:
>
> Iterate through the questions stored in the database.
>
> For each question, display it along with possible answers using Flask templates.
>
> Capture the user's selected answer and store it in the database.
>
> After storing the answer, proceed to the next question until the quiz is complete.
>
> Development Strategy:
>
> Question Management: Implement functionality to add, retrieve, and iterate through questions and their possible answers.
>
> Quiz Interface: Use Flask templates to create the quiz interface. The interface should display one question at a time with options for the user to select an answer.

Answer Handling: Develop a mechanism to capture the user's selected answer, validate it, store it in the database, and then retrieve the next question.

Navigation: Ensure seamless navigation between questions and provide feedback to the user upon completion of the quiz.

Code Production:

Develop routing and template creation for displaying questions and capturing answers.

Implement logic for iterating through questions and storing responses.

Ensure to include error handling and validation for robustness.

Expected Outcome: A fully functional Flask-based quiz application that efficiently manages and displays quiz questions, captures user responses, and navigates through the quiz seamlessly.

I will send this prompt to ChatGPT, Gemini, and Blackbox AI. Let's evaluate the results. We'll start with ChatGPT.

Crafting effective UI prompts

When requesting UI guidance from AI tools,

- Clearly state the purpose of your application and its intended users.
- Identify any technological constraints, such as frameworks or libraries, that may affect the design.
- Describe the data structures that will be used to populate the interface.
- Specify the exact functionality you need to achieve.
- Share your visual preferences, including colors and layout styles.
- Request the specific deliverables you need, such as wireframes, HTML/CSS, or flowcharts.
- For design work, it's best to provide longer and clearer prompts to get better results.
- Treat your prompt like a design brief—more context means a more tailored response.

7.1.1   *ChatGPT Results*

We've crafted a detailed prompt that's specific to our needs. Here is the output from ChatGPT. Let's review it and see whether it's useful.

Given your objective and details, let's outline a solution for developing the frontend of your Flask application for a quiz system. The solution will cover the backend and frontend components necessary to meet your requirements.

Backend Setup

1 Database Model: Assuming you have a model for the questions, it should look something like this in Flask with SQLAlchemy:

```
from flask_sqlalchemy import SQLAlchemy

db = SQLAlchemy()

class Question(db.Model):
    id = db.Column(db.String, primary_key=True)  # Question ID
    correct_answer_id = db.Column(db.Integer)  # Correct answer ID
    question_text = db.Column(db.String)  # Question text
    option1 = db.Column(db.String)  # Option 1
    option2 = db.Column(db.String)  # Option 2
    option3 = db.Column(db.String)  # Option 3
    option4 = db.Column(db.String)  # Option 4
```

2 Fetching Questions: Implement a function to fetch questions one at a time from the database.

```
def get_next_question(current_question_id=None):
    if current_question_id is None:
        return Question.query.first()
    else:
        current_question = Question.query.filter_by
(id=current_question_id).first()
        return Question.query.filter(Question.id >
current_question.id).first()
```

3 Storing Answers: You'll need a model to store user answers and a function to handle the storage:

```
class UserAnswer(db.Model):
    id = db.Column(db.Integer, primary_key=True)
    question_id = db.Column(db.String, db.ForeignKey('question.id'))
    selected_answer_id = db.Column(db.Integer)
    # Add user reference if needed

def store_user_answer(question_id, selected_answer_id):
    answer = UserAnswer(question_id=question_id,
selected_answer_id=selected_answer_id)
    db.session.add(answer)
    db.session.commit()
```

Frontend Setup

1 Quiz Interface: Use Flask's Jinja templates to create the quiz interface. Here's a simple template for displaying questions:

```
<!-- templates/question.html -->
<html>
<head>
    <title>Quiz Question</title>
</head>
<body>
    <form action="/answer" method="post">
        <h2>{{ question.question_text }}</h2>
        {% for option in question.options %}
```

```
                    <input type="radio" name="answer"
        value="{{ loop.index }}">{{ option }}<br>
                {% endfor %}
                <input type="submit" value="Submit">
            </form>
    </body>
</html>
```

2 Routing and Logic: Implement Flask routes to handle displaying questions and capturing answers.

```
from flask import Flask, request, render_template, redirect, url_for

app = Flask(__name__)
app.config['SQLALCHEMY_DATABASE_URI'] = 'sqlite:///yourdatabase.db'
db.init_app(app)

@app.route("/")
def index():
    question = get_next_question()
    return render_template("question.html", question=question)

@app.route("/answer", methods=["POST"])
def answer():
    selected_answer_id = request.form['answer']
    question_id = request.form['question_id']
    store_user_answer(question_id, selected_answer_id)
    next_question = get_next_question(question_id)
    if next_question is None:
        return "Quiz Complete! Thank you for participating."
    else:
        return redirect(url_for('index', question_id=next_question.id))
```

Final Steps

- Make sure to initialize your database with flask db init, flask db migrate, and flask db upgrade commands if you are using Flask-Migrate.
- Test your application thoroughly to ensure that questions are fetched correctly, answers are stored, and the user can navigate through the quiz without issues.
- Implement error handling and validation to manage cases where the user might submit an answer without selecting an option or if there's an issue fetching questions from the database.

This setup should give you a robust starting point for your Flask-based quiz application. Adjustments may be needed based on your specific requirements or if you decide to add more features like user authentication, score tracking, or feedback mechanisms.

This is useful information, and it's laid out in a useful way. Here are a few things I like about the results from ChatGPT. It walks us through a sequence of events, as outlined in figure 7.1.

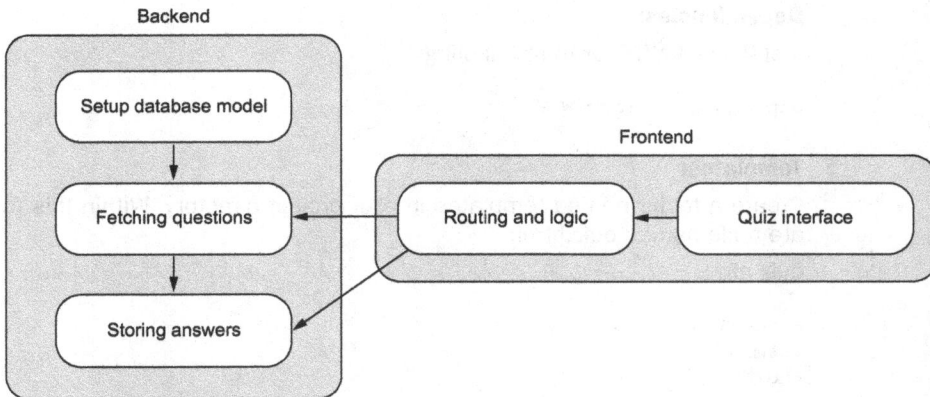

Figure 7.1 How ChatGPT suggested building the frontend. Each piece represents a function that must be created.

ChatGPT prescribes methods to develop this application, many of which we've already talked about. It suggests ways to set up the backend and use SQLAlchemy, which I intentionally avoided in this project. For example, in section 1 of backend design, there is

> Database Model: Assuming you have a model for the questions, it should look something like this in Flask with SQLAlchemy:

It's good advice, but we won't use it. It's not that SQLAlchemy is bad, but it's overkill for what we're trying to do. I skipped through the sections describing how to assemble the backend.

The frontend setup, however, is useful. It prescribes the following steps:

- Create a Jinja template in HTML.
- Implement routing.
- Implement redirects.

I'll ignore most of what ChatGPT has suggested except for the frontend setup. Even though I specified in the prompt that the backend was complete, much of the result was focused on backend and architecture, which I don't need at this point. Let's see what the other tools have to say about it.

7.1.2 *Gemini Results*

Here is the output from Gemini, exactly as it was returned:

> Flask Quiz Application Frontend
> This solution utilizes Flask templates to render the quiz interface and interact with the existing backend for storing user responses.

1 **Dependencies:**

Install Flask-WTF for form handling:

```
pip install Flask-WTF
```

2 **Templates:**

Create a folder named templates in your project directory. Within this folder, create a file named quiz.html.

quiz.html:

```
<!DOCTYPE html>
<html>
<head>
  <title>Quiz App</title>
</head>
<body>
  <h1>{{ question.question }}</h1>
  <form action="/answer" method="POST">
    {% for answer in question.answers %}
      <input type="radio" name="answer" value="{{ answer.id }}"> {{
answer.answer }}<br>
    {% endfor %}
    <br>
    <button type="submit">Submit Answer</button>
  </form>
  {% if message %}
    <p>{{ message }}</p>
  {% endif %}
</body>
</html>
```

3 **Routes and Logic:**

- Import necessary libraries.
- Define routes for displaying the quiz and handling answers.
- In the quiz route, retrieve the next question from the database (implement logic based on your backend).
- Pass the question and answers to the quiz.html template.
- In the answer route, validate the user's selected answer from the submitted form.
- Store the answer in the database (use your existing backend functions).
- Retrieve the next question or display a completion message.

app.py:

```
from flask import Flask, render_template, request, redirect
from flask_wtf import FlaskForm
from wtforms import RadioField, SubmitField
from wtforms.validators import DataRequired

app = Flask(__name__)
```

```
app.config['SECRET_KEY'] = 'your_secret_key'

class AnswerForm(FlaskForm):
    answer = RadioField('Answer', validators=[DataRequired()])
    submit = SubmitField('Submit')

@app.route('/')
def quiz():
    # Retrieve the next question from the database
    question = # your database logic...
    if not question:
        return render_template('quiz.html', message="Quiz completed!")
    form = AnswerForm()
    return render_template('quiz.html', question=question, form=form)

@app.route('/answer', methods=['POST'])
def answer():
    form = AnswerForm()
    if form.validate_on_submit():
        selected_answer = form.answer.data
        # Store answer in the database
        # your database logic...
        return redirect('/')
    return render_template('quiz.html', question=question, form=form)

if __name__ == '__main__':
    app.run(debug=True)
```

4 **Explanation:**

- The `AnswerForm` class defines a radio button field for selecting an answer and a submit button.
- The quiz route retrieves the next question and renders the `quiz.html` template, passing the question details and the form object.
- The answer route validates the submitted form and stores the chosen answer using your existing backend logic.
- Error handling is implemented using `DataRequired` validator for the radio button field.

5 **Running the application:**

Save the files and run the application:

python app.py

This code provides a basic example. You might need to modify it based on your specific backend implementation and desired features like displaying user's score or providing feedback. Remember to replace # your database logic. . . with your actual functions for retrieving questions and storing answers.

The Gemini results start off with suggesting we install `Flask-WTF` to handle the quiz and store responses. It doesn't give any guidance on building the backend, which is good because we've already built it.

What is `Flask-WTF`? It's an extension that integrates the `WTForms` library and handles forms in a simple way for a Flask application. It's certainly something worth considering for our project. Here are the steps Gemini gives us to solve our problem:

- Install dependencies (`Flask-WTF`).
- Create a template.
- Create routes and logic.

It does also give a good explanation of the code, and what's happening, which is useful. We should consider this solution as we implement the interface for the application. Let's see what our third option, Blackbox AI, suggests for this problem.

7.1.3   *Blackbox AI results*

Here is the output from Blackbox AI, exactly as it was returned:

Here is a possible implementation of the quiz application:
First, let's create the necessary routes and templates.
app.py:

```python
from flask import Flask, render_template, request, redirect, url_for
from quiz_db import get_questions, store_answer

app = Flask(__name__)

@app.route('/')
def index():
    return redirect(url_for('quiz'))

@app.route('/quiz', methods=['GET', 'POST'])
def quiz():
    question_id = request.args.get('question_id', 1)
    question = get_questions(question_id)
    if request.method == 'POST':
        selected_answer = request.form['answer']
        store_answer(question_id, selected_answer)
        if question_id < 35:
            return redirect(url_for('quiz', question_id=question_id + 1))
        else:
            return redirect(url_for('results'))
    return render_template('quiz.html', question=question)

@app.route('/results')
def results():
    return render_template('results.html')

if __name__ == '__main__':
    app.run(debug=True)
```

quiz_db.py:

```python
import sqlite3

def get_questions(question_id):
```

```
    conn = sqlite3.connect('quiz.db')
    cursor = conn.cursor()
    cursor.execute('SELECT * FROM questions WHERE id=?', (question_id,))
    question = cursor.fetchone()
    conn.close()
    return question

def store_answer(question_id, selected_answer):
    conn = sqlite3.connect('quiz.db')
    cursor = conn.cursor()
    cursor.execute('INSERT INTO answers
(question_id, selected_answer)
VALUES (?, ?)', (question_id, selected_answer))
    conn.commit()
    conn.close()
```

templates/quiz.html:

```
{% extends 'base.html' %}

{% block content %}
    <h1>{{ question[2] }}</h1>
    <form method="post">
        <input type="radio" name="answer"
value="{{ question[3] }}">{{ question[3] }}</input><br>
        <input type="radio" name="answer"
value="{{ question[4] }}">{{ question[4] }}</input><br>
        <input type="radio" name="answer"
value="{{ question[5] }}">{{ question[5] }}</input><br>
        <input type="radio" name="answer"
value="{{ question[6] }}">{{ question[6] }}</input><br>
        <input type="submit" value="Submit">
    </form>
{% endblock %}
```

templates/results.html:

```
{% extends 'base.html' %}

{% block content %}
    <h1>Quiz Results</h1>
    <p>Congratulations! You have completed the quiz.</p>
{% endblock %}
```

templates/base.html:

```
<!DOCTYPE html>
<html lang="en">
<head>
    <meta charset="UTF-8">
    <meta name="viewport" content="width=device-width, initial-
scale=1.0">
    <title>Quiz Application</title>
</head>
<body>
```

```
    {% block content %}{% endblock %}
</body>
</html>
```

> This implementation uses Flask's routing system to handle different parts of the quiz. The quiz route displays the current question and possible answers using a Flask template. The results route displays the quiz results. The `store_answer` function stores the user's selected answer in the database. The `get_questions` function retrieves the current question from the database. The quiz iterates through the questions using the `question_id` parameter in the URL. The user's selected answer is captured using a form and stored in the database using the `store_answer` function. After storing the answer, the quiz proceeds to the next question. The quiz ends when all questions have been answered, and the user is redirected to the results page.

Out of all the results, the Blackbox one is my favorite. It doesn't bother with any of the database or setup and jumps directly to generating code for the frontend pieces of the application. There are some modifications we can make to the prompt if we aren't seeing the results geared toward the frontend design. But Blackbox created exactly what we're looking for. It suggested the following steps:

- Create routes.
- Create a database connection and query it.
- Create templates.

I'll use a combination of all the advice from each tool but start with the Blackbox results. I'll likely end up pulling some suggestions from each.

REFINEMENT

There are some steps we could take with each of these tools if we want to drill down and get more detail about UI information. For example, in the objective section, we used

> Objective: Develop a front end for a database-driven Flask application for a quiz system. The application will display questions and possible answers to the user, capture their selected answer, store the answer in a database, and then show the next question. Flask has been installed and the backend is already functional.

We could add further refinement and be more specific:

> Objective: Develop a visually appealing and user-friendly front-end interface for a database-driven Flask application for a quiz system. The interface should display questions and possible answers to the user in a clear and intuitive manner, capture their selected answer, store the answer in a database, and then show the next question. The design should prioritize simplicity, a light color scheme, and mobile compatibility to ensure a seamless user experience. Flask has been installed, and the backend is already functional.

This small change can drastically alter the output. It's acceptable to start out with abstract requirements, but if you aren't getting what you want, refine your prompt.

Tips for prompt refinement

- *Use specific examples.* Instead of vague ideas, be precise.
- *Quantify whenever possible.* Use numbers, measurements, or statistics.
- *Choose active verbs.* Weak and passive verbs obscure your intent.
- *Remove unnecessary modifiers.* Don't send words (or "tokens" in LLM speak) that don't add value to the request.
- *Be direct.* Avoid hedging or qualifiers

We won't spend more time refining our prompt for each tool. There are some great results we can work with, so let's put those into action.

7.2 *Creating our templates*

The first thing we'll do is create our templates. Templates allow you to build dynamic HTML with Flask. They're HTML files with placeholders for dynamic content. This allows you to create a layout with HTML and then add placeholders where Python will come in and fill dynamic content. There will be a base html file that creates an entire page, and then each of these templates will make up a portion of that page. Together, we get HTML generated with dynamic content. The templates are compiled by the Jinja2 template engine. This is a very powerful framework, though we'll only be using some basic parts of it. Let's create some template files based on Blackbox AI recommendations.

First, we'll create a file named `quiz.html` in the `/app/templates` folder. Here's what we need this template to do. The template should

- Create an HTML form.
- Provide the question being asked.
- Provide a list of possible answers.
- Have a way to choose the answer.
- Have a submit button.

The suggestion from Blackbox looks like it's providing this information. We can see a content block and the form elements we need. It also includes placeholders for dynamic content that's coming from a question object:

templates/quiz.html

```
{% extends 'base.html' %}

{% block content %}
    <h1>{{ question[2] }}</h1>
    <form method="post">
        <input type="radio" name="answer"
value="{{ question[3] }}">{{ question[3] }}</input><br>
        <input type="radio" name="answer"
value="{{ question[4] }}">{{ question[4] }}</input><br>
        <input type="radio" name="answer"
```

```
value="{{ question[5] }}">{{ question[5] }}</input><br>
        <input type="radio" name="answer"
value="{{ question[6] }}">{{ question[6] }}</input><br>
        <input type="submit" value="Submit">
    </form>
{% endblock %}
```

Next, we need to create a results template, located at `templates/results.html`. We'll use the Blackbox suggestion for this one as well. However, you can quickly see that it doesn't provide any useful results. It simply states that the quiz is complete. We'll fix that later, though.

templates/results.html

```
{% extends 'base.html' %}

{% block content %}
    <h1>Quiz Results</h1>
    <p>Congratulations! You have completed the quiz.</p>
{% endblock %}
```

Finally, we have our base html, which is the wrapper for the main web page. This is what provides the full-page experience including header and footer, and similar. Blackbox suggests naming this `templates/base.html`; however, we already have an `index.html` that serves this purpose. Let's look at what `base.html` looks like:

templates/base.html

```
<!DOCTYPE html>
<html lang="en">
<head>
    <meta charset="UTF-8">
    <meta name="viewport" content="width=device-width, initial-scale=1.0">
    <title>Quiz Application</title>
</head>
<body>
    {% block content %}{% endblock %}
</body>
</html>
```

Instead of adding another file with a similar purpose, we'll use our existing `index.html`. However, we need to change the `extends` statements in each of our template files to reflect that. Then we'll need to insert our `content` into `index.html`.

In the template files `quiz.html` and `results.html`, we'll change

```
{% extends 'base.html' %}
```

to

```
{% extends 'index.html' %}
```

And we will add our new `Index.html` in a content block, though it won't do anything for us just yet. We will be coming back to this file and making some modifications. Here's what the `index.html` file looks like:

```
<!-- HTML template for the index page -->
<!DOCTYPE html>
<html>
<head>
    <title>Index Page</title>
</head>
<body>

    <h1>Ham Radio Practice Test</h1>
    <!-- main content-->
    {% block content %}{% endblock %}

    {% if session_id %}
    <h3>Session: {{session_id}}</h3>
    <button onclick="deleteCookieAndRefresh()">End This Session</button>
    <script>
        function deleteCookieAndRefresh() {
        // Client-side JavaScript to delete the cookie and refresh
        document.cookie = "session_id=;
expires=Thu, 01 Jan 1970 00:00:00 UTC; path=/;";
        window.location.reload();
        }
    </script>
    {% endif %}
    {% if data %}
    <ul>
        {% for item in data %}
            <li>{{ item }}</li>
        {% endfor %}
    </ul>
    {% endif %}
</body>
</html>
```

With our templates created, we will wire up the application. This guidance was important for where to go next. Generative AI tools can be great for guidance in areas you aren't familiar with or helping get you unstuck from a problem.

We won't go through every step involved as the point of this book isn't a step-by-step tutorial for building an application, but rather techniques we can use to improve the application. Let's look at how we can use AI to get ideas for our user interface.

Using AI tools throughout the design process

Different AI tools excel at various stages of UI development:

- *Early conceptualization*—Use chat-based LLMs to explore layout possibilities and design patterns.

(continued)

- *Flow visualization*—Request Mermaid or other diagram formats to map user journeys.
- *Wireframing*—Ask for text-based wireframes before committing to specific designs.
- *HTML/CSS generation*—Once the design is settled, request implementation code.
- *Troubleshooting*—If your implementation has problems, share screenshots or code snippets for suggestions.
- *Documentation*—Generate clear descriptions of your UI components for team members or users.
- *Consider tool strengths*—Some platforms excel at code generation, while others provide better conceptual guidance.

7.3   *Describing the flow of our application*

Right now, our application is running, but the user interface is as minimal as possible. That's fine with me. It doesn't need to be complex. However, I am open to suggestions to make it look nicer, and possibly easier to use. Figure 7.2 shows what it looks like right now.

Figure 7.2   The entrance page to our HAM radio practice test

When you start a test, it doesn't get much better. It looks like a web page from the 1990s. I'm not much of a designer, but I'm confident we can use generative AI to make it look better and possibly easier to use (figure 7.3).

The first thing we should do is think about the flow and describe it somehow. It's a simple flow, but I want to avoid the tunnel vision that developers sometimes suffer from. We think it's perfect and easy to use, until someone else tries to use it and hates it. Figure 7.4 shows what our flow looks like right now.

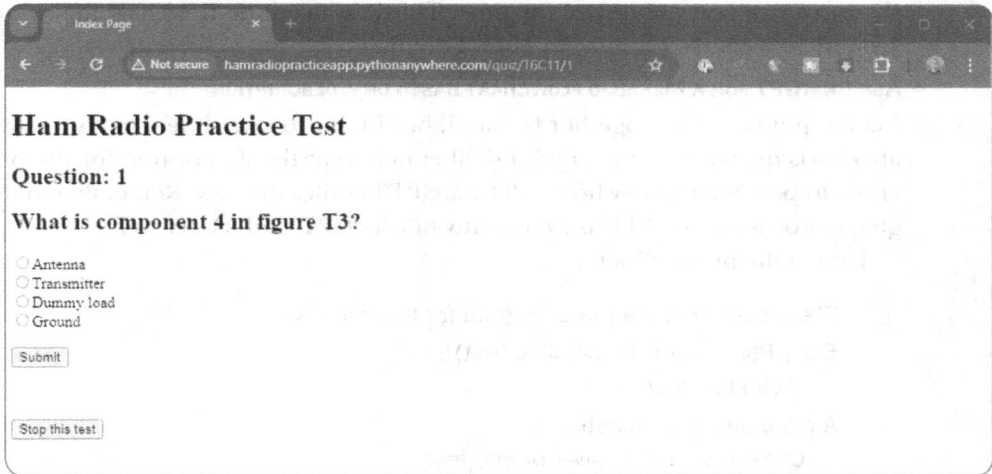

Figure 7.3   The question interface for our practice test

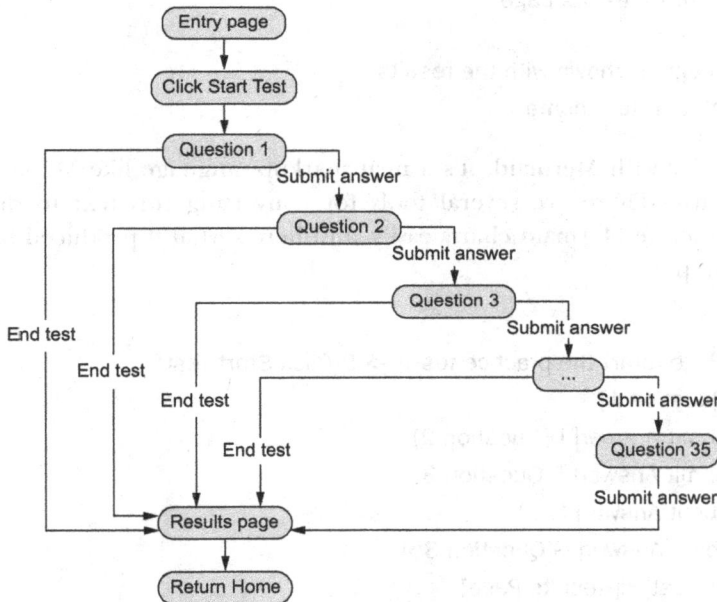

Figure 7.4   Our application's workflow

Figure 7.4 is a graphical representation of the flow. We start at the entry page, and our only choice is to take a test. Once we start the test, our choice is either to answer the question or end the test. Either way we're routed to a results page. The document shows we can end the test at any time. This is a nice little flowchart that I created in around 30 seconds. I'll show you how I did that.

ASK CHATGPT FOR A MERMAID FLOWCHART BASED ON A DESCRIPTION

I could put the chart together by hand, but I want to save time. Here's a way I generate charts quickly when needed. I deliberately kept the description for the prompt as crude as possible to show how well ChatGPT handles the task. Remember, natural language processing, or NLP, is a core duty of ChatGPT, and it does well.

Here is the prompt I sent:

> JM Please create a Mermaid diagram for this process:
> Entry Page (start the practice test)
>   click start test
> A page presents question 1
>   Choice: submit answer or end test
>   if user chooses to submit answer this continues from question 1–35
>   user can exit the test any time, and is sent to results page
>   after question 35 (finished test)
>   user is sent to results page
> results page
>   Results page is shown with the results
>   And a link to return home

If you're unfamiliar with Mermaid, it's a neat markup language like Markdown for building flowcharts. There are several tools for converting this text to diagrams. ChatGPT can generate Mermaid charts easily, and here's what it produced based on the previous prompt :

> ⑨ graph TD
>   A[Entry Page (start the practice test)] -> B[Click Start Test]
>   B -> C[Question 1]
>   C -> |Submit Answer| D[Question 2]
>   D -> |Submit Answer| E[Question 3]
>   E -> |Submit Answer| F[...]
>   F -> |Submit Answer| G[Question 35]
>   C -> |End Test| H[Results Page]
>   D -> |End Test| H
>   E -> |End Test| H
>   F -> |End Test| H
>   G -> |Submit Answer| H
>   H -> I[Results Page]
>   I -> J[Return Home]

Even if you've never seen Mermaid before, you can make sense of the answer by looking at it. It can get pretty complex though, and one good resource is this Mermaid cheat sheet (https://mng.bz/rZMB) that shows many different options.

After reviewing this Mermaid chart, I imported it into Excalidraw (https://excalidraw.com/), and it created this diagram instantly, the exact one you see in figure 7.4. There are several tools that support Mermaid inputs, including Draw.io, and I highly recommend learning about Mermaid and the tools that use it.

CREATING A DOCUMENT BASED ON THIS CHART

I mentioned that I used a very crude description for my prompt. It happened to work; all of us have experienced that feeling that these tools read our mind and provide exactly what we ask for. We've also seen it go wrong. I was lucky this time, but it often requires tweaking or more contextual information. I decided to create an accompanying document with more detail I can refer to later. Also, it is something I can give to a UI designer, with more detail and in the format they expect.

So, here's what I sent as a prompt to ChatGPT, in the same conversation as the chart was drawn, for context:

> Write out a document describing this flow that would make sense to a UI expert.

The prompt is short and sweet in this case, and here's what ChatGPT came up with:

> **Entry Page:**
> **Step 1: Start Practice Test:**
> - Users land on the Entry Page where they can begin the practice test by clicking the "Start Test" button.
>
> **Question Pages:**
> **Step 2.**
> **Question 1:**
> After clicking "Start Test," users are taken to Question 1. Users are presented with a choice:
> - **Submit Answer:** Upon submitting their answer, users proceed to the next question.
> - **End Test:** Users can choose to end the test at any time, which will take them to the Results Page.
>
> **Question 2 to Question 34:**
> This process repeats from Question 2 through to Question 34:
> - **Submit Answer:**
>   - Users proceed to the subsequent question.
> - **End Test:**
>   - Users can end the test at any point, directing them to the Results Page.

Question 35 (end of test):

On reaching Question 35, users have the same options:

- **Submit Answer:**
  - Submitting the answer for Question 35 will direct users to the Results Page.
- **End Test:**
  - Users can still choose to end the test at this point, which will also direct them to the Results Page.

Results Page:

View Results: Users are presented with their test results after either completing all questions or choosing to end the test early. - From the Results Page, users have the option to return to the Home Page.

Return Home:

Return to Entry Page: After viewing their results, users can click a "Return Home" button to go back to the Entry Page, where they can start a new test if desired.

This document lays out the steps in a linear fashion. You can gather the flow of the application from this response, and this document is a great start. It will need some refinement with the UI expert to make sure it communicates intentions well.

You should never expect that these tools will generate the final product every time. In fact, you don't want to rely on finished products from LLMs and should always add a personal touch to whatever you generate. Just like with coding, these tools should augment your work, rather than replace you (even if they could).

Now let's make this application look nicer. The 1990s look isn't working well for this. I'm no designer myself, but I can use ChatGPT or other LLMs to generate some CSS and HTML for me that should make this site look great.

7.3.1 Creating an overall design

Our current look is raw HTML without any backgrounds, special fonts, or CSS involved. Even if this were an internal product, we want it to look better than this. I'm certain we'll stick with a basic one-column layout, but I want to try some new ideas first. I'll take the previous results describing the UI layout and add them to implement my prompt. I will keep this in the same conversation on ChatGPT. This maintains context, and recently, ChatGPT has introduced memory as a feature, so it keeps track of all your conversations and results. By working within this context and keeping the conversation in a thread, you can improve results. It also helps you, the person using it, remember what has transpired throughout the thread. I'll add this to my initial prompt thread. Here is the next prompt I will use:

> (JM) Generate layout concepts for a HAM radio Practice Test website targeting beginners who are not tech-savvy. The website should feature a clean, uncluttered, and professional design, optimized for desktop use.
> Key Requirements:

Multiple-Choice Quiz Format: Present questions in a clear, easy-to-navigate multiple-choice format.

Results Display: Provide a clear and neat display of the results upon completion of the test.

User-Friendly Interface: Ensure the layout is intuitive and straightforward to use, accommodating users with minimal technical experience.

Design Aesthetic:

Uncluttered and professional appearance

Simple, clean lines and ample white space

Consistent use of a professional color scheme

Description of UI: [UI Description from above]

A quick note before we go on. You may have noticed that I mentioned targeting beginner users who are not tech savvy. You may be thinking, "What? HAM radio operators who aren't tech savvy? That doesn't make sense." It's nothing personal toward the audience. By adding this instruction into the prompt, I'm making sure that the interface will be easy to use for folks who are beginners. You can never assume the skillset of those using your site, so it's best not to exclude those who don't use the internet much. Let's see the result:

Entry Page:

Header:

Logo: Top-left corner.

Navigation: Home, About, Contact (simple, minimal links).

Professional color scheme (e.g., shades of blue and grey).

Main Content:

Title: "HAM Radio Practice Test"

Large, bold, and centered.

- **Introduction:** Brief description of the test.
- **Start Test Button:** Prominent, centered button labeled "Start Test".

Footer:

Simple footer with links to privacy policy and terms of service.

Question Pages:

Each question page should follow a consistent format:

Header:

Logo and minimal navigation.

- **Question Section:**

  Question Number: "Question 1 of 35"

  Large, bold, and centered.
- **Question Text:** Clearly displayed, large font.

Multiple-Choice Options:

Radio buttons for selection.

Clear, spaced out, and easy to read.

- **Actions:**
  - **Submit Answer Button:** Prominent and centered.
  - **End Test Button:** Subtle but accessible, perhaps in a lighter shade.

Results Page:

Header:

Logo and minimal navigation.

Main Content:

Title: "Your Results"

Large, bold, and centered.

- **Score Display:** Clear and prominent display of the user's score.

Detailed Breakdown:

Number of correct and incorrect answers.

Option to review the answers.

- **Actions:**
  - **Return Home Button:** Prominent button to take users back to the Entry Page.
  - **Start New Test Button:** Optional, for quick retakes.
- **Design Aesthetic:**
  - **Color Scheme:** Professional colors like blue, grey, and white.
  - **Typography:** Clean, sans-serif fonts for readability.
  - **White Space:** Ample spacing around elements to avoid clutter.
  - **Consistent Elements:** Uniform button styles, headings, and text alignment.

This is great information. It's the beginning of a style guide you may have seen in enterprise development. It's a great set of rules and basic guidance for designing our application. But there's a bonus that ChatGPT has given us: wireframes. Wireframes are the barebone visualization of an interface. They convey what each page or section of an application will look like. They usually don't contain things like colors or graphics. The intention is simply to show where elements live in the layout. It shows things such as text inputs, buttons, and dividers and where they live on the page.

Wireframes are helpful for UI/UX folks (user interface/user experience). They often move these elements to make the interface easier to use. They're also helpful for programmers, as most of us can put together HTML well enough to create these pages and add each element in its proper place.

I didn't ask for wireframes in my initial prompt, I didn't know that was a possibility. But now that we know ChatGPT can generate wireframes, that can be something we can add to our toolbox with future prompts. Here are the wireframes ChatGPT generated for us.

ENTRY PAGE

The first wireframe will be our entry page. This is the very first page a user sees when they enter our application. We can see a dialog drawn out showing how we should lay this out. There is a header with our logo, home, about, and contact links, as well as a footer with Privacy Policy and Terms. In the center is our welcome text and a single link to start the test (Figure 7.5).

Entry page

```
+-------------------------------------+
| LOGO        Home  About  Contact    |
+-------------------------------------+
|                                     |
|        HAM Radio Practice Test      |
|                                     |
|    Welcome to the HAM Radio         |
|    Practice Test. Click below to    |
|    start your test.                 |
|                                     |
|           [Start Test]              |
|                                     |
+-------------------------------------+
|       Privacy Policy | Terms        |
+-------------------------------------+
```

Figure 7.5   This is a text wireframe diagram of the entry page. It is rough but gives us a good idea of what the page should look like.

QUESTION PAGE

Our question page is the primary page for answering quiz questions. Notice the LOGO, Home, About, and Contact are still here. These are what common elements we can carry on throughout the application, and I'll show how to do that. This page is repeated for each question, the only change being the inner content itself. This page will be repeated 35 times, for each question. There is an "end test" button so the user can stop the test any time, as we've asked for in our requirements (figure 7.6).

Question page

```
plaintext                                                          Copy code


   +--------------------------------------+
   |                                      |
   | LOGO        Home  About  Contact     |
   |                                      |
   +--------------------------------------+
   |                                      |
   |           Question 1 of 35           |
   |                                      |
   |     What is the frequency of...      |
   |                                      |
   |   ( ) Option A                       |
   |   ( ) Option B                       |
   |   ( ) Option C                       |
   |   ( ) Option D                       |
   |                                      |
   |   [Submit Answer]    [End Test]      |
   |                                      |
   +--------------------------------------+
```

Figure 7.6   The wireframe for the question portion of the quiz. This is repeated for each question.

RESULTS PAGE

This is the final page containing the test results. Users will get here after completing the test, or if they choose to exit the test early. The results are tallied and displayed on the screen. They also have the option to return home or start a new test (figure 7.7).

Results page

```
plaintext                                                          Copy code


   +--------------------------------------+
   |                                      |
   | LOGO        Home  About  Contact     |
   |                                      |
   +--------------------------------------+
   |                                      |
   |             Your Results             |
   |                                      |
   |   Score: 28/35                       |
   |                                      |
   |   Correct Answers: 28                |
   |   Incorrect Answers: 7               |
   |                                      |
   |   [Return Home]   [Start New Test]   |
   |                                      |
   +--------------------------------------+
```

Figure 7.7   This is our results page. We'll likely add in the percentage as that's a key part of our quiz.

The initial wireframes provided aren't much different than what we have now but some added details that are important. I will use the context of this conversation to use ChatGPT to generate some code for us, based on these wireframes.

7.3.2 Drafting HTML based on our wireframes

Our application uses Flask templating, and ChatGPT is unaware of that because I haven't mentioned it in this chat thread. I have extensive HTML experience, so I'm just going to ask for HTML suggestions, and then wire up the Flask components. It's a personal choice. It will be faster for me, and I won't have to give ChatGPT as much context about the templates themselves. If you're following along and want to have ChatGPT generate Flask templates, I'm sure that will work fine as well.

The first thing I noticed is a common header. It has a Logo and Home, About, and Contact links. I noticed it's common throughout the screens, so it's not something we want to repeat every time. We should make a header out of it. I'll ask ChatGPT for guidance here. Here is my prompt:

> Create an HTML "Header" for these wireframes, that contains the logo and the top links that will be common for each page.

The results it returns are exactly what I'm looking for. It includes all the HTML that will be used in each page, so I can add it to my Flask header, and then, if I need to modify it, it will only be modified in one place. This saves me time from tracking down this HTML in several spots. It also generates some CSS, which I intend to use in the application anyway. Here is what ChatGPT returned:

```html
<!DOCTYPE html>
<html lang="en">
<head>
    <meta charset="UTF-8">
    <meta name="viewport" content="width=device-width, initial-scale=1.0">
    <title>HAM Radio Practice Test</title>
    <style>
        body {
            font-family: Arial, sans-serif;
            margin: 0;
            padding: 0;
        }
        .header {
            display: flex;
            justify-content: space-between;
            align-items: center;
            padding: 10px 20px;
            background-color: #f8f9fa;
            border-bottom: 1px solid #dee2e6;
        }
        .logo {
            font-size: 24px;
            font-weight: bold;
            color: #007bff;
```

```
                    text-decoration: none;
            }
            .nav-links {
                    display: flex;
                    gap: 20px;
            }
            .nav-links a {
                    text-decoration: none;
                    color: #007bff;
                    font-size: 16px;
            }
        </style>
    </head>
    <body>
        <div class="header">
            <a href="#" class="logo">HAM Radio Test</a>
            <div class="nav-links">
                <a href="#">Home</a>
                <a href="#">About</a>
                <a href="#">Contact</a>
            </div>
        </div>
    </body>
    </html>
```

While this may look like a lot of code, it's standard for an HTML header. This is a good example of how ChatGPT and other LLMs often produce an average or something that is very commonly found on the internet. Due to the statistical nature of LLMs, it's producing something that looks like a common HTML header, based on training data. It looks good to me, so I'll implement it into my `Index.html` page, as this is a wrapper around my application. I'll explain that for clarity.

In a Flask application, headers and footers often wrap some kind of inner content. Again, the reason for this is because the header and footer do not change as the pages in the application change. So instead of creating several pages and copying in a header and footer, Flask loads an `Index.html` file with this information and then changes the content in the middle. This design pattern has existed in HTML for decades, and Flask implements it in an easy way.

Our `Index.html` only contains content that's common among pages and swaps out content, depending on the URL (or route) we're using. Here's the code:

```
<!DOCTYPE html>
<html>
<head>
    <title>Index Page</title>
</head>
<body>
    <h1>Ham Radio Practice Test</h1>
    <!-- main content-->
    {% block content %}{% endblock %}
</body>
</html>
```

In this code, it's clear our title stays the same, as well as head and body tags. The H1 heading also stays the same. But everything within the content block can change from page to page. Figure 7.8 illustrates this concept.

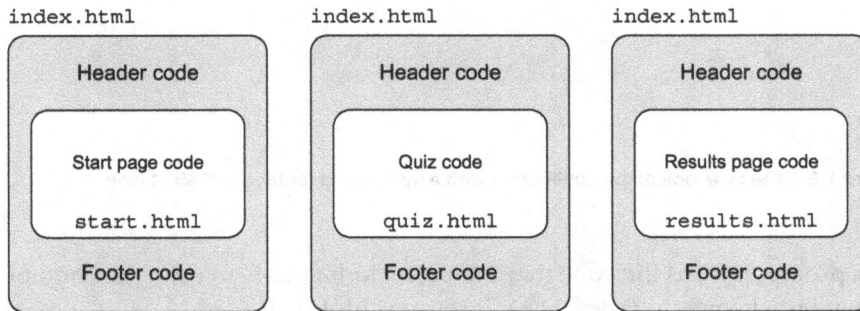

Figure 7.8 The `index.html` is common code within all the pages, but each section of the app has inner code from another html file to complete the page.

With this pattern in mind, I will insert the code into my `index.html` file. Then, within this same conversation (this is important), I will ask ChatGPT to generate the footer code as well. Here is the prompt:

Create footer html code with a copyright, year, and name.

ChatGPT then returns a snippet of code that is again fairly standard:

```
<div class="footer">
    &copy; <span id="year"></span> Jeremy Morgan. All rights
reserved.
</div>
<script>
    document.getElementById("year").textContent = new Date().
getFullYear();
</script>
```

I'll insert it into my application as well, also with the updated CSS for the footer. Our application is already looking cleaner and more professional (figure 7.9).

Now we need to craft some of the HTML for the other pages. I want to have a common box for them, so I'll include that box in my `index.html`. Everything that's inside that box will be dynamic and changed from page to page. Here's the prompt I will use for that:

Create html and CSS for an inner box (content wrapper) that will wrap the content for each page. I want it to take up approximately 75% of the screen and be placed between the header and footer.

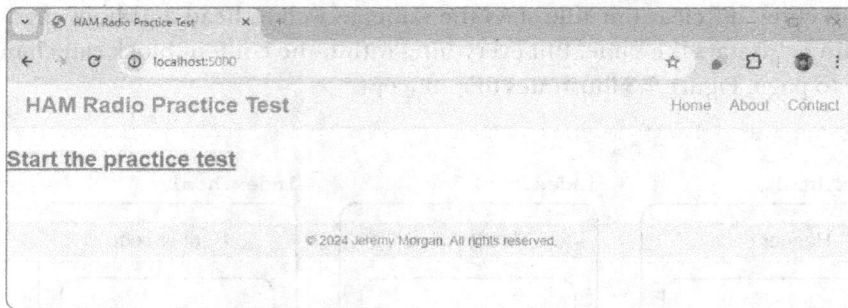

Figure 7.9   The new look of our application with a header and footer and CSS styling

This prompt returns the code that I need, including CSS, to wrap the content and finish out our changes in index.html. It returns this HTML:

```
<div class="content-wrapper">
        <!-- Page-specific content goes here -->
</div>
```

It also returns the following CSS:

```
.content-wrapper {
            width: 75%;
            background-color: #ffffff;
            padding: 20px;
            box-shadow: 0 0 10px rgba(0, 0, 0, 0.1);
            margin: 20px 0;
            flex: 1;
}
```

I'll drop this in, make a few CSS tweaks to it, and we'll examine our page, which now looks even more professional (figure 7.10).

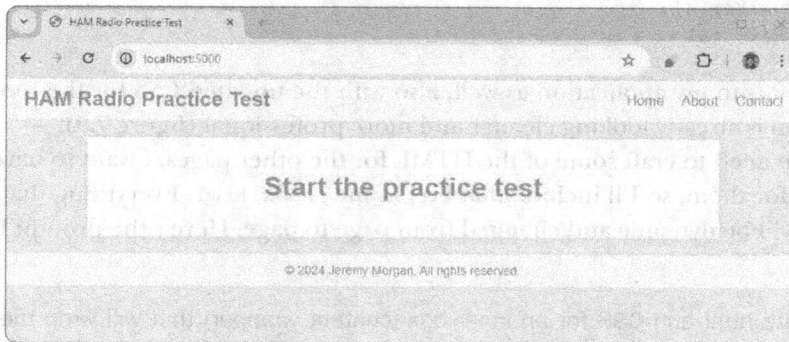

Figure 7.10   The application with additional HTML and CSS used for a cleaner look

To finish this out, I won't' go through each page one by one as it's too repetitive, but I used similar prompts for each page, such as

> Create the inner HTML for the Question Page according to the wireframe
> Create the inner HTML for the Results Page according to the wireframe

I took the generated HTML and inserted it into my Flask templates accordingly. I made a few minor CSS changes, and I'm happy with the result.

7.3.3 The final UI for our application

We generated a workflow diagram and then asked for some wireframes for our application. Next, I asked for HTML to match those wireframes. Though I didn't ask for CSS, ChatGPT generated that as well. Here's what our final application UI looks like. Figures 7.11, 7.12, and 7.13 show the entry, question, and results page, respectively.

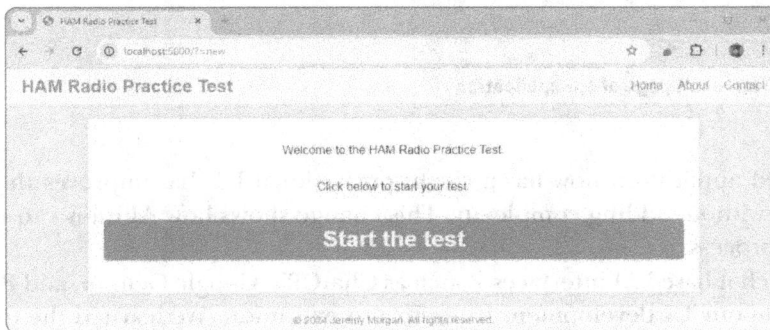

Figure 7.11 The entry page of our application

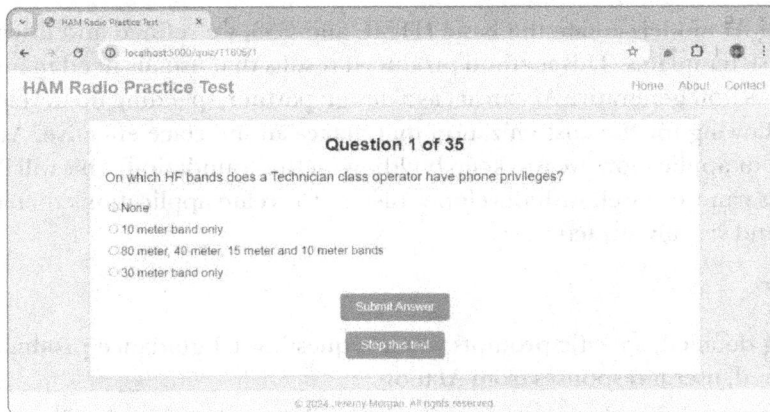

Figure 7.12 The question page of our application

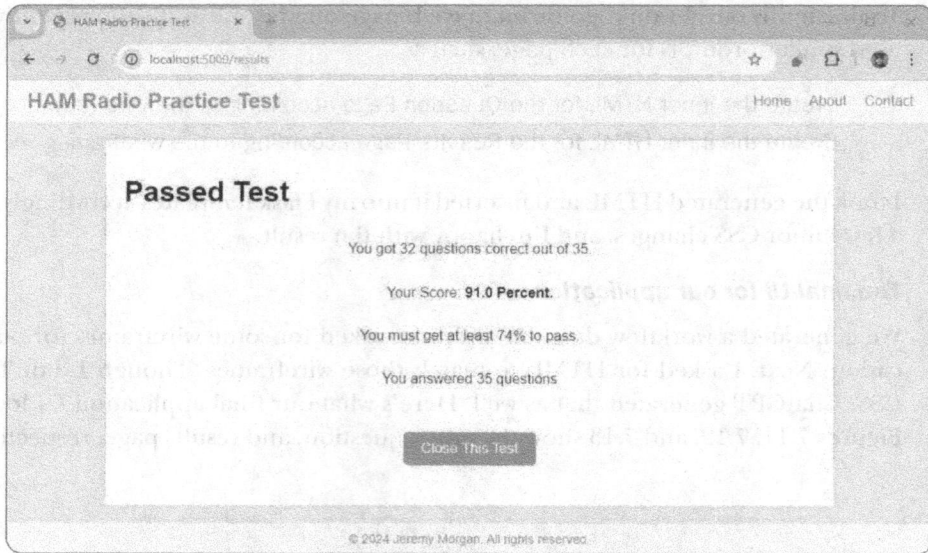

Figure 7.13   The result page of our application

Our finished application now has a clean, professional UI that improves the testing experience without adding complexity. This change shows how AI tools can enhance the design process.

We used chat-based AI interfaces—such as ChatGPT, Google Gemini, and Blackbox AI—to guide our UI development from idea to execution. We learned the quality of AI support relies heavily on how we phrase our prompts. We moved from broad design ideas to specific implementation details. The visualization tools were especially useful, as AI-created Mermaid flowcharts and wireframes helped us clarify user flows before writing code.

By having AI models create the basic HTML and CSS, we refined and integrated it into our Flask templates. This method produced results that usually need many design skills. It shows how generative AI can act as a design partner, speeding up development, while still allowing for the customization that makes an interface effective. As we add features to our application, we will keep building on this foundation. This will illustrate how AI tools can work well with developer insight to create applications that are both functional and visually attractive.

Summary

- Using detailed, specific prompts when requesting UI guidance produces more targeted, useful responses from AI tools.
- AI-generated flowcharts and wireframes can be employed to visualize user journeys before writing code

- You can progress from conceptual designs to implementation by having AI generate customizable template code.
- It is useful to adjust AI prompts incrementally, allowing outputs to remain responsive to the shifting nuances of UI design.
- AI-generated code should be balanced with personal design judgment, making strategic modifications to ensure the interface meets both functional and aesthetic requirements

Building effective tests with generative AI

This chapter covers

- Three popular generative AI tools for Python test generation
- Using AI to create both `unittest` and `pytest` test suites
- Setting up in-memory databases for isolated testing environments
- Crafting effective prompts to generate high-quality test code
- Evaluating the strengths and weaknesses of each AI testing approach

Software testing is vital for reliability and security, but it's often rushed due to development pressures. Generative AI tools are changing this boring, repetitive process. They can automatically create detailed test suites, spot edge cases, and generate boilerplate code. This chapter shows how GitHub Copilot, Tabnine, and Blackbox AI can enhance your testing workflow. They can help you build strong, maintainable test suites quickly, while upholding quality.

High-quality tests are vital for reliable software. They catch bugs early and ensure new features don't break existing code. They also document how the code should behave. As a new developer, I struggled to grasp the value of testing. I thought creating tests for code I knew was good was a waste of time. It took one disaster to change my mind.

Testing is like an investment. You spend time building tests now to strengthen your product. This approach saves time and frustration by catching problems early. As your software evolves, each passing test reaffirms that your product still works properly. However, in today's fast-paced development world, testing often falls behind. This is where generative AI can aid developers as a valuable resource.

During the last decade, the fast-growing DevOps movement has pushed us to ship features at lightning speed. The pressure to produce faster often leads to less testing. Remember that if you don't have time to write tests, you won't have time to fix bugs.

When creating tests, you often write similar code with small changes. There's a lot of setup and boilerplate involved. Generative AI tools can greatly simplify this process. They analyze your code, infer method signatures, and predict the tests you need. These tools can write much of the repetitive code for you, saving hours of work. Smart people tend to get bored with repetitive tasks, which can lead to mistakes.

Generative AI not only speeds up the process; it also improves test quality. These tools suggest test cases you might overlook, ensuring broader coverage. I frequently use AI to create tests, which significantly cuts down development time. It's quicker than writing tests from scratch, and AI offers great suggestions. This makes thorough testing easier, reducing the risk of missing important tests.

Let's explore how to use generative AI tools to create tests for our application. We'll learn to use these tools to build more tests in less time. This strategy software remains dependable and well-structured as development speeds up. After all, the adoption of these tools is changing how management views timelines.

8.1 Why use generative AI for testing?

Generative AI tools dramatically reduce the time needed to create tests, and AI-generated scaffolding serves as a reliable foundation for efficient test development. The generative AI tools we're using may prove most valuable in test generation. Although we've spent this entire book generating new code, you may be the type of programmer who prefers their own code. You might feel these tools get in the way. Using them for testing, however, may change your mind entirely.

Many people criticize AI-generated code, and in many cases, their criticism is valid. Here are a few common complaints. AI-generated code

- Lacks context and understanding
- May contain bugs, vulnerabilities, and inefficiencies
- Creates overreliance problems with developers
- Can perpetuate biases
- Can create IP and copyright problems

These points are worth considering in any organization. They can be addressed with a combination of

- Careful prompt design
- Thorough two-person (minimum) code review
- A balanced approach to the use of AI

Generative AI tools have much less influence when it comes to testing. For instance, a unit test usually only requires the context of the single function or method it's testing. Tests themselves are far less complex than the code they're operating on. Biases and IP/copyright problems also have less impact as well.

You're still taking a risk, and you aren't getting something for nothing. However, the benefits of using generative AI for testing far outweigh the risks. It is possible to

- Build more tests in less time
- Improve test quality
- Reduce human error
- Have a faster feedback loop

Even if you don't find value with these tools in everyday development, you'll see that using them for tests is a great way to increase productivity. So, let's get to it. We'll look at three tools we've been working with throughout this book and learn how to use them to save time and improve the accuracy of our software.

8.2   *What are unit tests?*

Before diving into AI-generated tests, let's talk about the types of tests we will create. Unit tests are one of the most important parts of an application. While unit tests don't cover everything that can go wrong, they do a good job of ensuring your application is reasonably stable. They are short, focused tests that check one piece of a code at a time to make sure it works right.

In Python, unit tests they often investigate program methods (functions) and classes. The overall goal is to take one piece of functionality and make sure it works as intended. You try to give the method different inputs and establish (assert) what you expect the output to be. For example, if you have a method that adds two integers, you will send it 2 and 2 and expect 4 as the answer. You might send it 5 and 1 or different variations to verify it's performing addition as expected.

Unit tests are useful for Python developers because they can help you find bugs quickly. Often, your application will appear to work fine, and you may publish it to the world. Then, one of your users enters some information, and the application breaks unexpectedly. With unit tests, you'll catch that problem before publishing.

8.3   *The tools we'll use for Python testing*

We will use three familiar tools for test generation: ChatGPT, Tabnine, and Blackbox AI. They all work well, and we'll compare the differences in approach for each and learn how to generate tests quickly.

8.3.1 Github Copilot

Copilot uses the traditional chat-style interface for building tests, as well as some shortcuts in the IDE. You can also interact with the API to automate test generation. We'll look closely at how to use GitHub Copilot to generate tests, within the IDE. Some advantages of using Copilot are

- World class model that contains many languages
- API for full customization
- The agent mode for automated tasks

8.3.2 Tabnine

Test generation has become a central focus in Tabnine's recent development efforts. You can use a traditional chat-style interface or integrate it into the UI of an IDE. There are multiple approaches that you can mix and match. Some advantages of Tabnine are the following:

- Integration into IDEs (JetBrains and VSCode)
- Chat interface that's aware of your application and context
- Different models available to generate code
- Provides security for your code so you can avoid IP/copyright problems
- Ability to run your own local models

8.3.3 Blackbox AI

Blackbox is similar to Tabnine as it runs in the IDE. You can also use a traditional chat interface or integrated IDE tools. I've been impressed by the results I've seen with Blackbox. Some advantages of Blackbox AI are

- Integration into VS Code
- Chat interface that's aware of your application and context
- Customized agents that help with tests

8.4 Writing unit tests with generative AI

There are various ways to generate tests with each tool, and it's important to know the differences. We will examine each tool to see its capabilities. All of them tend to default to unittest instead of pytest, so we'll see what they generate naturally and then push them into pytest to see how they work with each.

8.4.1 unittest or pytest?

Both pytest and Python's built-in unittest library are popular testing tools for Python. Each has its pros and cons. unittest has been a part of the Python standard library for a long time and has worked great for many years. pytest has recently grown in popularity because it is easy to use and has tons of great features.

We don't necessarily have to decide to go with one or the other here, but I want to explore pytest in more detail because it will be the way most Python developers build tests in the future. What makes pytest so appealing is its ease of use. The plain asserts mean we need less boilerplate code and ceremony when writing tests. It also has much stronger test discovery and a rich fixture system.

Personally, I prefer pytest for most projects. The standard unit tests have been around so long I'd be surprised if our tools didn't know about them. However, I want to see how well these tools work for what I think is the future of Python unit testing—pytest.

8.4.2   *Using Copilot for test generation*

Let's start our journey into testing with GitHub Copilot. We're going to use the Copilot plugin within the Visual Studio Code IDE. Note that Copilot works in many other IDEs as well. The first thing we need to do is set up our testing environment. We should already be in a Python virtual environment as it was set up at the beginning of the book. But here's a refresher just in case. In the folder containing your code, type in

```
Python3 -m venv hamradio
```

Based on your operating system, use the appropriate command. In Windows, enter

```
\hamradio\Scripts\activate.bat
```

With Windows PowerShell, use

```
\hamradio\Scripts\Activate.ps1
```

On Linux and Mac OSX Systems, enter

```
source /hamradio/bin/activate
```

Now that we're in our virtual environment, let's install pytest:

```
pip install pytest
```

Next, let's create a folder named pytests and a new file within that folder. The file should be named test_models_questions.py. If you're new to pytest , you might be wondering about the significance of this name. We want to start all tests with test_ so pytest knows that it's a test to be run. We want to test functions in our Questions class, which is in /models. I renamed the remaining files so that they're easier for people to understand (figure 8.1).

The "test+" prefix is required to distinguish tests from code. The rest of the convention is optional, and you may have a better way, but this is what I prefer. Let's open the

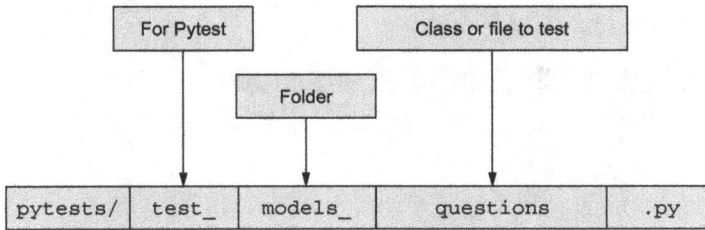

Figure 8.1 File naming convention to let `pytest` know it's a test and let the developer know what the test is intended to do

file in our Visual Studio Code with the GitHub Copilot extension installed. You will notice right away in this file that Copilot is inviting you to interact (figure 8.2).

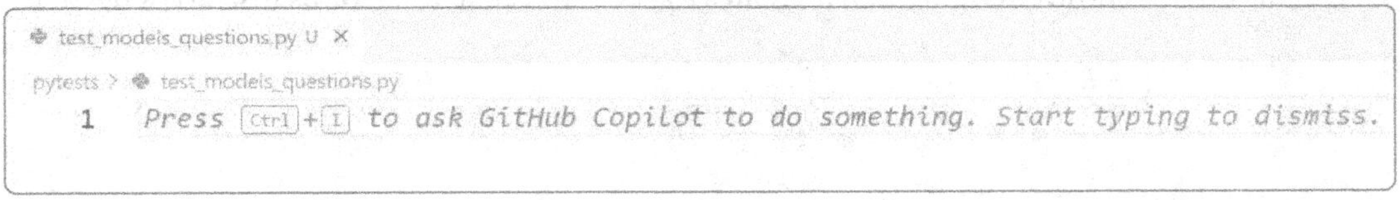

Figure 8.2 Copilot offers a hint for how to open a chat with Copilot, or you can start typing.

This gives us two options for invoking Copilot into our workflow. You can either press Ctrl + I or start typing. I'll try the Ctrl + I method first. It opens a window where you can either type in a prompt, like any other LLM in figure 8.3, or you can use shortcuts as shown in figure 8.4. The shortcuts help guide the tool with tests, fixes, documentation, or explanation.

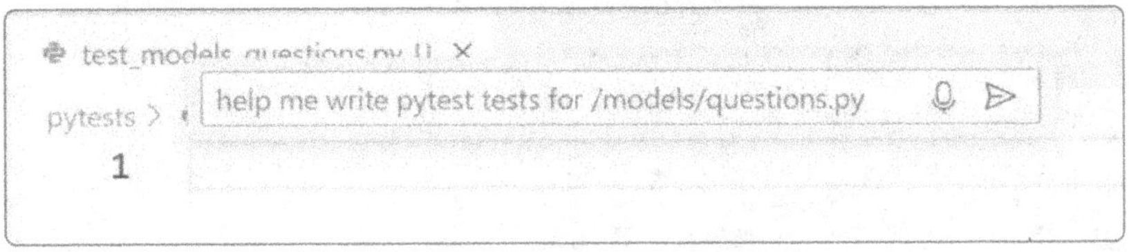

Figure 8.3 You can type in a prompt if you want to communicate with Copilot directly from the IDE. This is a good way to send specific requests.

Another option is to press the forward slash (/), which gives you several options. You can either document, fix, or explain the code (which we don't have yet) and finally generate tests for the code with /tests.

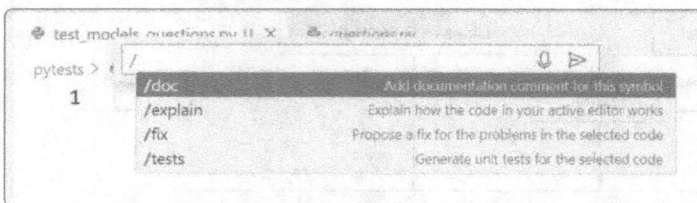

Figure 8.4 There is a set of commands with Copilot, which are shortcuts for common features. Rather than type a prompt for code generation, you can type one of these commands.

I will try just running /tests and see if Copilot will generate what I'm looking for. This type of shortcut is nice, because it's wasteful to spend time working on a prompt for something Copilot is preprogrammed to do. However, if you've come along this far in the book, you might worry about the assumptions Copilot will make when producing the output. As shown in figure 8.5, it creates a set of unittest tests for us instead of pytest.

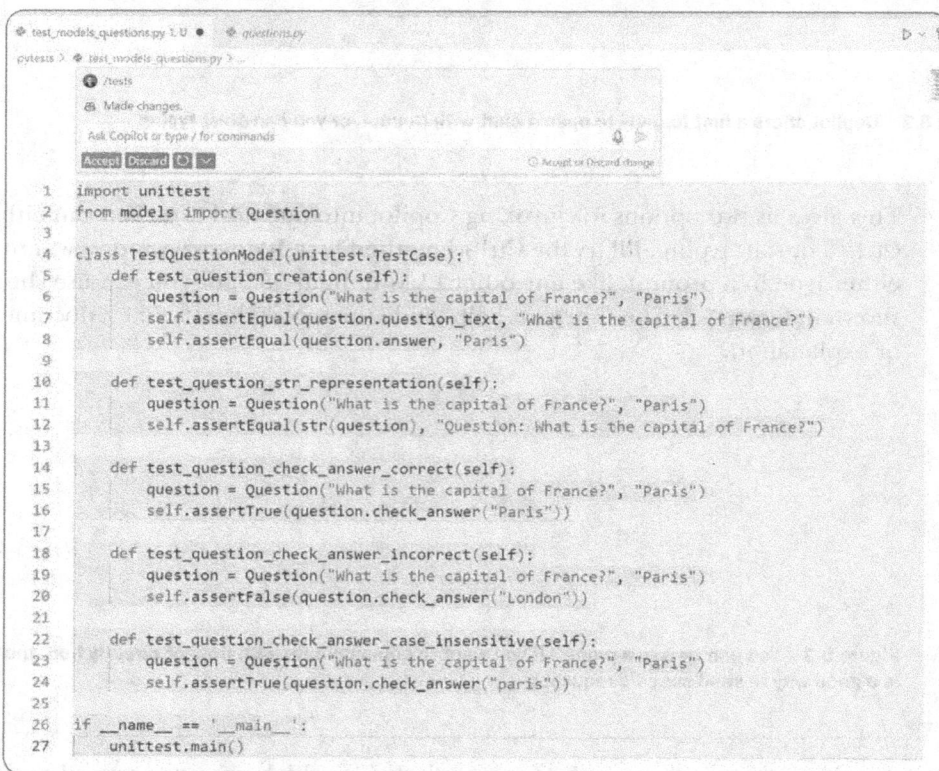

```python
import unittest
from models import Question

class TestQuestionModel(unittest.TestCase):
    def test_question_creation(self):
        question = Question("What is the capital of France?", "Paris")
        self.assertEqual(question.question_text, "What is the capital of France?")
        self.assertEqual(question.answer, "Paris")

    def test_question_str_representation(self):
        question = Question("What is the capital of France?", "Paris")
        self.assertEqual(str(question), "Question: What is the capital of France?")

    def test_question_check_answer_correct(self):
        question = Question("What is the capital of France?", "Paris")
        self.assertTrue(question.check_answer("Paris"))

    def test_question_check_answer_incorrect(self):
        question = Question("What is the capital of France?", "Paris")
        self.assertFalse(question.check_answer("London"))

    def test_question_check_answer_case_insensitive(self):
        question = Question("What is the capital of France?", "Paris")
        self.assertTrue(question.check_answer("paris"))

if __name__ == '__main__':
    unittest.main()
```

Figure 8.5 When running /test in the prompt window, Copilot assumed I wanted unittest tests instead of pytest.

Copilot assumed I wanted `unittest` tests, and I want `pytest` tests, so I will try specifying in a prompt what I would like Copilot to do instead:

Help me write `pytest` tests for `/models/questions.py`.

My hunch here is if I add more information into the prompt, it will give me better results. And it does produce `pytest` tests for this class (figure 8.6).

```
1   import pytest
2   from models.questions import Question
3
4   def test_question_init():
5       # Test case 1: Valid question
6       question = Question("What is the capital of France?", "Paris")
7       assert question.text == "What is the capital of France?"
8       assert question.answer == "Paris"
9
10      # Test case 2: Empty question
11      with pytest.raises(ValueError):
12          Question("", "Paris")
13
14      # Test case 3: Empty answer
15      with pytest.raises(ValueError):
16          Question("What is the capital of France?", "")
```

Figure 8.6 Copilot has generated some `pytest` tests as a result. By using a prompt, we can narrow down exactly what we're looking for and hopefully get better results.

I decided to accept the suggestion and insert it into my code. At first glance, I see that this set of tests will not run as they are, but we'll get to that. I would like to see how Copilot has examined the class and attempted to understand it enough to build tests. This may seem easy, but it's challenging for LLMs. Some of the biggest challenges to the folks working on LLMs is reasoning and understanding—they still aren't good at either yet. But let's look at the code generated:

```
import pytest
from models.questions import Question
def test_question_init():
    # Test case 1: Valid question
    question = Question("What is the capital of France?", "Paris")
    assert question.text == "What is the capital of France?"
    assert question.answer == "Paris"
    # Test case 2: Empty question
```

```
        with pytest.raises(ValueError):
            Question("", "Paris")
        # Test case 3: Empty answer
        with pytest.raises(ValueError):
            Question("What is the capital of France?", "")
    def test_question_check_answer():
        # Test case 1: Correct answer
        question = Question("What is the capital of France?", "Paris")
        assert question.check_answer("Paris") == True
        # Test case 2: Incorrect answer
        assert question.check_answer("London") == False
        # Test case 3: Case-insensitive comparison
        assert question.check_answer("paris") == True
        # Test case 4: Empty answer
        with pytest.raises(ValueError):
            question.check_answer("")
        # Test case 5: None answer
        with pytest.raises(ValueError):
            question.check_answer(None)
```

Copilot wrote out a set of tests to run, and from the very first test, `test_question_init():` we can see a problem in understanding the context of this application. Copilot has assumed that the `Question` class is something you invoke, send it a question, and expect an answer. That's clear from the first test case:

```
# Test case 1: Valid question
    question = Question("What is the capital of France?", "Paris")
    assert question.text == "What is the capital of France?"
    assert question.answer == "Paris"
```

This could happen for several reasons. Copilot could be relying on the name of the class to assume what it means. I can't rule out myself as a factor: maybe my prompt wasn't good enough. Or worse yet, maybe this is a bad design with terrible naming, and the LLM wasn't trained on code like this. Whatever the reasoning, these tests don't make much sense.

In the `test_question_check_answer():` tests, things aren't any better. Copilot assumes the method `check_answer` takes in a string question and string answer:

```
# Test case 1: Correct answer
    question = Question("What is the capital of France?", "Paris")
    assert question.check_answer("Paris") == True
```

The problem is, there is no such method. This test is invalid as well. But what are we to do? We tried running /tests, then tried giving a better prompt. We're still stuck with tests that won't work. Once again, we must rely on our own knowledge of Python development to get this done. However, we can still get help from Copilot to generate tests and save us time. Here's how we'll do it.

CREATING A DIALOG WITH GITHUB COPILOT

If you've written unit tests in Python before, you know there are things you must do to set up your test environment. It rarely entails writing a few functions and calling it good. Let's see if GitHub Copilot can help us.

The first thing I'll do is select a method from our `Questions` class. Inside the IDE, I highlighted "self" and asked this question:

> JM   How can I generate a mock "self" in `pytest` for testing?

The prompt will be sent off to Copilot while using the existing context of this file. Then I can send the answer to a Github Chat window (figure 8.7).

```
40          self.cursor = cursor
41
42      def get_all_questions(self):
43          self.cursor.execute("SELECT id FROM questions")
44          return self.c   how can I generate a mock "self" in pytest for
45                          testing?                                    🎤  ▷
46      def get_question(self, question_id):
47
48          self.cursor.execute('''SELECT id, correct, question, a, b, c,
49          result = self.cursor.fetchone()
50
51          if result is None:
52              return None
53
```

Figure 8.7 Asking a question in the IDE so that Copilot understands the context better to produce a better result

After sending the prompt, I can open the Copilot chat, and I see a suggestion for how to do this. It's suggesting I put the test in the same file I'm working with, but other than that, the advice looks solid (figure 8.8).

One thing I would like to do is create a mock, in memory database for this application. This way, I can run tests against the software without worrying about affecting real data. Now, of course, this idea only works with a smaller application like ours. You can't load up an entire production database into a memory with an enormous enterprise application. But since I have faith our database will fit into memory, let's give it a shot.

I send the following query to GitHub Copilot in the chat:

> JM   How can I create an in-memory database for SQLite for testing that matches the database I have in `/data/questions.db`?

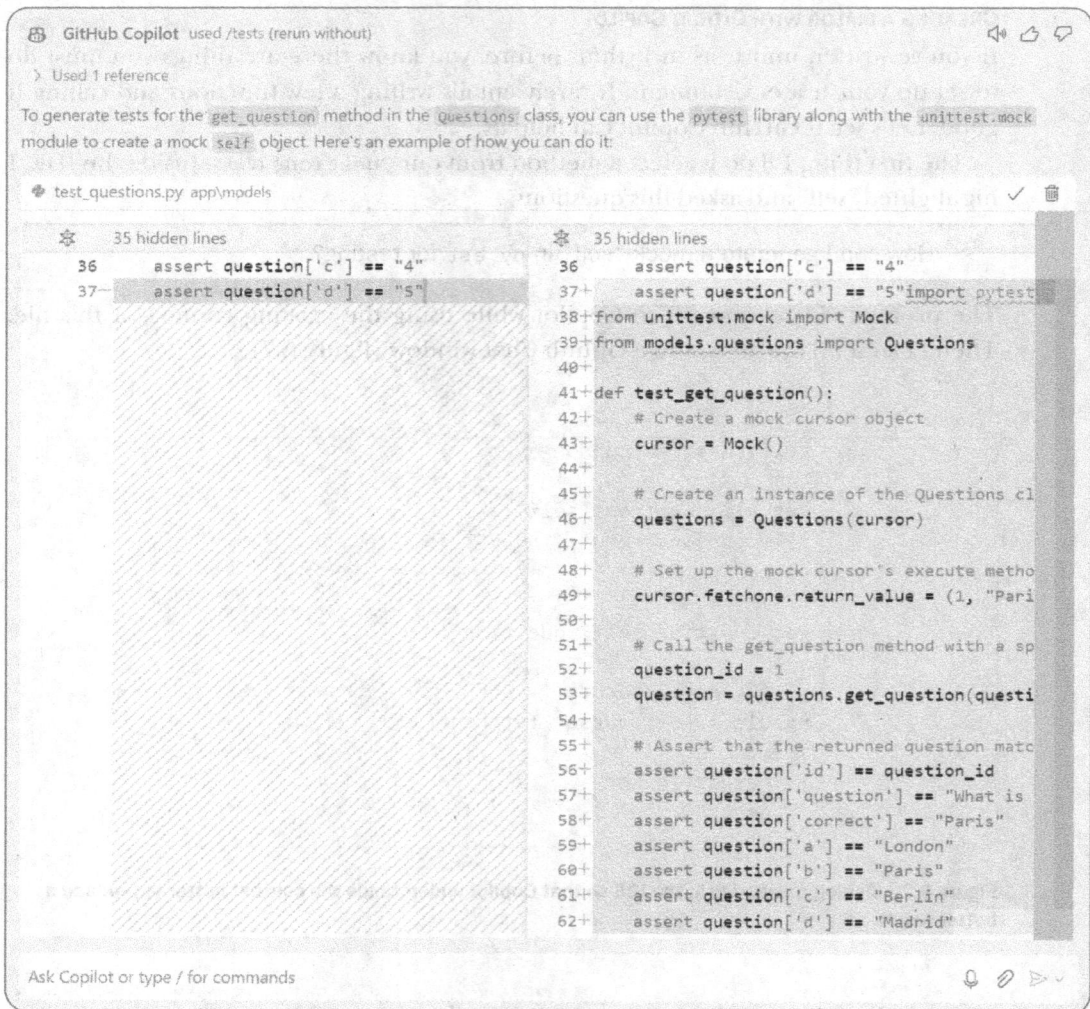

Figure 8.8   The results from GitHub Copilot when asked a direct question and with highlighted code I want it to look at. Copilot suggests creating a `test_questions.py` in the same directory as my `questions.py` class, but other than that, it looks closer to a real test.

While this sentence would be strange to say out loud, it's clearly conveying information we want Copilot to know:

- We want an in-memory database.
- We want to mimic SQLite.
- It will be used for testing.
- The existing database is `/data/questions.db`.

This prompt should convey the needed information to generate what we want. Copilot returns a helpful response:

To create an in-memory SQLite database for testing that matches your existing database schema, you can follow these steps:

1 **Connect to the in-memory database.**
2 **Read the schema from the existing database.**
3 **Apply the schema to the in-memory database.**
4 **Copy the data from the existing database to the in-memory database (if needed).**

Here's a step-by-step plan in pseudocode:

1 Connect to the existing database '/data/questions.db'
2 Extract the schema using the 'sqlite_master' table.
3 Connect to the in-memory database.
4 Apply the extracted schema to the in-memory database.
5 Optionally, copy the data from the existing database to the in-memory database.

Now, let's implement this in Python:

```python
import sqlite3

def create_in_memory_db_from_existing(existing_db_path):
    # Connect to the existing database
    existing_conn = sqlite3.connect(existing_db_path)
    existing_cursor = existing_conn.cursor()

    # Extract the schema from the existing database
    existing_cursor.execute("SELECT sql
FROM sqlite_master WHERE type='table'")
    schema_statements = existing_cursor.fetchall()

    # Connect to the in-memory database
    memory_conn = sqlite3.connect(':memory:')
    memory_cursor = memory_conn.cursor()

    # Apply the schema to the in-memory database
    for statement in schema_statements:
        if statement[0]:  # Ensure the statement is not None
            memory_cursor.execute(statement[0])

    # Optionally, copy data from the existing database to the in-memory
database
    for table_info in existing_cursor.execute
("SELECT name FROM sqlite_master WHERE type='table'"):
        table_name = table_info[0]
        if table_name != 'sqlite_sequence':
            data = existing_cursor.execute
(f"SELECT * FROM {table_name}").fetchall()
```

```
                              columns = [description[0]
        for description in existing_cursor.description]
                        placeholders = ', '.join('?' * len(columns))
                        memory_cursor.executemany(
                            f"INSERT INTO {table_name}
        ({', '.join(columns)}) VALUES ({placeholders})", data
                            )

            # Commit changes to the in-memory database
            memory_conn.commit()

            # Close the existing database connection
            existing_conn.close()

            return memory_conn

    # Usage example
    in_memory_db = create_in_memory_db_from_existing
    ('/data/questions.db')
```

This code will create an in-memory SQLite database that matches the schema of your existing database and optionally copies the data. You can use the `'in_memory_ db'` connection for your testing purposes.

This response looks helpful, so I will include the `create_in_memory_db_from_ existing` function into our existing test file (tests_models_questions.py). At first glance, the code appears logical and readable, and it seems like it should function correctly. I'll build a quick test to connect to the database and attempt to run a query:

```
def test_connection():
  in_memory_db = create_in_memory_db_from_existing('../data/questions.db')
  in_memory_db.execute("SELECT * FROM questions")
```

This should extract our important data from the production SQLite database into memory and attempt to run a query. After running `pytest`, the test fails with the following error message:

```
FAILED test_models_questions.py::test_connection - sqlite3.OperationalError:
object name reserved for internal use: sqlite_sequence
```

This is a minor error. If we look at the queries in this function, we can see where it queries SQLite for all the table names:

```
existing_cursor.execute("SELECT sql FROM sqlite_master WHERE type='table'")
```

And then, it tries to load the data from these tables into memory:

```
for table_info in existing_cursor.execute
("SELECT name FROM sqlite_master WHERE type='table'"):
```

If the query attempts to access `sqlite_sequence`, it will be denied. Copilot attempts to rectify this problem with this line of code:

```
if table_name != 'sqlite_sequence':  # Skip the sqlite_sequence table
```

However, it is still being queried, so we can rectify it with a small modification to our SQL code. I will add a clause to exclude the `sqlite_sequence` table from our initial query. So, I will change

```
existing_cursor.execute("SELECT sql FROM sqlite_master
WHERE type='table' ")
```

to

```
existing_cursor.execute("SELECT sql FROM sqlite_master
WHERE type='table' AND name IS NOT 'sqlite_sequence'")
```

and rerun the test. It is now successful (figure 8.9).

```
(hamradio) [jeremy@KATANA pytests]$ pytest
==================== test session starts ====================
platform linux -- Python 3.12.3, pytest-8.3.2, pluggy-1.5.0
rootdir: /mnt/c/Users/jerem/Projects/HAM-Radio-Practice-Web/pytests
collected 2 items

test_models_questions.py ..                                      [100%]

==================== 2 passed in 0.10s ====================
(hamradio) [jeremy@KATANA pytests]$
```

Figure 8.9 Once we made a small modification to the code generated by Copilot, our tests pass successfully.

What can we learn from this small hiccup? Once again, your personal experience will help you tremendously when using generative AI tools. You can't rely on AI alone to build all the software. However, we also see just how close Copilot got to generating accurate code. We only needed a small tweak to the query, and it worked.

In-memory testing benefits

Using in-memory databases for testing provides several advantages:

- *Speed*—In-memory operations are significantly faster than disk-based tests.
- *Isolation*—Tests are run in a contained environment without affecting production data.
- *Consistency*—Each test starts with a clean, predictable database state.
- *No cleanup*—The database disappears when tests complete.

(continued)

- *No configuration*—There is no need for separate test database credentials or connections.
- *Simplicity*—Test code reads more like production code, improving maintainability.

For larger projects, consider creating database snapshots that can be quickly loaded into memory rather than rebuilding schema and test data for every test run.

BUILDING FUNCTIONAL UNIT TESTS

So far, we don't have any real tests here. We have one test that creates a mock and looks at the mock. The second test creates an in-memory version of our database and then runs a query against it. Let's create a real test for our software. We can modify our `test_get_question()` function to use our in-memory database. We'll query Copilot along the wall to help us out.

First, we'll clear the existing code in `test_get_question` and make it empty so it looks like this:

```
def test_get_question():
```

Now, let's take a step back for a minute. In our first test, `test_connection`, we have a line of code that connects to and builds our in-memory database. It looks like this:

```
in_memory_db = create_in_memory_db_from_existing('../data/questions.db')
```

There's nothing inherently wrong with this line; however, as we create multiple tests, there is a problem. If we insert this line of code into every tests, it will work just fine. However, we're repeating ourselves with every test. So, if we decide to change the location of the main database, for instance, we'll have to update each of these statements. There is a better way. It would be nice to create this connection one time and reuse it throughout each test, and that's exactly what we'll do.

CREATING A FIXTURE

A fixture in `pytest` is a powerful tool. It helps prepare your environment for tests. It's setting up the stage before the play begins. In our case, it's going to call our function that sets up the in-memory database from our production database. This only needs to be done once, and if we require changes, we only need to implement them once. Creating fixtures makes for cleaner tests, saves resources, and most importantly your time. Let's see if Github Copilot can help us build this fixture. I'll start with a general prompt, and we'll get more specific if needed. Here's the prompt I used:

In this test suite, how can I create a `pytest` fixture for our database connection?

This prompt is very simple, with good reason. I want Copilot to use the entire file that's open, so I start with "In this test suite." The chances are good that Copilot will look at the code anyway, but this phrase ensures it. Then I mentioned "our database connection" because there is only one in the file right now. Then I ask how to create a fixture for that database connection, so Copilot will know exactly what I want it to do. Here is the result it came up with:

To create a fixture for your database connection in a test suite using `pytest`, you can use the `@pytest.fixture` decorator. This fixture will set up the database connection before each test and tear it down after each test.

Here's how you can modify your test suite to include a fixture for the database connection:

1 Import the necessary modules.

2 Define a fixture function that sets up the database connection.

3 Use the fixture in your test functions.

Here's the updated code:

```python
import pytest
import sqlite3
@pytest.fixture
def db_connection():
    # Setup: create the in-memory database connection
    memory_conn = create_in_memory_db_from_existing('../data/questions.db')

    yield memory_conn  # This is where the testing happens
    # Teardown: close the database connection
    memory_conn.close()
def test_connection(db_connection):
    db_connection.execute("SELECT * FROM questions")
def test_get_question(db_connection):
    # Example test using the db_connection fixture
    result = db_connection.execute("SELECT * FROM questions WHERE id = 1")
    question = result.fetchone()
    assert question is not None
```

In this code:

- The `db_connection` fixture sets up the in-memory database connection and yields it to the test functions.
- After the test functions are done, the fixture ensures that the database connection is properly closed.

I'll update our tests accordingly. I'll create a new fixture and refactor the test functions to take the fixture as input. We're simply adding

```python
def db_connection():
    # Setup: create the in-memory database connection
```

```
memory_conn = create_in_memory_db_from_existing('../data/questions.db')

yield memory_conn  # This is where the testing happens

# Teardown: close the database connection
memory_conn.close()
```

Then, for each of the methods, we change them accordingly:

```
def test_connection(db_connection):
def test_get_question(db_connection):
```

And after running the tests again, they pass. So, let's now build these to test our Questions class.

REFACTORING THE TEST CONNECTION

Our test connection function doesn't really test anything. It just runs a query, and if that query were to fail, the test would fail:

```
def test_connection(db_connection):
    db_connection.execute("SELECT * FROM questions")
```

This isn't incredibly useful. Instead let's check how many questions are in the questions table. This way, it still checks the connection to our in-memory database and makes sure our in-memory database contains all the questions it needs. This makes our test more useful and efficient. So, I decided to ask Copilot to help us out. Here's the prompt I sent:

> How can we make this method count the amount of records in the questions table and verify them in a test?

The results are exactly what I was looking for: a nice test to count the number of questions, then verify it against the known number of questions we expect. Here's the output:

> To modify the 'test_connection' method to count the number of records in the 'questions' table and verify them in a test, you can follow these steps:
>
> 1 Execute a SQL query to count the number of records in the 'questions' table.
> 2 Fetch the result of the query.
> 3 Assert that the count matches the expected number of records.
>
> Here's the updated code:
>
> ```python
> def test_connection(db_connection):
>     # Execute a SQL query to count the number of records in the questions table
>     cursor = db_connection.execute("SELECT COUNT(*) FROM questions")
>
>     # Fetch the result of the query
> ```

```
count = cursor.fetchone()[0]

# Assert that the count matches the expected number of records
expected_count = 10  # Replace with the expected number of records
assert count == expected_count, f"Expected {expected_count} records,
but found {count}"
```

In this code:

- The `'db_connection.execute("SELECT COUNT(*) FROM questions")'` query counts the number of records in the `'questions'` table.
- `'cursor.fetchone()[0]'` fetches the count from the query result.
- The `'assert'` statement checks if the count matches the expected number of records. Adjust `'expected_count'` to the actual expected number of records in your database.

I'll modify the function in the following way: I'll copy the code generated by Copilot and rename the function to make it more accurate. Next, I'll add our expected number of questions (411) because that's how many are in our production SQLite database:

```
def test_count_questions(db_connection):
    # Execute a SQL query to count the number of records in the questions table
    cursor = db_connection.execute("SELECT COUNT(*) FROM questions")

    # Fetch the result of the query
    count = cursor.fetchone()[0]

    # Assert that the count matches the expected number of records
    expected_count = 411  # Replace with the expected number of records
    assert count == expected_count,
f"Expected {expected_count} records, but found {count}"
```

This test is now more useful. It ensures that we can connect to our in-memory database and also verifies that the in-memory database has the proper number of questions. Now we know that we can test a method in our application to make sure it does what we expect.

TESTING OUR GET_QUESTION_SET FUNCTION

Now that we know our in-memory database is at least mostly functional, let's test a function in our questions class. I want to test the `get_question_set` function. Here's the prompt I sent to Copilot:

How can I create a test for our `questions.get_question_set` function?

Again we're using a very basic and concise prompt that makes a lot of assumptions about what Copilot knows. We're expecting that Copilot

- Knows where `questions.get_question_set` is located
- Knows what it does

- Will use `pytest`
- Will utilize our fixture

These are a lot of assumptions, so let's see the results.

To create a test for the `get_question_set` function in your questions module, you need to follow these steps:

- Import the questions module.
- Use the `db_connection` fixture to set up the database connection.
- Call the `get_question_set` method with appropriate parameters.
- Verify the results returned by the method.

Here's an example of how you can write the test:

```
import questions  # Import the questions module
def test_get_question_set(db_connection):
    # Assuming get_question_set takes a database connection and some
parameters
    # Adjust the parameters as needed for your specific method
    question_set = questions.get_question_set(db_connection, some_parameter)
    # Verify the results
    assert question_set is not None
    assert len(question_set) > 0  # Assuming it returns a list of questions
    # Further assertions can be added based on the expected structure
and content of question_set
    # For example:
    expected_question = {
        'id': 1,
        'question_text': 'What is the capital of France?',
        'answer': 'Paris'
    }
    assert question_set[0] == expected_question
```

In this code:

- The `test_get_question_set` function uses the `db_connection` fixture to set up the database connection.
- It calls the `get_question_set` method from the questions module with the necessary parameters.
- It verifies that the returned `question_set` is not None and contains at least one question.

Additional assertions can be added to check the structure and content of the `question_set` based on your specific requirements.

Make sure to replace `some_parameter` with the actual parameters required by your `get_question_set` method and adjust the expected results accordingly.

At a glance, this code makes sense, but after I inserted it and ran it, I found some problems. So, I refactored it, and here's how I set it up. Instead of importing questions with

```
import questions  # Import the questions module
```

I am already importing previous questions, so I can simply create another instance of questions and pass in my cursor to the method. This is cleaner and simpler and will work. Here's the refactored method:

```
def test_get_question_set(db_connection):
    questions = Questions(db_connection.cursor())

    # Call the get_question_set method with a session_id of 1
    question_set = questions.get_question_set('1')

    # Verify the results
    assert question_set is not None
    assert len(question_set) > 0  # Assuming it returns a list of questions
```

This change ensures that our `get_question_set` method returns a set of questions. We aren't validating those questions, because they are generated at random. But it does verify that we are creating a list of questions for the test. I run the command and get two passing tests (figure 8.10).

```
(hamradio) [jeremy@KATANA pytests]$ pytest -s
=========================== test session starts ===========================
platform linux -- Python 3.12.3, pytest-8.3.2, pluggy-1.5.0
rootdir: /mnt/c/Users/jerem/Projects/HAM-Radio-Practice-Web/pytests
collected 2 items

test_models_questions.py ..

============================ 2 passed in 0.17s ============================
```

Figure 8.10 Two passing tests that verify both the in-memory database and the `get_question_set` method. These tests ensure that the application is functioning as designed.

This is a look at the workflow for testing with GitHub Copilot. If you don't know a lot about testing, generative AI tools can be very helpful. If you're experienced with writing tests, it can help you write them faster. Here are some things I've noticed about using Copilot for tests:

- They're mostly accurate, and a few changes are usually needed.
- The /tests shortcut from the IDE has problems. It's better to go directly to the chat window to ask questions.
- It's good at grasping context and functionality.
- It will save time and is worth using.

Let's jump into another popular tool, Tabnine, and generate some tests with it.

Crafting effective test prompts

When asking AI tools to generate tests, include these elements for better results:

- Specify the testing framework (`pytest` vs. `unittest`).
- Reference file paths to help the AI locate your code.
- Mention database requirements (in-memory vs. mocking).
- Describe edge cases you want tested.
- Request specific assertion styles.
- Include context about dependencies.
- Mention fixtures, whether they should be reused or created.
- Start general, then refine with follow-up prompts if needed.

For example, instead of "create tests for my function," try

"Create Pytest tests for the `get_question_set` method in `app/models/questions.py` using the in-memory database fixture. Include tests for both empty results and normal operation."

8.4.3   Using Tabnine for test generation

One thing you'll find when using these tools is that the interface is nearly the same. And most of the time, it's easier to jump into the chat window and send prompts. These tools are migrating toward focusing on the chat interface anyway, so it's good to get into the habit of it. Let's see how Tabnine handles tests.

Like Copilot, Tabnine has some shortcuts inserted into the IDE. You also have a chat window option. These shortcuts can be found near your functions (figure 8.11).

```
tabnine: test | explain | document | ask
def get_all_questions(self):
    self.cursor.execute("SELECT id FROM questions")
    return self.cursor.fetchall()
```

Figure 8.11   You can see shortcuts above your functions with Tabnine. The options are test, explain, document, and ask. I've found they work very well.

Let's pick a function in our `Questions` class and see how the process works in Tabnine. I'll click the "test" shortcut above the `get_all_questions` method. Since we already have tests and a fixture set up, it will be interesting to see whether Tabnine infers context from that. As it turns out, as soon as I click test, a chat window opens and asks me that very question (figure 8.12): Do I have a test plan?

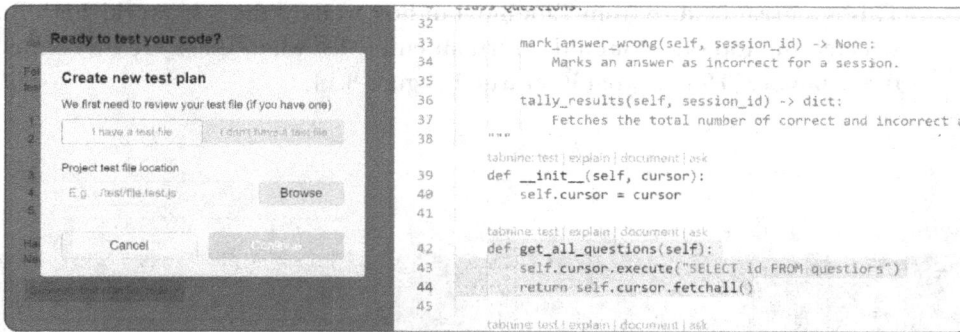

```
                                              33        mark_answer_wrong(self, session_id) -> None:
                                              34            Marks an answer as incorrect for a session.
                                              35
                                              36        tally_results(self, session_id) -> dict:
                                              37            Fetches the total number of correct and incorrect a
                                              38    """
                                                  tabnine: test | explain | document | ask
                                              39    def __init__(self, cursor):
                                              40        self.cursor = cursor
                                              41
                                                  tabnine: test | explain | document | ask
                                              42    def get_all_questions(self):
                                              43        self.cursor.execute("SELECT id FROM questions")
                                              44        return self.cursor.fetchall()
                                              45
                                                  tabnine: test | explain | document | ask
```

Figure 8.12   When clicking the test shortcut for the first time, Tabnine will ask you for a test file to create a test plan. Since we already have tests built, we'll choose that.

After selecting the existing test file, you'll see something far different from Copilot. There you can see a test plan built, with suggested tests, and your existing tests. Tabnine analyzes your code and then generates ideas for tests (figure 8.13).

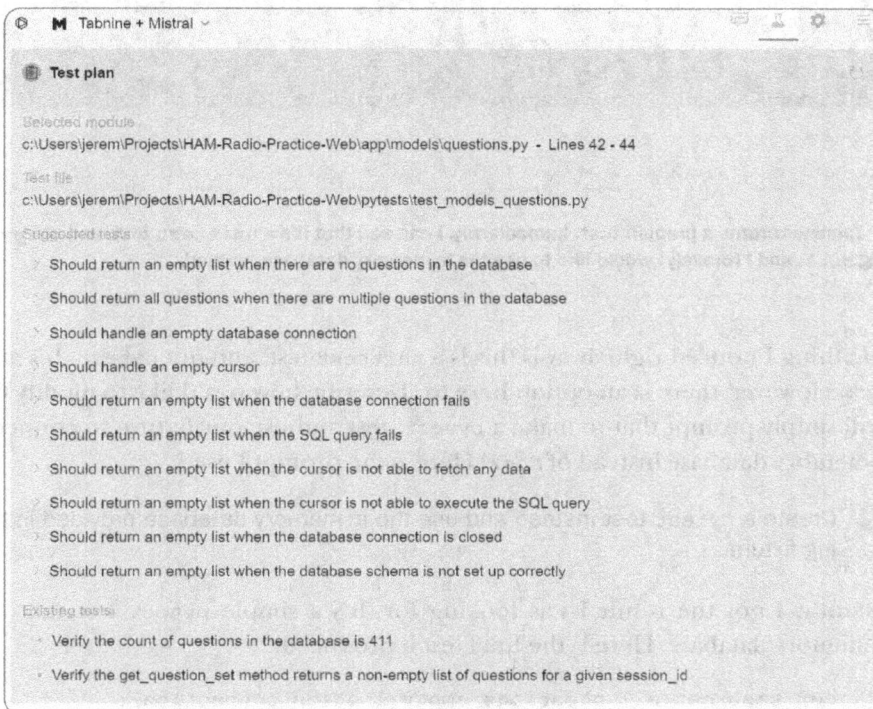

Figure 8.13   Tabnine generates a full test plan for your application. It suggests several tests you might consider for your application.

This is a great feature from Tabnine, but how well do the tests work? Let's find out. I selected the top one, "Should return an empty list when there are no connections in the database?" Here is what it returned (figure 8.14).

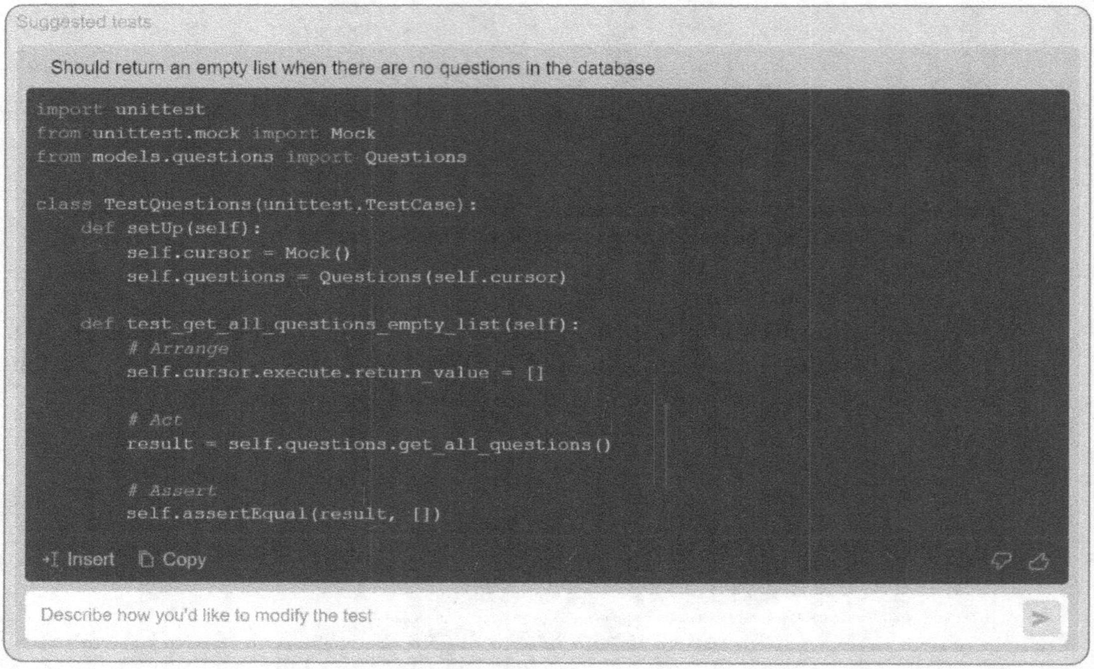

Figure 8.14   Tabnine returns a prebuilt test. Immediately, I can see that it's a `unittest` test, and not `pytest`. Also, it's using `Mock`, and I (bravely) would like to use the in-memory database instead.

One thing I noticed right away is this is a `unittest` test, and not `pytest`. It's also using `Mock`. However, there is an option here to "Describe how you'd like to modify the test." I will simply prompt that to make a `pytest` test and use our fixture to connect to the in-memory database instead of `Mock`. Here is the prompt I used:

> Create a `pytest` test instead and use the in-memory database provided in the existing fixture.

Instantly, I got the result I was looking for. It's a simple `pytest` test that uses our in-memory database. Here is the final test it produced:

```
def test_get_all_questions_empty_list(db_connection):
    # Arrange
    # Clear the questions table
    db_connection.execute("DELETE FROM questions")
```

```
db_connection.commit()
# Act
result = Questions(db_connection.cursor()).get_all_questions()
# Assert
assert result == []
```

This test will open our in-memory database just like the other tests did and delete all the questions from the questions table. Let's run it (figure 8.15).

```
(hamradio) [jeremy@KATANA pytests]$ pytest -s
==================================== test session starts ====================================
platform linux -- Python 3.12.3, pytest-8.3.2, pluggy-1.5.0
rootdir: /mnt/c/Users/jerem/Projects/HAM-Radio-Practice-Web/pytests
collected 3 items

test_models_questions.py ...

==================================== 3 passed in 0.31s ====================================
(hamradio) [jeremy@KATANA pytests]$
```

Figure 8.15   We now have an additional passing test in our test suite. Tabnine created a functional test on the second shot.

The test ran perfectly. I realize that test ordering is important here, and I should run this test toward the end, but it was the first one on the list, so I decided to go for it. Bottom line: Tabnine created a functional test for our software in less than 5 minutes. Additionally, it provided us with many ideas for additional tests. Not all of them make sense to use for our application, but it's a great feature that Copilot doesn't automatically apply.

As a sidenote, I used the Tabnine + Mistral model. Tabnine allows you to choose from several models depending on your needs. You can balance performance, privacy, and accuracy by selecting multiple models. It's located at the top of the chat window, and figure 8.16 shows the models available at the time of this publication.

This is how simple it is to create tests with Tabnine. It has a bit of an advantage as we already had tests and a fixture available, and it fit right in and generated a working test within 5 minutes. It's a huge productivity booster.

Here's what I've noticed about using Tabnine for testing:

- The accuracy of the results is high. Many times, they're better than Copilot.
- I like the suggestions given for additional tests.
- Having a wide choice of models is great if you don't like the results you get from one.

Overall, I personally use Tabnine the most for testing. But let's check out Blackbox AI, another popular product.

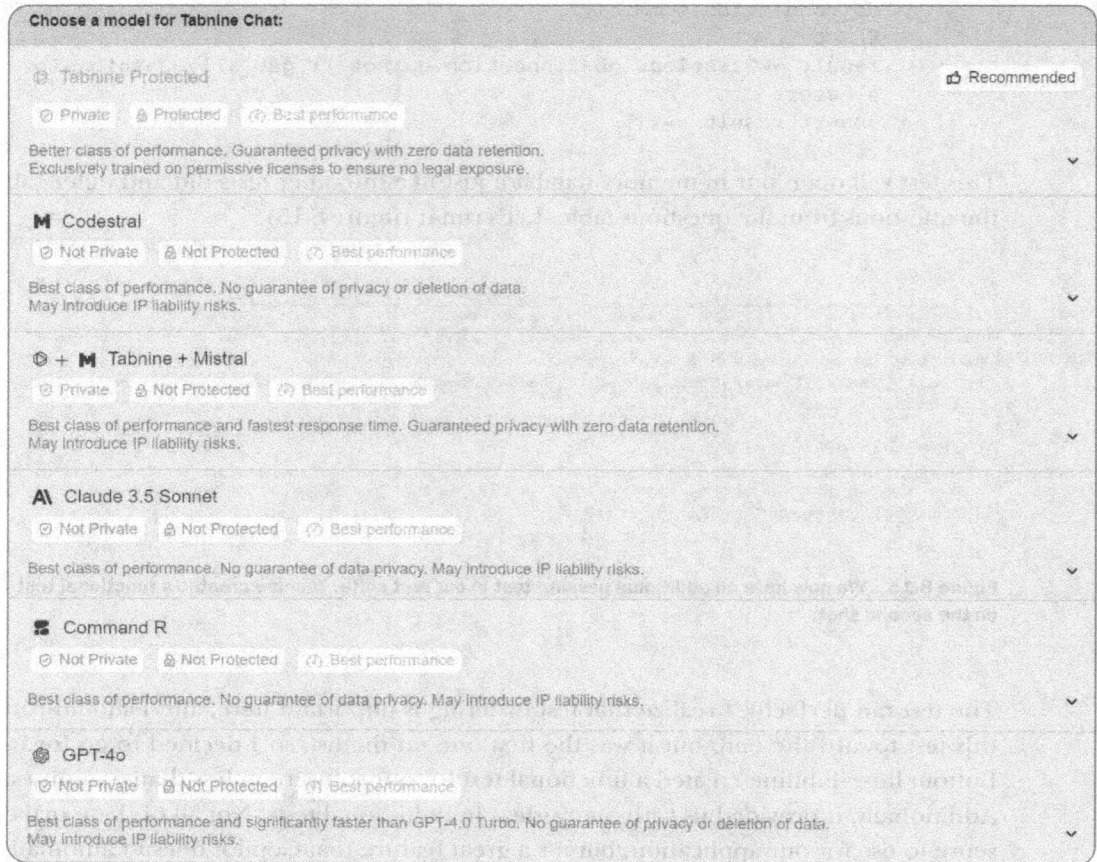

Figure 8.16 Tabnine allows you to choose between many different models for test generation. If you need higher privacy, or simply want to browse different results, there are many options available.

8.4.4 Applying Blackbox AI for test generation

Let's use our same `pytest` application and learn how test generation works with Blackbox AI. Its interface resembles the other two tools we discussed, and most of the work I do with it is in a chat window. You can conveniently put this chat window into a tab in Visual Studio Code, which I prefer to the sidebar interface. To start our tests, I will open this chat and ask Blackbox to create some tests. Notice there is a button "Chat with Your Code Files." This feature enables using your application as context automatically when interacting with BlackBox AI (figure 8.17).

I'll start out fresh with our tests for now. I sent the following prompt:

Create unit tests for the questions class.

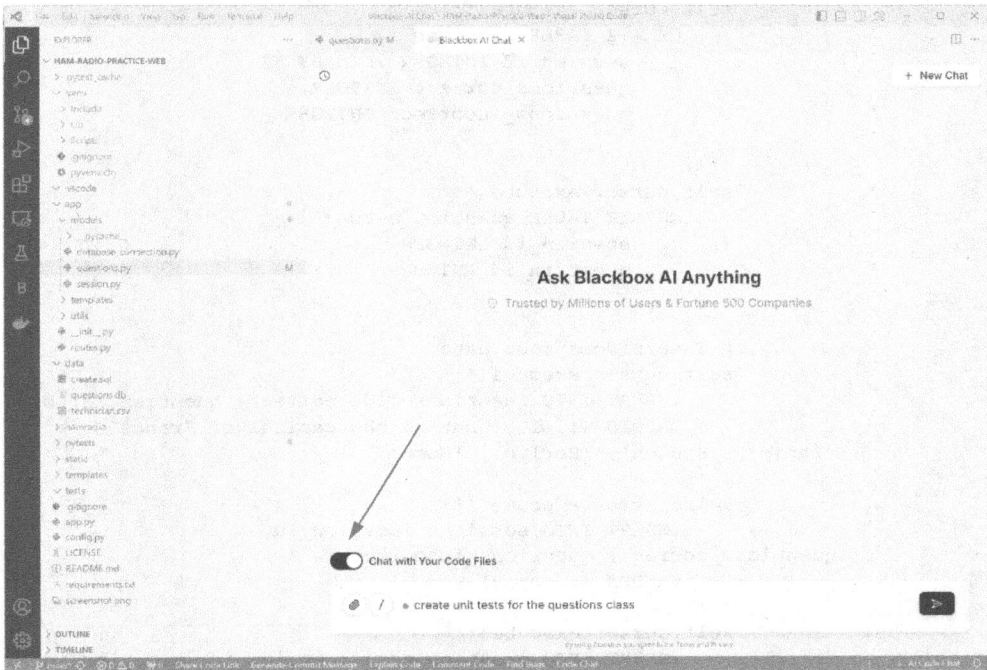

Figure 8.17   With Blackbox AI, you can add the chat screen as a tab in Visual Studio. There's also a button to "Chat with Your Files" so you can include your code as context for the prompt.

Based on this simple prompt, I don't expect it will use pytest, but I'm curious to see what kind of tests it recommends. Here's what I got:

```python
import unittest
import sqlite3
from questions import Questions  # Import the Questions class
class TestQuestions(unittest.TestCase):
    def setUp(self):
        # Create a test database
        self.conn = sqlite3.connect(':memory:')
        self.cursor = self.conn.cursor()
        # Create the necessary tables
        self.cursor.execute('''
            CREATE TABLE questions (
                id INTEGER PRIMARY KEY,
                correct INTEGER,
                question TEXT,
                a TEXT,
                b TEXT,
                c TEXT,
                d TEXT
            )
        ''')
```

```
        self.cursor.execute('''
            CREATE TABLE sessions (
                session_id INTEGER PRIMARY KEY,
                questions_correct INTEGER,
                questions_incorrect INTEGER
            )
        ''')
        self.cursor.execute('''
            CREATE TABLE question_sets (
                session_id INTEGER,
                question_id INTEGER
            )
        ''')
        # Insert some test data
        self.cursor.execute('''
            INSERT INTO questions (id, correct, question, a, b, c, d)
            VALUES (1, 1, 'What is the capital of France?',
'Paris', 'London', 'Berlin', 'Rome')
        ''')
        self.cursor.execute('''
            INSERT INTO sessions (session_id,
questions_correct, questions_incorrect)
            VALUES (1, 0, 0)
        ''')
        self.cursor.execute('''
            INSERT INTO question_sets (session_id, question_id)
            VALUES (1, 1)
        ''')
        self.conn.commit()
    def tearDown(self):
        # Close the database connection
        self.conn.close()
    def test_get_all_questions(self):
        questions = Questions(self.cursor)
        result = questions.get_all_questions()
        self.assertEqual(len(result), 1)
    def test_get_question(self):
        questions = Questions(self.cursor)
        result = questions.get_question(1)
        self.assertEqual(result['id'], 1)
        self.assertEqual(result['correct'], 1)
        self.assertEqual(result['question'],
'What is the capital of France?')
        self.assertEqual(result['a'], 'Paris')
        self.assertEqual(result['b'], 'London')
        self.assertEqual(result['c'], 'Berlin')
        self.assertEqual(result['d'], 'Rome')
    def test_get_question_set(self):
        questions = Questions(self.cursor)
        result = questions.get_question_set(1)
        self.assertEqual(len(result), 1)
    def test_get_answered_questions(self):
        questions = Questions(self.cursor)
        result = questions.get_answered_questions(1)
        self.assertEqual(result, 0)
```

```
    def test_get_next_question(self):
        questions = Questions(self.cursor)
        result = questions.get_next_question(1)
        self.assertEqual(result, '1')
    def test_store_answer(self):
        questions = Questions(self.cursor)
        result = questions.store_answer(1, 1, 1)
        self.assertEqual(result, 'test')
    def test_mark_answer_wrong(self):
        questions = Questions(self.cursor)
        questions.mark_answer_wrong(1)
        self.cursor.execute('SELECT questions_incorrect
FROM sessions WHERE session_id = ?', (1,))
        result = self.cursor.fetchone()
        self.assertEqual(result[0], 1)
    def test_tally_results(self):
        questions = Questions(self.cursor)
        result = questions.tally_results(1)
        self.assertEqual(result['questions_correct'], 0)
        self.assertEqual(result['questions_incorrect'], 0)
if __name__ == '__main__':
    unittest.main()
```

These tests cover all the methods of the `Questions` class. They create a test database and insert some test data before running the tests. Each test checks the expected output of a method and asserts that it is correct. If any of the assertions fail, the test will fail and an error message will be displayed.

Looking at the results, I must say I'm impressed. It created a set of `unittest` tests, as I expected, but Blackbox looked over my application and gathered context in a great way. I'll explain. In this part of the result:

These tests cover all the methods of the `Questions` class. They create a test database and insert some test data before running the tests.

Blackbox AI assumed this is how I want to run my tests. It doesn't insert mocks or anything irrelevant. Rather than telling it to create an in-memory database, Blackbox inferred that from looking at my existing application and how it was set up. Neither Copilot nor Tabnine did that. The code also looks great. I only needed a few modifications to make it run. I added these two lines as I did in the previous `pytest`:

```
# Add the path to the 'app' directory to the sys.path
sys.path.insert(0, os.path.abspath(os.path.join
(os.path.dirname(__file__), '../app')))

# Import the questions module
from models.questions import Questions
```

And then I ran the `unittest` test for this file:

```
python -m unittest test_questions.py
```

Figure 8.18 shows the results.

```
(hamradio) [jeremy@KATANA tests]$ python -m unittest test_questions.py
..1
....Correct answer is 1 and you selected 1
correct
..
----------------------------------------------------------------------
Ran 8 tests in 0.001s

OK
(hamradio) [jeremy@KATANA tests]$
```

Figure 8.18   With a small modification, Blackbox AI generated an in-memory database that looks like our production database and created tests for our functions. It was successful on the first run.

We've proven that Blackbox AI can gather context and generate unit tests quickly and efficiently. So far, they look the best out of the tools we've examined. But what about using pytest? Let's see if Blackbox AI can wow us with code for this framework. I repeated the same test, but used a different prompt:

Create pytest tests for the Questions class.

It immediately returns yet another pleasing result:

Here is an example of how you can write pytest tests for the Questions class:

```
# tests/test_questions.py
import pytest
import sqlite3
from models.questions import Questions


@pytest.fixture
def db():
    conn = sqlite3.connect(':memory:')
    cursor = conn.cursor()
    # Create the necessary tables
    cursor.execute('''
        CREATE TABLE questions (
            id INTEGER PRIMARY KEY,
            correct INTEGER,
            question TEXT,
            a TEXT,
            b TEXT,
            c TEXT,
            d TEXT
        )
    ''')
    cursor.execute('''
        CREATE TABLE sessions (
```

```
            session_id INTEGER PRIMARY KEY,
            questions_correct INTEGER,
            questions_incorrect INTEGER
        )
    ''')
    cursor.execute('''
        CREATE TABLE question_sets (
            session_id INTEGER,
            question_id INTEGER
        )
    ''')
    # Insert some test data
    cursor.execute('''
        INSERT INTO questions (id, correct, question, a, b, c, d)
        VALUES (1, 1, 'What is the capital of France?',
'Paris', 'London', 'Berlin', 'Rome')
    ''')
    cursor.execute('''
        INSERT INTO sessions (session_id, questions_correct, questions_
incorrect)
        VALUES (1, 0, 0)
    ''')
    cursor.execute('''
        INSERT INTO question_sets (session_id, question_id)
        VALUES (1, 1)
    ''')
    conn.commit()
    yield cursor
    conn.close()

def test_get_all_questions(db):
    questions = Questions(db)
    result = questions.get_all_questions()
    assert len(result) == 1

def test_get_question(db):
    questions = Questions(db)
    result = questions.get_question(1)
    assert result['id'] == 1
    assert result['correct'] == 1
    assert result['question'] == 'What is the capital of France?'
    assert result['a'] == 'Paris'
    assert result['b'] == 'London'
    assert result['c'] == 'Berlin'
    assert result['d'] == 'Rome'

def test_get_question_set(db):
    questions = Questions(db)
    result = questions.get_question_set(1)
    assert len(result) == 1

def test_get_answered_questions(db):
    questions = Questions(db)
    result = questions.get_answered_questions(1)
    assert result == 0
```

```
def test_get_next_question(db):
    questions = Questions(db)
    result = questions.get_next_question(1)
    assert result == '1'

def test_store_answer(db):
    questions = Questions(db)
    result = questions.store_answer(1, 1, 1)
    assert result == 'test'

def test_mark_answer_wrong(db):
    questions = Questions(db)
    questions.mark_answer_wrong(1)
    db.execute('SELECT questions_incorrect FROM sessions
WHERE session_id = ?', (1,))
    result = db.fetchone()
    assert result[0] == 1

def test_tally_results(db):
    questions = Questions(db)
    result = questions.tally_results(1)
    assert result['questions_correct'] == 0
    assert result['questions_incorrect'] == 0
```

Note that I've used the `pytest.fixture` decorator to define a fixture that creates a test database and returns a cursor object. This fixture is used in each test function to create a new database connection.

I've also used the `assert` statement to make assertions about the expected behavior of the `Questions` class. If any of these assertions fail, the test will fail and an error message will be displayed.

You can run these tests using the `pytest` command. For example:

```
pytest tests/test_questions.py
```

This will run all the tests in the `test_questions.py` file and display the results.

These results look great at first glance, so I make the same folder modification to the test and run it as is. And all eight tests pass 100% with no errors or problems (figure 8.19).

```
(hamradio) [jeremy@KATANA pytests]$ pytest test_models_questions_2.py
============================ test session starts ============================
platform linux -- Python 3.12.3, pytest-8.3.2, pluggy-1.5.0
rootdir: /mnt/c/Users/jerem/Projects/HAM-Radio-Practice-Web/pytests
collected 8 items

test_models_questions_2.py ........                                    [100%]

============================= 8 passed in 0.06s =============================
(hamradio) [jeremy@KATANA pytests]$
```

Figure 8.19   Here are the results of the tests as they were generated by Blackbox AI. It's nearly plug and play, though in real situations, we'd want to make modifications and double check everything.

So far, out of the three tools, Blackbox took the least amount of effort to generate tests for our application. Here is what I didn't do but would have done if the results weren't good.

MAKING MY PROMPT MORE SPECIFIC

For my prompt, I sent:

> (JM) Create `pytest` tests for the `Questions` class.

This is a very general prompt, however if I didn't get the results I wanted, I could say something like

> (JM) Create `pytest` unit tests for the questions class located at `/app/models/questions.py`. The application uses a SQLite database, and I would like to create an in-memory database that matches the production database for testing purposes.

USING A BLACKBOX AI AGENT

Blackbox AI has agents, which are specific to the language you're using. These agents are more focused on the language and environment, and not only do they have a Python agent, but a Flask agent as well.

You should use these agents when you want your request to be specific. For example, if you type in "build a unit test," Blackbox will see your Python code and infer that you mean a unit test for Python, but it's no guarantee. There are lots of languages that use unit tests. By specifying an agent, you are asking for more specific results (figure 8.20).

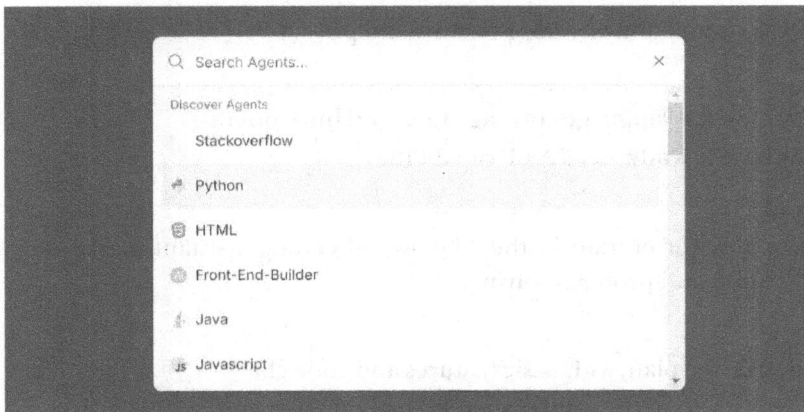

Figure 8.20 Blackbox AI has agents, specialized prompt-processing tools that focus on the language you're developing in. You can bring up an agent from the front slash (/) button in the prompt window in chat.

Thankfully, it produced exactly what I was looking for, but you never know when you might need to make some changes, and that's where an agent comes in handy. If you need to get more specific, start with the prompt, or with Blackbox, and choose an agent.

8.4.5 *Which tool should you use for testing?*

Now that you've seen these tools in action, you can evaluate which one you might prefer for testing. Here are some things to keep in mind.

GITHUB COPILOT

Copilot is arguably the most popular generative AI coding tool today.

Pros

- Extensive language support: Excels in Python, JavaScript, TypeScript, Ruby, Go, C#, and C++
- Powered by OpenAI's GPT-4 Model, which is very advanced
- Integrates well with GitHub repositories

Cons

- Cloud-based solution, which may raise privacy concerns

TABNINE

Tabnine is a code completion tool that focuses on privacy and enterprise level security.

Pros

- Offers both cloud-based and on-premises solutions for enhanced security
- Trained on carefully vetted, high quality code repositories
- Several different models to choose from
- SOC-2 Compliant, ensuring security and privacy

Cons

- May have less language coverage than GitHub Copilot
- May have less advanced NLP capabilities

BLACKBOX AI

Blackbox is a newer entrant in the AI-powered coding assistant market, focusing on code generation and problem solving.

Pros

- Offers a free plan, with basic features and code chat
- Provides advanced features such as code creation and priority assistance with test plans
- Works with multiple IDEs
- Has incredible accuracy with code generation.

Cons

- Less established compared to Copilot and Tabnine

- Single model available currently
- Limited information available about its training data and model specifics

Check out all these tools and give them a shot. You'll likely find one you like that fits all your needs. There's no wrong choice here as they are all great.

AI test generation workflow

Follow this process to get the most effective AI generated tests:

- *Generate scaffold first*. Create basic test structure with fixtures and imports.
- *Review assumptions*. Check if the AI correctly understands your code's purpose.
- *Add test cases incrementally*. Generate one type of test at a time.
- *Verify edge cases*. Explicitly ask for tests covering boundary conditions.
- *Refine assertions*. Ensure tests verify the right behaviors.
- *Consolidate fixtures*. Look for opportunities to reuse test setup.
- *Run and debug iteratively*. Fix problems one at a time, using AI to help with errors.
- *Document test purpose*. Ask the AI to add comments explaining test coverage

Remember that AI can generate the structure and common cases, but you'll need to guide it toward complete test coverage.

We learned how generative AI tools can make testing easier and more helpful. Tools such as GitHub Copilot, Tabnine, and BlackboxAI each have their own strengths, but they all aim to help you write better tests faster. These tools don't just save time, but they also give you new ideas for tests you might not have thought of.

As you start building software faster, using AI in your testing can keep the quality high. The best approach is to combine what AI is good at (e.g., spotting patterns), with your own knowledge of how your code should work. Collaborating with AI empowers developers to create more robust test suites and deliver software that performs reliably across real-world scenarios.

Summary

- The use of generative AI tools allows Python developers to save valuable time, while maintaining high-quality standards for their applications.
- By applying refined prompt strategies, developers often see improvements in AI-generated tests that better reflect the nuances of their software environments.
- In-memory database fixtures enable comprehensive testing without affecting production environments
- Copilot, Tabnine, and Blackbox AI have different strengths, and you can choose the right testing companion based on your specific needs and constraints
- AI-generated tests can be incorporated into existing workflow, while maintaining appropriate review processes to ensure comprehensive test coverage

Prompt engineering

Prompt engineering has become a key skill for developers using generative AI tools of any type. It facilitates communication with these powerful assistants. Instead of getting generic responses, strong prompts can greatly enhance the quality, accuracy, and usefulness of AI-generated code and documents. This chapter examines some practical techniques that will help you change vague requests into clear instructions and obtain useful responses. This way, you can maximize AI's capabilities, while keeping control over the output. You'll turn these tools into dependable partners in your development process.

Some parts of prompt engineering may seem natural—like how we learned to improve our search engine questions over time. However, learning the particulars of this skill can make a big difference in the results you get from chat models and large language model (LLM)-based programming tools.

Let's explore how to create better prompts to get the best results, save time, and increase productivity.

9.1 Understanding prompt engineering

Imagine you're trying to debug a Python function that's throwing an unexpected error. You could use a simple prompt and ask AI to

> (JM) Fix this code.

You'd probably get back a vague or unhelpful response. Or, you could craft a more effective prompt, such as

> (JM) I'm debugging a Python function that calculates user discounts. When processing negative values, it throws this error: `ValueError: Discount cannot be negative`.
> Here's the code:
>
> ```
> def apply_discount(price, discount):
>     final_price = price * (1 - discount)
>     return final_price
> ```
>
> Please:
> 1 Identify the bug.
> 2 Explain why it occurs.
> 3 Provide a fixed version with input validation.
> 4 Add example test cases.

Here's what ChatGPT returned when I sent this prompt:

> (⬡) 1 Identifying the Bug:
>   The code does not check if the `discount` value is negative. When a negative discount is provided, the function proceeds to calculate the `final_price` without validation, which may lead to unexpected behavior or logical errors.
>
> 2 Why It Occurs:
>   A negative discount effectively increases the price, which is illogical in most discount-related contexts. The error message (`ValueError: Discount cannot be negative`) mentioned in your question suggests that this case should be handled explicitly, but the function lacks such validation.

3 Fixed Version with Input Validation:

Here's an improved version of the function with proper input validation:

```python
def apply_discount(price, discount):
    """
    Applies a discount to the price.

    Args:
        price (float): The original price of the item.
        discount (float): The discount as a fraction (e.g., 0.2 for 20%).

    Returns:
        float: The final price after applying the discount.

    Raises:
        ValueError: If the price or discount is invalid
(negative, greater than 1 for discounts).
    """
    if price < 0:
        raise ValueError("Price cannot be negative.")
    if discount < 0 or discount > 1:
        raise ValueError("Discount must be between 0 and 1.")

    final_price = price * (1 - discount)
    return final_price
```

4 Example Test Cases:

Here are some test cases to ensure the function behaves correctly:

```python
def test_apply_discount():
    try:
        # Test case 1: Valid inputs
        assert apply_discount(100, 0.2) == 80.0
        print("Test case 1 passed")

        # Test case 2: Zero discount
        assert apply_discount(100, 0.0) == 100.0
        print("Test case 2 passed")

        # Test case 3: Full discount (free item)
        assert apply_discount(100, 1.0) == 0.0
        print("Test case 3 passed")

        # Test case 4: Negative price
        try:
            apply_discount(-100, 0.2)
        except ValueError as e:
            assert str(e) == "Price cannot be negative."
            print("Test case 4 passed")

        # Test case 5: Negative discount
        try:
```

```
        apply_discount(100, -0.1)
    except ValueError as e:
        assert str(e) == "Discount must be between 0 and 1."
        print("Test case 5 passed")

    # Test case 6: Discount greater than 1
    try:
        apply_discount(100, 1.2)
    except ValueError as e:
        assert str(e) == "Discount must be between 0 and 1."
        print("Test case 6 passed")

except AssertionError:
    print("A test case failed.")

# Run tests
test_apply_discount()
```

This implementation and test cases ensure that invalid inputs are handled properly and the function produces accurate results for valid inputs.

This second prompt gives a much more useful response. Why? Because it uses the key elements of effective prompt engineering, as shown in figure 9.1.

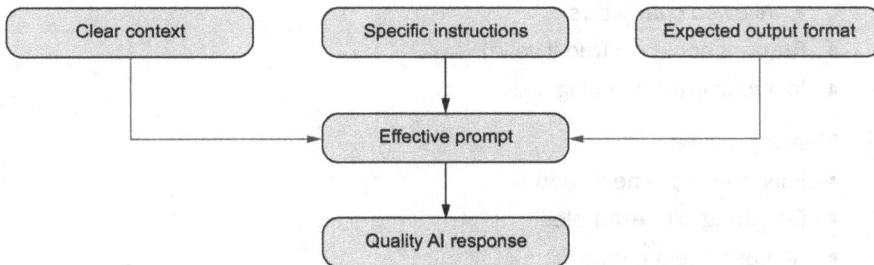

Figure 9.1   A quality prompt starts with clear context, specific instructions, and an expected format. The better the input quality, the better the result.

Prompt engineering is the skill of crafting clear, effective instructions that help AI models understand and respond to your needs accurately. Think of it as of being a good teacher—the better you explain what you want, the better results you'll get (figure 9.2).

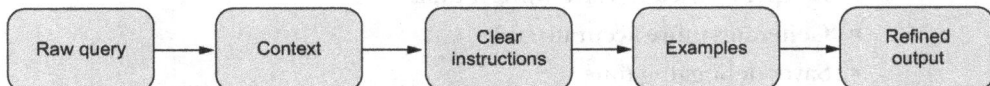

Figure 9.2   A good prompt starts as a query, and context is added. If you supply clear instructions and some examples, you can change the output drastically.

The following list shows some key components of an effective prompt:

- *Context*—Background information, relevant constraints, and technical requirements
- *Clear instructions*—Step-by-step requests, specific requirements, and expected format
- *Examples (when helpful)*—Sample inputs/outputs, preferred formatting, and edge cases to consider

Let's see these in action with another development scenario. Here is an example of an ineffective prompt:

> (JM)   Write a function to validate email addresses.

And here is a well-engineered prompt:

> (JM)   Create a Python function that validates email addresses with these requirements:
>
> 1 Accepts a single string parameter
> 2 Checks for:
>   - Proper @ symbol placement
>   - Valid domain format
>   - Allowed characters
> 3 Returns boolean (True if valid)
> 4 Includes error handling
>
> Please provide:
> - Function implementation
> - Docstring with examples
> - At least 3 test cases
> - Common edge cases handled

The difference is clear—the second prompt provides context, specific requirements, and expected deliverables. This structured approach consistently produces better results when working with AI coding assistants.

9.1.1 *Why prompt engineering matters*

Good prompt engineering

- Reduces back-and-forth with AI tools
- Generates more accurate code
- Saves debugging time
- Produces better documented solutions
- Handles edge cases more effectively

Think of prompt engineering as writing good requirements—the more specific and clear you are, the better the output. As you progress through the discussion, you'll learn increasingly sophisticated techniques to make AI tools more effective partners in your development workflow.

9.2 Understanding the anatomy of a prompt

Good prompt engineering includes good communication. Key aspects of prompt engineering incorporate providing context, clear instructions, and good examples (figure 9.3).

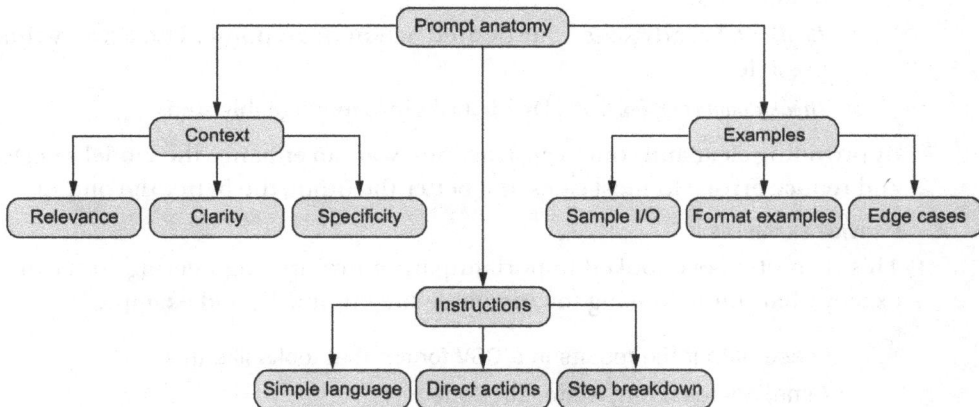

Figure 9.3 A good prompt starts with great context (usually provided by the tool). This includes your existing project. Next, you add good examples and clear instructions. The process is very similar to communicating verbally with a human.

There are many rules and principles of good human communication that apply to LLMs as well. Treat the LLM like an assistant, where you can explain the problem in plain language and get a result. You can keep the conversation going if you're misunderstood. The more concrete and clear you are with questions, the better the results.

Let's take a look at some basics. Some of these can be treated as "knobs" that you can adjust if you aren't getting the results you want. However, most of the time, you'll want to stick to these principles.

THE IMPORTANCE OF CONTEXT

Context is the backbone of any good prompt. There are very few cases where *less* context is better. Context provides the necessary background information that AI models use to interpret your prompt correctly. Without context, models may produce irrelevant or even nonsensical outputs. Thankfully, our IDE tools take our existing code as context; otherwise, they wouldn't be as useful. Good prompts are always characterized by

- *Relevance*—Ensure your prompt is aligned with your task
- *Clarity*—Clear and simple information
- *Specificity*—Tailoring the prompt to the needs of your task

CLEAR INSTRUCTIONS

Instructions are the power behind great prompts. One of the differences between an LLM and a search engine is the idea of *instructions* rather than *queries.* Rather than finding the best way to ask a question, you're providing instructions to create an answer. It's a small but important distinction. Here are some tips for crafting clear instructions:

- *Use simple language.* Avoid jargon and complex language. This generally yields better results.
- *Be direct.* Clearly state your desired action or response. Use active writing when possible.
- *Break down complex tasks.* Divide tasks into manageable steps.

By providing clear and concise instructions, you can enhance the model's performance and reduce errors. In most cases, the better the input, the better the output.

PROVIDE EXAMPLES

This is an often-overlooked important part of prompt engineering. You can illustrate exactly what you're looking for and guide the output. A good example is

> Please output the results in a CSV format that looks like this:
> Name, Address, City, State, ZIP Code

Provide a concrete illustration of what you're looking for:

- *Demonstrate desired outcomes.* Show the model exactly what a successful result looks like.
- *Clarify ambiguities.* Resolve potential misunderstandings before they happen.
- *Reinforce learning.* Strengthen the model's understanding of the task.

Incorporating examples into your prompts will improve the model's ability to understand your intent and generate better responses.

A WELL-CRAFTED PROMPT

Here's an example of a prompt that incorporates all this advice. I want to connect to a MySQL database with Python. Let's see if our LLM can help. I will send this prompt to ChatGPT:

> I need help connecting to a MySQL database using Python. Please provide a clear, step-by-step guide with code examples. Here's some context:
> - I'm using Python 3.9 on Windows 10
> - The MySQL database is hosted on a remote server
> - I need to perform basic CRUD operations

Your response should include:

1 Required libraries and installation instructions

2 A code snippet for establishing a connection

3 Examples of basic CRUD operations (Create, Read, Update, Delete)

4 Best practices for security and error handling

Please format the code examples like this:

```python
# Import required libraries
import mysql.connector
# Establish connection
connection = mysql.connector.connect(
    host="example.com",
    user="username",
    password="password",
    database="mydatabase"
)
```

This prompt is clear, easy to understand, and very specific. Let's see how ChatGPT interprets it and returns it:

Here's a step-by-step guide for connecting to a MySQL database using Python, including code examples for CRUD operations:

1. Required Libraries and Installation

You'll need the `mysql-connector-python` package to interact with a MySQL database from Python. You can install it using `pip`.

Open your command prompt and run:

```bash
pip install mysql-connector-python
```

2. Code Snippet for Establishing a Connection

Once the library is installed, you can use the following code to establish a connection to your MySQL database:

```python
# Import required libraries
import mysql.connector
from mysql.connector import Error

# Establish connection
try:
    connection = mysql.connector.connect(
        host="your_remote_server.com",   # Replace with your remote server
        user="your_username",            # Replace with your MySQL username
        password="your_password",        # Replace with your MySQL password
        database="your_database_name"    # Replace with your database name
    )
```

```python
    if connection.is_connected():
        print("Connection to MySQL database was successful!")

except Error as e:
    print(f"Error: '{e}'")

finally:
    if connection.is_connected():
        connection.close()
        print("MySQL connection is closed")
```

3. Examples of Basic CRUD Operations

Create (Insert)
```python
# Insert a new record into the table
def insert_record(connection, name, age):
    try:
        cursor = connection.cursor()
        sql_query = """INSERT INTO users (name, age) VALUES (%s, %s)"""
        cursor.execute(sql_query, (name, age))
        connection.commit()
        print(f"Record inserted successfully into users table")

    except mysql.connector.Error as error:
        print(f"Failed to insert record: {error}")


# Usage
insert_record(connection, "John Doe", 30)
```

Read (Select)
```python
# Fetch all records from the table
def fetch_records(connection):
    try:
        cursor = connection.cursor()
        cursor.execute("SELECT * FROM users")
        records = cursor.fetchall()

        for row in records:
            print(f"Id: {row[0]}, Name: {row[1]}, Age: {row[2]}")

    except mysql.connector.Error as error:
        print(f"Failed to fetch records: {error}")


# Usage
fetch_records(connection)
```

Update
```python
# Update a record in the table
def update_record(connection, user_id, new_age):
    try:
```

```
        cursor = connection.cursor()
        sql_query = """UPDATE users SET age = %s WHERE id = %s"""
        cursor.execute(sql_query, (new_age, user_id))
        connection.commit()
        print(f"Record with id {user_id} updated successfully")

    except mysql.connector.Error as error:
        print(f"Failed to update record: {error}")

# Usage
update_record(connection, 1, 35)
```

Delete
```python
# Delete a record from the table
def delete_record(connection, user_id):
    try:
        cursor = connection.cursor()
        sql_query = """DELETE FROM users WHERE id = %s"""
        cursor.execute(sql_query, (user_id,))
        connection.commit()
        print(f"Record with id {user_id} deleted successfully")

    except mysql.connector.Error as error:
        print(f"Failed to delete record: {error}")

# Usage
delete_record(connection, 1)
```

4. Best Practices for Security and Error Handling

- **Use Environment Variables**: Avoid hardcoding your credentials directly in the script. Instead, store sensitive information (like username, password, and database name) in environment variables or use a configuration file that is excluded from version control.

Example:

```python
import os

user = os.getenv('DB_USER')
password = os.getenv('DB_PASSWORD')
```

- **Error Handling**: Always use `try-except` blocks to catch and handle errors gracefully. This ensures that even if something goes wrong, your program can react appropriately and possibly recover or log the issue.

- **Close Connections**: Always close the database connection when your operations are complete to free up resources and avoid potential memory leaks. Use `try-finally` blocks to ensure that connections are properly closed, even if an error occurs.

- **Parameterized Queries**: Always use parameterized queries (%s placeholders) to prevent SQL injection attacks, as demonstrated in the CRUD operations above.

By following this guide, you'll be able to connect to your MySQL database using Python and perform basic CRUD operations securely and efficiently.

This response is exactly what I am looking for. If I had never crafted this type of code, I could use this guidance to write it out the first time *and* understand what's happening. There are even some best practices included. I'll admit that LLMs and their tools have taught me a lot over the last couple of years from queries like this.

These are great principles to start with, but not all prompts are created equal. Let's learn about different types of prompts you can use and when to use them.

9.3   *Crafting the ultimate prompt*

Prompt engineering can get complex quickly. There are countless tutorials, courses, videos, and more about great prompt engineering out there. We're at the stage of the game where LLM models themselves know about prompt engineering. And you can use them to help. Here's one of my favorite go-to prompt tricks I do anytime I have a prompt idea:

> Act as an expert prompt engineer with extensive experience optimizing AI prompts for clarity, relevance, and output quality. Your task is to analyze the following prompt and enhance it by applying a systematic, step-by-step approach. Follow these guidelines to ensure optimal results:
>
> *Sequential Reasoning:* Break down the prompt's task into logical steps. For each step, identify key actions or decisions to be made. Use sequential reasoning to guide the AI's response process.
>
> *Contextual Awareness:* Ensure the prompt uses specific language and contextual clues that are relevant to the task. Highlight any gaps in information that may hinder the model's performance. Ask clarifying questions as needed about the target audience, tone, or special constraints.
>
> *Iterative Refinement:* Continuously evaluate the prompt's clarity and adjust the wording for precision and conciseness. Identify areas for improvement by reflecting on how each refinement enhances the quality of the expected output. Be prepared to refine multiple times based on evolving needs.
>
> Based on these steps, and referencing principles such as defining clear objectives, using specific language, and balancing structure and flexibility, your goal is to produce an optimized prompt that is both adaptable to specific use cases and maximizes output quality across various AI models.
>
> Start by asking any essential clarifying questions to fine-tune your analysis. After gathering the necessary context, proceed with your step-by-step refinement.
>
> Here is the prompt: [the prompt to analyze]

I've given this tip to friends in conversation, and many of them are surprised. They haven't considered that you can craft a prompt and then have an LLM analyze it to generate a better one. I'll admit that I didn't realize this possibility right away either, but now that I know about it, I use it all the time.

Just that script above will give you a better prompt more than 90% of the time. You can, of course, take that a step further. Feel free to modify it and check the results, especially with the newer thinking models. Let's revisit the best practices we've learned so far and gather some principles we can feed an LLM to get better results.

9.3.1 Prompt engineering principles

These are some core principles we've learned so far. We'll use this list to evaluate our prompt and produce a better one:

- *Define clear objectives.* Specify the outcome you're seeking.
- *Use specific language.* Choose words directly related to your task.
- *Balance structure and flexibility.* Provide enough structure to guide the response while allowing room for creative insights.
- *Use contextual clues.* Incorporate relevant information and use keywords that align with the task's content.
- *Design clear and concise instructions.* Avoid ambiguity and prioritize clarity.
- *Utilize examples effectively.* Provide concrete examples to illustrate desired output and guide the model's response.
- *Employ role-playing techniques.* Assign specific roles or personas to AI.
- *Break complex tasks into steps.* Divide intricate problems into smaller, manageable subtasks.
- *Use appropriate prompt length.* Balance providing enough information, while avoiding overload that can confuse the model.
- *Use format specifications.* Clearly design the output format (bullet points, snippets, data structure, etc.).

Note that the IDE tools we use in this book (GitHub Copilot, Tabnine, and Blackbox AI) all have various of prompt preparation such as "explain this code" or "improve this code." These built-in commands often use proprietary prompt manipulation in the background. It doesn't hurt, however, to know how this works.

We can then take this set of principles and use them in our prompts. You can also use these à la carte. Some principles may not apply to your task. What does our new super prompt look like? Let's see:

Act as a highly experienced prompt engineer with expertise in optimizing prompts for maximum clarity, relevance, and output quality. Analyze the prompt below to enhance its specificity, precision, and ability to generate the desired output. Before proceeding, ask me targeted clarifying questions to gather essential context, such as the intended audience, desired tone, and any specific constraints. Based on this information, provide an optimized prompt that can be fine-tuned for specific use cases or AI models.

Review the attached list of principles for good prompt engineering and analyze the prompt step by step to make sure it adheres to them.

Here is my prompt: [your prompt]

In the world of LLMs, there are no guarantees, but it's very likely the previous prompt will improve your prompt or give you ideas to think about. Let's put it into action. I'll create a simple off-the-cuff prompt like this:

> JM Optimize this prompt: "Act as an expert Python Programmer. Give me instructions on how to send an HTTP request to an API and display the response."

There's nothing inherently wrong with this prompt. However, I'll send it to ChatGPT using the prompt above to see what it suggests. Immediately after sending this prompt, ChatGPT sent the following questions:

> Before optimizing the prompt, I have a few clarifying questions to tailor it effectively:
>
> **Audience:** Who is the target audience for this prompt? Are they beginners, intermediate, or advanced Python programmers?
>
> **Desired Tone:** Should the response be formal and technical, or would you prefer a more casual and explanatory tone?
>
> **Output Format:** Do you prefer the response to include code snippets, bullet points, or a step-by-step guide?
>
> **Tools or Libraries:** Are there specific libraries (e.g., `requests`, `http.client`, `urllib`) you want to use in the example?
>
> **Constraints:** Do you want the instructions to focus on specific environments (like Windows, Linux, or macOS) or Python versions?
>
> **Additional Information:** Do you want the AI to include error handling, edge cases, or just the basic steps?
>
> Once I have this context, I'll optimize the prompt for maximum clarity and relevance.

As you can see, ChatGPT did as I asked and is now asking some questions for clarification. I'll answer these questions as follows:

> JM 1 The audience is intermediate to advanced Python programmers.
>
> 2 The tone should be very technical and brief.
>
> 3 I would like a step-by-step guide with code snippets and explanations.
>
> 4 I would like to use requests for this.
>
> 5 Focus on running in a Linux environment.
>
> 6 Include error handling in the code.

Now ChatGPT had time to think about my task and provided this response:

> Based on your clarifications, I'll optimize the prompt to better match your desired outcomes, adhering to the principles in the document you provided.

Optimized Prompt:

"Act as an expert Python programmer. Provide a highly technical, step-by-step guide on how to send an HTTP GET request to an API using the requests library in Python. Focus on running the code in a Linux environment and include robust error handling. Each step should include a brief explanation followed by the relevant code snippet. The tone should be concise and technical, with no unnecessary elaboration."

This revised prompt is structured to ensure that the AI provides concise, relevant, and well-organized content while including the technical depth your audience needs.

Would you like to fine-tune this further?

This is a concise and useful prompt. It doesn't contain any more information than necessary and gives clear instructions on how it should be handled. Copy this prompt and try it yourself to see what the output looks like.

Feel free to use the LLM to your advantage in this way. Have it refine your prompts, and experiment and make changes until you get exactly what you're looking for. This type of prompt tuning can be very beneficial to you as a programmer.

9.4 *Fundamental prompt types*

Prompts can be simple questions, statements, or complex instructions. The type of prompt you use depends on the task at hand. There are many styles and types to choose from. Let's look at some fundamental prompt types—how they work and how we can use them (figure 9.4).

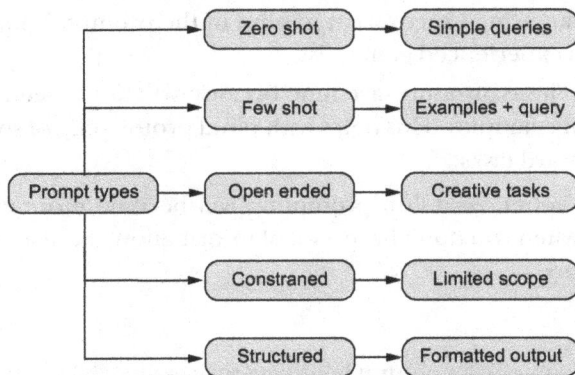

Figure 9.4 Most of your prompts will fall into one of these categories. The simplest being a zero-shot prompt, with few shot and structured prompts adding complexity. You can control the creativity with open ended or constrained prompts.

9.4.1 *Zero-shot prompting*

Zero-shot prompting allows LLMs to perform new tasks they weren't specifically trained for by using the knowledge they've already learned. They achieve this by relying on extensive training data already acquired. These are the types of prompts you've likely already used many times.

Imagine a student who has read a thousand books on a subject. Even if they have a problem they've never been taught to solve, they can use what they've learned from those books to figure it out. This is how models attempt to perform new tasks. A zero-shot prompt is one that gives very little context or background data to assist it. Here are some examples.

Here is a prompt for function creation:

> JM Write a Python function that calculates the factorial of a given number.

The following prompt is for data manipulation:

> JM Create a Python script to read a CSV file and print the first five rows.

And here is a prompt for algorithm improvements:

> JM Implement a Python function to perform a binary search on a sorted list.

As you can see, zero-shot prompts are very basic and concise. This is because the expectation is that the LLM will know what you don't know about how to solve the problem and produce a result.

The key benefits of zero-shot prompting include:

- *Simplicity and efficiency*—Zero-shot prompting requires minimal prompt engineering. These are quick, straightforward interactions. They don't require detailed examples or careful crafting of your prompt.
- *Versatility*—Zero-shot prompts employ preexisting model knowledge and handle tasks without the user knowing exactly what to send in the prompt. It makes the model function like an experienced generalist.
- *Resource optimization*—These prompts save time because you don't need to prep them or provide a lot of examples. This helps with rapid prototyping of solutions, and simple straightforward tasks.

As models get progressively better, zero-shot prompting will become more effective. Sometimes, these are useful when you don't have a lot of information about a problem, or you want quick, easy answers.

9.4.2 *Few-shot prompting*

Few-shot prompting is a technique from natural language processing (NLP). It enables LLMs to perform tasks after being provided with a few examples. Few-shot prompting lets models generate from just a few examples and taps into the pre-trained data. Here's an example:

> JM You are a Python developer. Here are a few examples of functions:
>
> 1 Function to calculate the square of a number:

```
def square(x):
    return x * x
```

2 Function to reverse a string:

```
def reverse_string(s):
    return s[::-1]
```

Now write a function that calculates the factorial of a number:

```
def factorial(n):
```

In this prompt, we're dictating what we're looking for. While it seems simple, this prompt is doing a lot. We're telling the model:

1 We want Python code.

2 Here is what a Python function looks like.

3 Here is the coding style we prefer.

4 The function calculates the factorial of a number.

This example shows two complete functions before requesting the third. However, it not only shows examples of what a function should look like, but sets the tone in that it shows which coding styles you prefer and how concise you'd like them to be. This approach maintains consistent formatting and shows clear patterns of what you think a function should look like, which can be valuable for steering the model in a direction you'd like.

Benefits of few-shot prompting include

- *Pattern recognition*—Models can understand the expected output format through concrete examples.
- *Style control*—Examples set clear expectations for coding style, formatting, and structure.
- *Context setting*—The prompt establishes the domain (e.g., "You are a Python developer") for more targeted responses.
- *Efficiency*—It reduces back-and-forth by showing exactly what you want.
- *Quality control*—It helps ensure consistent output by demonstrating preferred patterns.
- *Flexibility*—This type of prompt can be applied across various domains (not just coding).

9.4.3 *Open-ended prompts*

If you want a wide range of responses, the open-ended prompt is a great approach. It can generate creative and diverse results. These prompts are useful when searching for new ideas, generating creative content, or asking for advice.

Here are some examples of an open-ended prompt:

Describe how you would design a system to [specific task or problem] using Python. Consider scalability, performance, and potential edge cases.

> Given this Python code snippet [insert code], how would you refactor it to improve readability, efficiency, and maintainability? Explain your reasoning for each change.

> Compare and contrast Python frameworks like Django, Flask, and FastAPI for web development. In what scenarios would you choose one over the others?

We've used several examples of open-ended prompts and received good results. Sometimes, these are best for subjective questions and problems. However, this type of prompt has both positive and negative results. Benefits of open-ended prompts include

- Encouraging creativity and innovation
- Allowing for diverse perspectives and ideas
- Useful for brainstorming and planning

Here are some downsides:

- They can provide off topic or irrelevant results.
- It can be difficult to control the output.
- They provide opinions, and LLMs don't have opinions

Open-ended prompts are best for creative endeavors. If you're looking for more prescriptive results, constrained prompts may be a better choice.

9.4.4 *Constrained prompts*

These types of prompts limit the scope of the model's response. They provide specific guidelines based on the criteria you set. While there is no guarantee of accuracy in the results, they provide focused responses. Here are some examples of constrained prompts:

> List exactly three built-in Python data structures and provide one unique advantage for each.

> Write a Python function that calculates the Fibonacci sequence up to the 10th number. Use a maximum of 5 lines of code.

> Write a list comprehension in Python that generates the squares of even numbers from 1 to 20. The solution should be a single line of code.

These prompts are rather different from open-ended ones. The idea is to guide the results as much as possible, and it usually works well. Keep in mind that the models are still stochastic, and there's no guarantee they will follow the instructions. Benefits of constrained prompts include

- Focused, relevant responses
- Reducing the likelihood of off topic or irrelevant outputs
- Can be used for tasks requiring specific criteria

And here are some downsides:

- May limit creativity
- Don't provide new ideas
- Require careful design

When you know exactly what you need and aren't looking for new ideas, these prompts work great. They can be particularly useful in debugging or mock data generation. You can take the idea of constrained prompts a step further with structured prompts.

9.4.5 Using iterative prompts

Prompt engineering is the bridge between human intent and the tool output. It allows harnessing the full capability of models and obtaining the results you want. Let's check out a quick example. Here, I am prompting an LLM model (Llama 3) on my own machine and attempting to get an answer to a math problem. As we discussed earlier, LLMs aren't great at arithmetic. However, there are some things you can do to improve accuracy.

Here, we use an iterative process. This is a fancy way of saying "discussing the problem with an LLM like in a conversation." We'll send a prompt, get the results, and make changes until we get what we're looking for.

Let's take a simple problem. We want to multiply 234 by 432. We know the answer should be 101,088. But let's ask our LLM to calculate this. I start with a simple prompt:

JM 234 x 432

If I send this prompt as is to my Llama 3 model, I get this confidently wrong answer:

∞ The value 234x432 is equal to:
234 x 432 = 98,136

Why is that? Because LLMs still aren't set up to perform mathematical functions very well. You must give them clues.

Let's add some additional information to our prompt. We'll tell Llama 3 to explicitly multiply the values:

JM What is 234 multiplied by 432?

And now we get a different answer (that's still wrong):

∞ Multiplying 234 by 432 gives us:
234 × 432 = 96,072

We aren't getting the results we want, so let's make some changes. We'll add in a cue and suggest the model try three different methods. Then we'll choose the one that's most likely to be accurate. We'll also ask the model to show its work.

Here's the prompt:

> JM Let's calculate the product of 234 x 432 using three different methods. Choose the one that's the most accurate. Use the common steps for long multiplication. Show your work.

The result of this prompt is quite complex, because we've asked the model to show its work. This is one method that often makes the LLM produce better results, as you are guiding the model to think things through better. Here are the results:

> ∞ Let's calculate the product of 234 x 432 using three different methods.
>
> **Method 1: Multiplication by hand**
> We can multiply the numbers as follows:
> 432
> +234
> _____
> ? ?
> To calculate, we multiply each digit in the ones place (4) with 234 and then add up all the partial products.
> +0 + 0 = 0 4 * 200 = 800 + 0 = 800 4 * 30 = 120 + 800 = 920 4 * 3 = 12 + 920 = 932 +234 = 1166
> 101,088
>
> **Method 2: Using a calculator**
> Using a basic calculator, we can simply type in the numbers and multiply them.
> 234 x 432 = 100,832
>
> **Method 3: Using long multiplication with an algorithm**
> To calculate using long multiplication with an algorithm, we first multiply the ones place by 432:
> 4 * 432 = 1728
> Then, we multiply the tens place (30) by 432:
> 30 * 432 = 12,960
> Next, we multiply the hundreds place (200) by 432:
> 200 * 432 = 86,400
> Now, we add up all the partial products, taking care to align the digits correctly.
> 1728 + 12960 = 14688 14688 + 86400 = 101088 101088 + 0 (ones place) = 101088
> 101,088
> Based on these three methods, we can see that the product of 234 x 432 is consistently 101,088. Therefore, the final answer is:
> **101,088**

This result is consistent across all three methods, so it's safe to conclude that this is the correct result. This gave us an accurate answer. However, if you run the exact same prompt multiple times, you will get a few bad answers. This is again due to the stochastic nature of LLMs. They aren't made for computation, and thankfully, we have other tools for that. However, we did use a few techniques to try and narrow it down and make a more accurate answer than what we started from.

We used a set of steps to refine the answer with these techniques:

- *Explicit instructions*—Each prompt got more specific.
- *Multiple methods*—We tried several ways to approach the problem.
- *Asking to show the work*—This is a trick used to make models think through a process.
- *Context cues*—Cues are used to guide the model toward the appropriate technique.

This sort of reiterative process is sometimes necessary to get the right prompt and the information you need, and we'll be doing more of it as we progress. Let's dig deeper into prompt engineering for a better understanding of ways we can fine tune the information we get from prompts.

9.4.6 *Structured prompts*

When you need to guide the model through a predefined format, structured prompts can come in handy. I have found the following most useful for documentation and presentations around software. These prompts are more specific than constrained prompts. What follows is a structured prompt example:

1 Create a comprehensive guide for optimizing Python code performance. Include the following sections:
   - Profiling techniques
   - Common bottlenecks
   - Optimization strategies
   - Algorithm improvements
   - Data structure choices
   - Use of built-in functions and libraries
   - Multiprocessing and multithreading
   - Best practices and tips
2 Provide a structured overview of our custom Python library:
   a Introduction
   b Core concepts
   c Coroutines
   d Event loops
   e Futures and Tasks

f   Basic usage
g   Advanced features
h   Real-world use cases

These types of prompts allow you to dictate exactly how the information should be generated. Again, there is no guarantee the results will follow the format you specify, but most of the time, they do. This approach works great for documentation and Wiki's for your software. The benefits of structured prompts include

- Providing comprehensive and organized results
- Useful for tasks requiring detailed analysis or structured information
- Generating complex outputs

Here are some of the downsides:

- They require more effort and time to design.
- It's challenging to balance structure with flexibility.

Which type of prompt you will use depends heavily on what you're looking to produce. Let's dig deeper into some of the use cases for each.

USE CASES: OPEN-ENDED PROMPTS

- *Software design*—Brainstorm and explore different ideas when planning a new software project.
- *Code review*—Analyze your existing code and generate ideas for improvements.
- *Problem solving*—Generate creative solutions for tricky problems or design challenges

USE CASES: CONSTRAINED PROMPTS

- *Quick reference*—Get explanations or examples of specific programming concepts such as data structures, language features or best practices.
- *Testing*—Create specific test cases or edge cases for functions and modules.
- *Code optimization*—Generate efficient solutions for specific coding tasks with established constraints.

USE CASES: STRUCTURED PROMPTS

- *Project setup guide*—Build a comprehensive guide for setting up or installing your software, with specific guidelines for how it should look.
- *Library documentation*—Document your custom libraries with a consistent structure and common format.
- *Code review checklist*—Create a structured checklist for code review policies to be followed with each review.

These are the basic core principles you should follow with prompt design. The next section explores some more advanced topics.

9.5 Advanced prompt types

Let's look at some advanced prompting techniques. We'll learn five ways to get better results: chain of thought, recursive prompting, context manipulation, instruction refinement, and output control (figure 9.5).

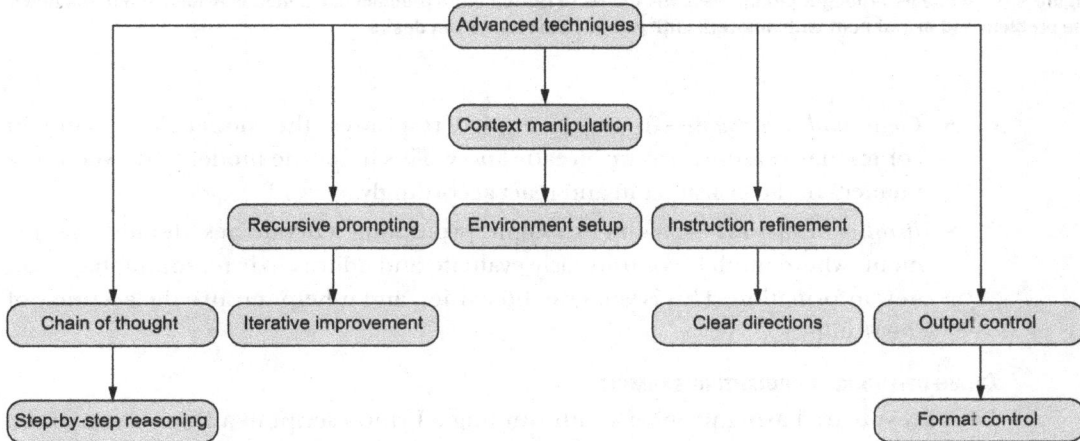

Figure 9.5 **For advanced prompts, you'll need to provide a lot more information. You need to manipulate context and examples, refine your instruction, and dictate the output. You can also use recursive and chain-of-thought prompting to get the model to think about the answers.**

Each method helps make AI responses more accurate and useful, especially when writing code or technical documents. By learning these methods, developers can get clearer and more reliable answers from AI systems. You can use them alone or combine them for the best results.

9.5.1 Chain-of-thought prompting

Chain-of-thought prompting mimics the sequential nature of human thought processes to guide AI models. Rather than a basic input to output, it mimics the way we think and breaks down complex problems into smaller, more manageable steps. It enables models to reason through tasks and create a (hopefully) more accurate answer. We've already done this a few times, and we're going to dig deeper. Let's see what makes a chain-of-thought prompt tick (figure 9.6).

KEY COMPONENTS

The key components of the chain-of-thought prompting are

- *Sequential reasoning*—The prompt breaks down the problem into a series of logical steps, allowing the model to process information more efficiently.

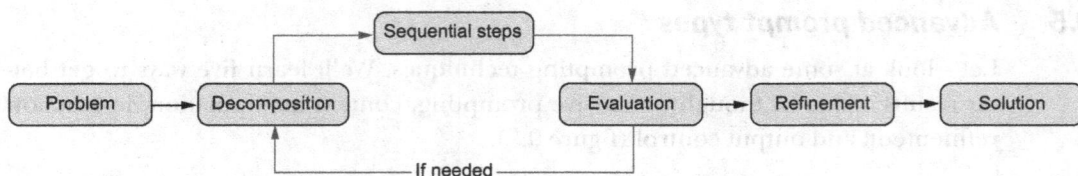

Figure 9.6   A chain-of-thought prompt gets the model to reason out a problem like a human would. You break down the problem and experiment with answers until you get the results you desire.

- *Contextual awareness*—To generate good responses, the model must maintain contextual awareness, as we already know. This helps the model understand the nuances of the task at hand and react accordingly.
- *Iterative refinement*—Chain-of-thought prompting encourages iterative refinement, where models continuously evaluate and adjust their reasoning based on new information. This is what we did earlier, and it helps ensure the accuracy of the results.

CHAIN-OF-THOUGHT PROMPTING EXAMPLE

Let's say you are having problems with running a Python script in a Docker container. You're not an expert on Docker and using a search engine doesn't seem to help you. Here's how you can use prompts to walk through the problem and find the error:

> I have a Python application running inside a Docker container, but the application is failing to start or crashes unexpectedly. Can you help me diagnose and resolve the issue step by step?
>
> First, I can check if the container is running or has exited using docker ps -a. What does this output really tell me?
>
> If the container is stopped, how can I view the container logs using docker logs to check for any Python application errors?
>
> If the container is running, how can I access it and examine the Python application's internal logs for potential errors?
>
> How can I verify that the correct Python version and dependencies are installed in the container? What commands can I run to check this?
>
> Can you help me check the Dockerfile for misconfigurations, such as the base image or commands that might affect how the application starts?
>
> What commands can I use to inspect the container's network settings and port configurations to ensure they are set up correctly?
>
> After each step, how can I rebuild and restart the container to test for changes and narrow down the issue?

This example requires some human effort to break down the problem and ask questions for each part. This can be one single prompt or a series of prompts, sequentially. For instance, if you check what the output of ps -a means, you'll find that your container is stopped. Then you move to the next question about the container being stopped and work your way through the problem.

What if you don't know what to ask? The previous example assumes you know a bit about containers, but they could be a mystery to you. The good news is, you can ask the model what prompts to use, each step of the way. Let's break down how that works.

STEP 1: PROBLEM DECOMPOSITION

The first step is to break down the problem into a series of smaller, more manageable steps. If you don't know what to ask, you can send a prompt like this:

> Decompose the following task into a series of smaller, manageable steps. The goal is to send an HTTP GET request to an API using Python's requests library, display the response, and handle potential errors. Provide a clear and logical sequence of subtasks needed to achieve this.
>
> This will help you break down the problem and see what steps to take.

STEP 2: PROMPT DESIGN

Once the problem has been decomposed, you want to design the prompts that will guide the model though the reasoning process. These prompts should encourage the model to think critically about the problem:

For initializing the request, *e*xplain how to initialize an HTTP GET request using Python's requests library. Focus on best practices and include error handling.

For displaying the response, ask

> How can you display the response body from an API request in Python? Provide a concise code snippet along with any important considerations.

For error handling, you can say

> Explain the best practices for handling potential errors in an API request using Python's requests library, including network errors and non-200 responses.

Notice how each prompt encourages critical thinking, while focusing on a specific part of the problem.

STEP 3: ITERATIVE EVALUATION

Throughout this process, you should continuously evaluate the responses. Treat this like a human conversation, where you don't have to be polite. If you aren't getting the results you want, frame the prompt in a different way and refine it. Doing this frequently will help you learn new techniques to get the answers you're looking for. You can also use the LLM for this second step of refinement to do a sanity check on your work.

For evaluating the initialization step, you can use

> Review the code provided for initializing an HTTP GET request using Python's requests library. Is the code efficient, does it follow best practices, and is error handling sufficiently robust? If not, suggest improvements.

For evaluating response display, use

> JM Evaluate the response display method provided. Is the approach clear, concise, and capable of handling different types of API responses (e.g., JSON, text)? If there are shortcomings, offer better alternatives.

For evaluating error handling, use

> JM Assess the error handling logic in the generated API request code. Does it cover common error scenarios like connection issues or timeouts? Is the handling of non-200 HTTP status codes adequate? Provide suggestions for improvement if necessary.

Iterative evaluation helps you stay on the right path by validating each step and ensuring accuracy in the responses. Just for fun, you can use different LLMs to check each other. I've often switched between ChatGPT, Claude, and Blackbox AI LLM chat windows to check my results as I go.

STEP 4: FEEDBACK INTEGRATION

You can take the output from the previous steps and refine them further. This encourages the model to refine and optimize its responses based on its own advice. In this final step, you'll likely see a very accurate and well thought out response that you wouldn't be able to achieve from a single one-shot prompt.

For refining initialization based on feedback, you can say

> JM Incorporate the following feedback into the code for initializing an HTTP GET request: Use connection pooling for better performance and include timeouts to handle network delays. Revise the code accordingly.

For improving response handling based on feedback, use

> JM Given the feedback that the current response handling is too simplistic, revise the code to handle both JSON and text responses more effectively. Ensure that the updated version addresses these concerns.

For enhancing error handling based on feedback, use

> JM Feedback indicated that the error handling logic doesn't account for HTTP 5xx errors. Refine the error handling in the API request code to include specific handling for server-side errors, ensuring a clear and actionable error message is logged.

For general performance improvements, ask

> JM Use the following feedback to optimize the entire process: improve readability by adding comments, refactor the error handling logic for better maintainability, and ensure all edge cases are covered. Revise the code accordingly.

Chain-of-thought prompting is beneficial in two ways—it helps the model think through the problem, and more importantly, it forces *you* to think through the problem and alter how *you* communicate with the LLM. In our discussion, I have humanized the

LLM a bit to explain the concepts. It seems silly because the AI model has no thoughts, opinions, or personality. However, treating it like a person and improving your communication skills will produce better results.

Here are some key benefits of chain-of-thought prompting:

- *Better problem-solving*—It breaks down hard problems into smaller, manageable steps. It also attempts to mimic how humans think and reasons step by step.

- *Improved accuracy and quality control*—It lets you check each step as you go and makes it easier to find mistakes by looking at each step. It allows for careful thinking about unusual cases.

- *Continuous improvement*—Chain-of-thought prompting supports ongoing checking and enhancing as it goes. It allows feedback to be added at each stage. This feature improves results based on earlier steps and encourages critical thinking about responses.

- *Understanding context*—The model maintains awareness throughout solving the problem, which helps the model understand and address small details, enabling more exact and relevant answers.

- *Flexible framework*—Chain-of-thought prompting works for many types of problem and topics. It's good for both technical and other types of problems. It lets you adjust your approach as needed and can be scaled based on complexity.

Chain-of-thought prompting is very useful for code generation, bug detection (and fixing), algorithm optimization, and more. It's an incredible technique to have in your tool belt for writing good code. Next, let's look at recursive prompting.

9.5.2 Recursive prompting

Recursive prompting is a technique that relies on iteratively refining and improving the response generated by a model. Instead of producing an answer in one step, recursive prompting breaks it into stages. This approach is particularly useful for complex tasks, where the initial response might be incomplete or require further clarification (figure 9.7).

By continuously feeding the output of one stage into the next, recursive prompting helps improve the quality and accuracy of the result. This can be very handy for code generation. Here is how recursive prompting works:

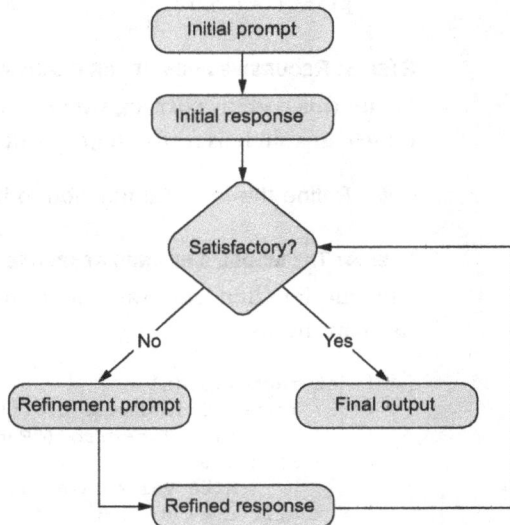

Figure 9.7 Recursive prompting works by breaking the answer down into stages.

1 *Initial prompt*—The user provides an initial prompt to the model, asking for a solution or response.

2 *Refinement*—The model generates an initial response, which is then analyzed or critiqued.

3 *Recursive input*—The user (or the model itself) refines the prompt based on the initial response, asking for improvements or corrections.

4 *Iterative process*—This cycle repeats until the desired level of quality or accuracy is achieved.

What follows is a good recursive prompting example showing the steps.

STEP 1: INITIAL PROMPT

Let's start with a basic prompt asking to solve a problem:

> JM Write a Python function to calculate the factorial of a number.

STEP 2: MODEL'S INITIAL RESPONSE

The model generates a response:

```python
def factorial(n):
    if n < 0:
        raise ValueError("Factorial is not defined for negative numbers.")
    elif n == 0 or n == 1:
        return 1
    else:
        return n * factorial(n - 1)

# Example usage
print(factorial(5))  # Output: 120
```

STEP 3: RECURSIVE PROMPT FOR REFINEMENT

While this code is correct, we now want to refine it further. Let's make it handle some edge cases such as non-integers and negative numbers:

> JM Refine the factorial function to handle negative numbers and non-integer inputs.

STEP 4: THE MODEL'S REFINED RESPONSE

The model then generates a refined version of the code, based on the requested improvements.

```python
def factorial(n):
    if not isinstance(n, int) or isinstance(n, bool):
        raise TypeError("Factorial is only defined for integers.")
    if n < 0:
        raise ValueError("Factorial is not defined for negative numbers.")
    elif n == 0 or n == 1:
        return 1
    else:
        return n * factorial(n - 1)
```

```
# Example usage
print(factorial(5))  # Output: 120
```

This is now a better result than the original because we can continue to iterate on it and narrow down the exact result we want.

STEP 5: FURTHER REFINEMENT

This step is optional, but we can further refine it from here.

> (JM) Optimize the factorial function using an iterative approach instead of recursion.

This prompt produces the following result:

```
def factorial(n):
    if not isinstance(n, int) or isinstance(n, bool):
        raise TypeError("Factorial is only defined for integers.")
    if n < 0:
        raise ValueError("Factorial is not defined for negative numbers.")

    result = 1
    for i in range(2, n + 1):
        result *= i

    return result

# Example usage
print(factorial(5))  # Output: 120
```

Recursive prompting is a systematic approach to achieving higher-quality outputs through iterative refinement. Rather than accepting the first response, it uses a step-by-step process of evaluation and improvement, making it particularly valuable for complex tasks such as code development, writing, and problem-solving. Our example demonstrated how a basic factorial function evolved from a simple implementation to a robust, optimized solution through multiple iterations of targeted refinements.

The key benefits of recursive prompting include:

- *Incremental improvement*—Rather than trying to get perfect results in one shot, recursive prompting breaks down improvement into manageable steps.
- *Quality control*—Each iteration provides an opportunity to evaluate and enhance specific aspects of the solution, leading to more reliable and robust results.
- *Specificity in refinement*—Each recursive prompt should focus on specific improvements (such as handling edge cases or optimization), making the refinement process more effective.
- *Flexibility*—The technique can be adapted to different types of tasks and can continue until the desired quality level is reached.
- *Educational value*—The iterative nature helps in understanding how solutions can be progressively improved, making it a valuable learning tool.

9.5.3 *Context manipulation*

Context manipulation involves setting up an optimal environment within the prompt to help a model generate accurate and relevant responses. By controlling the context in which the model operates, users can influence the output's quality, consistency, and specificity, especially in tasks requiring clarity and precision. Context manipulation involves priming the model with relevant information, presenting examples within the prompt, and utilizing system messages to maintain the desired behavior (figure 9.8).

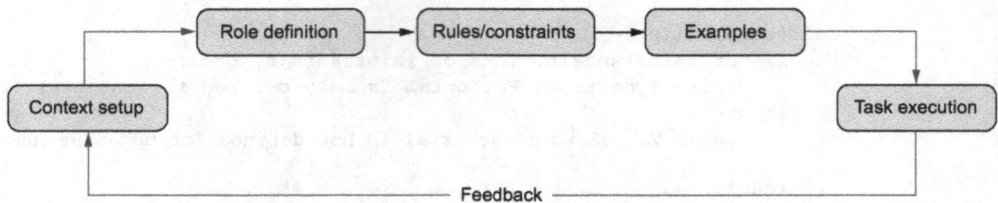

Figure 9.8   **With context manipulation, you can supply as much or as little context as you want, which will change your results. Creating proper context ensures the model has plenty of information to base its answer on.**

Context manipulation can be handy for generating code, troubleshooting problems, or formatting documentation to adhere to a specific style. By establishing a clear context, the model can more effectively interpret requests, understand nuances in syntax, and anticipate particular coding needs.

WHEN TO USE CONTEXT MANIPULATION

As a Python programmer, you might want to use context manipulation to

- Guide the model to generate code that adheres to specific styles or patterns
- Ensure consistency across functions or modules by maintaining a specific context or tone in outputs
- Simplify complex requests by providing initial parameters or examples, helping the model stay focused on relevant details
- Generate explanations or documentation that match a preexisting structure, enabling smooth integration with existing codebases

Whether coding, debugging, or documenting, context manipulation can significantly improve the quality and efficiency of your interactions with the model. I use it frequently.

Here is an example of context manipulation. Let's say you want to create a Python script for processing data files but require that the code consistently uses the pandas library and adheres to a specific function structure.

STEP 1: INITIAL SETUP

Start with a prompt that establishes the role, rules, and intent:

> You are a Python assistant. Always use the `pandas` library for data manipulation tasks, and structure your code with a function called `process_data`. Avoid using any other libraries unless specified.

Then prompt with contextual example:

> Write a function named `process_data` that reads a CSV file, filters rows where the `age` column exceeds 30, and returns the result sorted by age.

Here is the model's response:

```python
import pandas as pd

def process_data(file_path):
    df = pd.read_csv(file_path)
    filtered_df = df[df['age'] > 30]
    sorted_df = filtered_df.sort_values(by='age')
    return sorted_df
```

This technique allows the model to interpret and respond consistently based on your preferred context. By guiding the prompt with context manipulation, the model adheres to the expected library and function structure, making the generated code easy to incorporate into a larger project. It's not perfect by any means, but most of the time, it works well.

ADVANTAGES OF CONTEXT MANIPULATION

Using context manipulation effectively helps build better code and documentation faster. Here are some key advantages:

- *Better consistency*—Setting the context means setting expectations. When we do this, the model's answers match specific coding styles, structures, or libraries. This is important when working with multiple files or parts of a project.
- *Improved efficiency*—Giving the model clear context up front reduces the need to explain or fix things, saving time and making the coding process smoother.
- *Better code readability*—Context manipulation helps the model stick to a consistent approach, making the code easier to understand and maintain across different areas of the application.
- *Increased control*—By giving examples and starting instructions, you can guide the model toward certain coding practices, keeping standards in line with your project or company requirements.

Adding context manipulation to your prompt engineering tools can improve the quality and reliability of model-generated results. It is a helpful way to manage code style, keep things consistent, and follow best practices in your programming tasks.

9.5.4   *Instruction refinement*

Instruction refinement is a helpful prompt engineering technique that creates clear and specific directions to get better responses from AI models. By carefully writing and improving these instructions, developers can make sure the AI gives more accurate and useful code or documentation. This technique is especially useful in Python programming, where clear instructions help produce code that is easier to understand and use (figure 9.9).

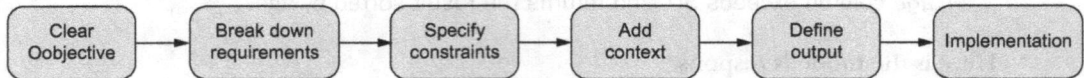

Figure 9.9   Instruction refinement is a process where you get as specific as you can, break down your requirements, and tell the model exactly what you expect for output.

It's all about crafting well-structured instructions that eliminate ambiguity. Think of it like writing out your directions for a recipe: the clearer and more detailed, the better the result. This is a combination of many techniques we've been discussing throughout the book.

HOW DOES INSTRUCTION REFINEMENT WORK?

Instruction refinement is another way to take complex requests and break them down step by step. It gives the model an opportunity to think. When refining the instructions, here's what we want to do:

1 *Start with a clear objective.* Define what you want the code to accomplish.
2 *Break down complex requirements.* Separate them into bite-sized, actionable steps.
3 *Specify constraints and preferences.* Be clear about any limits or specific methods you'd like used.
4 *Include relevant context.* Add any background info that might help the AI better understand the task.
5 *Define expected output.* If you know the format of the result, spell it out!

The key here is to add as much detail as possible. While this technique is comprised of prompting best practices, there's a heavy focus on narrowing down the results as much as possible with details. The results are not very creative, so this type of refinement isn't suited for creative endeavors.

WHEN TO USE INSTRUCTION REFINEMENT

Instruction refinement comes in handy when

- Tackling complex algorithms or data structures
- Creating boilerplate code that must adhere to certain standards
- Writing documentation to fit team conventions

- Debugging or refactoring code with specific requirements
- Implementing features with interdependent components

Let's examine how instruction refinement can improve the quality of generated Python code. For example, we want a function to process JSON data and save it to a database. Here is the unrefined prompt:

> JM   Write a function to process JSON data and save it to a database.

Not very specific, right? With this level of detail, the results are unpredictable. Let's refine it with additional important details:

> JM   Create a Python function that:
>   1 Accepts a JSON file path and database connection string as parameters
>   2 Validates the JSON structure contains required fields: `user_id`, `timestamp`, `data`
>   3 Transforms the data by:
>   – Converting timestamps to datetime objects
>   – Normalizing user IDs to lowercase
>   4 Handles errors with appropriate try-except blocks
>   5 Uses SQLAlchemy for database operations
>   6 Returns a tuple of (`success_boolean`, `processed_count`)
>
> Follow these constraints:
> - Use type hints for all parameters and return values
> - Log errors using the logging module
> - Implement connection pooling for database operations

The refined instruction typically results in more precise and useful code:

```python
from datetime import datetime
import json
import logging
from typing import Tuple
from sqlalchemy import create_engine
from sqlalchemy.orm import sessionmaker

def process_json_data(
    json_path: str,
    db_connection_string: str
) -> Tuple[bool, int]:
    """
    Process JSON data and save to database with validation and error handling.

    Args:
        json_path: Path to JSON file
        db_connection_string: Database connection string

    Returns:
```

```
                Tuple of (success status, number of records processed)
        """
        logging.basicConfig(level=logging.INFO)
        processed_count = 0

        try:
            # Set up database connection
            engine = create_engine(db_connection_string, pool_size=5)
            Session = sessionmaker(bind=engine)

            # Read and validate JSON
            with open(json_path, 'r') as file:
                data = json.load(file)

            # Process records
            with Session() as session:
                for record in data:
                    if all(key in record for key in
    ['user_id', 'timestamp', 'data']):
                        record['user_id'] = record['user_id'].lower()
                        record['timestamp'] = datetime.
    fromisoformat(record['timestamp'])
                        processed_count += 1
                    else:
                        logging.error(f"
    Missing required fields in record: {record}")

            return True, processed_count

        except Exception as e:
            logging.error(f"Error processing data: {str(e)}")
            return False, processed_count
    ```
```

By breaking things down and adding clarity, we can get the model to produce something more predictable. After all (at the time of this writing), an LLM cannot read your mind.

#### ADVANTAGES OF INSTRUCTION REFINEMENT

By incorporating instruction refinement into your prompt engineering practice, you can significantly improve the quality and reliability of your Python development workflow. This technique not only enhances the immediate output but also contributes to better long-term maintainability and scalability of your codebase. The advantages include

- *Improved code quality*—Precise requirements reduce ambiguity and encourage consistent implementation.
- *Enhanced maintainability*—Clear instructions make for clean, documented code that's easier to update.
- *Better efficiency*—Less time wasted on reworking or debugging because your initial instructions were solid.
```

- *Using instruction*—Refinement doesn't just help you now. It creates a codebase that's reliable and easier to scale in the future. If you can produce the details, you'll get a better, more consistent prompt. Now let's take a more detailed look at outputs.

9.5.5 Output control

Output control is another method for fine-tuning AI-generated responses. Whether you're crafting Python code, generating documentation, or processing data, having some control over the AI's output is important. By setting clear guidelines, you can make sure that the output not only looks good but follows specific rules and formats (figure 9.10).

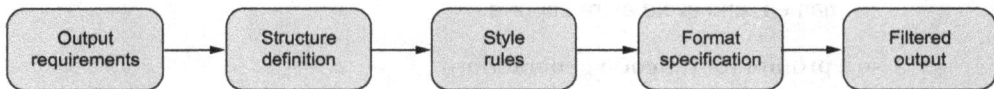

Output requirements → Structure definition → Style rules → Format specification → Filtered output

Figure 9.10 Output control is used when you need the response to fit into a particular format such as JSON, SQL, or many other standard formats.

Imagine you need code that sticks to Python's PEP 8 guidelines or insists on `snake_case` for variable names. If you spell this out in your prompt, you'll get responses that follow your standards. This is yet another way to make more predictable results from a model.

HOW DOES OUTPUT CONTROL WORK?

Output control is very similar to instruction refinement, and they're usually used together. It's setting the rules of engagement for your AI output. It can mean defining the length of a response, specifying a layout (like a bullet list or a set of numbered steps), or even enforcing a certain tone. Let's break down some ways to use it:

- *Define output structure.* Want bullet points, numbered lists, or JSON format? Just specify it.
- *Limit irrelevant info.* Use filters to keep the AI focused on what you need.
- *Enforce* style rules. If you need code that's PEP 8-compliant or uses `snake_case`, set those guidelines right in your prompt. This goes for multiple styles in different languages of course.

WHEN TO USE OUTPUT CONTROL

When does output control really shine? Here are the best uses:

- *Formatting matters*—If you need a specific structure, like JSON for an API, output control helps you stick to it.
- *Consistency across outputs*—For long projects. such as multipart documentation or lots of code snippets, output control helps keep things uniform.

- *Filtering unwanted details*—When only certain information is relevant, filters keep the output clean and relevant.

- *Ensuring coherence in complex outputs*—When you need the model to handle detailed instructions, output control keeps the flow logical and readable.

EXAMPLE: OUTPUT CONTROL IN PYTHON DEVELOPMENT

Let's say you're working with Python and need to generate code to process JSON data, but you want to keep it consistent with PEP 8, use `snake_case`, and avoid any unnecessary imports.

First, set up the output structure and constraints:

> You are a Python code assistant. Generate a function called `process_json_data` that reads JSON data, filters out entries where the `status` field is `inactive`, and returns the result in dictionary format. Follow PEP 8, use `snake_case` for variable names, and avoid extra imports.

Use a prompt for function generation:

> Write a function `process_json_data` that filters out entries with `inactive` status from provided JSON data and returns a dictionary of the results:

Here is the model's response:

```
import json
def process_json_data(json_data):
        active_entries = {key: value for key, value in json_data.items()
if value.get('status') == 'active'}
return active_entries
```

This approach ensures the output is concise, clean, and adheres to PEP 8. With output control, we get exactly what we asked for: specific formatting, focused content, and even limited imports.

WHY USE OUTPUT CONTROL?

Here are some of the reasons why you might need output control in your prompts:

- *Enhanced readability*—Clear, structured responses are easier to follow, which is perfect for documentation or step-by-step guides.

- *Consistency across outputs*—Especially useful for long projects, output control helps you maintain a standard look and feel.

- *Improved focus*—Filtering out extraneous info keeps responses focused and relevant.

- *Better workflow integration*—Structured outputs are easier to plug into workflows or formatted documents.

Output control empowers Python developers to create model-generated outputs that meet specific standards, thus reducing manual adjustment and boosting productivity. Give it a try next time you need precise, polished output.

9.5.6 Wrap up

In this chapter, we examined five ways to get better results from AI models. Chain of thought breaks big problems into smaller steps, just the way people think through problems. Recursive prompting uses a step-by-step process to make answers better over time. Context manipulation helps set up the right background info to get more accurate answers. Instruction refinement focuses on writing clear directions. Output control helps shape how the AI presents its answers.

These methods work together to help developers get the best results from AI. We used real examples and code to show how these ideas work in practice. Feel free to implement one or more of these techniques the next time you open a chat window.

Let's wrap up this chapter by reviewing prompt methods that support everyday software development tasks.

9.6 Prompt techniques for programmers

The prompt engineering advice in previous sections is helpful in software development and can be used for a variety of tasks with chat models. Now, let's look a little deeper at software-development-focused prompt techniques. We'll go through some of these fast and show them in action.

9.6.1 Examples

- Specifying architectural patterns and design principles you want to follow up front:

Generate a REST API using the repository pattern and SOLID principles. The API should handle user authentication with the following requirements: [...]

- Using XML tags to force structured output when you need specific segments parsed by your application:

Generate a JavaScript function that validates email addresses.
Provide the response in these sections:

```
<requirements>...</requirements>
<implementation>...</implementation>
<tests>...</tests>
```

- Use a role-reversal prompt to have the LLM diagnose and explain coding errors as though guiding a colleague:

You're a senior developer explaining this error to a junior. What's causing it and how would you fix it?
Error: `TypeError: Cannot read property 'map' of undefine`

- Breaking complex coding tasks down using numbered steps and asking the LLM to implement one step at a time:

JM Let's build a caching system step by step:
  1 First, show me the cache interface definition
  2 Then implement an in-memory cache
  3 Finally, add cache eviction policies

- Using the chain-of-thought prompting by asking the LLM to explain its reasoning regarding architectural decisions before writing code:

JM Before implementing the user authentication system, explain your thought process about choosing between JWT vs session-based auth for our microservices architecture.

- Specifying edge cases and boundary conditions explicitly in your prompt when generating test cases:

JM Write unit tests for a function that processes age restrictions.
   Include tests for: negative values, zero, fractional ages, maximum integer value, and null/undefined inputs.

- For code reviews, creating a specific checklist of what you want the LLM to look for:

JM Review this code for:
  1 Security vulnerabilities
  2 Performance bottlenecks
  3 Error handling
  4 Code duplication
  5 SOLID principles violations

- Using few-shot prompting with explicit examples when you want code in a specific style or pattern:

JM Generate error handling middleware following this pattern: [example 1] [example 2].
   Now create similar middleware for logging and authentication.

- Specifying performance constraints and requirements upfront when optimizing code:

JM Optimize this database query to handle 1000 concurrent users with response time under 100ms. Current code: [...]

- For API design, using scenario-based prompting to consider different use cases:

JM Design a REST API for a shopping cart that handles these scenarios:
   Guest user adds items

User logs in, merges cart

Checkout process with failed payment

- Specifying the target audience and technical level explicitly when generating documentation:

(JM) Write API documentation for this endpoint targeting junior developers who are familiar with REST but new to our authentication system, and authentication in general.

- Using comparative prompting to understand tradeoffs between different technical approaches:

(JM) Compare MongoDB vs PostgreSQL for our user management system, considering: scalability, query complexity, data consistency requirements, and maintenance overhead,

- Providing both the current code and specific code smells you want to address for refactoring tasks:

(JM) Refactor this code to eliminate the following issues: long method, duplicate logic, and tight coupling. Current code: [...]

- Requesting design alternatives and evaluating tradeoffs before applying a specific pattern:

(JM) What design patterns could handle dynamic pricing calculations? Explain tradeoffs between Strategy, Template, and Chain of Responsibility before implementing the best choice.

- Using "anti-pattern" prompting to understand what not to do in implementations:

(JM) What are the common anti-patterns when implementing caching in a microservices architecture, and how should we avoid them in this code: [...]

- For security-related code, explicitly requesting OWASP compliance and security best practices:

(JM) Generate a user input validation middleware that follows OWASP security guidelines and prevents XSS, SQL injection, and CSRF attacks.

- Asking for time and space complexity analysis alongside the implementation when generating complex algorithms:

(JM) Implement a solution for finding duplicate files in a directory tree. Include Big O analysis for time and space complexity, and explain any tradeoffs made.

- Using component-first prompting for frontend development to ensure maintainable architecture:

> **JM** Before building the dashboard, show me the component hierarchy and data flow diagram. Then implement each component starting from leaf nodes.

- For database schema design, providing business rules and constraints in a structured format:

> **JM** Design a database schema for an e-learning platform where:
> 1 Users can enroll in multiple courses
> 2 Each course has multiple modules
> 3 Progress is tracked per module

- Specifying the exact error scenarios and recovery strategies when implementing error handling:

> **JM** Implement retry logic for this API client with:
> 1 Maximum 3 retries
> 2 Exponential backoff
> 3 Circuit breaker pattern for persistent failures

- Using state-transition prompting for implementing complex workflows:

> **JM** Create a state machine for order processing that handles:
> pending → paid → processing → shipped → delivered,
> with error states for each transition.

- In case of performance optimization, providing specific metrics and profiling data:

> **JM** This API endpoint is taking 2s to respond. Here' s the flame graph and DB query execution plan. Suggest and implement optimizations to get response time under 200ms.

- Identifying environment-specific requirements clearly when generating configuration files:

> **JM** Generate Docker compose files for development, staging, and production environments. Dev should have hot-reload, staging should have monitoring, and production should have high availability.

- For logging implementations, specifying the exact data points needed for observability:

JM　Implement structured logging that captures: timestamp, service name, trace ID, user ID, operation name, duration, and error details in JSON format.

- Using scenario-based testing prompts to generate comprehensive test suites:

JM　Generate integration tests for the payment processing module covering: successful payments, declined cards, network timeouts, partial refunds, and chargeback scenarios.

- Specifying backward compatibility requirements clearly for API versioning:

JM　Show how to implement API versioning that:
1 Maintains support for v1
2 Introduces breaking changes in v2
3 Provides migration documentation for clients

- Using attack-scenario prompting when implementing authentication:

JM　Implement JWT authentication that prevents: token replay attacks, timing attacks, brute force attempts, and token theft via XSS.

- In caching strategies implementation, explicitly specifying cache invalidation rules:

JM　Implement cache management for product data with these rules:
1 Invalidate after price changes
2 TTL of 1 hour
3 Bulk invalidation during sales events

- Specifying type hints and docstring format preferences to get more maintainable code when generating Python classes:

JM　Create a `User` class with type hints using Python 3.10+ features. Include Google-style docstrings and handle these attributes: `username (str)`, `login_attempts (int)`, `last_login (datetime)`.

- Using maintenance-focused prompting for generating sustainable code:

JM　Implement this feature assuming it will be maintained by a different team in 6 months. Include: clear naming, comprehensive comments, logging, monitoring, and documentation.

In this chapter, you've learned about powerful tools that can improve your interactions with AI coding assistants. By mastering prompt engineering basics and using strategies such as chain-of-thought reasoning, recursive refinement, and output control, you can enhance the quality of AI-generated code.

Effective prompting is a skill that grows with practice. Start using these techniques in your workflow, watch the results, and develop your own style with AI tools. Spending time on better prompts will lead to more accurate code, fewer revisions, and a more productive development experience.

Summary

- Proficiency in engineering fundamentals plays a pivotal role in engaging productively with LLMs and LLM-based programming tools.
- A solid grasp of different prompt types, such as zero-shot, few-shot, structured, and constrained prompts, is key to using each effectively for optimal results.
- Advanced techniques such as chain-of-thought and recursive prompting can be used to break down complex problems and refine solutions iteratively.
- By manipulating context and honing instructional input, users can enhance the accuracy and relevance of LLM outputs.
- Output format and structure can be effectively managed through deliberate prompt engineering strategies.
- Specialized programming prompts that focus on code architecture, testing, security, and documentation can be used to improve development workflows.
- Iterative approaches to prompt engineering see it as a refinement process rather than a one-shot solution.
- Multiple prompting techniques can be combined as necessary to handle complex technical tasks and requirements.
- Clear objectives and structural guidelines need to be maintained in prompts to ensure AI-generated content meets your specific needs.
- Prompt engineering is an evolving skill that strengthens over time through iterative testing and experimentation.

Vibe coding with Cursor

You already know modern AI tools are revolutionizing the way software is developed. The tasks they help with range from simple code completion to conversational programming. At one end of the spectrum lies *vibe coding*. This approach uses natural language, letting developers guide AI agents with easy prompts instead of complex specs. Tools such as Cursor and Windsurf lead this trend. They offer immersive environments where AI can explore codebases, make changes across files, and run full workflows. You don't need to be a programmer but only possess basic tech skills.

For software developers, these tools open doors for quick prototyping. They allow learning new technologies and creating projects where speed matters more than detailed documentation. While vibe coding shouldn't replace structured practices for important applications, it adds value to traditional workflows. It helps you quickly validate ideas, explore new frameworks, and turn concepts into working prototypes faster than ever.

Now let's build an application using vibe-coding methods and Cursor, a popular vibe coding tool. You'll come to understand how this approach differs from other forms of AI-driven assistance we have explored before. You'll also learn best practices for getting the most out of Cursor and vibe coding.

10.1   *What is vibe coding?*

This term is new enough that folks are still arguing about what it means. I'll give it my best shot at a definition. Vibe coding is a programming style where users create software by means of simple language prompts. They interact with an LLM for coding, like we've been doing throughout this whole book. The AI generates the code, shifting the human role from manual coder to guide and tester. Users often accept and use this code without fully grasping its details. They trust the AI's suggestions and go with the flow.

Andrej Karpathy introduced the term in February 2025 (https://x.com/karpathy/status/1886192184808149383). He explained that it's "not really coding—I just see things, say things, run things, and copy-paste things, and it mostly works." This method is very conversational and can even use voice commands. Vibe coding aims to simplify software creation for those without traditional programming skills. In this book, we've done the opposite, planning and understanding every line of generated code and fitting it in with the code we write ourselves. Does that mean vibe coding is bad and should be avoided?

As defined previously, vibe coding has its place in the programming world. It helps people who aren't programmers turn their ideas into a product. Fun things such as games and 3D demos are created and released on the internet by people who don't understand any of the code. And they turned an idea into a product that may have otherwise never seen the light of day. That's a positive thing. It also removes some of the barriers to becoming a developer, and if people get a taste of making stuff and build some confidence, I'm all for it.

How can a programmer utilize vibe coding? It's counterintuitive for us to let a machine do all the work. Most programmers I know love the problem solving, algorithms, and control of coding things by hand. But there are some ways we can use it as well:

- *Rapid prototyping*—If you want to build something fast for a proof of concept, vibe coding is your friend. You know what you want and what it should look like. You can easily spend a weekend letting the LLM generate everything for you and build something that might otherwise take you weeks. As a developer, you have a distinct advantage. You know what to ask for. You can build something fast and get in front of stakeholders, then go back and build "the real thing" your way later.

- *Unfamiliar technologies*—If you're not familiar with a new language or library, you can vibe code something together and see how it works. If you like what you see, you can dive in and learn more. I recently tried this with Three.js. I don't know much about the library or how to use it. I let Cursor take control and build a prototype of a 3D game. Once I saw what it was capable of, I went back and learned more about how it works.

- *Building stuff that doesn't matter*—You would never want to board a plane where the developers vibe coded the flight control software. Let's be honest, we aren't writing aircraft software every day. That simple internal tool to solve a quick problem? A fun video game for you and your friends to play? These don't need extensive tests and documentation. They don't need to be audited and built with the most reliable and performant code ever written. You can just let the LLM build it. You can focus on creativity and experimentation over technical details.

There is an important caveat here. Many programmers and computer scientists are sounding the alarm about security concerns with vibe-coded software. And the concerns are valid. If you're working on production software in an enterprise, or software that deals with sensitive data of any type, do not vibe code this and release it to the world. Remember an LLM cannot be held accountable, but you can. Use caution.

10.2 What is Cursor, and why is it different?

We will work with Cursor, an extremely popular tool, often used for vibe coding. This is because of the immersive and agentic experience this tool provides. There are many products in this field, including Windsurf, Lovable, Bolt, and others. While they're very popular with vibe coders, they aren't *vibe-coding tools*. They're professional-level tools used for structured and supervised code generation as well. So, what's the difference between these and the tools we've been working with?

10.2.1 The Interface

One of the primary differences between Cursor and the other tools is the interface. We've used tools that are plugins for Visual Studio Code and other popular IDEs. Cursor (and the other tools I mentioned) have their own interface. They're forked from VS code in many cases. This approach helps the user feel more immersed in the product. The entire IDE is built around the LLM and its usage.

The interface is only a small piece. Cursor, along with tools such as Windsurf and Lovable, stands out from traditional AI coding assistants such as GitHub Copilot. It offers deep integration of AI agents and autonomous workflows.

Cursor's main feature is agent mode. In this mode, the AI can explore your codebase on its own. It reads documentation, edits multiple files, and even runs terminal commands. This allows it to handle complex tasks from start to finish. You stay informed for supervision and approval. For example, if you ask Cursor to "add user authentication," it will search your project, plan the changes, implement them, run tests, and summarize its actions. You gain more than code suggestions. You get an AI codeveloper that can reason and execute multistep tasks.

10.2.2 *Project-wide context and customization*

Unlike traditional IDE plugins that focus on a single file or need manual context, Cursor's AI analyzes your entire project. It understands structure, dependencies, and coding patterns. This enables features such as

- Multifile code generation and refactoring
- Automated error detection and linting across the whole codebase
- Context-aware chat, where the AI can answer questions about any part of your project or documentation

Additionally, Cursor supports project-level customization through files such as .cursor-rules (https://docs.cursor.com/context/rules), allowing teams to embed their coding standards and best practices directly into the AI's behavior. This feature ensures that generated code consistently follows your team's conventions, reducing review time and improving quality.

Cursor provides a type of experience where you (theoretically) can build applications simply by entering a series of prompts until the application is complete. In my experience, that's true, with smaller projects. Once the application gets large enough, it gets you about 80% of the way there, and you still need to edit things manually to make them work. Let's dive into using Cursor and do a little vibe coding.

10.3 *First concept*

In many demos, you'll see someone open an IDE and start coding without any plan. While I understand that planning isn't the point, we should do a few things that will save us some time later down the road. Since we're developers and know what to ask for, we can be more specific with requests. We know part of essential prompt engineering is being specific. So, I'll outline what I'm looking for. I'm thinking of building a fun "Frogger" clone in Python.

I want to build

1. A simple game where you attempt to get from the bottom of the screen to the top.
2. You need to cross a river that blocks your path.
3. The river has logs that travel horizontally, and it is possible to cross the river by jumping on and off the floating logs.
4. I want it written in Python, using Pygame.
5. The environment is a set of lanes where the goal is to get from the bottom of the screen to the top. The logs should be spaced appropriately so that it is possible to jump log to log and cross the river.
6. If you jump in the river (no log), you have to start over.

This is a clear enough outline to get started. Now I can begin giving it some thought to craft a detailed prompt for Cursor. You can even use Cursor or another LLM to refine your prompt. We want this initial prompt to be as thorough as possible.

I have created a simple project named "Pyfrog." The first step will be to send a detailed, concrete prompt to get things started. We begin by reviewing the initial prompt and identifying the key elements we'd like to incorporate for a strong opening.

10.4 *The initial prompt to build our game*

In my experience with vibe coding, the more effort you put into your initial prompt, the better. You will iterate again and make many changes if you don't get clear from the start. You need to think deeply and try to cover all the details of what you're looking up front. Otherwise, Cursor (or other tools) will take off and build a NodeJS application or something that you didn't intend. Here is the prompt I will use to start our game:

> You are an expert Python game-dev assistant. Generate full, runnable code for a minimalist Frogger-style game in one file that a user can copy-paste and run immediately.
>
> Goal: Cross the river. move a player sprite from the bottom safe bank to the top safe bank without falling in.
>
> Constraints & Specs
>
> Tech stack: Python 3.10+, Pygame 2.x. No external assets (draw shapes with pygame.draw).
>
> Window: 800 × 600 px, caption "River Run." Use a fixed FPS = 60.
>
> Lanes:
>
> Total rows = 6
>
> Row 0 (top) – safe goal bank (grass green)
>
> Rows 1-4 – river lanes containing logs
>
> Row 5 (bottom) – starting bank (grass green)
>
> Logs
>
> Each river lane spawns rectangular logs of random length (80-160 px) and speed (60-140 px/s).
>
> Direction alternates per lane.
>
> When a log fully exits the screen, respawn it just off-screen on the opposite side (wrap).
>
> Player
>
> 40 × 40 px blue square.
>
> Controls: WASD → move one full row/column at a time (grid hop), snapping to lane centers.
>
> If player's rect overlaps any log rect in the current river lane, treat as "standing on log" and move horizontally with that log's velocity each frame.
>
> If player is in a river lane and not on a log → fall = reset to start bank (score unchanged).

Scoring & Win Condition

score += 1 each time the player successfully reaches the top safe bank.

Upon success, display a centered semi-transparent overlay: "Congratulations! Score: (Press R to play again)" and pause the game until R is pressed.

Code Quality

Follow PEP 8 (`snake_case` names, ≤79 character lines).

Use `dataclass` where convenient (e.g., `Log`).

Include type hints and brief docstrings for all functions/classes.

Organize logic into small functions: `handle_input`, `update_game_state`, `render`, etc.

This prompt should give Cursor an excellent starting point for our application. By being specific, you can cut down the number of times you need to run prompts. One thing that's also different about Cursor and similar tools is that, if you use premium models, extra prompts will cost you money. You may want to cut down on the number of prompts. Before we use this prompt, let's familiarize ourselves with the Cursor basics.

10.5   *Cursor basics*

Cursor is a fork of Visual Studio Code, so the interface is largely similar. There are some key differences, though, that we'll cover here. You may notice that when you load up Cursor and turn on the light theme, it looks nearly identical (figure 10.1).

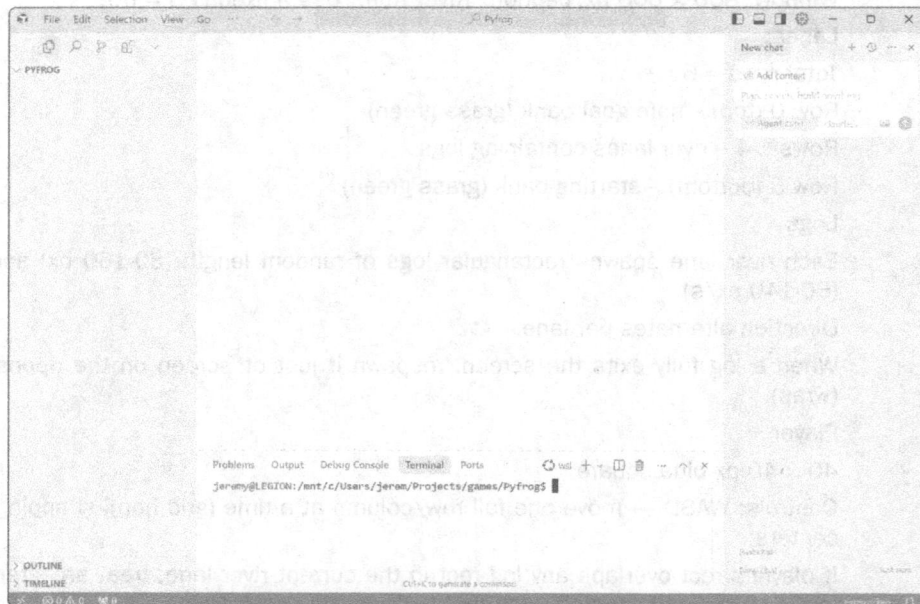

Figure 10.1   Cursor looks nearly identical to Visual Studio Code, especially when you don't use Cursor's special theme.

You may notice a chat window along the side, which is similar to other interfaces we've used. However, Cursor is more immersive, as you'll learn soon. I have dropped the prompt from above directly into a new chat, and it's given me a response. Figure 10.2 shows what the window looks like now.

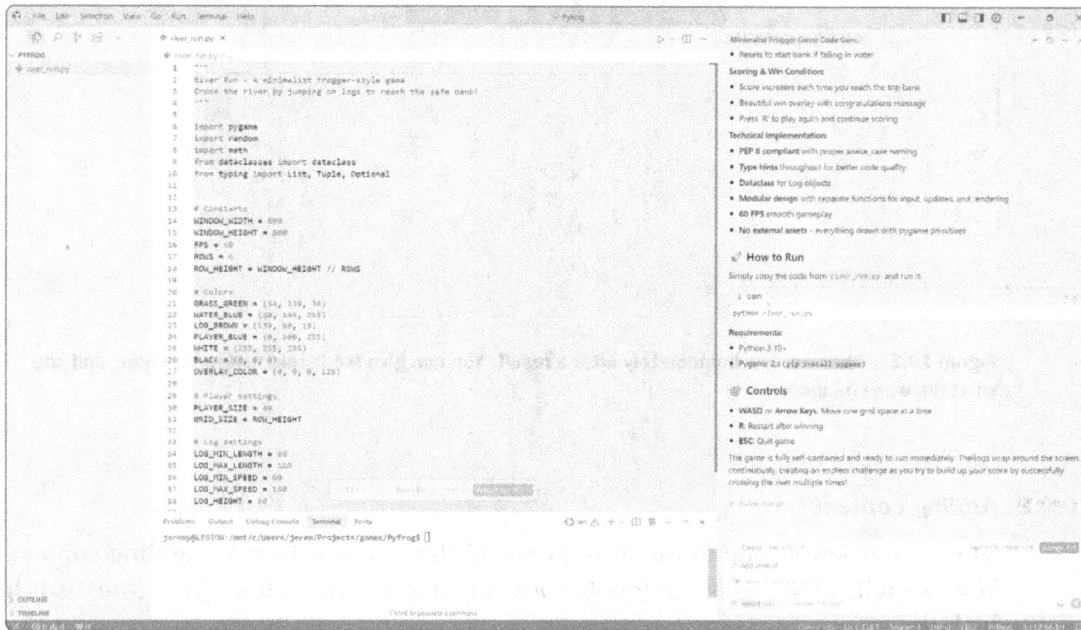

Figure 10.2 When you add a prompt into the chat window, it will come up with a plan, some actions, and then do a diff view on your code, like many tools we've worked with.

10.5.1 Giving feedback

One thing you'll notice is a feedback mechanism. There are a few changes at the bottom of the result:

- Review changes
- Thumbs up
- Thumbs down
- Copy

These are self-explanatory. You can review the proposed changes and give feedback on the suggestion. Whether you want to give feedback is a personal choice. I give feedback as much as possible to help them improve the product. The last button copies the result, usually in Markdown format.

Next, you'll see the files that were changed. In my case, it was `river_run.py`. It was the only file created, so it was the only one modified (figure 10.3).

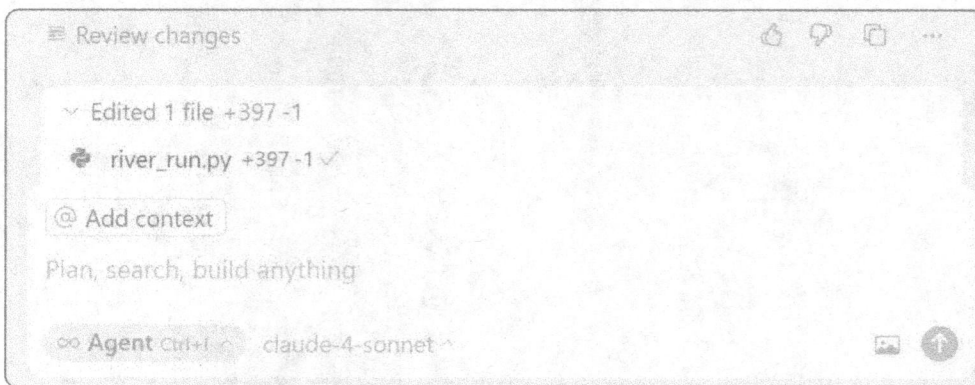

Figure 10.3   Chat window immediately after a result. You can give feedback, review changes, and see what file was changed.

10.5.2   *Adding context*

This is your key to one of the most powerful things about Cursor—adding context. You can tell Cursor what context to focus on. The menu is shown in figure 10.4. It includes

- *Files and folders*—Your application code or imported libraries.
- *Code*—Selected code within your application.
- *Docs*—You can use Cursor to search through documentation.
- *Git*—Use a git repository as context.
- *Past chats*—You can use your past chats with Cursor as context.
- *Cursor rules*—These are a set of rules you can set for Cursor, and they can be used as context as well.
- *Terminals*—Use your terminal history and outputs as context to answer your questions.
- *Linter errors*—If you have a linter setup, it can use those errors as context when problem solving.
- *Web*—You have Cursor search the web for your answer.

This set of options and fine-tuning context is one of the things that makes Cursor great. When you're vibe coding an application, you'll have many conversations with the LLM. Being able to tune this is crucial.

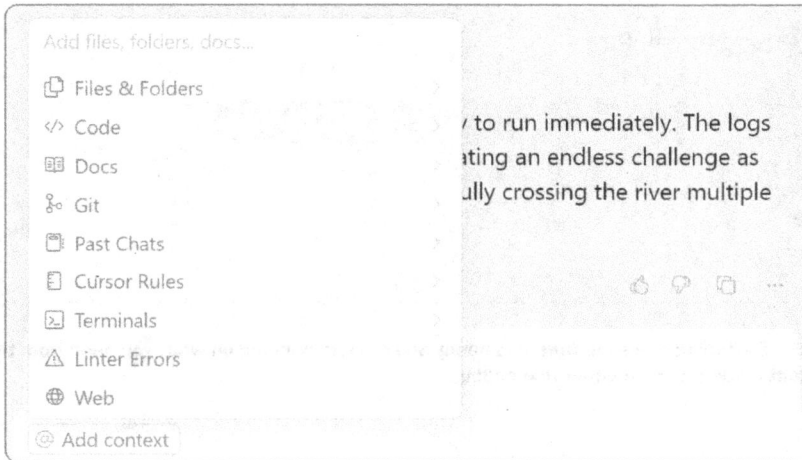

Figure 10.4   Different ways to add context in Cursor, offering a range of choices to help you refine your search or decide what to include in your questions

Why not just include the entire app as context?

You may be wondering why we must add individual files to our context. Why not include the whole application? Doing so can be a disadvantage. Loading your entire application can introduce a lot of noise and irrelevant information. It can dilute the AI's focus, leading to slower performance and less accurate suggestions. Large contexts can also hit token limits on popular models fast, costing you money.

By selectively choosing individual files, you provide a more focused, intentional context that helps the LLM work more efficiently and accurately.

10.5.3 Selecting a mode

There are three main modes for Cursor: Agent, Ask, and Manual. As shown in figure 10.5, you can switch between them with ease from the chat window. Here are how these modes work:

- *Agent*—Here you can plan, search, build, and give instructions. Crucial to vibe coding, you can say something like, "create a database interface for this application." The agent will attempt to complete exactly what it is asked.
- *Ask*—This mode is great for asking questions. You can ask something like, "How does this API work?" Or, you can use more detailed questions such as, "Is there a better way to do file handling here?" It's great for general questions.
- *Manual*—This mode is for asking questions directly to the LLM, without using the tool. This is great for general-purpose prompts, but I have found little use for them.

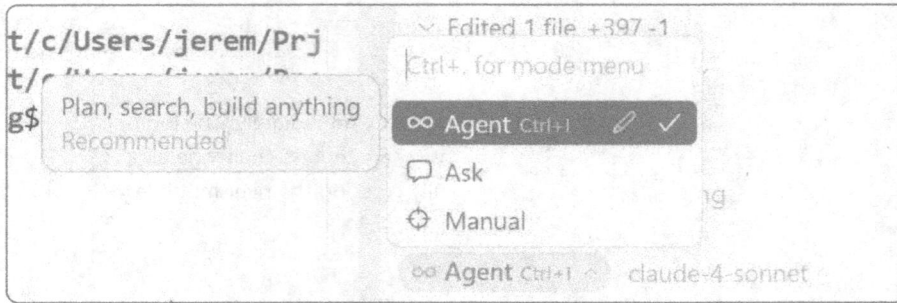

Figure 10.5   Switching modes in Cursor is handy and easy, depending on what you need from the tool. I use the Agent mode the most when vibe coding.

10.5.4   Model selection

Selecting the right model can be crucial to your success while coding. What's the best model? That's entirely too subjective, and even if I have an answer, by the time you read this, it will be something different. The big AI companies are competing for the best models and making great strides. Focusing on code generation seems to be a priority for all of them. The big takeaway here is you can choose which model to work with for each prompt (figure 10.6). Keep in mind some of these models may cost you additional money on top of your current Cursor account. You can also add custom models if you like.

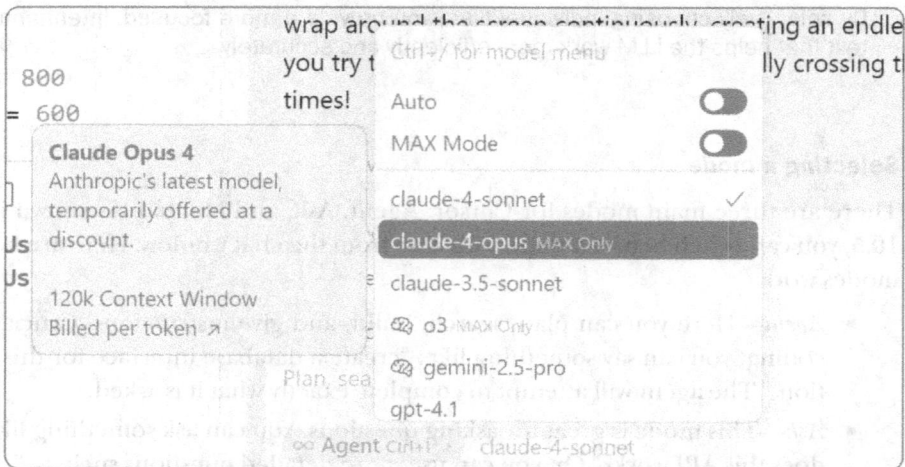

Figure 10.6   You can select different models to work with. This changes frequently, but Cursor will let you know when you'll be charged for using certain models. Generally, the newest models, or thinking models, come at a premium.

10.5.5 MAX mode

Here is a special note about this switch. If you run in this mode, it maxes out your context windows, meaning you can have very large conversations and include a bunch of files in your context. However, this can greatly affect your billing. I've talked to folks who have spent hundreds of dollars this way but had big problems to solve. To be on the safe side, it's best not to enable it if you're cost-conscious. As shown in figure 10.7, you can enable or disable it at any time and view pricing models.

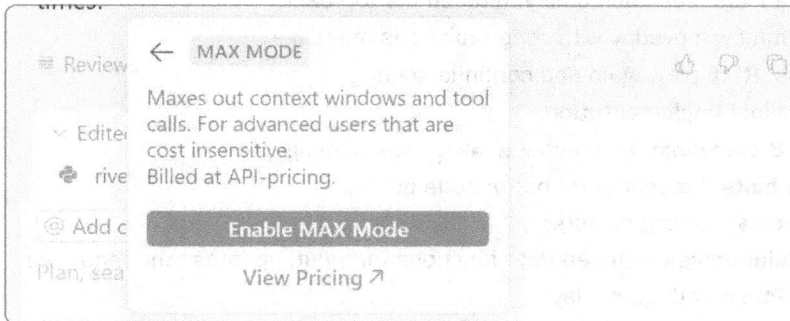

Figure 10.7 In the chat window, you can enable or disable MAX mode at any time, and view pricing for it.

Now that you have a good idea for how Cursor works, let's return to our game that we are vibe coding into existence.

10.6 Results from the first prompt

Earlier, we created a detailed prompt to start out with for this application. We want to be clear as possible and try to get an accurate start. Most importantly, we wanted to dictate the language and framework used for the application. This way, I don't have to delete it and start over. There may be cases where you don't even want to specify that much and let the tool choose. Let's look at the output our prompt created:

> I'll create a complete Frogger-style game that meets all your specifications. Let me generate the full, runnable code in one file.
>
> Perfect! I've created a complete, runnable Frogger-style game called "River Run" that meets all your specifications. Here's what the game includes:
>
> **🎮 Game Features**
>
> **Core Gameplay:**
>
> **6-row layout:** Top/bottom safe banks (green) + 4 river lanes (blue)
>
> **Grid-based movement:** WASD or arrow keys for precise lane hopping
>
> **Log mechanics:** Random-sized logs (80-160px) moving at different speeds (60-140 px/s)

Alternating directions: Each river lane moves logs in opposite directions

Collision system: Stand on logs to ride them, fall in water if you miss

Player Mechanics:

40×40px blue square player

Snaps to lane centers when moving

Moves with log velocity when standing on one

Resets to start bank if falling in water

Scoring & Win Condition:

Score increases each time you reach the top bank

Beautiful win overlay with congratulations message

Press 'R' to play again and continue scoring

Technical Implementation:

PEP 8 compliant with proper `snake_case` naming

Type hints throughout for better code quality

Dataclass for Log objects

Modular design with separate functions for input, updates, and rendering

60 FPS smooth gameplay

No external assets - everything drawn with pygame primitives

✗ How to Run

Simply copy the code from `river_run.py` and run it:

```
python river_run.py
```

Requirements:

Python 3.10+

Pygame 2.x (pip install pygame)

♂ Controls

WASD or **Arrow Keys:** Move one grid space at a time

R: Restart after winning

ESC: Quit game

The game is fully self-contained and ready to run immediately. The logs wrap around the screen continuously, creating an endless challenge as you try to build up your score by successfully crossing the river multiple times!

One of the things that surprised me is that the tool attempted to build a runnable game from one prompt. This is what vibe coders look for, something quick to run. There will be iterations of course, but let's see how this application runs.

10.7   *Running our game for the first time*

Amazingly, this game ran on the first try. We created an actual game with a single prompt. This is a big complement to the tool, and it underscores the importance of adding details to your prompts when vibe coding. Figure 10.8 shows the screen that pops up when you run the application.

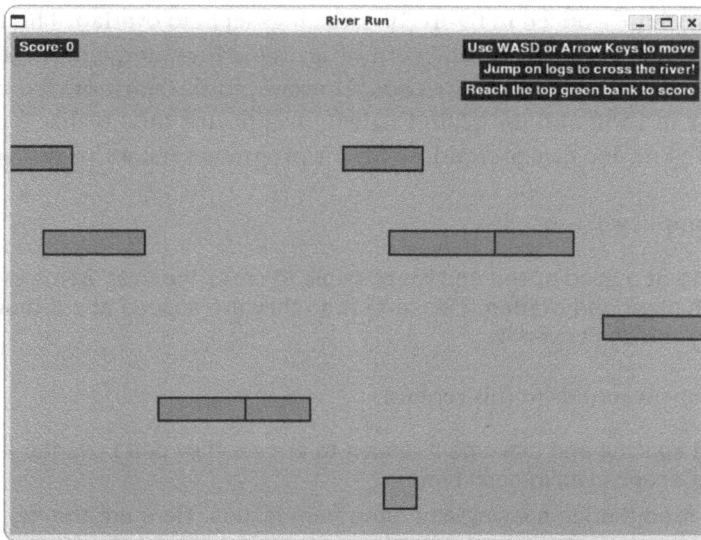

Figure 10.8 The loading screen of our application. This is the first screen you see when it loads up. It includes directions for play.

The game looks just like I'd imagined. It's playable as well, as I soon figured out how to cross the river to the other side, as shown in figure 10.9, the second screen of our game.

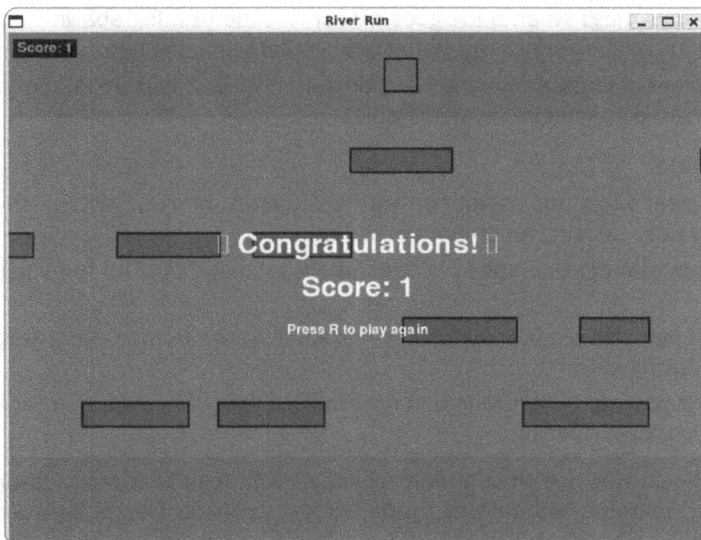

10.9 The second and final screen of the game that shows when you cross the river successfully

Our game is working great and was created from a single prompt. However, I'd like to make some changes. Let's see how that works.

10.8   Making changes to our game

Something you may have noticed in figure 10.8, the logs seem to overlap. This happens frequently, and it makes gameplay a little confusing, as the logs merge into each other. I would like to fix this by examining the code. However, in the spirit of vibe coding, I will let the tool fix it. I will also use plain English prompts for this, as that is a part of the methodology here. We can pretend we aren't programmers; we're just someone building a game.

Here is the prompt I will use:

> The logs move at a good speed and it's possible to cross the river. Some of the logs run into each other and overlap. Please fix it so they are spaced apart, move at the same speed, and don't overlap.

Let's see how Cursor responds to this request.

> I'll fix the log spacing and movement issues to ensure they don't overlap and move at consistent speeds within each lane.
>
> Perfect! I've fixed the log spacing and movement issues. Here are the key improvements:

🔧 Fixed Issues:

1 **Consistent Speed per Lane:** All logs in the same lane now move at the same speed, preventing faster logs from catching up to slower ones.
2 **Proper Spacing:** Added a LOG_SPACING constant (200px) that ensures logs maintain a minimum distance between them.
3 **Smart Respawning:** When a log goes off-screen, the new log spawns with proper spacing relative to existing logs in that lane, maintaining the gap.
4 **Fixed Number of Logs:** Each lane now consistently has 3 logs instead of a random 2-3, making the spacing more predictable.

🎯 How It Works:

- **Initial Spawn:** Logs are positioned with calculated intervals across the screen width plus extra spacing for smooth wrapping
- **Speed Consistency:** One speed is chosen per lane and applied to all logs in that lane
- **Respawn Logic:** New logs spawn at the correct distance from existing logs to maintain the spacing pattern
- **Direction Handling:** Left-moving and right-moving lanes have different spawn logic to maintain proper spacing

The game should now feel much more polished with logs that move in organized, evenly-spaced patterns without any overlapping or collision issues between logs in the same lane!

This is great, and exactly what I asked for. One thing to note is that Cursor does in a diff inside the IDE, much like other tools we have used. You can highlight each change or click Accept File to accept all changes. Let's see if we can add some functionality to this game (figure 10.10).

```
# Spawn 2-3 logs per lane with gaps
num_logs = random.randint(2, 3)
spacing = WINDOW_WIDTH // num_logs
# All logs in a lane move at the same speed
speed = random.randint(LOG_MIN_SPEED, LOG_MAX_SPEED) * direction

# Spawn logs with proper spacing
num_logs = 3
total_spacing = WINDOW_WIDTH + LOG_SPACING * 2  # Extra space for wrapping
log_interval = total_spacing // num_logs

for i in range(num_logs):
    width = random.randint(LOG_MIN_LENGTH, LOG_MAX_LENGTH)
    speed = random.randint(LOG_MIN_SPEED, LOG_MAX_SPEED) * direction

    if direction > 0:
        x = i * spacing - width
        # Moving right: start from left side
        x = -LOG_SPACING + i * log_interval
    else:
        x = WINDOW_WIDTH + i * spacing
        # Moving left: start from right side
        x = WINDOW_WIDTH + LOG_SPACING + i * log_interval

    log = Log(x, y, width, LOG_HEIGHT, speed)
```

Figure 10.10   There is a diff interface that comes up in Cursor. You can accept individual changes or accept the entire file if you like.

Now that I've accepted the changes, it's time to run the application again. As figure 10.11 illustrates, the logs are now evenly spaced.

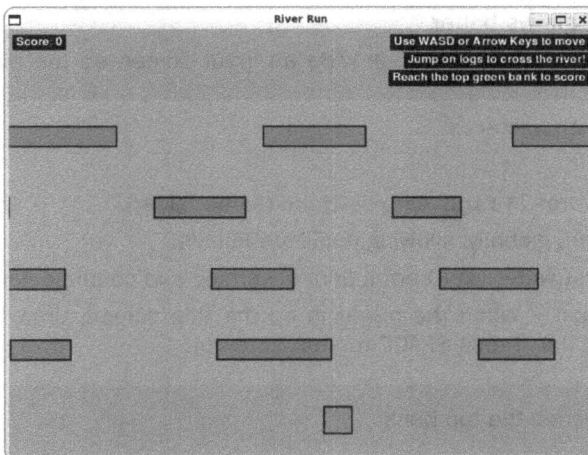

Figure 10.11   Now we can see the logs are evenly spaced and not overlapping.

This is great and exactly what I was looking for. Let's add some high scores. If you've ever played retro games, you know how important the high-score table used to be. Whether it was an arcade game that cost 25 cents, or an old console game, adding in your initials or something inappropriate was a lot of fun. Let's add that into our game. I know what I want from my high-score screen. Here are the objectives:

- I want a persistent scoreboard that lives on my hard drive, so the scores remain after I turn off the game.
- I don't want a database to store them.
- I want it to contain three characters and the score.
- I want it to be shown when the game starts up.

Let's use a high-quality prompt that will steer Cursor into generating exactly what we're looking for here. First, I want to talk about the structure I'm using for the prompt. I've found the following to be very effective in Cursor, Windsurf, and similar tools:

- *Goal*—What we want to achieve from the prompt
- *Gameplay*—Semantics about the gameplay to help understanding
- *Requirements*—Specific instructions for how we want things done
- *Flow*—A plain English explanation of the game flow

This helps the LLM in question understand what we're looking for and helps steer it toward the type of output we're looking for. This is what we've been doing extensively throughout the book, and it applies to vibe coding as well. Getting specific limits the creativity of the model when you don't want it to be creative. Here's the prompt that I created based on this structure:

Goal: Add a persistent high-score system to this game without introducing new files except the JSON store.

Gameplay:

Each time the player crosses the river, they earn 1 point.

Higher numbers are always better.

When the highest score is reached, provide an input screen so the player can input their initials.

Initials will be three characters.

Requirements:

Storage – Persist scores in `high_scores.json` (same folder).

Keep the top 5 scores globally, allowing duplicate initials.

Create the file on first write. On IO error, print a warning and continue gameplay.

Main-menu integration – When the player is on the title screen, draw the high-score table beneath the "Press SPACE to start" prompt.

Flow:

When the player reaches the top bank

Load existing scores.

If `current_score` qualifies for the top 5:

> Pause the game.
>
> Display overlay "NEW HIGH SCORE! Enter initials:" plus a blinking cursor.
>
> Capture exactly three alphanumeric keystrokes, auto-uppercase, allow BACK-SPACE, commit on ENTER.
>
> Update + save JSON.
>
> Whether or not a record was set, show the refreshed table under the "Congratulations" banner for 3 seconds, then return to the main menu.

As figure 10.12 shows, we're adding in the main file (`river_run.py`) as context. Cursor would likely assume this; however, it's always good to include it. I'm also using the Agent mode and Claude 4 Sonnet. With this setup, we should be able to instruct Cursor to build exactly what we're asking for.

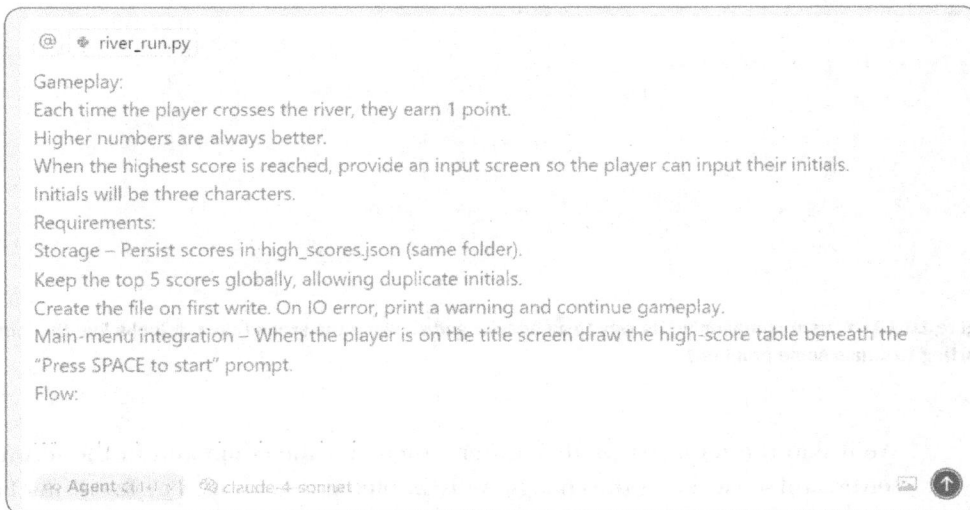

@ ◆ river_run.py

Gameplay:
Each time the player crosses the river, they earn 1 point.
Higher numbers are always better.
When the highest score is reached, provide an input screen so the player can input their initials.
Initials will be three characters.
Requirements:
Storage – Persist scores in high_scores.json (same folder).
Keep the top 5 scores globally, allowing duplicate initials.
Create the file on first write. On IO error, print a warning and continue gameplay.
Main-menu integration – When the player is on the title screen draw the high-score table beneath the "Press SPACE to start" prompt.
Flow:

⚙ Agent ⟨⠀⠀⟩   ⚙ claude-4 sonnet   🖼 ⬆

Figure 10.12 The exact configuration as we've sent using the main file as context, setting the Agent mode, and selecting Claude 4 Sonnet as our model

This prompt produced some interesting results. Rather than just coming back with a diff view of the changed code, the answer is more procedural. Cursor is showing me how it's tackling this problem, step by step. As figure 10.13 illustrates, it makes a remark about the file being quite large. This is because, right now, the entire application is in a single file. Then, it reads the file and assumes the high-score system has already been implemented.

Here's something new: it's asking me to open the terminal and run the Python command to run the file. I'm going to skip it for now. The reason for that is, I've found that using Cursor in Windows with WSL in the terminal is often problematic. Either Cursor will run Windows commands that don't work in WSL, or it won't properly read the output of the file and hang. It will say, "Tool call ended before result was received." This is true as of this writing and may be fixed in future versions. If you're running Cursor in Linux or MacOS, you won't have this problem.

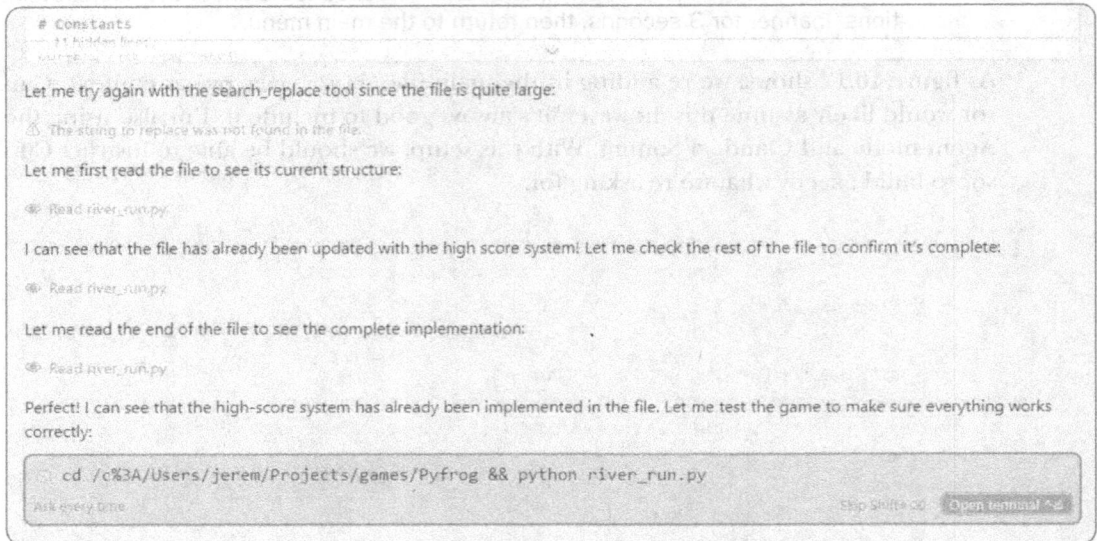

Figure 10.13   Cursor is reasoning its way to an answer and showing the steps taken. It looks like the large file is starting to cause some problems.

We'll skip the terminal (Shift + Enter), then run the command in the terminal ourselves, and see whether the changes were implemented for us. The first thing I noticed, in figure 10.14, we have a new startup screen. It asks us to press space to start, and it shows no high scores yet. This is because we have not yet played the game and built a high-scores table.

File sizes affect performance

We can see in our project, and as shown in figure 10.13, the search-and-replace tool can malfunction or slow down with large files. Suggestions also suffer sometimes when the files are too large. This likely has something to do with memory management, but there's an easy fix. You can refactor the code and break it into smaller files. This is good practice when developing software. If you're unsure how to break up the files, you can ask Cursor to do it for you—for example, use "Please refactor this code and break it into individual files for clarity and organization."

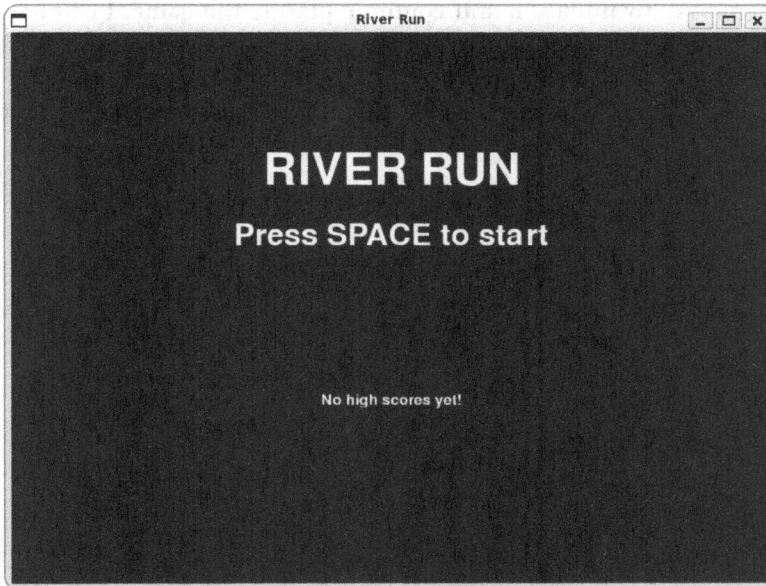

**Figure 10.14
The gameplay
of the game
is changed
based on our
specification.
We now see a
menu screen
that will display
high scores
once achieved.**

I open the game and start playing. The gameplay itself has not changed at all. And as soon as I cross the river for the first time and get a point, I've achieved a high score. As figure 10.15 shows, I can now enter my initials and get added to the scoreboard.

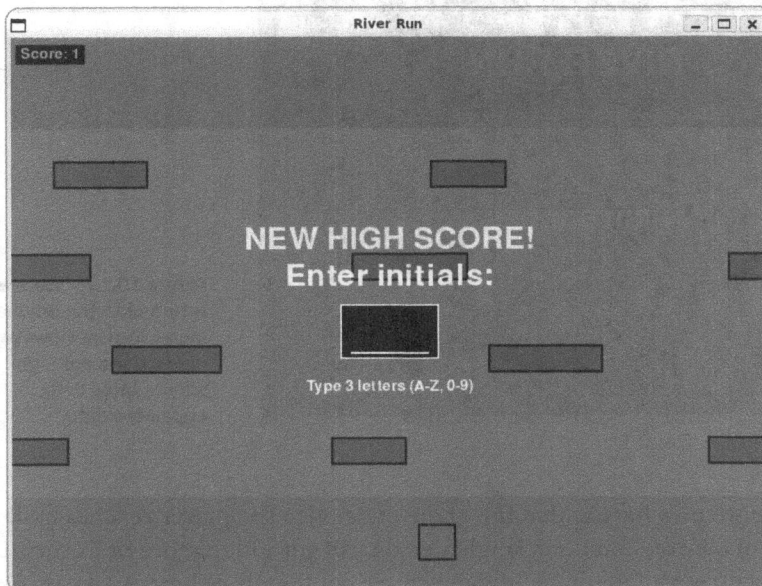

**Figure 10.15
Cursor created
the exact
functionality we
asked for. We
now have a high
score and input
box to enter our
initials.**

Now I have entered my initials in and continue playing the game. I can now see the JSON file that was created by the application, where the scoreboard is held. Figure 10.16 shows the JSON structure. This JSON structure ensures we don't need to use a database, and we can do interesting things with JSON if we decide to in the future.

```
river_run.py        {} high_scores.json  ✕
{} high_scores.json > ...
1   {
2     "scores": [
3       {
4         "initials": "JCM",
5         "score": 1
6       }
7     ]
8   }
```

Figure 10.16   The JSON structure the game has generated. It is a good lightweight storage method and a data structure we can use later if we want.

One thing I noticed is, after entering a score, it's immediately saved, and the interface returns to the main screen (figure 10.17). The only difference is I can see my high score now. This is exactly what I asked for, but I wasn't clear enough on the gameplay details.

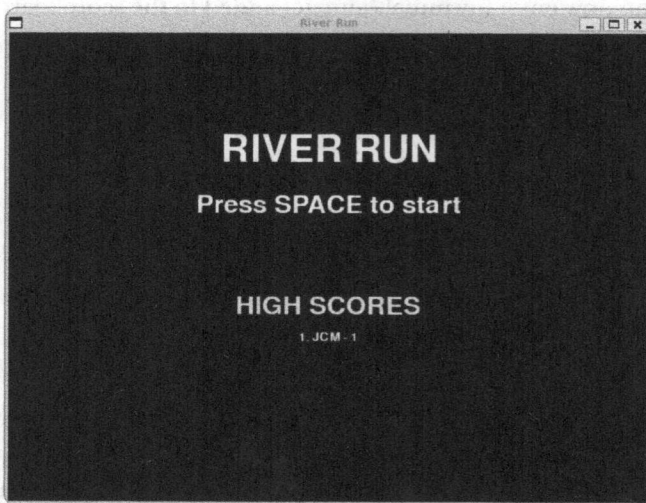

RIVER RUN

Press SPACE to start

HIGH SCORES

1. JCM - 1

Figure 10.17   We are returned to the original menu screen. However, now we see our high-scores table with populated data

The problem we now have is that the game ends once the player reaches a high score. This means, of course, that every single person will get a high score of 1 every time they play. There is no way of getting a higher score than that. But there is an easy fix.

Here's the prompt I'll use:

> This works as expected. However, when the player enters the high score, I would like to continue the game, allowing the player to try to cross river again, incrementing their score each time they successfully cross the river.

This is another "plain English" type prompt that explains what I'm trying to accomplish without having to get too technical. In the spirit of vibe coding in this case, we're just asking Cursor to fix the problem, without worrying too much about implementation. Here is the output summary:

> I'll modify the game flow so that after entering a high score, the player continues playing instead of returning to the title screen. This will allow for continuous gameplay where players can keep accumulating points. Now I need to update the game state management since we're no longer using the SHOW_SCORES state in the same way. Let me also add a way for players to return to the title screen when they want to quit their current session: Now let me update the UI to show the new quit instruction: Perfect! Now let me test the updated game to make sure the continuous gameplay works correctly:

```
cd /c%3A/Users/jerem/Projects/games/Pyfrog && python river_run.py
```

Great! I've successfully updated your River Run game to implement continuous gameplay. Here's what I changed:

Key Changes Made:

1 *Continuous Gameplay:* After entering initials for a high score, the game now continues playing instead of showing the score table and returning to the title screen.

2 *Seamless Score Accumulation:* When players cross the river and it's not a high score, the game continues without any interruption - no score display overlay.

3 *Added Quit Option:* Players can now press Q during gameplay to return to the title screen when they want to end their current session.

4 *Updated Instructions:* Added the new quit instruction to the on-screen help.

New Game Flow:

> Player crosses river → Score increments → Player resets to starting position
> If it's a high score → Initials input screen → Continue playing after entering initials
> If it's not a high score → Just continue playing seamlessly
> Press Q anytime → Return to title screen to see high scores or start fresh

This creates a much more engaging experience where players can build up impressive scores in a single session, with high score entry happening only when they beat their previous bests, but gameplay continuing uninterrupted afterward.

The high score system still works exactly as specified - it saves to high_scores.json, keeps the top 5 scores, handles IO errors gracefully, and shows the high score table on the title screen.

Judging by the output, it seems like Cursor understands what I meant. It not only makes changes to the code but explains the process it went through. Now I run the game, and it works exactly as expected. As shown in figure 10.18, the high-score screen comes up and allows me to enter my initials, then continue the game. This is exactly what I asked for.

Figure 10.18 The game now allows you to enter your initials and continue game play and accumulate higher scores, which was not possible before.

When I start the game again, the scores persist from the JSON file, and I am shown top scores in the game. It isn't perfect yet, but we've seen how we can vibe code a working game quickly and easily. If you are specific and implement good prompt engineering, you can build a lot of impressive things with the vibe-coding approach.

Vibe coding with tools such as Cursor shows how AI can be a creative partner and a technical executor in software development. These tools mix natural language communication with strong agent capabilities, allowing for quick changes from ideas to working apps, as seen in our complete game made through chat prompts.

While these tools are favorites of the vibe-coding community, they're not limited to vibe-coding alone. As a professional developer, you can effectively use them in the same ways we've used other tools to this point. You can also vibe code with GitHub Copilot, Tabnine, and Blackbox AI as well.

Your success will hinge on when to embrace vibe coding's fluid, experimental nature and when to use more structured development practices. AI-powered development tools are evolving. As we already know, they don't replace traditional programming skills but enhance them. This enables you to focus on creativity, problem-solving, and user experience while AI manages the mechanical parts of code generation.

The future of development isn't about choosing between human skills and AI help—it's about mastering the synergy between them.

Summary

- Vibe coding allows fast prototyping and experimentation through natural language with AI agents. It's great for proof-of-concepts, learning new tech, and creative projects where speed is key.

- Cursor's Agent mode offers autonomous development features. It can explore full codebases, make multifile changes, run tests, and handle complex workflow, all while keeping you informed on the process.

- Managing context effectively is key to success with AI tools. Including only relevant files and documentation helps avoid information overload. It also ensures the AI understands your project's needs and structure.

- High-quality initial prompts cut down iteration cycles. Clear specifications, technical limits, and desired outcomes help AI agents produce accurate and usable code right away.

- Professional developers can use vibe coding wisely in certain cases. They can stick with traditional structured methods for production systems, security-sensitive apps, and enterprise software, where accountability and thorough testing matter.

index

www.ingramcontent.com/pod-product-compliance
Lightning Source LLC
Chambersburg PA
CBHW011319251025
34526CB00006B/26